WITHDRAWN FROM
MACALESTER COLLEGE
LIBRARY

EUROPEAN POLITICAL CO-OPERATION

EUROPEAN POLITICAL CO-OPERATION

SIMON J. NUTTALL

CLARENDON PRESS · OXFORD
1992

Oxford University Press, Walton Street, Oxford OX2 6DP
Oxford New York Toronto
Delhi Bombay Calcutta Madras Karachi
Petaling Jaya Singapore Hong Kong Tokyo
Nairobi Dar es Salaam Cape Town
Melbourne Auckland
and associated companies in
Berlin Ibadan

Oxford is a trade mark of Oxford University Press

Published in the United States
by Oxford University Press, New York

© Simon J. Nuttall 1992

All rights reserved. No part of this publication may be reproduced,
stored in a retrieval system, or transmitted, in any form or by any means,
electronic, mechanical, photocopying, recording, or otherwise, without
the prior permission of Oxford University Press

British Library Cataloguing in Publication Data
Data available

Library of Congress Cataloging in Publication Data
Nuttall, Simon J.
European Political Co-operation / Simon J. Nuttall.
p.   cm.
Includes bibliographical references and index.
1. European Political Co-operation. 2. European Economic Community
countries—Foreign relations. 3. European federation. I. Title.
KJE5105.N88 1992   321'.04'094—dc20   92-4063
ISBN 0-19-827318-5

Typeset by Pentacor PLC, High Wycombe, Bucks.
Printed and bound in
Great Britain by Biddles Ltd,
Guildford and King's Lynn

To
The Memory of
Gerold von Braunmühl

ACKNOWLEDGEMENTS

The author would like to thank the following for their support, encouragement and frequently ignored advice: David Allen, Françoise de la Serre, Geoffrey Edwards, Christopher Hill, Jean-Marc Hoscheit, Hanns Maull, Jörg Monar, Roger Morgan, Jean Marie Palayret, Alfred Pijpers, Elfriede Regelsberger, Reinhardt Rummel, Helen Wallace, William Wallace, and Wolfgang Wessels.

He would also like to thank the following, who have kindly given up their time to shed light from personal experience on the functioning of EPC: Julian Bullard, Vicomte Étienne Davignon, Pieter De Haan, Adrian Fortescue, Louis Kawan, Horst Krenzler, Richard Lewis, Philip McDonagh, Emile Noël, and François-Xavier Ortoli.

The author would like to express his gratitude for their hospitality to the Library of the European Commission in Brussels, the Library of the European University Institute in Florence, and the Press Library of the Royal Institute of International Affairs at Chatham House, and in particular to Hazel Servais, who got out all the references.

SJN

Brussels – London
June 1989 – March 1991

CONTENTS

Introduction   1

1. THE MECHANICS OF EUROPEAN POLITICAL CO-OPERATION   11
2. THE ORIGINS   30
3. THE FORMATIVE YEARS (1970–1973)   51
4. BUILDING THE HOUSE (1973–1977)   81
5. EUROPEAN POLITICAL CO-OPERATION COMES OF AGE (1978–1981)   149
6. A BRIDGE TOO FAR (1982–1986)   182
7. THE SINGLE EUROPEAN ACT (1987)   239
8. EUROPEAN POLITICAL CO-OPERATION AND THE COMMUNITY   260
9. TALKING WITH THE WORLD   282
10. THE GREY AREA   294
11. CAN POLITICAL CO-OPERATION SURVIVE?   309

Bibliography   323

Index   331

Introduction

European Political Co-operation (EPC) is the process by which the Member States of the European Community co-ordinate their foreign policies. Although increasingly connected with them, it operates separately from the European Communities set up under the Treaties of Paris and Rome. It began in 1970 as a pragmatic way of achieving a foreign policy identity alongside the economic identity of the Communities, avoiding the institutional quarrels which had brought to nothing earlier attempts over a period of twenty years. This book sets out to describe the development of EPC and to trace the influences which have made it what it is today.

The question is an important and topical one. The foreign-policy arm of the European Community is increasingly significant both for the institutional development of the Community and for its impact on world events. As this book was being completed, the Inter-governmental Conference on Political Union was tackling the question of a common foreign, security, and defence policy, the results of which will be important both for the Community and internationally. The discussion must include an assessment of the achievements of Political Co-operation so far, and yet the procedures and political pressures which go towards shaping EPC are little known and frequently misunderstood. It is hoped that this book will improve understanding of a new form of diplomatic process, of great interest for the future, but which has barely begun.

It is too soon to write a complete history of EPC, nor would so voluminous a work be of general interest. In this book, only those events have been selected for study which cast a light on the way EPC has developed. Furthermore, the book has been written from the standpoint of Political Co-operation, frequently looking inwards on itself rather than outwards on the world. Inevitably, this approach emphasizes process rather than policy and gives a Eurocentric view of world events, neglecting related developments for no other reason than that they occurred in forums other than Political Co-operation. These are all omissions which the future historian will need to correct.

The account of Political Co-operation reveals three intertwining strands influencing its development. Now one comes into greater prominence, now another, but all were present throughout and none alone is an adequate explanation of what happened. Of the three strands, one is institutional, one political, and one organizational. The first is the tension between those who wanted a concert of sovereign nations expressing co-ordinated views on foreign-policy questions, and those who wanted a common foreign policy as the expression of a European Union; the second is the influence of the United States on West European foreign-policy making; and the third is the bureaucratic machinery which was gradually put into place in order to organize Political Co-operation's reaction to events.

The debate between inter-governmentalists and integrationists has surfaced at regular intervals. It was one of the main contributors to the failure of attempts in the 1950s and 1960s to find a workable framework for a West European foreign policy, whether in the shape of the European Political Community or in that of the Fouchet Plan launched by General de Gaulle. It can be seen again in the discussion on the Tindemans Report of 1975, the Genscher-Colombo initiative of 1981, and the Milan European Council leading to the Single European Act of 1987. It bids fair to be a main theme of the Inter-governmental Conference on Political Union of 1991. The question at issue is whether decisions on foreign policy, as on other policies, should in the long run be left in the hands of the individual governments, or whether mechanisms should be found to enable these decisions to be taken in common.

The line-up on this question has shifted over the years. In general, the United Kingdom, together with Denmark and Greece, has taken a consistently inter-governmental view. Italy, Germany, and the remaining smaller countries have been on the whole integrationist. France has frequently been inter-governmentalist—indeed General de Gaulle was the first to articulate the approach in a convincing way—but has nevertheless often taken the lead in launching the debate in order to push forward movement towards European Union, even if on a basis which may seem ambiguous. Political Co-operation was originally a French invention. Institutional progress has been at the French initiative, whether at the Summit of The Hague in 1969, the

Single European Act in 1987, or the Inter-governmental Conference of 1990. When France lost interest in the process, as in the late 1970s, EPC dragged its wing. When other countries tried to move things forward without active French support, as in the Genscher–Colombo initiative of 1981, the attempt was a failure. At the same time, France has best succeeded in its initiatives when it has secured German support.

The motives of successive French governments in promoting a European identity, whether along inter-governmental or integrationist lines, are complex and shifting. A consistent feature has been the need to find a way of expressing policies which are not those of the United States.

The relationship between the United States and its allies in Western Europe, and the view the Americans have taken of European efforts to build an integrated regional grouping, are the second determining factor in the shaping of Political Co-operation. The United States' view has fluctuated between support for a development which is in its long-term interest and suspicion of an emerging power which has not always followed the American lead. The Europeans for their part have been divided over the response to make to American policy, and have changed their views as US policy itself has changed. Most Europeans dealing with foreign affairs were mystified by policy under President Carter and found President Reagan's policy uncongenial. Whether for or against, no Member State of the Community could remain indifferent to the position of Washington, with direct consequences for the positions taken by EPC.

The European Defence Community of 1952 had been launched by France with the intention of containing a Germany rearming at the insistence of the United States in order to contribute to the defence of Western Europe. General de Gaulle's attempt a decade later to build an inter-governmental Europe foundered partly on opposition from the integrationists and partly from opposition, particularly from the Netherlands, to a system which did not contain an adequate place for the United States. Time and again after Political Co-operation had been set up, the Europeans had to face up to demands from the United States either for support on specific policy issues or to modify policies which the Americans believed not to be in their interests. Dr

Kissinger's 'Year of Europe' initiative was designed to redefine the transatlantic relationship, in a way which made clear the leadership of the American partner, faced with the growing profile of Political Co-operation. The Europeans' response was made more complicated by the war in the Middle East and the oil crisis, on which the United States demanded adherence to its policies. Later, the Americans sought support for Camp David, over the American hostages in Iran, over Poland, and, on international terrorism, against Libya. On each occasion, EPC policy was affected.

The third factor shaping Political Co-operation is the way in which machinery has been set up in a piecemeal way to cope with the challenges with which EPC was faced. There was no grand design; rather the way in which EPC reacted to events determined the type of organization it became. When EPC began in 1970, it was provided with the bare minimum of machinery and practically nothing in the way of rules of procedure. Both evolved over the years, and practice was from time to time codified to set Political Co-operation a stage further on the road, as in the Copenhagen Report of 1973 and the London Report of 1981. The system of Working Groups and of European Correspondents, the network of confidential telex communications, the co-operation at the United Nations and in third countries were all developed in this way. The process was also important for institutional reasons. Whereas, to begin with, the French in particular insisted that EPC should be kept totally separate from the European Community, it was soon found that the political and economic aspects of foreign policy were so intertwined that this was not practicable. There was no alternative but to allow the Commission to take part in at least some EPC activities, beginning with the economic aspects of the Conference on Security and Co-operation in Europe (CSCE) and the Euro-Arab Dialogue.

Later, the need for effective collective implementation of EPC policies obliged the Member States to turn increasingly to the economic instruments at the disposal of the Community, either for sanctions, as in the case of Poland, the Falkland Islands, South Africa, and Iraq, or for budgetary assistance, as in the case of Central America and South Africa again.

These three strands appear throughout the narrative, sometimes in a confused and tangled way which reflects reality, but does not make for an easy comprehension of the detailed description of what happened. Here, to guide the reader, is a broad picture of the sweep of events; inevitably it is a caricature.

The origins of Political Co-operation are to be sought in the immediate post-war period, when an idealist current of opinion determined to replace the political structures which had failed to prevent the war briefly coincided with the *realpolitik* necessity to create conditions in which Germany could safely be allowed to rearm. The move to create for this purpose a European Defence Community, which would have had attached to it a European Political Community with evolutive powers over foreign policy, failed essentially for reasons of French domestic politics. Instead, and after a decent interval, the Treaties of Rome conferred on supranational institutions responsibility for the conduct of limited areas of economic policy. What later became the 'Fouchet Plan', launched in the early 1960s, was an attempt by General de Gaulle to regain control for national governments of European policy-making and to give the Member States of the Community a more resonant, effective, and autonomous voice in international affairs. This initiative failed, as we have seen, because of opposition from integrationists and those who cherished the relationship with the United States. It was only under President Pompidou, at the Summit of The Hague in 1969, that a deal could be struck in which France's partners secured a number of concessions including the accession of the United Kingdom to the Communities in return for agreeing to set up a structure for foreign policy making on the intergovernmentalist lines of the Fouchet Plan.

Although the Luxembourg Report of 1970 which established EPC set up machinery which was essentially inter-governmental, it also stated that the intention was to 'give shape to the will to political union'. EPC was seen, at least by some, as a step on the road to European Union and not merely a convenient way to co-ordinate national foreign policies. The ambiguity has persisted to this day.

In its first three years EPC succeeded in forging a united position on the CSCE, a matter of particular concern to Germany, and, at the initiative of France, made surprising progress in bringing together divergent national views on the

Middle East. The discussions on the CSCE set the pattern of work for EPC, played an important part in the outcome of the Conference, and, contrary to French intentions, required the association of the Community in the shape of the Commission. The experience gained in these and other areas was consolidated in the Copenhagen Report of 1973, after the Paris Summit of the previous year had made it plain that EPC should henceforward get on with its foreign-policy job and leave to other bodies in the Community reflections on further steps towards European Union.

The year 1973 saw the enlargement of the Community and the need to face squarely up to the definition of the relationship with the United States. This was thrust upon the Nine by Dr Kissinger, who in the spring of that year launched the 'Year of Europe' in an attempt to preserve for the United States the political leadership of the transatlantic alliance. The Europeans' response was made yet more complicated by the outbreak of the October War and the call by the Americans to join an oil consumers' cartel led by them to counter the Arab oil embargo. Their response was mixed. The Member States except France joined the United States on the oil question in a position worked out in the Community framework, while, led by France in the EPC framework, they launched a dialogue with the Arabs which was originally intended to be political, but became economic, thereby once more bringing in the European Commission. The tension with the United States only relaxed in the spring of 1974 when a formula for consultations was agreed.

During this period EPC began to widen its scope under the pressure of events. The *coup d'état* and subsequent invasion of Cyprus in 1974 and the execution of Basque terrorists in Spain in 1975 forced the Nine into action. The events required a response because they took place in the back garden; EPC did not as yet feel the need to have a view on any and every event which took place in the world. The action over Cyprus was effective, at least to begin with, because the French Presidency made flexible use of the available mechanisms and because there was a broad convergence of views among the Nine. That over Spain was not, for the converse reasons.

In the same period, the Nine began to take an interest in Southern Africa, spurred on by the decaying situation in

Introduction

Portugal's ex-colonies, which it was feared offered fertile ground for Soviet influence, and by Dutch pressure to take action over the worsening situation in South Africa. The action taken—the adoption of a Code of Conduct on British lines in 1976—was intended by Member States with important economic interests in South Africa to ward off the need for more drastic action.

On the institutional side, the period 1973–7 was marked by the setting up of the European Council in 1974 and the commissioning from Prime Minister Tindemans of Belgium of a report on European Union. The European Council, which gave itself the job of ensuring overall consistency between the Community and Political Co-operation, was seen by integrationists as a step backwards from the Community method. The trend away from European Union, at the beginning of the years of Euro-pessimism as the economic situation worsened, was confirmed by the lukewarm reception given to the Tindemans Report, in spite of its unsensational recommendations.

The period 1976–81 was marked by stagnation, followed by a realization that the Nine risked seeing what they had achieved slipping away from them and by some initiatives to prevent that from happening. The achievements had been appreciable. Starting from nothing, EPC had in little more than five years made a name for itself in the world, contributed significantly to the process of *détente* in Europe through its participation in the CSCE, obliged the United States to think afresh about its relationship with its allies, begun a dialogue with its Arab partners, and extended its purview to its Mediterranean neighbours and to Southern Africa. Now this process seemed to come to a halt. The main reason was the diminished interest of France, on whom EPC had largely depended in the early years to push it forward. Now President Giscard d'Estaing, although convinced of the benefits of an effective European Community, preferred, for foreign-policy initiatives, smaller groupings of world statesmen.

EPC also suffered from a shortage of world crises to which to react. It was unlucky that the Soviet Union invaded Afghanistan just after Christmas 1979, a time of the year when the machinery was least able to function. The Nine were slow off the mark, acquiring some discredit thereby. With one eye over their shoulder at the Americans, their proposals for dealing with the situation were delayed for some months, and not followed up until a year later under the influence of Lord Carrington who throughout his period of office as British Foreign Secretary was a vigorous proponent of EPC. The attempt to work out a new policy on the Middle East was only partially successful, the Venice Declaration of 1980 having been deprived by the Americans of what had been intended to be its most telling component, a move in the Security Council to update Resolution 242. The Nine failed to come up to US expectations over the Iran hostage crisis, taking a decision on sanctions only when, unbeknown to them, President Carter had already decided to mount a rescue mission.

From 1978 on, as the negotiations for the enlargement of the Community first to Greece and later to Spain and Portugal proceeded, the Nine had to deal with the problem of how to organize parallel accession to EPC. The British suggested that the opportunity should be taken of strengthening the procedures of Political Co-operation, but this was blocked by the French. The British returned to the charge, however, alarmed by the inability of EPC to deal with crises as shown by the Afghanistan fiasco, and succeeded in securing the adoption of the London Report in 1981. This Report codified the accretion of procedure since the Copenhagen Report and provided for the full association of the Commission, but failed to bring security questions within the ambit of EPC discussions.

Similar concern about the apparent inability of the Nine (now Ten) to play an effective international role, especially at a time when American leadership under President Carter was seen to be weak, was shown by Foreign Minister Genscher of the Federal Republic, who in 1981 launched an initiative with his Italian colleague Colombo to extend the scope of inter-governmental consultations to cover questions of security and judicial co-operation. Subsequent discussions resulted in the Stuttgart Declaration of 1983, disappointing in that it marked scant progress. The reason was partly because some Member States distrusted the expansion of activities outside the Community framework, partly because Ireland, Denmark, and Greece were not prepared to go along with genuine discussions on security, and partly because France was lukewarm throughout.

The period 1982–6 was marked by a persistent deterioration in US–EPC relations, as many European governments found themselves increasingly out of sympathy with the 'Evil Empire' policies pursued by the Reagan Administration. The period began with what the Americans perceived as European pusillanimity in response to the imposition of martial law in Poland in the winter of 1981–2 and reached a climax with the American raid on Libya in 1986, which some maintained had been brought about by EPC's weakness in the previous weeks and months.

The Poland affair nevertheless enabled the Ten to test out new ways of implementing foreign-policy decisions by using Community instruments, and was the first of a series, by the end of which a procedure had been honed allowing the rapid imposition of sanctions in a combined EPC–EC operation. The other events in the series were the invasion of the Falkland Islands later in 1982 and the adoption of sanctions against South Africa in 1985 and 1986. The Falkland Islands crisis not only confirmed the use of sanctions at Community level, it allowed the Ten to display their solidarity with the United Kingdom and thereby demonstrated an important function of Political Co-operation. The South Africa sanctions were also significant, in spite of the long-drawn-out and public wrangling among Member States, because they showed that EPC as a mechanism had the ability to bring together in significant action national positions which at the outset had been widely separated. The experience gained in applying sanctions was put to rapid and uncontroversial use on the invasion of Kuwait in 1990.

The use of Community instruments by EPC was not confined to sanctions. Recourse was also had to the Community budget to provide financial incentives. The Ten's new policy towards Central America from 1982 on consisted largely in conducting a region-to-region dialogue which provided Central America with a political point of reference which was neither the United States nor the Soviet Union (an approach which did nothing to improve EPC–US relations). It could not have been launched, however, without the underpinning, albeit modest, of increased aid from the Community budget. Similarly, the sanctions against South Africa were accompanied by a series of 'positive measures', of which the most significant were financial support for the victims of apartheid provided from the Community budget.

Attempts to achieve institutional progress towards European Union had not been abandoned during this period, in spite of the failure of the Genscher–Colombo initiative. Moves in the European Parliament and, initiated by President Mitterrand, in the European Council, led first of all to the setting up of an *ad hoc* Committee on Institutional Affairs and later to the decision by the European Council in Milan in June 1985 setting in motion the process culminating in the Single European Act of 1987. The most significant feature of the Single European Act was that it was single: it combined in one legal text provisions for Political Co-operation and amendments to the Community Treaties, thus breaking the taboo of over thirty years. That this came about was in part owing to the fact that the two frameworks had been growing together, helped by the Commission's full association with EPC since 1981 and the series of events described above which encouraged interaction between EPC and the Community.

This growing together, or 'consistency', has continued since the coming into force of the Act, especially in response to the events in Central and Eastern Europe in 1989 and 1990. The extent to which this 'consistency' should or should not be converted into a common policy in a single framework is one of the main questions facing the Inter-governmental Conference in 1991.

1
The Mechanics of European Political Co-operation

This chapter describes how EPC is organized and what it does today.

First of all, a word about nomenclature. European co-operation in the sphere of foreign policy, to give it its correct name, is not the same as the European Community (EC), although its activities are frequently ascribed to the Community by those for whom the inner workings of the Community institutions remain impenetrably arcane. It is often referred to in abbreviated form as Political Co-operation, or by its initials, EPC. It is also known by the number of Member States it comprises, currently the Twelve. This can lead to confusion for the historian as successive enlargements took the original Six to Nine, then Ten, then Twelve. The practice in recent years has been to refer in formal declarations to 'the Community and its Member States'.

THE BASIS

For the first seventeen years of its existence EPC had no legal, or even formal, standing. It was based on a private agreement among Foreign Ministries to organize regular meetings and observe certain conventions. These were set out in three Reports, the Luxembourg Report of 1970, the Copenhagen Report of 1973, and the London Report of 1981. These Reports were never submitted to parliamentary scrutiny and in most cases authority to agree to them was not sought outside the Foreign Ministries of the Member States. Political Co-operation was a private club, operated by diplomats for diplomats, and the same ambience has persisted to this day. This has been a source of both weakness and strength: strength, because those responsible for foreign policy have felt committed to the agreements they have themselves made; weakness, because the closed nature of the system has denied it popular awareness and legitimacy and because movement is not generated from within the system, but depends on outside events.

The legal situation was altered in 1987 by the coming into force of the Single European Act, Title III of which contains Treaty provisions governing EPC. Political Co-operation thus acquired the status conferred on it by an instrument subject to international law and shared with the European Communities. The change in legal status did not, however, affect the way EPC conducted its business, through inter-governmental co-operation separate from the Community institutional order.

The pillars on which Political Co-operation rests are the inter-governmental method and the rule of consensus. The Member States take part in a highly developed process of consultation, without abandoning, at least in theory, a whit of their national sovereignty. All delegations are equal around the table, from permanent members of the Security Council, like France and the United Kingdom, to the smallest Member State, the Grand Duchy of Luxembourg. None of the Community institutions has a formal role. There are mechanisms for contacts with the European Parliament, and the Commission has been fully associated with EPC since 1981, but it does not play the institutional role it has in the Community. The Single European Act excluded Title III from the jurisdiction of the European Court of Justice, and the meetings of the Community Council and of Ministers in EPC are formally separate, although recent practice has eroded this principle.

All decisions are taken by consensus of the Twelve Member States. If any one of them objects, the decision is not taken. The effect of this is less negative than might be expected, and not so dissimilar from much of what happens in the Community. EPC does not operate under the perpetual threat of veto, and the participants make genuine efforts to reach a positive outcome. Past attempts to introduce an element of majority decision making have, however, failed.

EPC operates by talking incessantly. Every year upwards of a hundred meetings are held at all levels, during which the Twelve exchange information and analysis of international political developments. This forms the basis for common views, which influence national positions and, when made public, are studied attentively by Foreign Ministries around the world. The Twelve have a view on most subjects and make them known by declarations at frequent intervals. A useful compendium of their current views is found in the speech which the Foreign Minister of the Presidency makes each year on their behalf to the United Nations General Assembly, traditionally on the second morning of the 'New York week' at the end of September, on the heels of the United States and the Soviet Union.

EPC has been criticized as being limited to declaratory diplomacy. Declarations certainly form a high proportion of its activity, but they should not be disparaged for all that. They can sometimes be effective tools and substantial diplomatic events, like the Venice Declaration on the Middle East in 1980 or the declarations on Central America in 1983 and 1984. But it is true that the Twelve have few means of collective action at their disposal. They can decide to make a diplomatic *démarche* to a third country, either confidentially or publicly, as when EPC presented Israel with a questionnaire about its intentions after the invasion of Lebanon in 1982, or appealing for clemency or the release of political prisoners in South Africa in the years after 1984. There are more than 150 human-rights *démarches* a year. Since EPC does not have its own diplomatic service, these *démarches* are carried out by the Ambassador of the Presidency on the spot, either alone or according to the 'Troika' formula, in which the Presidency is joined by its immediate predecessor and successor together with the Commission.

Beyond this point, the traditional means of national diplomacy can scarcely be transposed to the European level. The Twelve therefore look, when their policies need to be implemented collectively, to the instruments available in the Community. These may be positive, like the aid programme for the victims of apartheid and support for regional projects in Central America, or negative, like sanctions against Argentina or South Africa.

The Twelve are debarred from collective military action, even for peace-keeping purposes. The failure of the attempt to provide political cover through EPC for European participation in the Sinai Multinational Force and Observers in 1981–2 was at least in part owing to EPC's self-denying ordinance on anything with a military flavour.

THE MACHINERY

The machinery of EPC is complex and active. At the apex is the European Council of Heads of State and Government, meeting twice a year or more often if required. The European Council was designed to be the body in which the streams of Political Co-operation and the Community came together, and was to give political directives to work in both forums. In fact this has rarely happened. The course of history has obliged the European Council to spend most of its time unravelling Community problems. Only rarely has it played an important role in an EPC question, one example being the Venice Declaration of 1980. It failed completely at The Hague in 1986 on sanctions against South Africa, and the matter was left to be settled by Foreign Ministers three months later.

Political Co-operation questions at meetings of the European Council are usually dealt with by Foreign Ministers at dinner the first evening and any texts to be adopted are submitted to Heads of Government the next day. Contrary to earlier practice, the European Council has in recent years shown some resistance to rubber-stamping routine EPC texts which do not reflect its own discussions.

Officials on the EPC side are included in the national delegations to meetings of the European Council. Since they do not usually have a great deal to do on these occasions, there is ample opportunity, often in agreeable surroundings, for the 'socialization' which oils the wheels of EPC.

At the level below the Heads of Government, the Foreign Ministers hold four EPC meetings a year, two in the capitals of successive Presidencies and two in Brussels and Luxembourg. The dates are fixed well in advance, which leads to some lack of flexibility in preparing the agenda. In the case of meetings in the capitals, the date chosen may not fit happily into the course of international events and declarations by Ministers could be better timed. Rather than cancellation, which might be the sensible course, the meetings usually take place anyway in order to cast lustre on the country holding the Presidency, and the need to produce something for the press may slant the discussion.

The same does not apply to the meetings of Ministers in Brussels and Luxembourg, which are held in tandem with the

General Affairs Council of the Community. By and large, the same Ministers attend both, and EPC affairs are regularly discussed at the monthly Council meetings without waiting for the formal EPC Ministerial Meetings to come round. In the past, the Community and EPC agendas were kept rigidly separate, although in practice the time available could be allotted flexibly. Since the Irish and Italian Presidencies in 1990, the agendas of Ministerial Meetings and the Council have been merged and there is no indication as to which point comes from EPC and which from the Community side. This was a reform, proposed at the time by the Italians, which was specifically rejected during the negotiation of the Single European Act in 1985. The merging does not, however, extend to the preparation of the Ministers' discussions, which is the responsibility of the Political Committee for EPC items and of the Committee of Permanent Representatives (Coreper) for the Community items, each according to its own rules and procedures.

The Foreign Ministers also meet informally over the weekend once in each Presidency. These are the so-called 'Gymnich-type' meetings, after Schloss Gymnich near Bonn where the first such meeting was held in 1974, but which has since been bought by the Japanese. The meetings always take place in some quiet spot in the country which holds the Presidency, in an ambience conducive to fireside chats. To add to the ambience wives are invited, but officials are not. Some Ministers evade this prohibition by bringing their assistants masquerading as interpreters. Because the proceedings are informal, no decisions are taken and no official record is made. Differing recollections of what has been said have shown the inconvenience of this, and since 1990 not only the Political Director of the Presidency, but also the Secretary-General of the Council and the Head of the EPC Secretariat have attended the meetings. The informality is rapidly becoming a memory, especially as the press corps hovers at a distance to glean what it can. Comments to the press are not encouraged by the Presidency, but it has been known for Ministers to give impromptu press conferences in muddy fields. There is no bar on subjects to be discussed in the meeting, and EPC and Community items have always been discussed together in this setting.

The EPC and Community streams divide at the level immediately below the Foreign Ministers, represented on the EPC side by the Political Committee. This body is the hub of Political Co-operation, preparing the Ministers' discussions, directing the work of the Working Groups at the level next below, and frequently taking decisions on its own responsibility. It is made up of the Political Directors of the Twelve Foreign Ministries and of the Commission who meet once a month except in August and more frequently if necessary.

The Political Directors are senior officials whose place in the hierarchy of their Ministry varies with the Member State concerned. In some countries, such as Belgium, the Political Director is responsible to the Minister for all the political work of the Ministry. In others he has more specific responsibilities and is on an equal footing with colleagues of the same rank. This is the case in the Federal Republic of Germany. The British Political Director, whose title had to be created for the purposes of Political Co-operation, is a Deputy Under-Secretary with departmental responsibilities, but moral authority over his colleagues because of his role in the Political Committee. In most Foreign Ministries, the British Foreign Office being a notable exception, the political section is separate from the economic section and the Political Director's writ does not run there, complicating co-ordination between EPC and the Community.

The Political Committee can play a decisive part in EPC because the Political Directors have the authority to engage in bargaining and to strike a deal. They may wish to check with capitals before committing themselves, especially on issues outside their normal field of operation, and a great deal of telephoning goes on during Political Committee meetings, but except for cases requiring a decision at the level of Ministers, compromises can usually be reached which the Political Directors then defend with their respective administrations.

The atmosphere in the Political Committee is friendly, almost casual. The Political Directors are on first-name terms and the discussions, although well ordered, are free from the stiff formality of Coreper. The Political Directors have dinner and lunch together at each meeting of the Political Committee, which provides an opportunity for personal discussions and fosters the club spirit.

The Political Committee continues to meet in the capital of the Presidency, as it has throughout the history of Political Co-operation. When the Single European Act was concluded it was foreseen that the Political Committee would move most of its meetings to Brussels. Political Directors had second thoughts, however, ostensibly fearing that the hawk-eyed Brussels press corps would penetrate the confidentiality of their proceedings (the press corps had only once descended *en masse* on the Political Committee, when it discussed South Africa in Luxembourg in August 1985), but more likely in order to preserve its separateness from the Community bodies, as well as to avoid the Presidency having to decamp to Brussels for each meeting with all the Chairmen of the Working Groups. It must be added that the facilities provided by successive Presidencies, in a spirit of healthy emulation, in the national capitals are superior to the functional, but uninspiring, surroundings of the Council building in Brussels.

The great mass of work in Political Co-operation is done in the Working Groups. There are upwards of twenty of these, either geographical like the Latin America, Middle East, or Asia Working Groups, or horizontal, like the Working Groups on the United Nations or Non-Proliferation. They are manned usually at the level of Head of Department, although there has been some downgrading recently, and, depending on requirements, will meet several times in each Presidency. The meetings used to take place in the national capitals, but since the Single European Act have moved to the premises of the EPC Secretariat in the Charlemagne building in Brussels.

The main function of the Working Groups is to exchange information, and on the basis of that shared information to arrive at common analyses. The Groups can then make recommendations for action to the Political Committee, or at least identify options. They do not take decisions themselves, reflecting the fact that the Member States' representatives at that level do not have the authority to agree to compromises without referring back. If a decision cannot wait until the next meeting of the Political Committee, it can be taken by the Correspondance européenne (Coreu) telex network.

The proceedings of Working Group meetings are summarized in an 'oral report', which is written. It is drafted on the sole responsibility of the Presidency, does not require consensus, and therefore in theory should not be amended at the request of partners, although exceptions are sometimes made when particularly delicate points are at issue. It was originally presented orally by the Working Group Chairman to the Political Committee, and for many years was religiously read out, even though the Political Directors had the written text before them. This excruciating practice has gradually been abandoned since the late 1980s, although the presence of the Working Group Chairmen at Political Committee discussions of items in their area remains an important operational feature of EPC.

MANAGEMENT FUNCTIONS

Since Political Co-operation is inter-governmental, it has had to develop its own management functions which are different from those of the Community. The leading role is played by the Presidency, which rotates among Member States, following the same rules as in the Community. The Presidency not only chairs all meetings, from the European Council down to the Working Groups, but also draws up the agenda and provides the intellectual input for the discussions, for example by circulating position papers. This is not an exclusive function, since any Member State can request that an item be put on the agenda or can circulate a paper, but the job is usually done by the Presidency.

The fact that each Presidency lasts for only six months has an effect on the way EPC works. On the one hand, there is often a drive to notch up achievements before the end of the Presidency, providing an element of dynamism which would otherwise be lacking from within the system, although some Presidencies, particularly those of the larger countries, prefer a low-key, managerial approach. On the other hand, the frequent change of Presidency makes a consistent presentation of policy difficult and practically excludes long-term planning. The fact that each Member State's turn now comes round every six years, instead of every three as in the early years, is an additional drawback.

The Presidency's other main function is to act as spokesman for the Twelve. As interest in EPC on the part of third countries has grown, this has become a time-consuming and wellnigh impossible task. The Ambassadors of many countries must be briefed after Ministerial Meetings and meetings of the Political Committee, diplomatic contacts have to be maintained, and *démarches* must be carried out. The ease of modern jet travel both enables and requires the Political Director of the Presidency to be frequently on the move. The obligations cannot be avoided and are an important means for Political Co-operation to assert its personality and make its views known.

A mechanism has been devised to support the Presidency in its contacts with third countries. This is the Troika, in which the Presidency is accompanied by representatives of the previous and next Presidencies and of the Commission. The Troika formula had been developed in the mid–1970s to negotiate texts with the Arab League for the purposes of the Euro-Arab Dialogue, was seen in 1978 to have special advantages for dealing with Turkey after the accession of Greece, and thereafter came to be a preferred way of denoting the collective personality of EPC. Although the Commission took part in the Euro-Arab Dialogue Troika, its presence as a general rule was only confirmed after the Gymnich meeting in April 1983. Member States' hesitations were not surprising. Apart from doubts about sharing EPC representational functions with a Community institution, they reflected that, whereas any one Member State was in the Troika for eighteen months only, and that at five-year intervals, the Commission would be a permanent member and would thus acquire undue influence.

Political Co-operation did without a Secretariat for the first seventeen years of its existence. The reason was historical: for twenty years previously successive initiatives to institute a European foreign policy had failed because of disagreement over whether it should be integrationist or inter-governmental. The setting up of a Secretariat, in Paris, had come to symbolize the extreme inter-governmental approach and was rejected by the integrationists for that reason. As a result, when EPC began, the Presidency had to provide its own Secretariat. This became an increasing burden as the volume of work grew, and various experiments were tried. The London Report of 1981 set up a Troika support team, in which young officials from the previous and the incoming Presidencies were lent to the current Presidency for its six months' term of office. The development was a promising one. As well as providing material help, a significant factor for the smaller countries, the support team had an important educative function. With one exception, it was physically housed in the Foreign Ministry of the Presidency, and the sight of foreign diplomats *intra muros*, taking part in national meetings and helping to form policy, was a revelation to many national officials. There were disadvantages too. The usefulness of the team depended on the extent the Presidency was prepared to make use of it, and in countries like Denmark and Greece there were inevitably linguistic constraints. The peripatetic nature of the arrangement placed a strain on the team members and was an easy target for criticism. The fact that the EPC archives had to be carried halfway across Europe in a suitcase every six months gave rise to particularly unfavourable comment. When French and German proposals in 1985 for a high-level EPC Secretariat for the European Council ran into the old integrationist objections, the obvious compromise was to enlarge the Troika to five members and site it permanently in Brussels. This was the decision incorporated into the Single European Act.

The new Secretariat had a difficult job to do. Its role was tightly circumscribed in the Ministers' decision of 28 February 1986, which made it plain that its task was to assist the Presidency and that it had no autonomous attributions of its own. It nevertheless had to overcome the suspicions of the Political Directors and of the Commission, both of whom scented a rival. It therefore concentrated on making itself useful and threatening no one. It did not seek a role of initiative like the Commission's in the Community, but was always ready to draft a paper at the request of the Presidency. After some initial confusion, it was always present at meetings with third countries and with the European Parliament and has thus acquired a continuity of memory without displacing the Presidency or the Troika as the spokesman of EPC. Reassured by the Secretariat's behaviour, successive Presidencies have been more inclined not only to hand over administrative tasks but also to allow it space to develop an individual role. This willingness to look beyond the subservience originally envisaged was deliberately encouraged by the Belgian Presidency which oversaw the first six months of the Secretariat's existence and set the tone for the coming years.

The Secretariat is made up of a Head of Secretariat appointed by the Ministers, five officials of diplomatic rank seconded from the Foreign Ministries of the 'enlarged Troika', five more seconded officials to serve as administration officer, archivist, and communications officers, and six secretaries, also seconded. The Secretariat is housed in its own quarters in the Charlemagne building of the Council in Brussels, where there is a meeting room for the Working Groups. Normal office services are provided by the Council Secretariat for a symbolic payment of 1 ecu each Presidency, under the terms of an exchange of letters of 21 July 1986 between Sir Geoffrey Howe as President-in-Office and the Secretary-General of the Council, Mr Ersbøll. Other costs are borne by the Presidency.

The members of the Secretariat do not become Community officials, but remain on the books of their national administrations and are attached for administrative purposes to one of their country's diplomatic missions in Brussels, usually the Permanent Representation to the Community. The most serious drawback to their position is that they do not have regular access to sources of information. Individual members may see telegrams from their home Ministry, but the information these contain varies from country to country, as does permission to share the information with colleagues in the Secretariat. The lack of a consistent and homogeneous source of information has been one of the main obstacles in the way of the Secretariat's undertaking the regular analysis of events which would be the foundation for any role of initiative.

The Secretariat's main tasks are to service EPC meetings, provide the draft replies to parliamentary questions, and act as the memory of Political Co-operation. The organization of meetings involves close liaison with the Presidency, in whose name agendas are circulated and oral reports and conclusions prepared. This work is complicated by the fact that, except during the Belgian Presidency, the co-ordination has to be done over a distance. Modern communications help, but EPC's obsession with confidentiality has meant that, although an encrypted fax link between Presidency and Secretariat has been added to the telex facility, the possibilities of video-conferencing have not been adequately explored. The personal advice which the secretary of a Working Group can give to his Chairman during the latter's presence in Brussels for meetings can therefore be influential.

Members of the European Parliament put down more than 500 questions a year for reply by EPC. The draft replies are prepared by the EPC Secretariat, cleared with the Presidency, and then submitted for approval to the Member States. When consensus has been reached, which may require some time and a succession of amendments, all of which in turn have to go through the same process, the Secretariat sends the reply to the Parliament via the Council Secretariat. A start has been made in the Secretariat in setting up the beginnings of an electronic archive, which helps ensure consistency in the Twelve's replies and minimizes difficulties in reaching consensus. By the same token, however, reliance on precedent tends to stifle innovation and is not highly appreciated by Parliament.

The same observation can be made about the Secretariat's role as guardian of the tablets of EPC. The successful development of Political Co-operation was possible because participants were prepared to find new answers to new problems. This presented few difficulties when precedent was both informal and frequently forgotten as one EPC generation succeeded another. The legal codification of EPC in the Single European Act formalized precedent, albeit at a high level of generality. There is a risk that the institutionalized memory of the Secretariat, in addition to its obvious advantages, will act as a dead hand on new ways of doing things.

The arrival of the Secretariat has detracted somewhat from the former importance of the Group of Correspondents, which previously advised on procedure and helped manage EPC. The Group is formed of the European Correspondents, who are the middle-grade officials in each Foreign Ministry, and the Commission, who act as the central contact point and as assistants to the Political Directors for all EPC questions. The Correspondents attend all Ministerial Meetings and meetings of the Political Committee. They hold a meeting on their own in the morning before the Political Committee begins, during which they go through the Political Committee's agenda, deal with the oral reports of any Working Group meetings which do not require attention at the level of the Political Committee, and discuss any questions relating to the organization of EPC. After the Political Committee meeting the Correspondents finalize at lunch its draft conclusions, which will have been prepared by the Presidency with the help of the Secretariat as the meeting progresses. This esoteric exercise can last well into the coffee, but is important because the Political Committee's conclusions are agreed by consensus and bind the Member States. Although the conclusions can later be amended within a fixed period, the Correspondents are supposed to do their work well enough to make this unnecessary.

Like the Political Directors, the Correspondents lunch together at their own table. The *esprit de corps* of the group is even stronger than that of the Political Directors and many of them become personal friends. These personal links serve an important operational purpose. It frequently happens that one Correspondent will telephone another to warn him of some difficulty looming on the horizon or to sort out a problem informally without causing a stir. The Correspondents have also been traditionally responsible for working out procedural ways of dealing with problems or encouraging the development of EPC. It was they who drafted the London Report, the instructions to missions in third countries, and the Ministers' decision of 28 February 1986.

Political Co-operation has its own communications network, without which the system would break down. This is the Coreu network, which allows the Member States to exchange confidential telex messages with extraordinary rapidity. Each of the Twelve Foreign Ministries, as well as the Commission and the EPC Secretariat, has a Coreu terminal which enables it to receive and send enciphered messages, which are then circulated within the Ministry, usually under the control of the European Correspondent. Most Coreus are copied to the diplomatic Missions of the Twelve in Geneva and New York as well as to the Permanent Representatives to the Communities in Brussels, but this is done manually, not by direct link. The Presidency is responsible for seeing that the Embassies of its partners in the capital of the Presidency are supplied with copies of Coreus direct.

When Political Co-operation started, messages were conveyed via the traditional diplomatic channels, the Embassies of the Member States in each other's capitals. This was soon found to be too cumbersome for the purposes of decision-making by consensus on which EPC relied. The Coreu network was therefore set up under the Danish Presidency in the second half of 1973. It is run from the Netherlands Foreign Ministry in The Hague, and the Danish and Dutch representatives have always been particularly active in the regular meetings of Heads of Communications through which the network is managed. The Commission joined the network with its own terminal after its full association with Political Co-operation had been accepted in the London Report of 1981, and the Secretariat on its being set up in 1987. The operating costs are shared equally among the participants.

Some 9,000 Coreus are currently sent annually, many of them concerned with the minutiae of EPC such as the calling of meetings, the exchange of day-to-day diplomatic information, the finalizing of reports and declarations, or the approval of replies to parliamentary questions. The sheer volume is impressive, and acts as a perpetual reminder of EPC to all those over whose desks Coreus pass. So also is the speed with which messages are exchanged. A telegram sent by one Foreign Ministry will within a few hours be studied and acted on in twelve others. In addition to providing an efficient service without which EPC could not function, the Coreu network has had the side effect of reducing the reporting work of the Embassies of the Twelve in each other's capitals, whose role in EPC has practically been reduced to contacts with the host country when bilateral deals are brewing.

Although not part of the management function of EPC, the Commission has acquired its own place in the mechanism. This is because of the increasing number of occasions on which there is interaction between EPC and the Community. The Commission then has a role to play, not only because of its powers to initiate Community action and execute Community policies, and in particular the budget, but also because under the provisions of the Single European Act it shares with the Presidency the responsibility for ensuring that consistency is sought and maintained between the external policies of the Community and the policies agreed in EPC.

This responsibility is carried out in a variety of ways. In the everyday run of work, the Commission must make sure that the participants in EPC are aware of relevant activities in the Community. This might seem superfluous, since the same Member States are present in both forums. However, the fact that many Foreign Ministries are divided into separate political and economic sections means that information does not circulate freely enough within a Ministry to ensure perfect consistency in European policy at national level. The problem is even greater between Foreign Ministries and Economics Ministries. There is an information gap which the Commission tries to fill. The process is helped by the fact that the same Commission representatives (unlike those of Member States) often participate in EPC Working Groups and in Groups of the Council, and that responsibility for EPC is situated in the Secretariat-General of the Commission, which has central co-ordinating powers with regard to other Commission services.

The same process works in the reverse direction. By its presence in EPC, the Commission is able to propose and execute Community policies with a fuller knowledge of the broader political framework as it emerges from the EPC discussions. Full records are made by the Secretariat-General of discussions in EPC and these are circulated to the Commissioners and departments concerned, helping to create a community of views within the Commission.

It is not so much a question of policy orientations being decided in EPC and executed in the Community as of the creation of a shared perception within which both sides can work. The process is not without its difficulties. There is a natural tendency on the part of the Working Groups to turn themselves into management committees for the execution of Community policy, a tendency which the Commission resists in defence of the Community institutional order. The positions taken by the Commission in cases like this are resented by the Member States, which ascribe them to excessive formalism and a determination to hang on to power.

CO-OPERATION IN THIRD COUNTRIES

Political Co-operation does not stop at the borders of the Community. Embassies of the Twelve in third countries also meet regularly and engage in co-operation on their own account. This process is not always mastered by the central administrations, and has led to attempts in the past to require Ambassadors to seek authorization before embarking on a joint report. There is a risk that an Ambassador whose policy recommendations have not found favour at home will seek to present them again, this time with the imprimatur of the Twelve. It is outweighed, however, by the advantages of encouraging activities which strengthen the identity of the Twelve, and central directives have more often gone in this than in a restrictive direction.

Co-operation abroad was slow to take off, but has intensified over the years, as can be seen from the references to it in the successive Reports produced by EPC. It had become an appreciable phenomenon by the time of the London Report, which stated that

> In view of the increasing activities of the Ten in third countries it is important that the Heads of Mission of the Ten maintain the practice of meeting regularly in order to exchange information and co-ordinate views. In considering their response to significant developments in the country to which they are accredited, their first instinct should be to co-ordinate with their colleagues of the Ten.

At the initiative of the United Kingdom, always looking for concrete and uncontroversial ways of consolidating Political Co-operation, the Political Committee issued in May 1984 a set of directives which listed the areas in which posts abroad were to seek to co-operate. This list was later taken over practically unchanged in the Ministers' Decision of 28 February 1986 which accompanied the Single European Act. Annex II of the Decision directed Member States' missions and Commission delegations to intensify their co-operation in third countries and international organizations in areas including the exchange of political and economic information, the pooling of information on administrative and practical problems, communications, security and consular questions, health, education, information, and cultural affairs.

The Ambassadors are bidden to meet at least once a month on political questions, and Embassy staff also meet in their own groups at regular intervals. The common identity is most often displayed in *démarches* made collectively or by the Troika. A mechanism frequently employed is for the Ambassadors to lunch together with the Foreign Minister from time to time or to request special briefings for the Twelve. In other areas such as cultural or information work much depends on the enthusiasm of one or two individuals. The Commission Delegation—the counterpart of Member States' Embassies in third countries—can play an important part in stimulating collective activity of a non-political nature, since by definition it has no national axe to

The Mechanics of EPC

grind and embodies the European presence. Attempts at concrete and cost-cutting co-operation measures, such as sharing buildings or services, have been less successful than might have been expected in spite of exhortations from the Political Committee. Missions have shown themselves resistant to advice from above, and co-operation has worked best where the need for it has been perceived locally. This has led to a rather uneven pattern of co-operation around the world.

Co-operation in third countries sometimes suffers from the lack of timely and regular information about EPC discussions centrally. Both the Presidency and other partners immediately inform their Embassies in a third country of any EPC decision or discussion directly affecting that country. Background information about decisions affecting other areas is more sporadic and depends on the practices of each Member State. Attempts to provide a regular flow of EPC information on a uniform basis have so far not succeeded in overcoming procedural obstacles.

The quality of Political Co-operation abroad also depends on the presence of the Member States. In countries where all or nearly all of the Twelve are represented and with regard to which there is an active EPC policy, co-ordination on the spot is well developed and the identity of the Twelve strongly affirmed. In countries where perhaps only two or three Member States are represented, the tendency is for co-operation to be unstructured and informal—as like as not at the side of the pool—and for the Twelve's personality to be poorly defined. Such countries tend to have difficult living conditions, which strengthens the solidarity of the small local diplomatic corps and encourages co-operation in wider groupings than the Twelve, thus blurring further the identity of EPC.

EPC AT THE UNITED NATIONS

The activity of the Twelve at the United Nations in New York and in the specialized agencies in Geneva is somewhat different from that in third countries. The object here is not so much to achieve a uniform presentation of policy to the host organization as to work out common positions on questions on which the central authorities of EPC do not provide sufficiently detailed guidance. The rhythm of work of the Member States' missions and the Commission

Delegation is intense, especially during the sessions of the General Assembly, when there are co-ordination meetings every day.

The success or otherwise of the co-ordination of the Twelve is often judged by the number of occasions on which they vote together in the General Assembly. Analysis of the statistics, which seem to show scant progress, can be misleading. Resolutions adopted by consensus are usually not included, and it is precisely on those which are not that national positions are likely to diverge. On the other hand, the figures alone do not reveal the fact that divergence is concentrated in a few areas, but ones of particular significance, such as disarmament, South Africa, or the Middle East. It is generally admitted that the accession of Greece to the Community has made voting together more difficult because of the insistence of the Greeks in sticking to long-held national positions at the expense of Community solidarity. This has had a knock-on effect with other Member States such as Ireland and Denmark, which have difficulty in justifying to their public opinion a vote against their national convictions for the sake of solidarity when another member of the Community is seen to break ranks. In the case of Denmark, Nordic solidarity is sometimes more compelling than its membership of EPC.

Member States are faced with the difficulty that in New York they cannot control the agenda. If the Twelve decide centrally to issue a declaration, they can concentrate on those aspects of the subject on which they are in agreement and pass over those on which consensus is difficult to reach. This is not possible in New York, where the drafters of resolutions are less accommodating, forcing the Twelve's divergencies into the open.

The co-ordination among the Twelve does not extend to the activities of the permanent members of the Security Council. For many years even discussion of this was taboo. That began to change in 1987, but France and the United Kingdom still take the view that their participation in Political Co-operation in no way restrains the exercise of their responsibilities as permanent members, nor requires them to act in that capacity as spokesmen of the Twelve.

This is a picture of Political Co-operation at the beginning of the 1990s. It is time to look at the brush strokes which went to make the picture over a period of nearly forty years.

The Mechanics of EPC

SELECTED READING

The most authoritative descriptions of how EPC worked in the 1980s are to be found in A. Pijpers, E. Regelsberger, and W. Wessels (eds.), *European Political Co-operation in the 1980s* (Dordrecht, 1988). This contains chapters by Bonvicini (mechanisms and procedures), de Schoutheete (the Presidency and the management of EPC), da Costa Pereira (the Secretariat), and Nuttall (the Commission). Another good overall view is given by Gérard (1987), a former European Correspondent of France.

More information about the EPC Secretariat can be found in Lak (1988) and Späth (1990), both former members of the Secretariat.

Co-operation in third countries is discussed in Bot (1984), a former European Correspondent and Dutch Ambassador in Turkey. Additional insight is given by Tomkys (1987), drawn from his experiences as British Ambassador in Syria. The most up-to-date work on co-operation at the United Nations is Stadler (1989), whose expanded doctoral dissertation on the subject is scheduled for future publication.

2
The Origins

European Political Co-operation did not spring fully armed from the head of Zeus in the Davignon Report of 1970. It reflected in its structure and approach twenty-five years of debate about the desirability of a political authority in Western Europe. Indeed, the reason why it is commonly known as European Political Co-operation, which does not accurately describe its foreign-policy function, is that its origins lie in the different attempts made to set up such a political authority, which would have foreign-policy responsibilities as one, but only one, of its attributes. This objective was more important than to achieve a European foreign policy as such. The first attempt was made on classical federalist lines; it failed. The second attempt, launched by General de Gaulle, was on inter-governmental lines; it also failed. The third attempt succeeded, by steering clear of the reefs on which the two previous attempts had foundered.

Although EPC since 1970 has concentrated on making practical progress, the debate between federalism and inter-governmentalism is still very much alive. The history of the quarter century before then shows the roots of this debate, as it does two other important features of EPC: the influence of the United States, and, whenever the United Kingdom absents itself from the European stage, the predominant role of France in alliance with the Federal Republic of Germany.

THE EUROPEAN POLITICAL COMMUNITY

The immediate post-war years were unusual in that they provided conditions in which federalist aspirations for a united Europe coincided for a brief moment with the pragmatists' need to find an effective response to the double challenge of post-war reconstruction and the Cold War. The federalists' aim was to set up European institutions to which national powers could be transferred, while the pragmatists wanted to restrict the transfer of sovereignty to the strict minimum. The result was that discussions took place in terms of institutional structures rather than functions. It might be thought that national governments would inevitably fall into the pragmatist camp and limit as far as possible their loss of national power. This was not at first the case. Italy frequently, Belgium and the Netherlands intermittently, followed a more federalist line. The strong initiatives taken from time to time by France had to be diluted when the government came to rely on Gaullist support. But the constellation of interests which made it possible for the European Coal and Steel Community (ECSC) and later the Economic and Euratom Communities to be set up was lacking in the case of a political community. There was nothing inevitable about the construction of Europe; much depended on the circumstances of the hour.

The call for a federal Europe was heard most clearly at the Congress of the European Movements in The Hague in May 1948. Yet even then national differences had begun to appear. Broadly speaking, the French, Belgians, Dutch, and Italians were federalists, while the British and the Scandinavians favoured a more prudent approach. When a year later ten governments, in response to the call of the Congress at The Hague, signed the Statute of the Council of Europe, originally designed to form an embryonic government in which a Committee of Ministers was controlled by a parliamentary Assembly, the British had ensured that the Committee of Ministers would limit itself to inter-governmental co-operation in the classical mould and the Assembly would be restricted to a consultative role. In any case, the Statute excluded defence, and by implication foreign policy, from the Council's field of action.

There were nevertheless good reasons, other than federalist idealism, to look for strong structures in the cold and dark Europe of the post-war years. The ravaged economies of Western Europe could not be rebuilt without the help of the Americans, and the United States made it plain that that help would be conditional on a co-operative effort on the part of the Europeans. This was why the Organization for European Economic Co-operation had been set up in Paris in April 1948. Although it provided a useful forum to compare economic policies and engage in effective co-operation, the United Kingdom, the Scandinavian countries, and Switzerland ensured that it did not have independent powers to control national reconstruction plans. This may have been no bad thing from the point of view of economic efficiency, but it did not satisfy the partisans of an institutional Europe.

In the view of the United States and the United Kingdom, the economic revival of Germany was an essential part of post-war economic reconstruction in Europe. This meant freeing the German economy, in particular the coal and steel industries, from the restrictions under which it lay as a result of the war. France, under pressure from its wartime allies, needed to find a framework for this revival which would prevent a recurrence of German aggression. This was the origin of the Schuman Plan of May 1950, inspired by Jean Monnet, for a European Coal and Steel Community. The ECSC was designed to serve a need, not to conform to a theoretical model. It had limited, but real, supranational powers, enough to ensure effective operation without exciting suspicion and opposition. Its powers did not extend to foreign relations, which remained the responsibility of Member States.

American pressure for effective European co-operation was even more marked when it came to defence. The onset of the Cold War made the defence of Western Europe a pressing necessity. European governments were in no position by their own efforts alone to counter the Soviet threat. The Brussels Pact of March 1948, which bound together the United Kingdom, France, Belgium, the Netherlands, and Luxembourg in a military accord which included an undertaking of mutual assistance in the case of armed aggression, made way the following year to the Atlantic Alliance which added to the five of the Brussels Pact not only the United States and Canada, but also Norway, Denmark, Iceland, Italy, and Portugal.

The Brussels Pact was endowed with institutions which gave it the potential to develop into a regional organization. It was not, however, foreseen that these would concern themselves with foreign policy separately from the common defence policy which was necessary to underpin the military nature of the Pact, and in any case these functions were in practice transferred to NATO on the latter's creation. There was thus no functioning, specifically European, framework for the discussion of foreign and security policy.

The Brussels Pact did not include defeated Germany; indeed, its preamble referred to the possibility of a renewal by Germany of a

The Origins

policy of aggression. But the defence of Europe against the Soviet threat was scarcely credible without the involvement of the new Federal Germany, which came into being in the summer of 1949. The crossing of the 38th parallel by North Korean troops in June 1950 gave rise to the spectre of a new world war, this time between East and West, in which Western Europe was inadequately prepared against Soviet attack. The rearmament of Germany had become a practical necessity, and one on which the United States increasingly insisted. The prospect was one which France in particular found hard to stomach, having been invaded by Germany three times in as many generations. The French fear of German rearmament not only led to the Schuman Plan of May 1950, but also provided the rationale for the Pléven Plan put forward in September of the same year.

This plan provided for the creation of an integrated European army in which German military forces would be subsumed under collective European control. The idea, already implied by the creation of the Atlantic Alliance, had been foreshadowed by Dr Adenauer, who in December 1949 had declared himself in favour 'not of an independent Wehrmacht but of a German contingent in a European force'. The Pléven Plan had been inspired by Jean Monnet, who applied to military questions the principles of the ECSC. The institutions would include a Board of Commissioners (the equivalent of today's Commission and of the ECSC High Authority), a Council of Ministers, an Assembly, and a Court of Justice.

The French proposal, which was open to all West Europeans, did not meet with an enthusiastic welcome. The United Kingdom, Denmark, and Norway were present at the discussions only as observers, as were the Netherlands at first. Although the Pléven Plan foresaw that the European army would be placed at the operational disposal of NATO, the Dutch were afraid that the United States' interest in the defence of Europe would wane if the Europeans developed too independent a defence personality. The British, for their part, were as attached to their Commonwealth links and as resistant to the transfer of sovereignty as they were in the case of the ECSC, which they had already declined to join.

Negotiations on the European Defence Community continued for a year, with strong support from the United States. The draft Treaty was signed on 27 May 1952. Although the independent powers of the institutions were less far-reaching than had been originally foreseen, the principle of an integrated army under joint command was maintained.

Had there not been a move for a European Defence Community Treaty, that for a European Political Community, which followed a step behind, would never have seen the light of day. It was argued that a defence community could not exist without a measure of democratic control through political institutions which went beyond the provisions of the EDC draft Treaty. The Italians had indeed argued without success in favour of provisions to that effect being incorporated in the Treaty itself, and had had to content themselves with a promise that the question would be looked at again within six months of the signing of the Treaty (Article 38). The failure of the EDC Treaty to make any specific provisions for the elaboration of a common foreign policy, without which it might be thought that a common defence policy did not make much sense, was thought at the time to be less important than the question of democratic control. A common foreign policy was addressed in the draft Treaty for a European Political Community as only one function of federal government among several.

The Article 38 process had to be brought forward. It was realized that there would be difficulties over ratification of the EDC Treaty unless more work was done on political institutions providing a measure of democratic control, particularly in the case of France, where even those socialists who supported the EDC strongly criticized the absence of such provisions. It was therefore decided that, pending the creation of the EDC Assembly (which depended on prior ratification of the Treaty), the ECSC Assembly in a suitably augmented *ad hoc* format should be asked to do the job. The opportunity was seized by the federalists. Thwarted by the inter-governmental character imposed on the Council of Europe, they saw their chance to relaunch the campaign for a federal Europe, this time from the ECSC parliamentary benches.

The *ad hoc* Assembly produced its draft by March 1953. The institutional structure it proposed reflected that of the ECSC, but with increased powers for the parliamentary element. The Political Community was to serve as a superstructure for, and later to absorb, the existing Coal and Steel and Defence Communities. For the first time, foreign policy provisions were included, but limited to the 'co-ordination of the external policy of the Member States'. However, the Executive Council (the equivalent of today's Commission) could conduct a foreign policy common to the Member States if it was so authorized by the Council of Ministers acting unanimously. This included the power to negotiate and conclude international agreements. The draft thus provided for consultation in the Council of Ministers for those foreign-policy questions for which Member States retained their national responsibilities, while for questions which by consensus had been removed to the European level the Executive Council was given delegated powers of both initiative and implementation.

The draft did not go uncontested in the *ad hoc* Assembly. Contrary to the original intention, the excessively federal approach alienated the French socialists, who withdrew from the discussions and did not take part in the final vote. The Gaullists, on the other hand, were confirmed in their total opposition. Led by M Michel Debré, they preferred a confederal system whereby each Member State retained its autonomy, particularly in foreign affairs. Attempts could and should be made to harmonize national views, but if these attempts failed, the discussion had to stop there. This was the mode which was ultimately chosen for European Political Co-operation. Although it has proved in practice to be less negative than the supranationalists feared, it stood little chance of acceptance in the federalist atmosphere of the *ad hoc* Assembly.

The Assembly's draft text, or 'Statute', was conveyed in March 1953 to the six governments who, however, showed little haste in taking the matter further. Robert Schuman had been replaced as French Foreign Minister by Georges Bidault, who was far from sharing his predecessor's enthusiasm. Moreover, the French government saw the Statute as more of a hindrance to ratification of the EDC Treaty than a help, and therefore adopted a cautious attitude from the start. Study of the draft was remitted to a diplomatic conference in which representatives of governments rather than parliamentarians conducted the discussion, and in which not only the French, but also the Italians after the fall of de Gasperi in July 1953, found themselves in a weaker position. The Germans, on the other hand, took a strong line in favour of the transfer of economic and monetary powers to the Community, while the Dutch were anxious for reasons of their own to include a customs union.

By the spring of 1954 it was clear that the French would have considerable difficulties in ratifying the EDC Treaty. There was thus little incentive to make progress on the drafting of the European Political Community text. Too much had changed since the EDC project had been launched. The situation in Korea had become stabilized; the death of Stalin in March 1953 had given rise to hopes of a relaxation of tension in the Cold War; and the vicissitudes of political life in France meant that successive governments could not dispense with Gaullist support, for which a price had to be paid. Public opinion in France was divided, but the suspicion of Germany went very deep and the proponents of the EDC were not able to show convincingly that it was the best answer to their fears. The French made some diplomatic moves to repair the situation by calling for amendments watering down the supranational provisions and by seeking to associate the United Kingdom more closely with the EDC to assist in providing a balance with a rearmed Germany. France's partners in the Six were reluctant to compromise, however, and the British remained unattracted by the supranational aspects of the EDC, still more by those of the European Political Community.

The crunch came on 29 August 1954 when the French National Assembly rejected the EDC Treaty. Work on the European Political Community Treaty immediately came to a halt. The gap thus left in European defence policy was filled on the initiative of the United Kingdom by the extension to Germany (and Italy) in October 1954 of membership of the Brussels Pact, which thereupon became the Western European Union (WEU), and by the accession of the Federal Republic to NATO. The gap in the construction of a political Europe, and thus of a common European foreign policy, was left unfilled.

The first phase of the post-war period had shown the difficulties of making progress along the federalist road towards a political authority with foreign-policy powers. In future different approaches would be tried. At the same time, some lessons could be learnt. The first was that the federalist approach, most often expressed through the drafting of texts by parliamentary bodies, could provide a stimulus for action, not always on the lines the federalists themselves desired, but could not itself directly bring about advances in institutional structures. The second was that the most effective stimulus to action was the presence of external circumstance. The EDC and its political corollary were the offspring of the Cold War and largely sprang from American pressure. This was to prove counter-productive in France where it helped to influence the Gaullist reaction. Finally, the position taken by France, as it swung from the positive to the negative, was crucial in determining the outcome in the face of a Germany still politically unsure of itself and a United Kingdom standing on the sidelines. The next initiative for a political Europe, ten years after the first, was again taken by France, this time by General de Gaulle. That it too failed was largely because the British could not be brought into the enterprise, and because the General's concept of Europe was as determinedly inter-governmental as the European Defence and Political Communities, in their initial form, had been supranational.

THE FOUCHET PLANS

The failure of the Defence Community, and with it the Political Community, meant that the high road to European unification was barred. The low road of functional integration was now tried with greater success, the Treaties of Rome setting up the European Economic and Euratom Communities coming into force in 1958. These Treaties did indeed contain provisions in the field of external relations—the EEC Treaty provided for the gradual transfer of responsibility for trade policy to the Community institutions—but left to one side the 'high politics' which were the traditional and glorious apanage of Foreign Ministries.

The low road was, however, anathema to General de Gaulle, who came to power in France on 1 June 1958. The European policy of the General consisted in providing Europe with an independent political authority capable of asserting itself in the world, to be achieved through regular consultations among governments. A text approved by the General in August 1958 stated that

l'Europe doit devenir pratiquement une réalité sur les plans politique, économique et culturel . . . La coopération européenne doit s'affirmer aussi en dehors de l'Europe, à l'égard des grands problèmes mondiaux... des consultations régulières auront lieu entre les gouvernements intéressés. Ce mécanisme de consultations pourra prendre un caractère en quelque sorte organique au fur et à mesure qu'il se développera.

This was the line General de Gaulle was to follow consistently and to bequeath to his political successors.

The General rejected the idea that a European foreign policy could exist simply as an attribute of a supranational European authority. It had to have an object, and that object was to assert Europe's independence of the United States in both European and world affairs. In particular, de Gaulle saw that the East European countries needed to be able to turn to their West European neighbours. This object could only be achieved through the force which came from democratic legitimacy. This meant that the sovereign powers of the Nation States which freely engaged in a co-operative enterprise had to be preserved, since only they, and not supranational institutions, enjoyed such legitimacy.

This independent foreign policy would be led by France. Like the United Kingdom, France was a permanent member of the Security Council, one of the Four Powers in Berlin, and from February 1960 was to be a nuclear power. It was only natural that she should take the foreign-policy lead, especially if she could secure the support of the Federal Republic. Already in September 1958 when General de Gaulle visited Bonn, Chancellor Adenauer showed an interest in permanent contacts with France on international questions; indeed it was de Gaulle who emphasized the need to go beyond the bilateral framework to draw in the other members of the Communities.

De Gaulle's vision of a political Europe had a second objective. This was to provide a higher authority through which the sovereign Member States would be able to exercise political control over the activities of the Community institutions. Although hidden from time to time by the meanderings of the negotiations over the next three years, this objective was always present in the General's mind. It is most clearly expressed in a text of April 1961: 'Institution d'un concert organique et périodique des Chefs d'État ou de gouvernement, institution d'un secrétariat de cet aréopage, non seulement distinct des "commissions" (Marché commun, CECA, EURATOM), mais encore [appelé à] les survoler en attendant de les coiffer.'

France's partners in the Community were attracted by the idea of a new attempt to introduce a European political authority with a foreign-policy capability, but resistant to many features of the General's thought. In the absence of the United Kingdom, Franco-German hegemony was an ever-present possibility, giving rise to suspicion and concern. The Netherlands in particular wanted the United Kingdom in the Community, also for economic reasons; British participation was of less importance to Chancellor Adenauer, given his understanding with General de Gaulle. Adenauer was also less interested in supranational dogma than his European colleagues, for whom the possibility of developing the Community method had to remain open. Finally, all France's partners, including Germany, were worried about the shift away from the United States and NATO which was the mainspring of de Gaulle's approach.

For the first year General de Gaulle was content to press his ideas through bilateral diplomacy and in a pragmatic way. Visiting Rome on 26 June 1959, he proposed to the Italians periodical meetings of Ministers of Foreign Affairs to discuss questions of international policy with a small joint secretariat to prepare the meetings, which the French intended should be in Paris. The Italians accepted that provided all Six were invited, as did the Germans. However, the broad scope of the discussions, including NATO questions, the risk that a Paris secretariat would detract from the Brussels institutions, France's refusal to countenance the presence of the Commission at the discussions, and the absence of the United Kingdom were all subjects of serious concern to the remaining three countries. It was only on the occasion of an EEC Council meeting in Strasbourg on 23 November 1959 that, following a compromise put forward by Germany, agreement could be reached on quarterly meetings of Foreign Ministers for consultations on international policy. 'Ces consultations porteront à la fois sur les prolongements politiques de l'activité des Communautés européennes et sur les autres problèmes internationaux.' Agreement was made possible by the stipulation that the consultations would be without prejudice to those in NATO and the WEU, and that the Commission would be informed and could be invited to take part when discussions touched on questions relevant to the Communities (the latter formula was to be resurrected in the Luxembourg Report). The permanent secretariat was dropped in favour of preparation of the Ministerial Meetings by the senior Foreign Ministry officials or Ambassadors (the forerunner of the Political Committee).

The series of meetings began in 1960 with a meeting on 25 January in Rome, followed by one on 9 May in Luxembourg and another on 18 July in The Hague. The apparent relaxation in Soviet policy, Latin America, the accession to the Community of Greece and Turkey, and the situation in the Congo were among the topics discussed. From the time of the first summit meeting in Paris in February 1961, the meetings of the Foreign Ministers became irregular and practically ceased after the collapse of the Fouchet negotiations in April 1962 (see the next section). The Fouchet Committee, by then chaired by the Secretary-General of the Italian Foreign Ministry, Attilio Cattani, met once in October 1962 in Brussels to discuss the Cuban crisis. This first series of Political Co-operation meetings was abandoned altogether after General de Gaulle's veto of the first British application to join the Communities in January 1963.

These hesitant beginnings did not deter General de Gaulle from pressing ahead with his project. He was all the more encouraged to do so as his proposals to reform NATO (he had proposed a Franco-US-British Directorate in September 1958) had finally to be abandoned after his meeting with President Eisenhower in December 1959. Moreover, both de Gaulle and Adenauer felt that Eisenhower, supported by the British, was not taking a tough enough line in resisting Soviet demands on Berlin. De Gaulle therefore launched a public campaign in a televised press conference on 31 May 1960 in which he declared that France would attach herself to

contribuer à bâtir l'Europe occidentale en un groupement politique, économique, culturel et humain, organisé pour l'action, le progrès et la défense . . . Sans doute, aussi, faut-il que les nations qui s'associent ne cessent pas d'être elles-mêmes et que la voie suivie soit celle d'une coopération organisée des États, en attendant d'en venir, peut-être, à une imposante Confédération. Mais la France . . . a reconnu la nécessité de cette Europe d'Occident . . . qui apparaît aujourd'hui comme la condition indispensable de l'équilibre du monde.

For the initiative to succeed, de Gaulle needed the support of the Federal Republic. This was secured at a meeting with Adenauer at Rambouillet on 29–30 July. De Gaulle called for 'organized co-operation' of States, beginning with France and Germany and extending to Italy, the Netherlands, Belgium, and Luxembourg; the reform of the 'supranational' institutions and their subjection to governments; and the placing of the Atlantic Alliance on a new basis to be proposed by Europe. As for the mechanism of 'organized co-operation', there were to be regular meetings of Heads of Government and Ministers prepared by four permanent committees of national civil servants (political, economic, culture, and defence). Adenauer balked at the reform of NATO, but accepted the rest, even preferring to restrict the whole affair to France and Germany.

When the scheme was revealed to the other partners, difficulties appeared which were to persist throughout the subsequent negotiations. These were the role of the United Kingdom, the relationship with NATO, and the status of the existing Communities. Even Adenauer found on his return to Bonn that he had gone further at Rambouillet than his Cabinet would have liked.

De Gaulle went over the heads of his partners by holding a spectacular press conference on 5 September.

Ce sont les États qui . . . sont les seules entités qui aient le droit d'ordonner et l'autorité pour agir . . . Assurer la coopération régulière de l'Europe occidentale, c'est ce que la France considère comme étant souhaitable, comme étant possible et comme étant pratique, dans le domaine politique, dans le domaine économique, dans le domaine culturel et dans celui de la défense. Cela comporte un concert organisé régulier des gouvernements responsables et puis, alors, le travail d'organismes spécialisés dans chacun des domaines communs et subordonnés aux gouvernements . . .

The prospect was not tempting to France's partners, for it left the General's objectives in no doubt. Yet it was difficult to resist such a resounding call. The Five therefore gave their consent to the basis for discussion set out by General de Gaulle at a meeting in Paris on 10–11 February 1961. This success had been assured by a meeting between de Gaulle and Adenauer the day before, at which assurances had been given about France's attachment to the Atlantic Alliance and the Communities. At the Conference, the Italians joined the consensus, as did Belgium and Luxembourg, having received the same assurances as Germany. Only Foreign Minister Luns of the Netherlands held out, suspicious of what he saw as a Franco-German deal. Giving the absence of the United Kingdom as a reason, and also concerned about NATO, Luns withheld consent to the principle of regular summit meetings and a permanent secretariat. The deadlock was broken by further work being entrusted to a 'study committee' of national diplomats chaired by the French Ambassador in Copenhagen, Christian Fouchet, who gave his name to the successive proposals later to be presented by France.

Luns could not hold out in isolation, although he declined to endorse the first report produced by the Fouchet Committee. By the time of the next summit meeting at Bad Godesberg on 18 July, a compromise could be worked out. France agreed to a reference to the Atlantic Alliance and the openness of the Communities to other European countries, while the Netherlands accepted the principle of regular summit meetings without insisting on British participation. Taking up an idea which the Italians had been promoting for some time, the development of political collaboration with a view to European union was mentioned in parallel with the continuation of the work of the Communities. The Fouchet Committee was directed to make proposals to give a statutory nature to the union of European peoples.

The Bonn Declaration was warmly welcomed and gave rise to hopes that the road to a political Europe had been found. But there was so far nothing beyond a declaration of principles. The Fouchet Committee went to work again to put flesh on the bones.

France presented a draft Treaty, which came to be known as Fouchet I, on 19 October 1961. This reflected fairly faithfully the position which had been worked out in Bad Godesberg. The objective was a common foreign policy and a common defence policy 'in co-operation with other free nations', as well as the development of co-operation in the fields of science and culture. The economic field was not mentioned, which implied that the 'Union of States' would forbear from imposing a new layer of political control on the activities of the Communities. A Council at the level of Heads of Government would meet every four months, and Foreign Ministers would continue to meet quarterly. The existing Assembly of the Communities could debate and

The Origins

make recommendations in any of the areas covered by the Union. A Political Committee made up of senior Foreign Ministry officials with its seat in Paris would prepare and implement the Council's decisions. The Treaty would be revised after three years to strengthen the Union in the direction of a unified foreign policy and the centralization of the Communities within the Union. Finally, members of the Communities could be admitted to the Union by unanimous decision.

In the negotiations which followed, France seemed disposed to make concessions to her partners who had not abandoned the concerns they felt before the Bonn Declaration. Luns, no longer isolated, was now joined by Spaak in his insistence on adequate provisions for the relationship with the Atlantic Alliance. The reason for the Belgian Foreign Minister's change of heart was twofold. France was at odds with her partners in the Atlantic Council over how to handle the situation following the erection of the Berlin Wall in August 1961. The United States and the other allies were disposed to negotiate with Khrushchev, while France took a firmer line. This alarmed Spaak, who supported the American position. Secondly, the British government had decided to apply for membership of the European Communities, stimulated at least in part by the discussions on political union. This led the Belgians and the Dutch to demand that the British should take part in the work of the Fouchet Committee. Their position was expressed most succinctly by Spaak the following April: 'Si vous voulez davantage d'intégration, nous sommes d'accord pour que les Anglais n'en soient pas. Mais, si vous ne voulez pas l'Europe integrée, alors il faut accepter l'Angleterre.' Spaak needed the guarantee of protection against Franco-German domination. This could be provided either by the presence of the British or by supranational institutions, but one of the two he had to have. The difficulty was solved for the time being at the meeting of Foreign Ministers in Paris in December 1961, the British having indicated they were disinclined to take part in the Fouchet discussions. Spaak abandoned his insistence on British involvement in the discussions on political union before the United Kingdom's accession to the Communities in favour of their obligation to take part afterwards. The principle of parallelism between accession to the Communities and participation in the Union was thus established.

The way was clear for the next meeting of the Fouchet Committee on 18 January 1962. In preparation for this the Quai d'Orsay produced a revised draft Treaty, dated 13 January, which took into account most of the objections raised by France's partners and which those involved in Paris had good reason to believe would be accepted by them. The defence policy was no longer to be undertaken 'in co-operation with other free nations', but would 'contribute to the strengthening of the Atlantic Alliance'; the revision of the Treaty after three years would lead to the progressive unification of defence as well as of foreign policy; and for the foreseen 'centralization' of the Communities was substituted their 'rationalization and co-ordination', thus guaranteeing their continued independence.

When this document was submitted to General de Gaulle, he personally made changes to it which nullified the concessions made to France's partners. The reference to the Atlantic Alliance was removed, the sector of the economy was reintroduced as one of the objectives of the Union, and in the section on Treaty revision the crucial phrase 'respecting the structures of the Treaties of Paris and Rome' was also removed. The General's original objective, of a political authority resistant to American dominance and controlling the activities of the supranational institutions, had been restored.

The text as amended by General de Gaulle, which came to be known as Fouchet II, was submitted to the Fouchet Committee on 18 January. It caused consternation, but the negotiations still did not break down. Various attempts were made to seek a compromise, including by General de Gaulle himself, and by the time the Ministers of Foreign Affairs met on 17 April 1962, successive French concessions had brought the text back almost to that prepared by the Quai d'Orsay on 13 January. What might have been agreed in January, however, could not be agreed in April; the General's *coup de théâtre* had sown too many doubts about France's real motives. Various further attempts were made to unblock the situation, without success. In the end, all that remained of de Gaulle's grand design for a political Europe of six States was the Franco-German Treaty of January 1963.

General de Gaulle's motives in amending the Quai d'Orsay's draft have been variously interpreted. One explanation is that the General felt the need for a firm reaction to President

The Origins

Kennedy's initiative for an Atlantic free-trade area including the British, launched in November 1960 and made more specific in the Trade Expansion Act announced on 11 January 1961 in the President's State of the Union address. This initiative in the economic sphere was reinforced by Kennedy's move towards a NATO multilateral force provided with a nuclear capability which presupposed the placing of nuclear weapons under NATO command. Alternatively, General de Gaulle might have been encouraged by the adoption of the principles of the common agricultural policy on 14 January 1961 to harden his stand, secure in the knowledge that this had now been achieved and determined to ensure that it could not in the future be reversed by majority vote. A third explanation is that he was convinced by Prime Minister Debré that Foreign Minister Couve de Murville and Fouchet had made too many concessions in the negotiations. The Germans had been given advance warning as early as 13 January that the Debré camp, supported by de Gaulle, were determined to reject the amendments demanded by the other countries, and were thinking of proposing that the Secretary-General should be *ex officio* French.

What is certain is that de Gaulle's underlying objectives never changed, however flexible he may have been over tactics. He may have felt that if he could secure the support of Adenauer, who was worried about the situation in Berlin, he could in the end impose his will on the other partners, just as he had at the Paris summit a year before. Adenauer did indeed make great efforts to save the agreement, at one stage even agreeing to include the economy among the domains of the Union, but to no avail. Indeed, the German Cabinet was divided on the issue. De Gaulle's tactics broke down in the face of determined opposition from the Netherlands and Belgium, supported on this occasion by Italy.

The reasons for the failure carried with them lessons for the future, which were heeded when the question of political union came up again nearly a decade later. It had proved vain to attempt to impose an inter-governmental superstructure on the Community order; the Davignon Plan which established European Political Co-operation did not attempt to do so. The United Kingdom could not be left out of the picture; its entry into the Community was part of the price paid at the Hague Conference in 1969 for the setting up of EPC on an inter-governmental basis. Only the need to pay proper attention to the relationship with the United States was not attended to in the Davignon Report, and this omission caused the first great crisis in EPC when Kissinger proposed the 'Year of Europe'. For the rest, much of the mechanism worked out in the Fouchet Committee was taken over by the architects of EPC, and has served without fundamental change up to the present day.

THE HAGUE CONFERENCE

If a political Europe could not be established with the Benelux countries, de Gaulle was prepared to make the attempt without them. France for a while promoted the idea of a tripartite system of consultations extended to the Federal Republic and Italy, but faced with the Italians' rejection of an arrangement which would have placed them in a position of permanent weakness, de Gaulle fell back on a bilateral agreement with Germany. The Franco-German Treaty of Co-operation of 22 January 1963 set up between the two countries the type of co-operation which de Gaulle had for so long hoped to see agreed among the Six: twice yearly meetings of Heads of Government and quarterly meetings of Foreign Ministers for co-operation on foreign policy, defence, and culture. The two governments were to consult before taking important foreign-policy decisions and as far as possible to reach common positions.

The setting up of a Franco-German bloc was the more strongly resented by the rest of the Six as it followed shortly after General de Gaulle's public refusal to entertain the United Kingdom's first application for membership of the Communities. Nevertheless, new plans to achieve a European political dimension continued to be launched. In September 1964 Foreign Minister Spaak of Belgium, using the platform of the WEU, suggested that a committee of independent personalities should be set up to work out in consultation with governments a Treaty on political union. Two months later, the German government proposed that negotiations for political union should be resumed, and that meanwhile there should be consultations on foreign policy, defence, and culture. Not to be outdone, the Italians proposed regular meetings of Heads of Government and Ministers prepared by a Political Commission appointed by governments, but with an

The Origins

independent personality with the right of initiative as Secretary-General.

None of these ideas was accepted by France, and after the crisis of 1965–6 (the Luxembourg compromise and France's withdrawal from the military structure of NATO) no further advances could be made as long as General de Gaulle remained in power.

The General laid down his office in April 1969 and was succeeded on 15 June as President of the French Republic by Georges Pompidou. Pompidou lost no time in setting in motion a new European policy which was Gaullist in its principles, but flexible in the way in which these were implemented. Already at a press conference on 10 July the President announced his determination to complete the common market by the scheduled date and strengthen it in areas so far neglected, and his willingness to consider British accession, provided that the Six agreed on the conditions in advance. The theme of 'completion, further development, and enlargement' was launched by Maurice Schumann, now Foreign Minister, at a Council meeting on 22 July and preparations began for a summit meeting at the end of the year.

A number of reasons have been given for Pompidou's move, although the real motivation of that secretive man remains shrouded in mystery. A main consideration was certainly cold calculation of national advantage. The provisional regime for the financing of the common agricultural policy was due to expire at the end of the year. For agreement to be reached to put it on a permanent footing, France would have to pay its partners a price. That price was the admission of the United Kingdom. The connection was admitted by President Pompidou in a television interview in 1971:

I could see that our partners did not want to go further, that there was very little hope, especially, of the common agricultural market's being renewed and, so to speak, definitively installed. That is why, at the Hague Conference, I confronted them with a clear choice. And I secured, on the one hand, that definitive arrangements should be made for the agricultural market, in exchange for the opening of relations with Great Britain, on the other.

At the same time, Pompidou was not unwilling to have the United Kingdom in the Community to balance Germany, whose weight had become much greater, especially after France had been weakened by the events of May 1968. The British were seen as less likely to be a Trojan horse for the Americans, with whom in any case relations had been improved even under General de Gaulle after the Soviet invasion of Czechoslovakia in 1968, as was shown by President Nixon's visit to Paris in February 1969. Indeed, the Soviet intervention in Prague had destroyed the assumptions of de Gaulle's East–West policy.

Finally, Pompidou's new approach to Europe helped him to master domestic political forces in France. Standing in the presidential election against the pro-European Poher, he had given assurances about a more open approach to the Communities to the Independent Republicans of Giscard d'Estaing and the centrist forces of Duhamel. The position had to be finely judged, to avoid alienating the Gaullists whose support remained essential and to avoid doing violence to his own Gaullist principles, but by keeping both camps in play, Pompidou could secure for himself greater freedom of action.

Pompidou remained a faithful follower of de Gaulle in his perception that Europe needed to develop a foreign-policy capability in order to contribute to the balance of an international order, and in his conviction that this could only be achieved through the free co-operation of sovereign States. The agreement at the Hague Conference to relaunch the movement towards political unification—confined for the time being to foreign-policy questions—on lines which were largely inspired by the Fouchet approach, was for President Pompidou an important part of the package, and one which he needed to balance the concessions he had made.

Following the French initiative, intensive discussions took place throughout the autumn in order to settle the conditions for a new summit meeting. To secure agreement, France made two concessions which proved significant for the shape ultimately taken by EPC: the Commission was to be invited to take part in the Summit for the economic discussions on the second day and there was to be no institutionalization of the meetings of Heads of Government, seen especially by the Dutch as posing a threat to the operation of the Community institutions.

The Summit Conference took place at The Hague on 1–2 December 1969. On the first day the atmosphere was not good. President Pompidou arrived in a bad temper, having been forced by bad weather in Paris to make the journey by train rather than fly. The Hague was bathed in sunshine. In spite of this inauspicious start, on the second day the deal was struck. The financing of the common agricultural policy was secured and the Community provided with its own budgetary resources; a move was made towards economic and monetary union; negotiations for the admission of the United Kingdom and the other candidate countries were to begin.

Europe's inability to speak with one voice on world affairs was felt by all the partners, not just by France alone. Indeed, President Pompidou's opening statement scarcely touched on the question, and was felt to be rather drab. Others made the point. Chancellor Brandt, who had taken office only two months previously, began by saying 'If all were well with Europe, we should not have met here today. If our Community could speak with one voice, our principal theme would be foreign policy: the question of a peace settlement in Europe, negotiations with the states of Eastern Europe, our interests with regard to the Middle East conflict.' Prime Minister Rumor of Italy said 'In the world dialogue, Europe as such is absent.' He cited the East–West Conference (later to become the CSCE) and the Mediterranean as areas of particular interest.

Pompidou proposed regular meetings of Foreign Ministers to discuss foreign-policy problems, Europe's relations with the rest of the world, and particularly the United States and Eastern countries, 'in order to try to harmonize our foreign policies and in any event to inform ourselves better of our respective policies.' The Conference did not wish to commit itself to a mechanism on the spot. At the suggestion of Brandt, it instructed the Ministers of Foreign Affairs 'to study the best way of achieving progress in the matter of political unification, within the context of enlargement.' The Ministers were to make proposals on this by the end of July 1970. With the entry of the United Kingdom now a possibility, the way was open for a form of political co-operation which owed much to the precedent of the Ministerial meetings between 1960 and 1963 and to the work done in the Fouchet Committee.

SELECTED READING

The best general introductions to the origins of the Community and of EPC are P. Gerbet, *La Construction de l'Europe* (Paris, 1988), and J.–C. Masclet, *L'Union politique de l'Europe*, in the series *Que sais-je?* Several editions of this exist, the most recent published in 1988, but it is worth consulting earlier editions for fuller details on the early period.

The best descriptions of the European Political Community are the chapters by Gerbet and Cardozo in R. Pryce (ed.), *The Dynamics of European Union* (London, 1987). Both belong to the federalist school. The classic work on the European Defence Community is Fursdon (1980).

The same book edited by Pryce contains a chapter by Gerbet on the Fouchet Plan negotiations. The other main works on this subject are Bloes (1970), Silj (1967), and Bodenheimer (1967). Soutou (1990) and Jansen (1986) contain interesting new material, including some from the personal papers of Jansen's father, who led the German delegation at the negotiations. Other eye-witness accounts are Fouchet (n.d.), and Cattani (1967).

The scant material on the Hague Conference and the Pompidou initiative can be traced through Couste and Visine (1974), and the chapter by de la Serre and Moreau Defarges in C. Hill (ed.), *National Foreign Policies and European Political Co-operation* (London, 1983).

3
The Formative Years (1970–1973)

ARGUMENT

The directives given by the Summit at The Hague were carried out within the year. The Luxembourg Report of October 1970 fixed the ground rules for Political Co-operation and the first Ministerial Meeting at Munich a month later set the ball rolling. Two subjects tested the new machinery: the Conference on Security and Co-operation in Europe, and the Middle East.

The Luxembourg Report had been drafted in such a way as to avoid the reefs on which the Fouchet Committee had foundered. In particular, the Community was to be kept at arm's length. EPC was not to interfere with it, and it was not to interfere with EPC. Reality was stronger than principle, however. The inclusion of an economic 'basket' in the CSCE demonstrated that the Commission's presence could not be dispensed with.

The Member States' Foreign Ministries took to EPC like ducks to water, and within three years sufficient progress had been made both in policy and in inventing procedures for it to be possible to produce a second report, the Copenhagen Report of July 1973, consolidating the achievement.

THE LUXEMBOURG REPORT

The Heads of State or Government had met in The Hague on 2 December 1969. Before the end of the following January, work on preparing the report for which the Summit had called had already begun. It was done by a group of senior officials from the Foreign Ministries of the six Member States—the Political Directors who later formed the Political Committee. Since Belgium had the Presidency for the first six months of 1970, the group was chaired by the Belgian Political Director, Viscount Davignon, after whom the Report is sometimes named.

As the initiators of the idea, the French, represented by the Political Director at the Quai d'Orsay, M. de Beaumarchais, took a leading role in the discussions. However, the Germans were not going to be left behind. By January a discussion paper on procedures for political co-operation had been prepared in the political section of the Auswärtiges Amt, where Berndt von Staden was Political Director, and had been circulated to Foreign Ministers.

The Ministers had been directed to prepare their report for the end of July. In fact it was not ready until the autumn, when it was adopted at the Conference of Foreign Ministers held on 27 October in Luxembourg. It is commonly known as the 'Luxembourg Report', and was the first of the three reports which laid down the procedures of European Political Co-operation before the Single European Act.

Ministers had not been asked to invent European Political Co-operation, but to 'study the best way of achieving progress in the matter of political unification, within the context of enlargement'. The mandate was quoted at the beginning of the Luxembourg Report, and the whole of Part One of the Report was devoted to the nature and responsibilities of a united Europe. An agenda was set: an increase in Europe's efforts for the benefit of the developing countries and respect for the liberty and the rights of men. Three considerations guided the proposals which were made: to give shape to the will to political union; to match the implementation of common (Community) policies with developments in the political sphere to bring the time nearer when Europe would speak with one voice; and to exercise Europe's growing responsibilities in the world.

The emphasis was on gradual progress. The construction of Europe was to 'proceed in successive stages', and 'the most appropriate method of, and instruments for, joint political action, should gradually develop.' In line with this gradualist approach, the Ministers decided that the present development of the Communities required Member States to 'intensify their political co-operation and provide in an initial phase the mechanism for harmonizing their views regarding international affairs.' First efforts should concentrate on the co-ordination of foreign policies.

The integrationist language of Part One of the Report was balanced by the down-to-earth, inter-governmental nature of the arrangements for the co-ordination of foreign policies set out in Part Two. These were profoundly influenced by the failure of

The Formative Years (1970–1973)

the Fouchet Plans. The collapse of the discussions in the spring of 1962 had left a deep scar. The difficulties which had brought about the collapse remained, and the authors of the Luxembourg Report, in order to avoid a repetition of the experience, skirted round them rather than tackling them head on. As the German Foreign Minister, Dr Scheel, later said, to insist on an ideal solution was condemned to failure. The Fouchet Plans had been based on an overarching structure which would have subsumed the Community institutions; the Luxembourg Report foresaw their existence in parallel. Fouchet had foreseen a permanent Secretariat; the Luxembourg Report stated that 'the host country will make the necessary arrangements to provide the secretariat and the material organization of the meetings.' The Luxembourg Report was confined to foreign-policy co-ordination; Fouchet would also have included economic policy (excluded because of the Community), cultural policy, and defence policy (excluded because of NATO). There were to be no institutional overtones, with everything as light and informal as possible. The Luxembourg Report was a report, not a Treaty.

The French knew that to insist on the Fouchet line would lead to a second collapse. They therefore did not do so, but insisted in return on safeguards to ensure that the new foreign-policy co-operation was not sucked into the Community. The Commission was not to be regularly associated, but 'Should the work of the Ministers affect the activities of the European Communities, the Commission will be invited to make known its views.' Links with the European Parliament were limited to a biannual colloquy with Parliament's Political Committee. Meetings were as a general rule to be held in the country whose representative was in the chair, and not in Brussels or Luxembourg, where the Council of the Communities met.

Part Two of the Report laid down the purpose of Political Co-operation ('to co-operate in the sphere of foreign policy') and its objectives. These owed more to rhetoric than to reality. The participants were to 'ensure, through regular exchanges of information and consultations, a better mutual understanding on the great international problems' and 'strengthen their solidarity by promoting the harmonization of their views, the co-ordination of their positions, and, where it appears possible and desirable, common actions.' The authors of the Report prudently set themselves a self-attaining objective. The impossible and the undesirable were excluded; the participants were the sole judges, by consensus, of what was possible and desirable, which was therefore automatically achieved. Fortunately the early actors in EPC did not allow their inventiveness to be confined by these texts. The first decade and a half of Political Co-operation has been marked by extreme conservatism in the drafting of theoretical papers and bold innovation on the ground.

The machinery which was set up was extremely simple. The Foreign Ministers would meet twice a year, under the chairmanship of the Foreign Minister of the country holding the Community Presidency. The Ministerial Meetings were prepared by a committee composed of the Directors of political affairs (the 'Political Committee'), which was to meet four times a year. The Political Committee was authorized to 'set up working groups to deal with special matters' and 'to appoint groups of experts to collect material relating to a specific problem and to present the possible alternatives', but by and large the Political Committee was conceived as working under the direct guidance of Ministers to prepare their meetings, and today's complex network of Working Groups was not foreseen.

Part Three of the Report dealt with the future. Here the Ministers returned to the task which had been set them, the search for progress in the field of political unification. Even though the French were not too happy about this, a second full report would be presented by Ministers not later than two years after the commencement of consultations on foreign policy, the report to contain an assessment of the results obtained.

Part Four of the Report set out the arrangements for associating the applicant countries with the work of Political Co-operation. The mandate of the Hague Summit had been firmly tied in with enlargement. Germany would have liked the United Kingdom to be brought in from the start, but France opposed this. The compromise reached was that Ministerial meetings were to be followed at a short interval by meetings of the Ten (Norway was an applicant at the time) and the Presidency of the Political Committee would provide information on the work of the Committee to the four applicants. In fact, more informal and closer forms of association were soon adopted.

The Report is adopted; the actors are on stage; the curtain on Political Co-operation is about to go up.

THE FIRST SUBJECTS TACKLED: THE CSCE AND THE MIDDLE EAST

The First Ministerial Conference in Munich

The Foreign Ministers of the Six met for the first time in European Political Co-operation barely a month after the adoption of the Luxembourg Report, on 19 November 1970 in Munich. The Conference took place in the evocative, but provisional, setting of the old Prussian Embassy to the Kingdom of Bavaria; the Gobelin tapestry which was found to hang on the wall depicted Amadis the Gaul, the knight errant of Gallic lore.

Why Munich, rather than Bonn? It is true that the Luxembourg Report only provided that 'the meetings will as a general rule be held in the country whose representative is in the chair', but ever since then, with very rare exceptions, meetings in the country holding the Presidency have taken place in the capital. The Chairman of the meeting, Dr Scheel, confessed to a sentimental desire to honour his family's Bavarian ties, but subsequently proffered as an explanation the imminence of the Bavarian Landtag elections.

The point is neither anecdotal nor trivial. Uncertainty about the proper place for an EPC Conference of Ministers (as the Ministerial Meetings were known at the time) merely showed that the ground rules for this new enterprise had not yet been set. The Ministers had never met before in that format; they were not certain what they were supposed to achieve nor in what conventions they would be operating; there had been some preparatory work for the meeting, but not the full-blown, professional preparation of the agenda which the Political Committee was to develop in later years. The setting of the agenda was by no means self-evident.

The two main topics discussed were the Middle East and the CSCE, which were to dominate the councils of EPC for the next few years and to determine the form in which it developed. Why was this so?

The two themes had one important characteristic in common:

they both concerned areas neighbouring the Community and had a pronounced European flavour. Political Co-operation did not at first busy itself with any and every topic of global concern, but started off with the problems of its own backyard. But for all that, the themes were not chosen for the sake of facility. The CSCE was a leap into the unknown, and the differences of the Member States with regard to the Middle East were all too familiar. There was a genuine desire, in embarking on these subjects, to achieve convergence of policy in the spirit of the Luxembourg Report, and a feeling that these were real problems on which EPC could, if it chose, be effective.

The Middle East was discussed for the simple reason that the French wanted it. General de Gaulle had brought about a sea change in France's policy towards the area. In 1956, France had taken part in the Suez operation in support of Israel; by 1967, de Gaulle was clearly on the Arab side. At the time of the June War in 1967, the Foreign Ministers of the Six had notably failed even to discuss the situation. France was determined to bring its partners closer to the French position and thus strengthen European support for the Arab cause. An added attraction was that such a movement, if it could be brought about, would assert European independence of American policy—in France's eyes one of the potential merits of European Political Co-operation. The move was supported by the Federal Republic of Germany because it could thus improve its relations with the Arab world without attracting undue criticism from Israel or the United States.

The choice of the CSCE theme was more complicated. The Soviet Union had for many years been trying to promote moves towards some sort of pan-European security system which would legitimate the post-war division of Europe and thus consolidate the Soviet sphere of influence. Resistant to this idea, the West had nevertheless agreed in principle to a Pan-European Security Conference, on condition that at the same time there were talks on force reductions. Western co-ordination on this subject had of course taken place within the Atlantic Alliance, EPC not yet being in existence.

This move was symptomatic of the atmosphere of *détente* in the late 1960s, which led to the twin-track approach of the Harmel initiative, combining vigilance with openness. Indeed,

M. Harmel, as Belgian Foreign Minister, was a prominent participant in the Munich Conference and was invited by the President, Dr Scheel, to introduce the specific discussion on the CSCE. A constructive attitude towards an initiative so redolent of détente as a Conference on security in Europe could scarcely avoid being a part of the emerging European identity. It was also a response to uncertainties about American policies towards Europe. The United States, their diplomatic energies concentrated almost entirely on the closing stages of the conflict in Vietnam, seemed strangely unconcerned about the idea. Moreover, the multilateral form of the CSCE did not appeal to Dr Kissinger's view of how global-power relationships should be handled. He considered the Conference 'at best significant for public opinion, but certainly not an essential component of the substantial make-up of the substance of détente'. The Americans were therefore inclined to let the Europeans handle this one by themselves—an attitude which changed in later years when EPC was seen to be the priority forum for co-ordination, taking precedence over NATO. In 1970, what became the CSCE was seen by many Europeans to be an opportunity to evolve a distinctively European policy.

Furthermore, Germany was particularly anxious that there should be a co-ordinated European position on this question to act as a counterbalance to what might otherwise be seen as disquieting features of its own *Ostpolitik*. The Federal Republic made it plain on a number of occasions that Europe-wide co-operation must not go forward at the expense of Community integration. Germany's return to the international community of nations was still too recent for it to be able to take the risk of a *rapprochement* with Eastern Europe without the comforting presence of its European partners in a similar policy enterprise.

Finally, there was, as so often in the development of the Community, an apparently technical, and politically unimportant, reason for doing something which nevertheless had far-reaching effects on the course of events. This was the fact that the transitional period, during which national trade policies towards the countries of Eastern Europe had been allowed to continue, was due to come to an end on 31 December 1972. After that date powers would be transferred to the European Community. In addition to being a powerful lever by which the European

Commission effected an entry into Political Co-operation, this meant that there was a pressing procedural reason for the Member States to elaborate in common an overall policy towards the countries concerned.

The CSCE

The Ministers' discussions at Munich about the proposed Conference on security in Europe fell into two parts. The first was concerned with the general approach of the Six to the question. The second, which lasted barely more than an hour, was devoted to the Community aspects. This part of the discussion was attended by a Commission delegation led by its President, Mr Malfatti. The Ministers' general approach largely reflected the communiqué already issued by NATO, emphasizing the free movement of people and economic, cultural, scientific, technical, and environmental co-operation. A number of Ministers warned against allowing the Soviet Union to interfere in the process of European integration. Launching the Commission's long battle for acceptance in EPC, Malfatti called for the participation of the Community as such in the CSCE, and was supported in particular by Dr Scheel and Mr Luns. France, however, for reasons of principle, took a more restrictive position; M. Schumann pointed out that the Conference would be mainly on security questions, rather than economic ones, and would be between States, not blocs. The Political Committee was asked to prepare both those aspects which had been dealt with in the NATO communiqué and the economic co-operation aspects.

Thus began the process which over the coming years was to take up a large part of the time of the participants in Political Co-operation, fix its organization and procedures, and give it a place on the map. It also ensured, because of the economic angle, that from the start there was a link with the Community and that the Commission was present for at least some of the discussions in EPC. For example, M. Schumann forwarded to the Commission President in April 1971 a draft document on CSCE economic co-operation prepared by the Political Committee and sought the Commission's views. Mr Malfatti was invited to the Conference of Ministers in Paris on 14 May and even (*O tempora, O mores*) to dinner the night before. The Commission would certainly not have received such an invitation had this item not been on the agenda; as it was, it did not take part in the discussions on the Middle East. Nor was it invited to the next Ministerial Conference in Rome in November, but merely informed in writing of those conclusions which concerned it.

The work of EPC in preparing the position of the Six with regard to the CSCE followed the phases into which the Helsinki Conference was itself divided. First of all there was discussion of the general approach to the Conference and preparation for the Multilateral Preparatory Talks (MPT) which took place in Helsinki from November 1972 to June 1973; then followed the first phase of the Conference proper, in Helsinki on 3–7 July 1973; the second phase of the Conference, in Geneva, lasted from September 1973 to June 1975 and was closed by the third phase in Helsinki on 1 August 1975.

The corresponding first phase in the work of the Six began with approval by the Foreign Ministers of principles for the multilateral preparatory phase, given at their Conference in Rome in November 1971. These principles were set out in a document which came up with the imprimatur of the Political Committee, prepared in its turn by the CSCE Subcommittee with input on economic questions from a paper submitted by the Commission. The document analysed the objectives of the Soviet Union—the maintenance of the status quo—and of the Community, which aimed at improved security, détente, and the encouragement of human rights and individual freedoms. Economic co-operation was seen as an important part of détente. Ideas were put forward for a structuring of the agenda which foreshadowed the later three baskets: on the political side there was to be a 'code of good conduct', designed to cover such questions as security and troop reductions; on the economic side, the Community should launch an economic initiative following the Political Committee's analysis; and the whole would be done under the general principles laid down by the Ministers.

A great deal of detailed technical work was done over the next year, the greater part being concentrated into the period from September 1972 until the opening of the MPT in February 1973. Meeting in Luxembourg at the halfway stage in May 1972,

Ministers gave broad approval to a report on progress in preparations which also contained orientations for the highly technical work done thereafter in the specialist groups. By October, the *ad hoc* group was tackling in some detail four broad areas of economic co-operation: industrial co-operation, trade co-operation, financial co-operation, and others including tourism, transports, and development. It is interesting that this activity was based on previous work done in NATO; indeed, the fiches prepared in NATO's Economic Committee provided the raw material for subsequent work by the Six. Not that there was much that was new in all this, since it also drew on discussions in the UN Economic Commission for Europe. Indeed, the Commission's experience in that forum helped establish its credibility in the new EPC exercise.

The Paris Summit of Heads of State and Government of the Community, convened by President Pompidou in October 1972, did not play a direct role in the preparation of the position of the Six with regard to the CSCE, although the two references to the Conference in the Summit's communiqué were an indication of its political importance. Significantly, the Heads of Government linked the CSCE to the Community's own policy towards Eastern Europe, in a passage redolent with institutional nuances:

> In order to promote détente in Europe, the Conference reaffirmed its determination to follow a common commercial policy towards the countries of Eastern Europe with effect from 1 January 1973; Member States declared their determination to promote a policy of co-operation, founded on reciprocity, with these countries. This policy of co-operation is, at the present stage, closely linked with the preparation and progress of the Conference on Security and Co-operation in Europe to which the enlarged Community and its Member States are called upon to make a concerted and constructive contribution.

The link between the CSCE and the Community's own policy towards the East European countries was not fortuitous. We have seen that the end of the transitional period for the continuance of national trade policies towards the state-trading countries on 31 December 1972 was one of the reasons for the Member States' enthusiasm for tackling the CSCE question in the new Political Co-operation framework. The governments of the Six intended that the political guidelines for the Community's common commercial policy should be set by them rather than

The Formative Years (1970–1973)   61

by the Commission. At the same time, the Commission was engaged in a struggle to prevent the common commercial policy towards the state-trading countries from being emptied of substance by separate national economic co-operation agreements. It failed in this: the Council decision of July 1974 providing for co-ordination of these national agreements was only formally applied.

The Political Committee as early as the end of 1971 set in hand work on the relationship between the Community and the Council for Mutual Economic Assistance (Comecon) and its members, including the attitude of the East European countries towards European unification. The work had progressed sufficiently by the autumn of the following year for a detailed document to be drafted. This was done by the United Kingdom, which tabled a paper in September 1972. (The United Kingdom had been associated with the work of the Six from an early stage and, as this example shows, was an active participant rather than an observer. The other candidate countries participated fully from March 1972.) The paper began with a factual description of the situation, drawing attention to the changes in commercial policy from 1973 on and Comecon's lack of formal powers, which differentiated it from the Community. It then set out a number of principles and drew the corresponding policy conclusions.

Although in theory the document was to be discussed in both the CSCE Subcommittee and the *ad hoc* Group, in practice the work was done in the former body, which had the effect of excluding the Commission. This was naturally not to the Commission's liking, and when the paper came up for approval by Ministers in their Session at The Hague in November 1972, the Commission President, Mr Mansholt, suggested that it should be added to the proposals on the economic aspects the Commission had sent to the Council the previous month. This suggestion was not followed; the Ministers did, however, decide to forward the document to the Council themselves, once it had been approved by diplomatic channels, as also the Political Committee's report on the economic aspects of the CSCE, 'approved in the presence of the Commission'.

To return to the preparation of the CSCE itself, the work in the specialized groups reached a climax in the early days of 1973 in order to enable the Six to table on 15 January a paper which in effect set a comprehensive draft mandate and agenda for the Conference. This determined the course of discussions for the whole of the MPT and indeed for the rest of the Helsinki Conference. The objective had been achieved: preparations for the Conference would go forward on the basis that it would tackle issues of substance, not empty declarations, and that a political volet would be balanced by both an economic initiative and a section on human liberties. Political Co-operation had passed its first test: it had shown that the Six could act together harmoniously and effectively.

How had this been achieved? A major factor was of course the will to succeed, but this would not have been enough if business had not been properly organized. The machinery which EPC set up in order to get through the work involved in preparing positions for Helsinki not only functioned efficiently, but also acted as a model for other policy areas and, by the intensity and frequency of the contacts among diplomats it involved, established at an early date the free and informal habits of working together which became the principal achievement of the system.

In order to carry out the mandate given to it by the Ministers in Munich, the Political Committee set up in February 1971 a Subcommittee on the CSCE with broad overall instructions to investigate all relevant aspects of the proposal for a Conference which might be of interest to the Community (avoiding, at any rate at that stage, any overlapping of work with NATO). The Commission was not invited to participate; we have seen that the draft document on economic co-operation which had been prepared by the Subcommittee was sent to the Commission for comments before the Paris Conference of Ministers, but the document had been prepared by Member States' experts alone.

Mr Malfatti raised at the Paris Conference the question of Community participation in both the preparation for the Conference and the Conference itself. He argued that the study of the substance of the economic questions should be carried out in the Community, a position which found some support, but also ran into objections grounded in the danger of thus enhancing the position of Comecon as an organization. As an alternative, it was suggested that the Commission should be represented in both the Political Committee and the CSCE Subcommittee for all points of Community competence. M.

The Formative Years (1970–1973)

Schumann, who as French Foreign Minister was in the chair, put forward the further compromise proposal that the Commission should make its comments available in writing to the Subcommittee, via the Political Committee, and also be invited to take part in a special group of experts on economic co-operation, which would be subordinate to the Subcommittee and report to it.

This was the genesis of the *ad hoc* Group, with the participation of the Commission, which soon took on in practice an institutional life of its own and reported direct to the Political Committee. It dealt, broadly speaking, with the economic aspects of the Conference while the Subcommittee dealt with the political aspects and overall tactics. In time the two groups grew closer together, for practical reasons, and began to hold some joint meetings, and as the Conference moved into the Geneva phase the *ad hoc* Group, meeting regularly on the spot in Geneva, took on greater overall importance.

The manner of operating of these groups established the pattern for Working Groups in the future. They were chaired by the Presidency and met in the Presidency's capital. Participants were the officials in Foreign Ministries who were involved on a day-to-day basis in setting national policies in the area concerned. The rhythm of meetings was very frequent, reaching at least one a month in 1972. All these were important features in fostering solidarity among the Six at an early stage.

The question of relations with NATO was one of some delicacy. Here again the institutional pattern was set early. The delegations of a number of Member States in the Subcommittee included experts from both the East European as well as the NATO sections of their political departments, many of whom knew each other from the six-monthly meetings of the NATO East European expert meetings. There was a move at the beginning of 1972 to include in the delegations to the Subcommittee members of the Permanent Representations at NATO. The Permanent Representatives of the Six at NATO were invited to co-ordinate among themselves, and the Subcommittee and *ad hoc* Group were bidden to make recommendations whenever they thought that a particular document should be communicated to NATO (the origin of the current 'usual distribution' system for selected documents). Ministers decided in May 1972 that decisions on whether or not to send documents to NATO would be taken on a case-by-case basis; the Presidency would, however, give informal information to NATO after each Ministerial meeting. The underlying disagreement about the proper relationship with the United States, which was to surface in 1973, can be seen here.

In spite of these precautions, there was some overlapping of work and jockeying for position. EPC came deliberately to organize its work in such a way that its position on a given question, particularly on the economic side, was fixed before discussions in NATO got under way. The NATO study of a science-and-technology initiative in the early part of 1973 was cautiously allowed to proceed, but with a failsafe mechanism for co-ordination in EPC in case things got out of hand. That there was not greater tension between the two frameworks was in large part because of the quiescence of the United States and because NATO co-ordination fell behind once the action moved to Geneva in the second phase of the Helsinki Conference. NATO had neither Secretariat nor permanent infrastructure in Geneva, which left the field clear for EPC in the all important daily co-ordination of tactics.

Relations with NATO were, however, as nothing compared with the complex issue of the role and status of the Community. From the beginning it was feared that to insist too much on the Community's powers would bring forth an undesirable reaction from the Eastern side. The Soviet Union did not recognize the Community; to ask for participation in the Conference by the Community might induce a parallel request on behalf of Comecon, which not only did not have the same powers as the Community, but was seen as an instrument of Soviet domination. These arguments were present in the minds of all the Six, but whereas some were prepared to face the difficulties, France found them a comforting bolster for its traditional Gaullist approach to the nature of the Community and the status of the Commission.

The French influence was at work at the Paris Ministerial Conference in May 1971, when it led to the setting up of the *ad hoc* Group as a means of confining within acceptable limits the indispensable input from the Commission. The same question had to be faced regarding the manner in which the Community

The Formative Years (1970–1973)

was to be represented in the various Helsinki meetings and whether it was to be able to make a statement. At its meeting in April 1972 the Political Committee decided that if a subject within the Community's competence was raised during the MPT phase, this should be done by the Presidency. Close co-ordination was therefore necessary, at the initiative of the Presidency, and with the participation of the Commission on each occasion on which points were raised which, in the opinion of all the Member States, affected Community competences. The Political Committee did not express a view on the presence at Helsinki of the Community as such, and the fact that the text of its decision was not finalized until over two months later (after Ministers had recognized in May the need for matters of Community competence to be handled by the Community Institutions) shows the delicacy and difficulty of the question.

The Political Committee's orientations were endorsed by Ministers meeting in The Hague in November 1972. The Ministers added that, during the MPT, proposals within the competence of the Community should only be tabled in the name of the Community and with the indication that their implementation depended on agreement within the Community. Concrete proposals in this area were to be decided through the normal Community procedures, and the Council should organize itself in consequence. Finally, the Ministers thought that the presence of a representative of the Commission in Helsinki was desirable, without taking a decision on the vexed question of participation. In practice, Commission officials attended the MPT as members of the delegation of the country holding the Presidency.

The question of whether a statement was to be made on behalf of the Community as such, at both the MPT and the Ministerial phase of the Conference in Helsinki, was equally tricky. The Commission proposed in February 1972 that such a statement should be made, and that it should be prepared by the Community Institutions. Ministers in March did not commit themselves to this (the French were opposed), but at least set in hand preparatory work on a text, and on a reply to be used in case the East European countries insisted on Comecon participation. The idea of a declaration at the MPT was not taken up, but in subsequent discussions the thought evolved that, in accepting the mandate, the country holding the Presidency should also approve it on behalf of the Community. This, in a watered-down form, was what was finally accepted. Opinions on a declaration at the Ministerial session were divided; most Member States thought that there should be a short reminder of Community competences, some wanted something more ceremonious, and one wanted nothing at all. In the event a declaration on behalf of the Community was approved and was read out in Helsinki by the Danish Foreign Minister, the first of the Nine to speak and from 1 July 1973 holding the EPC Presidency. Other Foreign Ministers were to refer to the Community declaration in their own speeches.

The Middle East

The work of the Six on the CSCE both created and exemplified the strength of European Political Co-operation. Their discussions on the Middle East were on the face of it less successful. The absence of a mechanism to reconcile widely diverging views prevented the Member States from forging an active policy in this area which would have served them in good stead in the difficult years to come. Yet their achievement should not be underestimated: the position of the Six did evolve towards one which occupied the middle ground, ironing out the extremes of the individual national positions. Admittedly, the shift towards the centre reflected a shift towards the Arab position in the traditionally pro-Israeli Member States which was probably taking place anyway. The fact remains that this tendency was fostered by the new consensus-building procedures of Political Co-operation.

A few years previously, the divergencies between the Middle East policies of the Member States could scarcely have been greater. France's initial strong support for Israel had been swung around by General de Gaulle, for a variety of reasons ranging from a high-flown theoretical approach to transatlantic relations to less high-flown considerations related to French arms sales. The policy of the Federal Republic was still confined within the straitjacket of guilt for the Nazis' treatment of the Jews, although some German politicians (including Scheel, in the chair at the Munich Conference) saw the advantages of a

The Formative Years (1970–1973)

degree of *rapprochement* with the Arabs. The Netherlands' support for Israel only wavered when considerations of national interest supervened. The Belgians did not want to have a policy at all, and were therefore staunch supporters of the United Nations, and Italy's line was more than usually dependent on the shifting kaleidoscope of the different factions within the government.

When the Six Day War broke out on 5 June 1967 the Member States of the Community took up positions consistent with their underlying attitudes. After having stopped the supply of arms to Israel, France condemned the Israeli action and gave the Arabs her full support. Germany's official position was one of neutrality, but this was accompanied by a strong moral commitment to Israel, at the cost of a hostile reaction from the Arab countries. The Italian government was divided, but at this time the pro-Israeli current prevailed. The Netherlands gave Israel strong support. Belgium played the UN card.

The Member States of the Community made no attempt to coordinate their positions. Heads of Government were meeting in Rome a few days before the outbreak of the war, and the German government had proposed that they should work out a joint position on the situation in the Middle East, although the meeting was designed to be only a ceremonial one marking the tenth anniversary of the signing of the Treaty of Rome. The Summit's failure even to discuss the question was roundly condemned by Chancellor Kiesinger after the war broke out. The French proposal for regular meetings of Foreign Ministers reminded the Benelux countries too vividly of the series of meetings which had preceded the failure of the Fouchet discussions, and was rejected. Although it is not entirely fair to blame the Heads of Government for failing to engage in an operation for which no procedure existed at the time and which was almost certainly doomed to failure, the public inability of the members of the Community to come together on such a vital question provided strong ammunition for those who wished to see a European foreign policy evolve, and meant that the Middle East stood a good chance of being on the agenda when Political Co-operation finally came into being.

Although national positions had already begun to shift, they were still sufficiently far apart for the discussion at the Munich

Conference in November 1970 to be a difficult one. The procedural outcome of the meeting appears to have been that the Political Committee was told to produce a joint paper for publication setting out the position of the Six. This work was undertaken in the early part of the following year, the principal items under discussion being what to do with the refugees, the proposed demilitarized zones on the border between Israel and Egypt and what forces should be deployed there, and the question of Jerusalem. Agreement was not easy, and many were taken by surprise when it became known that an agreed document, known as the Schumann document from its spiritual father, the French Foreign Minister, was in existence and that the French Presidency intended to submit this document to Ministers at their May meeting in Paris.

The paper was duly approved by Ministers on 13 May 1971, but at the price of agreement that it would not be made public, exacted by Germany and the Netherlands. Its subsequent publication in the Springer press, the result of a leak, was all the more serious a blow to the effectiveness of EPC and was the first of many crises of confidence as the result of a breach of confidentiality. It also caused serious difficulties to the German government, which was not yet ready to divulge to public opinion how far it had moved towards the French position. Heavily criticized by Israel and the Christian Democrat opposition, Scheel affirmed that the Schumann document was only a 'working paper', or even a 'basis for discussion', which considerably annoyed the French.

In the light of later declarations made in EPC, the Schumann document seems modest to a degree, and indeed did not provoke in the other Member States the storm to which it gave rise in Germany. It was consistent with UN Resolution 242 and did not indicate on the part of the Six any desire to go beyond this in order to carve out an individual European position on the Middle East. In particular the Six were not yet ready to talk about the 'Palestinians', who were referred to in the classic UN language as 'refugees'. The sea change here was only to come over two years later, under the pressure of the Yom Kippur War and the first oil crisis.

In the meanwhile the Political Committee, assisted by an expert group, quietly continued its work without the benefit of a publicly agreed document as a point of reference. There were

The Formative Years (1970–1973)

bilateral contacts with parties like the UN Secretary-General, Jarring, and interested third countries, based on a joint approach, but always within the framework of Resolution 242; co-ordination of the Six at the United Nations was strengthened, with the participation of the United Kingdom especially in view of the latter's membership of the Security Council; the idea of a European initiative was toyed with, but never taken up. Political Co-operation did, however, work on increased financial assistance for the refugees, and for this point, but for no other, the Commission was brought into the discussions.

So matters stood until the events of autumn 1973 threw the Nine into considerable disarray and obliged them to reassess drastically their policy on the Middle East.

Institutional Developments

Important and time-consuming as they were, the CSCE and the Middle East did not monopolize the attention of Political Co-operation in the early years. At the first meeting in Munich Ministers issued a communiqué on aid to Pakistan, and in the years which followed discussions at official level ranged over such widely varying topics as the relations between Cuba and the United States, the representation of China in international financial institutions, the political aspects of the Mutual and Balanced Force Reduction talks (MBFR), and the future role of the Council of Europe, the latter at a time when the organization in Strasbourg was having one of its periodic fits of self-doubt, brought on by the enlargement of the Community and the development of Political Co-operation. The Nine strengthened their co-ordination in Strasbourg.

Apart from these rather scattered subjects, the main topic of discussion was developments in the Mediterranean. A group of experts on Mediterranean questions was in existence by early 1972, and was engaged in a series of studies by geographical sectors shared out among the partners which were brought to the attention of the Political Committee and Ministers. The area was of some importance both because of its proximity to the Community and because of moves towards a Conference of the Mediterranean non-aligned countries and the relationship between this and Mediterranean participation in the CSCE. Nothing much of operational value came of the work, however, and in November 1972, following the Paris Summit, the Ministers decided that the political aspects of a global approach for the Community's relations with the Mediterranean countries should henceforth be treated by the Permanent Representatives to the Community. The Mediterranean Working Group's mandate was for the future to be confined to observing events in the region and the possibility of using a Mediterranean Conference as a channel through which non-European Mediterranean countries could be kept informed about developments in the CSCE. In fact the Mediterranean Working Group only came into its own in later years when it had to deal with the situation in Portugal, Cyprus, and later Spain.

Apart from the different groups dealing with the CSCE, the Middle East, and the Mediterranean, the only other groups which existed at this stage of EPC's development were those of the Heads of Protocol and the European Correspondents. The Heads of Protocol first met in October 1972, at the initiative of Germany, in order to harmonize protocol for state and official visits (they were still at it fifteen years later). The European Correspondents, on the other hand, established in the Luxembourg Report, soon showed that they were an indispensable element in the functioning of Political Co-operation. They were not at first called by that name, but appear as a Subcommittee of the Political Committee, their most important task being to finalize the conclusions of the meetings of the Political Committee and of the Ministers. They also did jobs like drafting joint directives to diplomatic missions abroad, looking after security, and doing much of the groundwork for what became the Copenhagen Report. Meeting in June 1972 in Luxembourg, the Correspondents produced a wide-ranging report on a number of organizational questions. It was in approving this report the following month that the Political Committee authorized the use of the term 'Groupe des Correspondants'. A particularly important role which devolved to them was to act as the contact point for the reception of EPC documents which were exchanged between partners, the Coreu system not yet being in existence.

Right from the start Member States were aware that Political Co-operation could not be confined to their capitals. In December 1971 instructions were given to Permanent Representatives in New York to concert their views, especially on the Middle East

The Formative Years (1970–1973)

(this concertation was extended to the Permanent Representative of the United Kingdom, on an *ad hoc* basis, on Middle East questions). Joint directives on co-operation in third countries were elaborated and updated on a number of occasions in the early years, enjoining Ambassadors to work with each other particularly regarding the impact of Political Co-operation in the countries to which they were accredited. Similarly, arrangements were made for third countries, especially Turkey, to be kept informed of what the Six, later Nine, were doing.

These procedural innovations, together with those mentioned in the course of this chapter which grew out of the organization of work on the CSCE, added up to a solid basis for the newly created EPC. When the time came to draft the follow-up report to the Luxembourg Report, there was already a great deal of institutional progress which could be put down on paper and systematized.

THE COPENHAGEN REPORT

The Paris Summit (October 1972)

In the Luxembourg Report the Foreign Ministers had given themselves a period of two years to prepare a second study of progress towards political unification, including Political Co-operation. The deadline thus fixed fell in November 1972, before enlargement. But the Ministers did not delay in setting about their renewed task. Arrangements for carrying out the study were being discussed already at the first Ministerial Conference in Munich; a year later memoranda from Germany and the Netherlands were on the table; in the following spring a Belgian paper on the functioning of EPC was being discussed by the Correspondents.

The functioning of EPC could still not be dissociated from the question of political union. On that subject, President Pompidou gave a press conference on 21 January 1971 in which he revived the idea of a confederal Europe. In Pompidou's view, the ultimate authority had to lie with the Nation States, represented by Ministers with special responsibility for European questions who in due course would evolve into a form of European government in which decisions would be taken collectively.

This body would be serviced, not by a supranational organ like the Commission in Brussels, but by a Secretariat under the direct control of the Ministers which, Pompidou later made clear, would have its seat in Paris.

The revival of the old spectre of an overarching political secretariat complicated the debate about progress towards political union and the functioning of EPC. Although the federalist aspirations of the age of the European Political Community had somewhat faded, the scars left by the discussions in the Fouchet Committee had not. The Federal Republic was committed to a federalist, rather than a confederalist, Europe. At the same time, Germany believed that a secretariat was necessary to enable the newly created EPC machinery to function properly. The organization of the early meetings must have been miracles of improvisation, and a standing infrastructure would have eased matters greatly. The United Kingdom, whose views had to be taken into account although it was not yet a member of the Community, was closer to the French position.

The prospect of a trilateral axis, Paris–Bonn–London, strengthened the resolve of the remaining Member States to resist any institutional developments which took Political Co-operation further down the inter-governmental road. This difference of approach found its expression in the argument over whether the secretariat should be established in Paris or in Brussels. In May 1972 the Netherlands Foreign Minister stated that the secretariat would have to be based in Brussels, in order to ensure adequate co-ordination with the Community Institutions. Shortly afterwards his French colleague insisted on Paris. In the end, the French had to abandon the idea of a political secretariat in Paris. Since they were not prepared to accept one in Brussels, which would have signalled a move towards a Community structure, EPC had to soldier on without a secretariat at all. The Ministers' Second Report did not mention the matter, and the European Parliament was told that it had not been raised in the preparatory work for the Paris Summit. The game had been played and lost outside the conference halls.

The idea of a new summit, to follow that held in The Hague, had been around for some time. The EPC Ministerial Conference held in Rome in November 1971 devoted much of its attention to

The Formative Years (1970–1973)

preparing such a meeting, which it was then planned to hold the following March. The purpose of the summit was to make further progress on the road to political union. To this end, the Belgian Foreign Minister, M. Harmel, proposed the discussion of five items: economic and monetary union, EEC–US relations, the CSCE, institutional questions in the enlarged Community, and the future of European institutions which did not derive from the Community Treaties. The Foreign Ministers agreed that a summit should be held as early as possible in 1972.

In fact the meeting was postponed mainly because of differences over relations with the United States. It was finally called for 19–20 October in Paris, at the invitation of President Pompidou, with an agenda focusing on three themes: economic and monetary union and social progress; strengthening the institutions and progress towards political union; and the Community's external relations and its world responsibilities. The Commission was to be associated with the preparation of these themes, with the exception of those bearing on progress to be made outside the Community framework, especially in political co-operation.

The Paris Summit produced a resounding declaration, but one which notably failed to be implemented in its more important elements. The Member States' commitment to 'transform before the end of the present decade the whole complex of their relations into a European Union' was to remain unfulfilled. Nevertheless, it was to achieve this aim that the Heads of State and Government requested the Institutions of the Community to draw up a report before the end of 1975 for submission to a further summit. At the same time, Foreign Ministers were asked to produce, not later than 30 June 1973, a second report on methods of improving political co-operation in accordance with the Luxembourg Report.

The distinction was crucial. Previously, the Foreign Ministers had been working on ways of moving towards political unification as foreseen by the Summit at The Hague. The Luxembourg Report itself had seen Political Co-operation as the initial stage in this wider process. Now, by entrusting the Community Institutions with the report on unification and leaving the Foreign Ministers to deal with the restricted area of EPC, the Heads of State and Government had recognized the *de facto* situation and ensured that Political Co-operation would continue down its independent road. EPC had taken the first step towards losing the role which some had foreseen for it as the motor of European Integration.

The Paris Summit did, however, recognize the need for consistency between EPC and Community policies. The Declaration stated that 'on matters which have a direct bearing on Community activities, close contact will be maintained with the Institutions of the Community.' The procedure was scarcely binding, and in fact went less far than the provisions of the Luxembourg Report. The scope of co-operation was refined, the definition now reading: 'to deal with problems of current interest and, where possible, to formulate common medium- and long-term positions, keeping in mind, inter alia, the international political implications for and effects of Community policies under construction.' This was an apparent advance on the Luxembourg formulation, since for the first time the possibility of common positions was admitted, but as usual in this type of text the language did not noticeably affect actual practice. One specific procedural improvement was introduced: the Foreign Ministers were henceforth to meet four times a year instead of twice.

The Copenhagen Report

The mandate to draft a second report was passed on to the Political Committee by Ministers at their meeting in November. By now it was fairly clear to all concerned what the broad lines of the report would be. There was no longer any question of a secretariat, and political co-operation was to develop on its own merits rather than as part of a grand scheme for political union. Given this, it became inevitable that the second report would build pragmatically on the foundations laid down in the first.

This was indeed what happened. Belgium took over the Presidency on 1 January 1973 and initiated work on the question. The Political Committee had before it at its March meeting a paper from its Chairman, Viscount Davignon, which already contained most of the substance of what later became the Copenhagen Report—which, like the Luxembourg Report, could with equal justice also have been called the Davignon Report. The Belgian draft took into account the line which had

The Formative Years (1970–1973)

emerged over the previous year. The second report was not to be a new one, but was to be complementary to the Luxembourg Report; it was to include a balance sheet of the first years' experience. The role of the Presidency in preparing the discussions of Ministers and in implementing their decisions was emphasized. Regarding administrative questions, it was thought that 'problems could most easily be solved within the Presidency for the time being.'

The question of relations between EPC and the Community was left for Ministers. This indeed proved to be a stumbling-block at the first round of discussions at the Ministerial meeting in March. However, by May the Political Committee had finalized a draft on which there was almost full agreement and this was submitted to the Ministers at their regular meeting in June. It was not approved then because of continuing differences of opinion on relations with the United States of America. This question, on which the Member States were sharply divided, all the more so after Secretary Kissinger's 'Year of Europe' speech in April 1973, held up agreement for some time.

Both questions were put off to a special meeting held in Copenhagen on 23 July. This was the famous meeting, quoted in all accounts of Political Co-operation, when Ministers met in Copenhagen in the morning to discuss EPC matters and then flew to Brussels to meet as the Council in the afternoon. It is often forgotten that such an event only happened once, and that the Ministers' meeting in June had taken place in Luxembourg in connection with a Council meeting without anyone apparently making any objection.

The procedural decisions taken by the Ministers at Copenhagen regarding relations with the United States—the decision to identify suitable subjects for dialogue and to draft a document on the European identity—made it possible to approve the second report on 'the European political co-operation as far as foreign policy is concerned'. Thus it was that the second report became the Copenhagen Report. Technically speaking, it was not adopted by the Ministers themselves, but by the Heads of State and of Government whose consent was sought by written procedure expiring in the course of August.

The Report was divided into three parts. Part I was an introduction setting out the general framework and objectives.

Part II listed the decisions to be taken. The third part, which was technically an annexe, described the results obtained from EPC so far. This apparently logical sequence needs to be taken in reverse order in order to represent reality. The achievements of the previous two years, as described in the annexe, were codified in a set of decisions which remained the ground rules of Political Co-operation for the next eight years, while the general principles in the introduction were drawn largely from previous summit positions. The Heads of State and Government were thus rather curiously invited to endorse on the one hand what they themselves had already said and on the other hand what had already been done without asking for anyone's approval. The Copenhagen Report should not, for all that, be underestimated. The innovations made since 1970 represented genuine progress and provided an adequate and not too constricting framework for developments in the years to come.

The annexe listed eight areas in which results had been obtained. The first concerned Ministerial meetings. The Paris Summit had doubled the initial frequency to four times a year. The Copenhagen Report now reserved the possibility of their consulting on specific subjects between meetings 'when they happen to come together on other occasions', in other words on the occasion of Council meetings.

Areas 2 and 3 were devoted to the organization of the Political Co-operation apparatus. The Political Committee had been meeting more frequently than the four times a year foreseen in the Luxembourg Report. The annexe revealed that it had met nine times in the previous twelve months. It had also set up a Subcommittee and an *ad hoc* Group to work on the CSCE, and three Working Groups on the Middle East, the Mediterranean, and Asia. The consultations preparatory to discussions in the United Nations family which had previously taken place in the WEU framework had been transferred to EPC, and the European Correspondents had been established as a Group.

The Copenhagen Report removed the limit on the number of meetings of the Political Committee, which henceforth could meet as frequently as the intensification of the work required. The Correspondents' Group was confirmed, and the Working Groups were given formal existence, but their life was limited to the time it took them to complete the particular task which had been assigned to them. Some nervousness can be detected here on the part of the Political Directors and the Ministers about creating transnational groupings which were not firmly in their control. Nevertheless, realities were faced by a provision which allowed the Presidency to ask the Political Committee to agree to bringing together senior officials from Foreign Ministries in the most important policy areas who had not met within the previous half year. These artificial restrictions soon became a dead letter and the Working Groups became permanent.

The Paris Summit mandate had set as an objective the formulation of common medium- and long-term positions. This had not previously been done in EPC. The Copenhagen Report provided that this type of work could be carried out according to circumstances either by the existing Working Groups or 'by entrusting the preparation of such studies to a special analysis and research group consisting normally of officials'. Neither formula worked, and planning has remained to this day one of the great lacunae in Political Co-operation.

Areas 4 and 5 of the annexe dealt with Political Co-operation activities outside the central organs. It had been found useful to organize contacts on EPC matters between the Ambassadors of the Nine in the respective capitals and the Foreign Ministry of the host country. This was particularly important in the capital of the Presidency. It should be recalled that at this stage the Member States were still dependent on the traditional channels of diplomatic communication for exchanging messages. The Copenhagen Report therefore legitimized this function of the Ambassadors, confirming that they should receive Community information from the Foreign Ministry of their country of residence and that they could from time to time be consulted collectively on specific subjects. The role of the Ambassadors became less important over the years, particularly after the Coreu system had been established. This confidential telex network linking the capitals of the Nine was inaugurated on 1 July 1973 at the start of the Danish Presidency. The decision was formalized in the Copenhagen Report itself.

A similar co-operation had been found useful among the Heads of the diplomatic Missions of the Nine in third countries and with international organizations. They could be asked by the Political Committee to supply reports and could regularly discuss among themselves problems of common interest. These arrangements were confirmed and even somewhat expanded in the Copenhagen Report. Early information was to be given to the colleagues of the Nine about important visits from the Member State concerned, and a debriefing given afterwards. The Permanent Representatives to the major international organizations were, on the basis of instructions, to seek common positions in regard to important questions dealt with by those organizations.

The consensus to leave to one side the question of a secretariat meant that the duties of the Presidency became of considerably greater importance. The Copenhagen Report therefore had to devote a section to this question, even though there was no corresponding section in the annexe describing achievements to date. The Presidency was asked to see that conclusions were implemented on a collegiate basis; to propose consultation (i.e. to set the agenda); and to inform the Ambassadors of the Member States of progress between meetings of the Political Committee. The whole question of the secretariat was brushed under the carpet in two laconic sentences: 'Experience has also shown that the Presidency's task presents a particularly heavy administrative burden. Administrative assistance may therefore be provided by other Member States for specific tasks.'

Areas 6 and 7 of the annexe dealt with relations with the Commission and the Parliament. The participation of the Commission in discussions on the economic aspects of the CSCE and the future role of the Council of Europe was noted, as were the colloquies with the European Parliament. The annexe mentioned a recently introduced procedure with regard to the latter, whereby the Political Committee of Parliament was notified in advance of the main subjects for discussion.

Relations with the Community were one of the most difficult areas of the Copenhagen Report, since they touched on the whole debate on the nature of Political Co-operation. The specific measures in the Report were not earth-shaking. The number of colloquies with the European Parliament was raised from two a year to four, in an act of measureless generosity by Ministers, who thus improved on the figure of three put forward by the Political Committee. The practice of sending Parliament an annual report was confirmed.

The Formative Years (1970–1973)

Throughout the Report the tension between the supporters of an inter-governmental system functioning independently and one capable of moving nearer to the Community in a process of European integration is continually surfacing in revealing half-phrases. The Ministers noted 'that the characteristically pragmatic mechanisms set up by the Luxembourg Report have shown their flexibility and effectiveness', and certainly the whole thrust of the Report was on these minimalist and practical lines. Yet Part II began by recalling the objective of the Paris Summit to transform the whole complex of the relations between the Member States of the Community into a European Union before the end of the decade, and ended by stating that co-operation on foreign policy must be placed in the perspective of European Union. And in approving the Report in July 1973, the Foreign Ministers envisaged that, together with the Luxembourg Report, it would be re-examined in the light of the report on European Union which the Community Institutions were due to present before the end of 1975. This did not happen.

The remaining operational section of Part II of the Report dealt ostensibly with the setting of priorities, but in effect essayed yet another definition of the scope and obligations of Political Co-operation. The purpose of the consultation was defined as being to seek common policies on practical problems, and the subject dealt with had to concern European interests, whether in Europe itself or elsewhere, where the adoption of a common position was necessary or desirable. Here the notion of obligation was introduced. On the questions so defined, each State undertook as a general rule not to take up final positions without prior consultations with its partners within the framework of the Political Co-operation machinery. In the absence of a supervisory authority, the undertaking was singularly unconstraining, the more so since it was qualified by the expression 'as a general rule', which with its sister expression 'in principle' has always served in Political Co-operation as a general licence to do as one pleases. The fact that it was thought worthwhile to include such an obligation in the text is nevertheless significant, as it showed that there was not only a general readiness to seek a community of views, but also an aspiration on the part of some to make the search more constraining and therefore more effective. A similar readiness for progress is shown by the provision in the same section that the Political Committee should submit to Ministers subjects among which the Ministers would select those to be given priority. Political Co-operation was now ready to deal with a widening range of subjects, and not just those which were forced upon it by immediate circumstance.

The Copenhagen Report was perhaps not the step forward towards European Union which had been envisaged by the Foreign Ministers when in October 1970 they commissioned a second report to follow on the Luxembourg Report. But it made public the considerable progress which had been made since then, which indeed, as the introduction to the Copenhagen Report said, constituted 'a new procedure in international relations and an original European contribution to the technique of arriving at concerted action'. It turned out to be a perfectly adequate basis for the rapid and substantial development of Political Co-operation over the next eight years. The most realistic assessment of the Copenhagen Report remains nevertheless that made by the Danish Foreign Minister, Mr K. B. Andersen, at the time: 'It is a sober piece of work, which has brought about a number of valuable improvements of the consultation machinery which like any other machinery is fundamental for the work that is going to be done.'

SELECTED READING

On the climate prevailing at the time of the Luxembourg Report, see Scheel (1988), who as German Foreign Minister chaired the first EPC meeting at Munich.

There is a wide literature on the CSCE process. The best way in is provided by Pijpers (1984 and 1990). Schwerin (1975) and von Groll (1982) have given valuable eye-witness studies.

Ifestos (1987) is particularly useful for the Middle East at all periods. Other works which provide a starting-point for the period 1970–3 are Greilsammer (1981) and Greilsammer and Weiler (1984).

On the Copenhagen Report, see Berger (1971).

4
Building the House (1973–1977)

ARGUMENT

Political Co-operation reached its first high point in July 1973, when the Copenhagen Report was approved and the Danish Foreign Minister spoke on behalf of the Nine at the opening of the Ministerial phase of the Helsinki Conference. Thereafter it found itself without a clear agenda for the future and facing the challenge of defining its relationship with the United States in response to the Kissinger 'Year of Europe' initiative, a task made more difficult by the oil crisis and conflict in the Middle East.

The October War and its aftermath brought the tensions with the United States to a peak. They were only removed when new procedures for consultation (the 'Gymnich' formula) had been agreed. Spurred on by the French, and in the teeth of the US opposition, the Nine's response to the Middle East problem was to launch the Euro-Arab Dialogue, which came to have an economic rather than a political content, thus strengthening the role of the Commission. EPC continued to make a decisive input into the CSCE, and the Final Act of Helsinki was signed in July 1975. The signatories included the Italian Presidency on behalf of the Community.

During this period EPC's scope began to widen. No longer confined to the CSCE and the Middle East, the Nine were confronted with crises in their Mediterranean neighbours as successively events in Cyprus, Portugal, and Spain demanded their attention. Their reaction posed the problem of how the Community's trade policy towards the countries concerned should be affected by political judgements. The Nine also began to concern themselves with Southern Africa following the break-up of the Portuguese colonial empire, but it proved more difficult to reach consensus in this area than on questions nearer home.

The Nine emerged from these ordeals, if not stronger, at least wiser from the shared experience of working together under fire. The future was secured by a strengthening of the co-operation procedures, not through institutional advances (the Tindemans Report did not provide the hoped for breakthrough), but by practical measures and by opening up new areas of policy discussion.

FORGING A PERSONALITY

The rise of an economic and potentially political entity in Western Europe was bound to pose difficult questions about the nature of the transatlantic relationship. The dilemma was being debated, and had exerted an influence on the course of European integration, long before Henry Kissinger made his speech on the 'Year of Europe' in April 1973. In the early 1960s differences over the nature of Europe's relationship with the United States, and General de Gaulle's unique perception of the issue, had played their part in the failure of moves towards closer foreign-policy co-operation. Whenever European Union was under discussion, the question of relations with the Americans was sure to be somewhere in the background. When Foreign Ministers met in Rome in November 1971 to prepare the Summit then due to be held the following March, the Belgian Foreign Minister, M. Harmel, included relations between the EEC and the United States as one of his five items for discussion at the Summit. The fact that the Summit was held six months later than planned was mainly because of differences over this question. After the Summit, President Pompidou expressed his reservations by a statement *ex contrario*: 'the very closeness of these links requires that Europe affirm its individual personality with regard to the United States. Western Europe . . . must not and cannot sever its links with the United States. But neither must it refrain from affirming its existence as a new reality.'

It would be wrong to suppose that European reluctance to build a closer relationship with the United States into its evolving political personality was entirely the effect of the dying throes of Gaullism. A number of perceptions of United States policy were widely shared. The certainties of nearly three post-war decades were beginning to crumble. The permanence of the US presence in Europe could no longer be taken for granted. The Mansfield amendment to withdraw US forces had been defeated in 1971 at the cost of renewed pressure on the Allies to assume a greater share of the burden of their own defence; Nixon and Brezhnev seemed to be inaugurating a new era of superpower dialogue which left the Allies out in the cold; the United States was establishing a cosy relationship with China from which others were excluded; above all, the continued engagement of the United States in Vietnam, with all the

Building the House (1973–1977)

horrors of the last stages of the war, had an impact on public opinion in Western Europe which swayed the policies of governments, even of such staunch supporters of the United States as the Netherlands.

On the economic side the situation was no better. Trade friction between the United States and the Community was rife; the United States had just brought to an end the Bretton Woods system which had provided financial stability since the end of the war; and the Nixon Trade Bill made it plain that the United States would not hesitate to adopt protectionist measures to safeguard its domestic interests.

The United States' perceptions of their partners in Western Europe were equally jaundiced. The Administration, committed to an allied defence policy, was resentful that its efforts to beat off calls for a reduction in the US military presence in Western Europe did not meet with a more helpful reaction from those principally concerned. European parochialism, accusations of which caused such offence after the Kissinger speech, was equally regretted on the other side of the Atlantic, as it meant that the Europeans did little to share the United States' global burden. The Community was building up a network of partnerships—with the European Free Trade Association (EFTA), with the Member States' ex-colonies through the Lomé Convention, with the Mediterranean countries through the Global Mediterranean Approach—which meant that it would one day count in the global balance of power, and in the meanwhile by its preferential arrangements effectively restricted access to the markets concerned. The Community itself had been enlarged, it had set up the embryo of a political organization which had been unexpectedly successful in the discussions leading up to the Helsinki Conference, and now, at the Paris Summit of October 1972, Heads of Government had committed themselves to 'transforming before the end of the present decade the whole complex of their relations into a European Union'. The difficulties through which the Community was to pass lay in the future; at the time, it was only a reasonable precaution to seek to define the nature of the relationship between this new political entity and the power which retained in large part responsibility for the defence of Western Europe.

We may therefore take with a pinch of salt Dr Kissinger's claim that the 'Year of Europe' initiative saw the light of day in the quintessentially French surroundings, still imbued with the ghostly presence of General de Gaulle, of President Pompidou's room in the Élysée Palace. In an interview with Pompidou on 8 December 1972, President Nixon's National Security Adviser received encouragement for his idea that Europe and North America should after two decades make a serious effort to chart their larger common purpose and to convene to this end a suitably prepared summit meeting of leaders of the Atlantic Alliance. A few days later President Pompidou gave an interview to the *New York Times* in which he said that he favoured consultations at the highest level to clarify economic, and above all political, relations among the democracies. He looked forward to discussions with his colleagues on both sides of the Atlantic to define and reaffirm the shared objectives of the United States, the European Community, and Japan in a new era.

President Pompidou's vision was one of world statesmen setting a broad political agenda for the new age. This had an immediate appeal to Nixon; Jean Monnet, however, whom Kissinger saw in January 1973, while agreeing on the need to tie the United States and Europe into a more coherent system on both economic and security issues, urged the Americans to begin treating Europe as a political unit, whether it was ready for it or not, and thus force the Community into institutional change. Other Europeans whom the Americans approached in advance of the Kissinger speech—Heath and Brandt—were evasive or opposed to the strengthening of transatlantic political consultations. For Heath, the priority was to strengthen the Community and its political arm. For Brandt, it was to continue the *Ostpolitik*.

The 'Year of Europe' speech was delivered by Dr Kissinger to the Associated Press Annual Luncheon on St George's Day, 23 April 1973, in the grand ballroom of the Waldorf-Astoria Hotel in New York. The speech was long on concept, but short on practical proposals. Its theme was, to quote its author,

that, a generation after World War II, the Western Alliance had to articulate a new sense of purpose; military defense remained crucial but no longer seemed a sufficient motivating force. The nations that shared democratic values needed to join in a reaffirmation of common ideals and common goals if we were to maintain our cohesion in a new era of

Building the House (1973–1977)

East–West diplomacy, economic and energy problems, and a changing military balance.

Dr Kissinger called for a new 'Atlantic Charter' to be worked out in time for President Nixon's trip to Europe towards the end of the year. The 'Agenda for the Future' was made up of three headings: economic ('a new equilibrium . . . in trade and monetary relations' and 'an open and balanced trading order with both Europe and Japan'); defence (proposals to 'give substance to the defence posture that our strategy defines' and to achieve 'a rational defence posture, at the safest minimum size and cost with burdens equitably shared'); and diplomacy ('to make the Atlantic relationship as dynamic a force in building a new structure of peace', 'to lay the basis for a new era of creativity in the West', and to evolve 'a new Atlantic Charter setting the goals for the future—a blueprint that . . . creates for the Atlantic nations a new relationship in whose progress Japan can share').

Dr Kissinger's purpose was to achieve linkage. The United States would continue to carry the burden of defending the free world against Communism, but in return expected support from its allies, not on the merits of each individual case, but in recognition of the obligation inherent in the status of ally.

We will continue to support European unity. Based on the principles of partnership, we will make concessions to its further growth. We will expect to be met in a spirit of reciprocity. We will not disengage from our solemn commitments to our allies. We will maintain our forces and not withdraw from Europe unilaterally. In turn, we expect from each ally a fair share of the common effort for the common defense. We shall continue to pursue the relaxation of tensions with our adversaries on the basis of concrete negotiations in the common interest. We welcome the participation of our friends in a constructive East–West dialogue. We will never consciously injure the interests of our friends in Europe or in Asia. We expect in return that their policies will take seriously our policies and our responsibilities.

The Kissinger speech was a conscious attempt to emulate General Marshall's Harvard Commencement address twenty-six years before, and to adapt the approach then set out to the new political and economic realities. Indeed it was hailed as such by the *New York Times*, whose correspondent, James Reston, had carried the interview with President Pompidou four months earlier. But the sober New England surroundings of Harvard were a world away from the razzle-dazzle of the Waldorf-Astoria, and President Truman a world away from a President Nixon about to sink deep and finally be engulfed in the mud of Watergate. Only a week later, the President announced the resignation of Haldeman and Ehrlichman. Already at the Waldorf-Astoria the press was more interested in Watergate than in Europe. From then on, Nixon became to the Europeans increasingly less reliable as a partner or attractive as a guest. The shuffling and tergiversation about the President's visit to Europe that autumn was as much because of this as because of difficulties over the Year of Europe and the Middle East. Kissinger was prevented from pursuing his initiative with the necessary diplomatic vigour and political support because of the Administration's absorption in growing domestic scandal.

The reaction of the Europeans to this speech was cautious and grudging. Two sets of difficulties were put forward as inhibiting a more open response.

The most commonly aired complaint was that Dr Kissinger took the view that the United States had a global role, but Europe only a regional one. Kissinger said: 'Diplomacy is the subject of frequent consultations but is essentially being conducted by traditional nation-states. The United States has global interests and responsibilities. Our European allies have regional interests. These are not necessarily in conflict, but in the new era neither are they automatically identical.' This hurt the pride not only of the traditional Nation States, but also of the nascent European political persona. The formulation revealed much about the light in which Kissinger saw the new Europe. The historian of the Congress of Vienna found it difficult to conceive of Europe organizing itself politically other than through a concert of the powers; the nations of Europe were the keys of an instrument only waiting for the touch of the maestro to produce harmonious chords. Political Co-operation had higher aspirations than that, and they were shared by the French who, under Pompidou, looked on themselves as having a proprietary interest in the enterprise. Kissinger recognized the primacy of France and therefore conducted his negotiations almost exclusively with that country. He was not, however, able to appreciate the French attachment to the idea of a political Europe and therefore made the mistake of ascribing the various moves made by Jobert only to a particularly devious variety of neo-Gaullism.

The other prima-facie reason for finding it difficult to respond positively to the American initiative was the lack of a sufficiently developed institutional framework. A strengthened political role for NATO in the transatlantic dialogue would not solve the problem of the Nine; the Community did not have an adequate mechanism for dealing with foreign Heads of State, even for matters for which it was competent, and, save for low-key contacts with Turkey, Political Co-operation had never been faced with the need to set up a mechanism for permanent political dialogue. Small wonder that the Member States of the Community took their time in working out their response.

The real difficulties lay deeper and could not be made to vanish by diplomacy or drafting. The first was the 'comprehensive approach' adopted by the Americans. Their idea was to secure acceptance of a new Atlantic Charter which would put all aspects of the allied relationship—political, economic, and defence—under the same roof. This caused immense problems, not only for institutional reasons, but also because the Europeans were not prepared to make economic concessions in payment for their defence. It was the rejection of the concept of linkage which led to the decision in December 1975 to have two separate transatlantic declarations, and to the damp squib of the purely NATO declaration which finally saw the light of day the following June.

Even more difficult than linkage was the American notion of preconsultation—the claim to be consulted before final positions were adopted by the Europeans. The advantage of political dialogue in American eyes was that potentially damaging differences of views could be averted by early consultation. The mechanics of Political Co-operation did not allow for this. The process of consultation within the Nine was so delicate that, once a view had been formed, it had to be stuck to through thick and thin. And to allow a non-member of the club to take part in the discussions at a stage when the collective view was still being formed would be to strike a blow at the identity of the Nine as a group; hence the need to define that identity, which was more than the delaying tactic Dr Kissinger thought it. The situation was made worse by the insistence of the Nine on conveying their official positions to the United States only through their accredited spokesman, the President of the day. By attempting to shut off the Americans' direct line to the Member States, EPC denied them a diplomatic advantage in a way bound to arouse suspicions.

Dr Kissinger's Waldorf-Astoria speech, the draft of which had been shown in advance to a number of partners, burst upon a European Community which was already grappling with the problem of EC-US relations. Ministers at the EPC Ministerial Meeting on 16 March had asked the Political Committee to prepare a discussion paper on the question together with the Permanent Representatives, with help from the Commission where the latter was concerned. The mandate was confirmed and made more precise at the meeting on 5 June. At the same time a number of partners were holding wary discussions with the Americans, but apparently content in the long run to leave the burden of the day to the French.

Agreement on a procedure for dealing with the American initiative was reached at the Ministerial Meeting in Copenhagen on 23 July 1973, thus allowing approval of the Copenhagen Report which had been ready for some time. The Ministers stressed the great importance they attached to the definition of a European identity to be recognized as such by the rest of the world. They charged the Political Committee to work on the definition which would serve as a basis for the constructive dialogue they wished to carry on with the United States. The European identity was to be based on the cohesion of the Community, the position and responsibilities of the Nine *vis-à-vis* the rest of the world, and the dynamic character of the construction of Europe.

The Political Directors worked through the summer on their report and on a draft 'Declaration of Principles' which, approved by Ministers at their meeting on 20 September, was given to the Americans on 25 September. It was thought weak by them, the atmosphere not being improved by the document's having been published in the *New York Times* the day before. It was drawn from the declarations of the Paris Summit of October 1972 and the principles of the Tokyo Round, and contained no reference to interdependence or Atlantic partnership. A separate draft Declaration was tabled on the NATO side—the Europeans were

Building the House (1973–1977)

determined to avoid linkage. This was more to the taste of Dr Kissinger, now Secretary of State, and discussion of it proceeded in the NATO framework.

The Americans replied with a counterdraft, also published in the *New York Times*. At their meeting on 20 November, the Ministers approved in substance the document on the European identity and handed it back to the Political Committee to be finalized in readiness for publication at the December Summit. By this time, the October War in the Middle East had taken place and the serious deterioration in relations between the Community and the United States as a result of the energy crisis, described below, made discussions on a Declaration hollow and unreal. The increasingly sterile exercise continued through the early months of 1974: the Americans continued to look for linkage, and their support of the Community was subordinated to its close co-operation with the United States. Above all, the Declaration was to be made by 'signatory states' free to pursue their interests bilaterally in the best traditions of *realpolitik*. On the Community side, a draft Declaration was agreed in March based on joint recognition of the new dimension conferred on transatlantic relations by the decision of the Community and its Member States to form a European Union. It was a dialogue of the deaf, and the Declaration of Principles never saw the light of day.

While discussions on joint declarations were running into the sand, the Document on the European Identity was published by the Nine Foreign Ministers meeting in Copenhagen on 14 December 1973 and endorsed by the Heads of Government in their communiqué the next day. While containing no operational clauses, the text is a substantive description of how the Nine wished to be seen, and should not be dismissed as empty rhetoric. It was the reverse of the sort of text the Americans had been aiming for, and would certainly not have been drafted but for the Kissinger initiative.

The purpose of the Document was to enable the Nine 'to achieve a better definition of their relations with other countries and of their responsibilities and the place which they occupy in world affairs'. The basis of the European identity was unity: 'they . . . have decided that unity is a basic European necessity to ensure the survival of the civilization which they have in common.' This unity was on the way to achievement through the Community Treaties and the system of political co-operation; it was a part of the European identity's originality and dynamism. Since present international problems were too difficult for any of the Nine to solve alone, Europe had to unite and speak increasingly with one voice if it wanted to make itself heard and play its proper role in the world.

Three principles were laid down to govern the Community's action as it progressed towards a common policy in relation to third countries:

- the Nine, acting as a single entity, will strive to promote harmonious and constructive relations with these countries. This should not however jeopardise, hold back or affect the will of the Nine to progress towards European Union within the time limits laid down.

- in future when the Nine negotiate collectively with other countries, the institutions and procedures chosen should enable the distinct character of the European entity to be respected.

- in bilateral contacts with other countries, the Member States of the Community will increasingly act on the basis of agreed common positions.

In other words, Europe was a collective entity greater than the sum of its parts, with a common policy as its goal. Its relations with third countries would reflect its individual identity and would be conducted in such a way as to strengthen its institutional personality. Europe had a global role; its relationship with the United States was one of 'co-operation . . . on the basis of equality and in a spirit of friendship', but was neither exclusive nor even at the head of the list of countries with which it was intended to conduct relations. Led by France, the Europeans announced their intention of conducting an independent policy in an area, the Middle East, in which the United States was looking for allied support.

Taking this document with the growing tension over Middle East and energy policy, it was scarcely surprising that negotiations with the Americans in the early months of 1974 went badly and that President Nixon accused the Europeans, in a speech in Chicago on 15 March, of ganging up on the United States. Yet a month later the problem had been solved, there was no more talk of joint declarations, and relations between Political Cooperation and the United States, in spite of disagreements over individual cases, have on the whole been good ever since.

The agreement was reached among Foreign Ministers meeting informally at Schloss Gymnich in Germany on 20–1 April. This was the first of the Gymnich meetings, an innovation of the current German Presidency. The agreement was not announced at the time; indeed, it seems not to have been brought to the knowledge of those Ministers who did not attend the meeting, including the Belgian Minister van Elslande. It was, deliberately, never written down, in order to maintain the pragmatic and flexible nature of the arrangement and to avoid jeopardizing it through drafting quarrels. The only official description of it is the wording used by Mr Genscher when he announced the results of the next formal meeting of Foreign Ministers on 10–11 June.

The second point is the question of consultations. The Ministers were agreed that in elaborating common positions on foreign policy there arises the question of consultations with allied or friendly countries. Such consultations are a matter of course in any modern foreign policy. We decided on a pragmatic approach in each individual case, which means that the country holding the Presidency will be authorized by the other eight partners to hold consultations on behalf of the Nine.

In practice, therefore, if any member of the EPC raises within the framework of EPC the question of informing and consulting an ally or a friendly State, the Nine will discuss the matter and, upon reaching agreement, authorize the Presidency to proceed on that basis.

The Ministers trust that this gentleman's agreement will also lead to smooth and pragmatic consultations with the United States which will take into account the interest of both sides.

This less than transparent arrangement, which left open the question of what happened if the Nine failed to reach agreement to consult (it was understood that in that event there would be bilateral consultations), nevertheless met with the approval of the United States, as Kissinger told Genscher when they met on 11 June in Bad Reichenhall. The reasons for the change have still not been satisfactorily explained.

It is certainly the case that matters were facilitated by the departure from the scene of a number of key figures on the European side in the early months of 1974. In the United

Kingdom, Edward Heath lost the general election and gave way to Harold Wilson, with James Callaghan as Foreign Secretary. Both these figures lacked Heath's mystic attachment to Europe, which he was prepared to place above the Atlantic relationship. In Germany, Brandt was forced to resign over the Guillaume affair and was succeeded by Schmidt, more of an Atlanticist and less connected in the American perception with a neutralist interpretation of the *Ostpolitik*. Scheel was replaced by Genscher, whose attachment to European integration was tempered by a more pragmatic readiness to accommodate political realities. Finally, President Pompidou died on 2 April and was succeeded by Giscard d'Estaing, whose eagerness to encourage personal contacts at the highest level applied equally to the United States and to his colleagues in the Community.

These changes may help to explain why relations between the United States and Political Co-operation improved, but they do not throw light on why agreement was reached at the Gymnich meeting on 20-1 April. The timing is wrong. In particular, although Pompidou was dead by the time of the Gymnich meeting, Giscard had not yet been elected and Pompidou's Foreign Minister, Jobert, had not yet been replaced by Sauvagnargues. Similarly, the change of government in Bonn did not take place until 7 May. A clue to what happened may be found in the nature of the Gymnich arrangement itself, which was limited to pragmatic procedure for consultation, leaving aside the vexed question of the nature of the Atlantic relationship, on which consensus was unlikely. The Europeans, and especially the French, now had an urgent operational need to come to an understanding with the Americans since pressure from Washington was preventing agreement in the Community on beginning the Euro-Arab Dialogue, which had become an important aim of French diplomacy. The Gymnich arrangement made it possible for the Dialogue to go ahead. On their side, the Americans were in no position, because of Watergate, to force the issue through to a finish, and had in any case secured important advantages from the Europeans, including recognition of the linkage between energy and security questions, at the Energy Conference in Washington in February; United States policy in the Middle East was also by now further advanced.

Matters had been brought to a head by the decisive movement of the Nine on 4 March towards a Euro-Arab Dialogue, of which

Secretary Kissinger claimed not to have been informed. On 7 March President Nixon wrote to Chancellor Brandt officially requesting that the United States should be associated with the European decisions; a further letter on 15 March following Brandt's unsatisfactory reply called a halt to further drafting work on the joint declaration. This was followed up by Nixon's Chicago speech on 15 March which set out what would happen if American requirements were not met ('The Europeans cannot have it both ways. They cannot have the United States' participation and co-operation on the security front and then proceed to have confrontation and even hostility on the economic and political fronts').

It is likely that no one, in the difficult days of energy shortages and the ever-present threat of conflict in the Middle East, was prepared for a showdown. Intensive bilateral diplomacy made a compromise possible. The Germans put to the Americans the suggestion that the Nine would no longer delay consultation until the Foreign Ministers had set the various projects in concrete; there could be consultations after the Political Directors had agreed, but before an issue had been put to the Foreign Ministers. This was not what was later announced as the Gymnich arrangement, but in practice was what happened; at any rate the Americans claimed to be satisfied.

The Gymnich arrangement marked the end of a contentious issue which had blown Political Co-operation off course for a year and at the same time led the Europeans to a clearer perception of the implications of claiming to adopt a common approach to foreign policy which did not wait upon American leadership.

THE WIDENING AGENDA

The Middle East and the Euro-Arab Dialogue

The October War

The Nine took no public initiative on Middle East policy and made no serious effort to bring their positions closer together following their failure to publish the Schumann document in May 1971. They were to regret this lethargy when the Egyptians and Syrians attacked Israel on 5 October 1973; the October War was upon them. The immediate reactions came not from EPC, but from the Member States, and they varied widely. On 6

October the Netherlands Foreign Minister issued a communiqué holding Egypt and Syria responsible for the inception of the war by breaking unilaterally the coexistence which had been observed since 1970. Three days later, M. Jobert affirmed that 'Tenter de remettre les pieds chez soi ne constitue pas forcément une agression imprévue.' It was only under pressure from the British and the French that the Nine finally issued a communiqué on 13 October calling for a ceasefire and negotiations on the basis of Security Council Resolution 242.

This was no doubt the most that the diverging positions of Member States would allow, but it was not enough to deal with the rapidly evolving situation. On 16 October the Gulf States announced that, until Israel returned to its pre–1967 frontiers and the Palestinians were able to exercise their right to self-determination, the price of oil would be increased by 70 per cent. The next day the Arab members of the Organization of Petroleum Exporting Countries (OPEC) decided in Kuwait on a monthly 5-per-cent cutback in oil production. On 20 October Saudi Arabia declared a total embargo on oil exports to the United States. On 4 November the Organization of Arab Petroleum Export Countries (OAPEC) announced production cutbacks of 25 per cent on September levels with further monthly 5-per-cent cuts and created three categories of consumers: friends, enemies, and neutrals. The French and the British were friends, and their supplies were untouched; the Netherlands were enemies, like the United States, and suffered a total embargo; the rest suffered the monthly 5-per-cent reductions.

In the meanwhile, spurred on by Secretary Kissinger's shuttle diplomacy, the United States and the Soviet Union appeared to be moving towards a solution in the Geneva Conference which would be limited to themselves and the parties to the conflict. This was deeply resented by the Europeans, who saw themselves being excluded from an area with which especially the French and the British considered themselves to have traditional ties. President Pompidou saw the dangers of this situation for France and for the Nine. At a press conference on 31 October he condemned the inertia of the Nine and called on them to show that they were capable of contributing to the settlement of global problems. It was agreed that there should be a Summit Meeting on 14–15 December in Copenhagen.

By this time, the Nine had realized that the gravity of the situation could only be met by common action. The line they took was to adopt a declaration which moved closer to the Arab position than the Schumann document of May 1971. This Declaration, issued with great difficulty in Brussels on 6 November 1973, urged disengagement in accordance with Security Council Resolutions and looked to the restoration of a just and lasting peace through negotiations in the framework of the United Nations. It called for a peace agreement based on an end to Israel's territorial occupation since 1967, respect for the sovereignty, territorial integrity, and independence of every State in the area and their right to live in peace within secure and recognized boundaries, and recognition that in the establishment of a just and lasting peace account must be taken of the legitimate rights of the Palestinians.

The main new feature of the Declaration in comparison with the Schumann document was the reference to the legitimate rights of the Palestinians. The emphasis on the United Nations, rather than the Geneva Conference, as the forum for negotiations and the setting out of principles for a peace agreement were also significant new elements.

The Brussels Declaration of 6 November was a success for French diplomacy, abetted by the British. The other members of the Nine had been brought further down the road towards a pro-Arab position than they would otherwise have gone had it not been for French pressure exerted within the Political Co-operation machinery. In particular the Netherlands found it convenient to justify a departure from its traditional policy, which it would have been difficult to uphold solely as a response to Arab pressure, by the need to stay in step with the Nine.

The effects of the Brussels Declaration were only partially satisfactory and to some extent unexpected. The Israeli condemnation was understandable and accurate: Mr Eban said that it meant 'Oil for Europe!' and not 'Peace for the Middle East!' The Americans saw the Declaration as a direct challenge to their own diplomatic efforts, which it countered in almost every respect. The Arabs, on the other hand, were sufficiently favourably impressed for the OAPEC oil ministers, meeting on 19 November, to decide not to continue with their 5-per-cent cutback to the Community. The embargo on supplies to the

Netherlands was not lifted, however, and the failure of the Netherlands' partners, for fear of once more alienating the Arabs, to show the Dutch the solidarity that the principle of free movement of goods in the Community might have been thought to require caused considerable offence to the latter. The dangers were more imagined than real. The Arab oil embargo proved to be remarkably ineffective, the major oil companies performing the function of 'laundering' and redistributing the supplies.

The Copenhagen Summit

The unexpected effect of the Brussels Declaration was the arrival unannounced at the portals of the tented enclosures in Copenhagen where the Heads of Government were holding their summit meeting on 14–15 December 1973, of a delegation of Arab Foreign Ministers anxious to cement their new-found friendship with the Europeans. The Arab Summit of 26–9 November in Algiers had welcomed the European change of heart and called on Europe to strive 'through all possible means towards the evacuation by Israel of all occupied territories, including Jerusalem, and the restoration of national rights to the Palestinian people'; the Summit also stated that 'Europe is linked to the Arab world through the Mediterranean by profound affinities of civilisation and by vital interests which can only be developed within the framework of confidence and mutually advantageous co-operation.' It was to propose to the Europeans a dialogue on these lines that the Arab Ministers came to Copenhagen.

The Heads of Government had to face up to another problem, which was how to organize co-operation in the energy crisis. Only two days before, Dr Kissinger had made a speech to the Society of Pilgrims in London which was primarily designed to launch an appeal to Europe and America to reaffirm their commitment to engage co-operatively in a common enterprise, removing some of the misunderstandings to which the 'Year of Europe' speech had given rise. The speech contained, however, an invitation to the industrial democracies to form an Energy Action Group with a mandate to develop within three months an initial action program for collaboration in all areas of the energy problem. Generously, the Secretary of State left it up to the Nine whether they preferred to participate individually or as the European Community.

The Copenhagen Summit's response to these challenges was threefold. The political line which had been taken in the Brussels Declaration of 6 November was confirmed, and this remained the Nine's basic position, with one or two variations, for the next four years. There was no agreement on the call for an energy dialogue among the industrialized nations. What the Americans had in mind was a consumers' cartel under their own leadership. This was opposed in particular by the French, who wanted co-operation between the consumers and the producers —an eminently reasonable approach, nevertheless vitiated in the circumstances of the time by the political concessions this would have required from the vast majority of the consumers. The split among the Nine on this question continued into the New Year. Although all the Nine, as well as the Community, took part in the Energy Conference in Washington in February, the event was marked by strong differences, especially between France and Germany; the results, based on the link between a continued American military commitment to Europe and the acceptance of American leadership on energy policy, were boycotted by France, as was the International Energy Agency to which the Conference ultimately gave rise.

The European position at the Conference and towards subsequent developments was worked out in the Community framework, not in Political Co-operation. Although the Treaties did not provide for a common energy policy, the matter was fairly clearly one of Community competence and the Council had for the previous two years been discussing without notable success a series of communications from the Commission on the subject. To have taken up the matter in Political Co-operation would probably have resulted in the absence of a common position at all. However, the fact that energy policy, on which the Community in the end followed the American line, and dialogue with the Arabs, on which the Nine followed the French line, were handled in two separate forums, made for a weak and aimless overall European policy.

The Euro-Arab Dialogue: Inception

This outcome was not inevitable. Although the Nine were in some disarray over the reply they were called on to give on the spot in Copenhagen to the Arab Ministers' request for a cooperative dialogue, the initial response was positive and it was firmly placed in the context of energy policy. In a document annexed to their communiqué, the Heads of Government 'confirmed the importance of entering into negotiations with oil-producing countries on comprehensive arrangements comprising co-operation on a wide scale for the economic and industrial development of these countries, industrial investments, and stable energy supplies to the member countries at reasonable prices.'

This concept of the dialogue with the Arabs was not to survive further discussion. The matter was complicated by the fact that, as we have seen, the response to the American initiative for an energy conference was co-ordinated in the Community framework, while what became the Euro-Arab Dialogue was assigned to Political Co-operation. This was not an obvious move. There was already a proposal on the table for co-operation with the Mediterranean countries, including a significant number of the Arabs. The 'Global Mediterranean Approach', which proposed co-operation agreements with most of the countries of the Mediterranean seaboard not members of the Community had been under discussion in the Council for twelve months, the initial proposals having been made by the Commission in September 1972, partially as a reaction to the growing strength of the Arab oil producers. Although little progress had been made, it would at least have been an option to build on the Global Mediterranean Approach for a dialogue with the Arabs. Indeed, during discussions of the Global Mediterranean Approach in the Council in 1973 the British had asked for a general political discussion on Mediterranean policy. This had been rejected by the French on the grounds that there should be no confusion between the Community and EPC. Similarly, a suggestion by the Commission before the Copenhagen Summit that it should be invited to put forward proposals for economic, technical, and financial measures to enable the Community to contribute to a just and lasting peace in the Middle East was not taken up.

Like the Arabs, the French looked on the Euro-Arab Dialogue in the first place as a political exercise, rather than an economic one. Indeed, they had been reflecting on the advantages of a dialogue with the Arabs even before the October War broke out,

Building the House (1973–1977)

and had been in bilateral contact about it with a number of Arab countries. If the political approach to the question was to be maintained, the Arab interlocutor had to be a universal one, namely the Arab League, and not the Arab countries individually, the approach favoured in the Commission's proposal. The institutional conclusion drawn by the French was to prefer the Political Co-operation channel, in which the Commission could be kept at a distance. It is ironic that, as things fell out, the Dialogue was obliged to exclude from its terms of reference both the political and the energy aspects, to concentrate on economic, technical, and trade co-operation. Nevertheless, it stayed within the Political Co-operation framework and because of its considerable economic content the Commission had to be involved. As in the case of CSCE, the Commission was able to strengthen its position in Political Co-operation because of the nature of the subjects discussed.

The Political Committee set to work in the New Year to discuss what had to be done to follow up the Copenhagen Summit. Although some thought was given, under British pressure, to the question of international guarantees and what role the Nine might play, most of the discussion turned on the nature of the dialogue with the Arabs. Some Member States, led by the Netherlands, took the view that the relationship should be essentially an economic and co-operative one, taking as a starting-point the plan for economic aid to the Palestinians (the 'Deniau Plan') which had been put forward by the Commission in 1972, and eventually broadening to cover economic support to the whole region. The French opposed this approach, which would have involved the Community as an institution and would have given insufficient importance to the political dimension of the Dialogue and removed the possibility of moving the EPC position on the Arab–Israel conflict closer to the Arab side. While not denying that there was an economic element in the relationship, they were in favour of launching a vast dialogue with the Arabs and responding to the requirements of the latter. The Arabs had made it plain at Copenhagen that they were interested in political support from the Nine, in return for which they would offer stability of energy supplies. After initial contacts, a series of joint meetings at working level could, in the French view, lead to a Ministerial Conference in the autumn.

This approach formed the basis of the eventual compromise in Political Co-operation, it being understood that the Community angle had to be fully taken into account. Arrangements were made to ensure that the Ministers were seized simultaneously of the reports prepared by the Political Committee and Coreper respectively and it was agreed, with some difficulty, that the Presidency, on behalf of the Nine or the Council as appropriate, and the Commission should act together in sounding out the Arabs. The decision was duly taken by the Ministers on 4 March 1974.

The violent reaction from the United States has been described in the previous section. As a result, doubts about the wisdom of undertaking the Euro-Arab Dialogue were already being expressed at the next meeting of the Political Committee. No date was set for a first meeting between Scheel and the Arab emissaries pending the views of the new British government, which had only just taken office at the time of the March Ministerial Meeting, and several other countries underlined that the Dialogue should make a contribution to the Kissinger peace efforts and the work of the energy co-ordination group, not get in their way. The Nixon–Brandt exchange of letters had been taken to heart. It was only after the Gymnich arrangement that preparations for the Dialogue were able to begin.

Policy Statements of the Nine

Much as France, and to some extent Italy, would have liked to move the Nine further towards recognition of the rights of the Palestinians as the key to progress on the Middle East question, this was not politically feasible for some time following the events of 1973. Concern not to cut across the efforts of the Americans, together with the traditionally more cautious approach of the Netherlands, Denmark, and Germany, condemned any attempt at a more striking approach to failure in advance. This meant that the burden of the Middle Eastern policy of the Nine had to be carried by the Euro-Arab Dialogue. Nevertheless, some opportunities for minor advances in response to developments in the area presented themselves.

The Geneva agreement on 4 September 1975 between Egypt and Israel provided the first of these opportunities. The French were quick to point out that the agreement removed one of the reasons for the Nine to hold back, namely the need not to cut across US peace efforts. The Ministers meeting in Venice on 11–12 September welcomed the agreement, praised the efforts of those concerned and called for the momentum to be kept up for new progress towards an overall settlement. Meeting shortly afterwards in Lucca, they agreed that the Palestinian problem was central and called on the Political Committee to develop new elements. The result of this work was noted by Ministers in Rome on 30 October as a useful basis for the Nine in international forums. The Italian Permanent Representative, speaking on behalf of the Nine, made use of the position when he announced before the UN General Assembly on 10 December that the settlement should include a recognition of the right of the Palestinian people to the expression of their national identity.

The question arose again when the Nine came to discuss the text which Mr van der Stoel, as the Netherlands President-in-Office, was to deliver to the General Assembly on behalf of the Nine on 28 September 1976. The French would have liked to refer to a 'territorial base' for the Palestinian identity, but the British and the Dutch were against this; a Belgian compromise formula ('the legitimate right of the Palestinian people to give effective expression to its national identity translated into fact') won the day. The Nine's position was edging imperceptibly forward—indeed, the expression 'territorial base' was admitted into the Nine's vocabulary only a month later and used in the United Nations on 7 December—but it was a process of internal evolution rather than a political act with any chance of making a mark on events.

At the beginning of 1977 the Political Committee took the view that the prospects for negotiation were more favourable and that the Nine should show their support; a draft declaration was submitted to Ministers. This largely took up previous statements, but incorporated the December UN addition ('the exercise of the right of the Palestinian people to the effective expression of their national identity could involve a territorial base in the framework of a negotiated settlement') and referred to the resumption of negotiations with the participation of representatives of the parties to the conflict, including the Palestinian people, and to the Nine's readiness to envisage taking part in a system of international guarantees for the implementation of a settlement.

Although the declaration was approved by Ministers, it was not published (although it was leaked verbatim in *Le Monde* and *Al Ahram*). The ostensible reason was that it would have been inappropriate to forestall the results of forthcoming visits to the region. It was true that both Mr Genscher and M. de Guiringaud were due to make such visits, but more to the point that Secretary Vance was too. The new Carter Administration had urged on the Nine that exploratory contacts with the Arabs were only just beginning, and it would be wrong to raise the question of Palestinian rights without ascertaining the Arab view on the matter. The Gymnich arrangement, in this case, worked to the satisfaction of the Americans.

The Nine did not move again until after the Israeli elections of May 1977 which brought to power the Likud led by Mr Begin. This, for different reasons, did nothing to improve relations with the Federal Republic and the United Kingdom, and encouraged the Nine to consider publishing a new declaration, which was designed to go a step further than the unpublished declaration of January by adding the crucial reference to a Palestinian homeland ('which would include the resolution of the question of a homeland for the Palestinian people'). The concept of a homeland, or *patrie*, had been part of the French political vocabulary for two years, but had not yet been endorsed by the Nine. The decision to do so made the resulting Declaration of the European Council meeting in London on 29–30 June one of the turning-points in the Middle East policy of EPC, putting the Palestinian question at the centre of the Middle East problem. The Declaration nearly came to grief at the last minute, again because of American intervention. Under the Gymnich arrangement, the Americans had been informed of the intentions of the Nine and had issued a *nihil obstat*. The State Department, temporarily following a policy more favourable to the Palestinians, then proceeded to upstage the operation by issuing a statement on 27 June which referred to the 'need for a homeland'. This caused considerable emotion in the Political Committee, which realized that the European formulation was less strong than the American. *In extremis*, a revised text was produced for the European Council ('which would take into account the need for a homeland for the Palestinian people').

The London Declaration, balancing the central role of the Palestinian problem with the need to recognize the right of Israel to live in peace within secure and recognized boundaries, remained the position of the Nine for the next three years until it was overtaken by the Venice Declaration. In the meanwhile, however, the Europeans' Middle East policy had been stymied by the Camp David process.

The Euro-Arab Dialogue: Structure

Few people can have thought, when the United States gave the green light for the Euro-Arab Dialogue to go ahead following the Gymnich arrangement in April 1974, that other obstacles lay in the way which would postpone the effective opening of the Dialogue for more than a year. These were the questions of whether or not there should be a political dialogue and a political committee to conduct it, and the status of the Palestinians at the conference table. To begin with, all went smoothly. The Ministers adopted the programme for discussions at their meeting on 10 June: this foresaw first of all the presentation of an *aide-mémoire* to the Arab governments setting out the Nine's concept of the Dialogue, and discussions to be concluded by a meeting between the Foreign Minister of the Presidency and his Arab counterpart; then the convening of a number of Working Groups to prepare the technical substance of the Dialogue, to be crowned by a meeting of the General Committee, to be composed of senior officials on both sides; then, if all went well, a meeting of both sides at Ministerial level could be envisaged. By fighting hard, and by taking the initiative of drafting good-quality working papers on the technical aspects, the Commission secured its participation in the meetings with the Arabs. The missions at the level of the officials were in theory conducted by the German Presidency and the Commission jointly; in practice a French representative was added to the delegation, given the imminence of the French Presidency and French interest in the subject.

The end of the first phase of preliminary contacts was marked by a meeting in Paris on 31 July 1974 at which the European side was represented by the French Foreign Minister M. Sauvagnargues, wearing both his EPC and Council President hats, and by the President of the Commission, M. Ortoli, and the Arab side by Shaikh Sabah Salim as-Sabah, the Foreign Minister of

Kuwait, as President-in-Office of the Arab League, and Mahmoud Riad, the League's Secretary-General. The Arab League Council had set up on 23 March a Commission of eleven Foreign Ministers and the Secretary-General to follow Dialogue affairs— an early example of other groups of countries being obliged to adapt their structures in order to be able to deal with the Nine. The expected procedural decisions were taken: Working Groups were to prepare a meeting of the General Committee which was scheduled for November 1974. The seeds of divergence were, however, already, discernible in the speeches made by the participants. Whereas M. Sauvagnargues stated that the object of the Dialogue was to organize long-term co-operation which would be economic, although in a political perspective, the Kuwaiti Foreign Minister placed the Dialogue firmly in the context of the Nine's declaration of 6 November 1973, especially regarding the rights of Palestinians.

While accepting that there were limits to the Europeans' freedom of manœuvre, the Arabs made it plain that the Dialogue was for them essentially a political event. In return for European support for their position in the Middle East conflict, they were prepared to envisage co-operation, including on energy questions. The Europeans were committed to a Dialogue, but could not accept that it should be a forum for political discussions related to the Arab-Israeli conflict. This was not just because the price would have been too high in terms of their relationship with the United States; the structure of Political Co-operation prevented the Nine from doing more, in their contacts with third countries, than repeating the positions which had been agreed in advance and were already well known to their interlocutors.

The Political Committee met after the summer holidays to decide on the structure which would be necessary to organize the European contribution to the Dialogue. So far, preparatory work had been done in the Middle East expert group, with the Commission taking part when required. This was not a satisfactory situation, given that the substance of the Dialogue was turning out to be more economic than political with subjects of Community competence directly involved and that the Commission did not in normal circumstances attend the meetings of the Middle East expert group. Apart from that,

Member States found themselves running into problems of co-ordination at home, as responsibility for the widely varied subjects of the Dialogue was spread over a number of departments. It was therefore decided that each Member State would appoint a senior official of the rank of Ambassador to co-ordinate Dialogue questions nationally. These officials would meet in a 'Co-ordinating Group', together with a representative of the Commission, to co-ordinate the Nine's position *vis-à-vis* the Arab League. The Co-ordinating Group would report on all matters to the Political Committee; it would also report, through the Presidency, to Coreper on matters of Community competence. The Commission confirmed that when it was called upon to exercise its right of initiative, it would do so following the ordinary procedure, not through the Co-ordinating Group. The Co-ordinating Group, like the expert groups, had its seat in the capital of the Presidency, but could meet elsewhere if necessary; in fact it met frequently in Brussels for the sake of convenience. To complicate matters further, Coreper set up its own subgroup to prepare its discussions on Dialogue questions. This was called the *ad hoc* Group and, apart from the Commission, had a different membership from the Co-ordinating Group.

As in the case of the CSCE, the operational requirements of the Euro-Arab Dialogue led to the setting up of machinery to handle the interaction between Political Co-operation and the Community and to the consequent involvement of the Commission in Political Co-operation to an extent which had not been originally foreseen. This role became an important one, not only because the Commission found itself chairing some of the joint Working Groups, but also because of its experience in preparing papers for technical discussions and of the dynamism of its representatives. The tasks of the Co-ordinating Group were defined in such a way, however, as to ensure that the overall operation remained a Political Co-operation one with technical input from the Community when necessary.

No sooner had the Nine reached agreement on these organizational points, when they were confronted with a new difficulty which bade fair to bring the whole enterprise to a halt. The Arab Summit at Rabat on 25 October instructed Mahmoud Riad to inform the Presidency that the Palestinians, represented by the Palestine Liberation Organization, would have to have an observer seat in the General Committee. This logically followed the Arab decision at Rabat that the PLO was the sole legitimate representative of the Palestinian people and as such a member of the Arab League.

The Arab demand threw the Nine into disarray. The French and the Italians had for some time taken a fairly forthcoming attitude towards the PLO, while other Member States were opposed to enhancement of its status. Germany in particular had suffered from Palestinian terrorism—the memory of the 1972 Munich Olympics was still strong. The Americans were also opposed. It took until the following spring to work out a solution in discreet contacts between the Presidency and the Commission and representatives of the Arab League. The compromise, first floated unofficially by the Arabs, but taken up by the Europeans, in particular the active new Irish Presidency from the beginning of 1975, was that for the Working Groups there would be only two delegations, one Arab and one European, and that the experts would take part in their personal capacity and not as national representatives. The question of what body or State Palestinians from the PLO represented was thereby side-stepped. The 'Dublin formula' was approved by the Foreign Ministers of the Nine on 13 February 1975 and by the Council of the Arab League on 26 April.

This incident and its solution took the Dialogue further away from its political origin. It showed the Nine's inability to revise their position on the Middle East conflict, and by postponing the meeting of the General Committee, for which the problem of participation had not been solved, it shifted the emphasis even more to concrete co-operation at expert level.

There was one further hazard before the ground rules of the Dialogue could be agreed between the two sides. Since July 1974 the Commission had had a mandate from the Council to negotiate agreements with a number of Mediterranean countries, including Israel, in the framework of the Global Mediterranean Approach. The negotiations with Israel had advanced rapidly and an agreement was initialled in January 1975 and signed on 11 May in the teeth of intensive lobbying by the Arabs. For a time there seemed a danger that the signature of the agreement would endanger the Euro-Arab Dialogue, but the difficulties were smoothed over, thanks to the position which the Nine had taken on the status of the occupied territories.

Building the House (1973–1977)

The incident cannot be compared in importance with the question of PLO representation, but it is significant in that apparently inconsistent policies were being pursued simultaneously on the Community and Political Co-operation tracks. Of course Member States in EPC were aware of the complications caused them by the negotiations with Israel, just as the Commission and Council were aware of the effect of their actions on the Euro-Arab Dialogue, but there was no one forum in which the relative merits of different courses of action could be weighed. This was untidy, but not necessarily bad for policy. Had the Member States been obliged to take a single decision, their differences would have been exposed and they certainly would not have ended up, as they did, with the best of both worlds—the agreement with Israel and the dialogue with the Arabs.

The ground rules of the Dialogue were finally laid down at a meeting between officials in Cairo on 10–14 June 1975, eighteen months after the idea had been first launched. The Arab side was represented by the Secretariat of the League, the Europeans by the Presidency and the Commission. A joint memorandum was adopted, which identified seven areas in which Working Groups would be active, and introduced the notion of a 'Steering Group' to deal with the difficulties of a General Committee as originally envisaged. One of the Working Groups was to deal with trade; this was a concession on the part of the Community, to compensate for the negative view it took on the substance of the Arabs' trade demands.

The meeting was followed by a second one in Rome on 21–5 July 1975, which, while less spectacular than the Cairo meeting, allowed the seven Working Groups to be launched with a number of concrete actions on their agenda. The third meeting took place in Abu Dhabi on 23–7 November. Further work was done on the technical side, especially on infrastructure, agriculture, and industry. However, the possibility of a dialogue on energy was finally buried, following a visit to the Persian Gulf by US Assistant Secretary to the Treasury Gerald Parsky, who urged the Gulf States to refrain from discussing the issue of petroleum supplies with the Europeans. More important, the way was cleared for a meeting of the General Committee at Ambassadorial level by the Arabs' acceptance of a proposal by the Europeans to use the same formula for participation by the PLO as for the expert groups.

The General Committee duly met in Luxembourg on 18–20 May 1976. For an event which had been so eagerly awaited and so difficult to bring about, the results were remarkably meagre. Although the Nine were prepared to exchange declarations on political questions, they were not willing to engage in dialogue on the Middle East conflict, nor, in spite of pressure from the French and the Italians, to go beyond their Declaration of 6 November 1973. The meeting was noteworthy for the fact that it took place at Ambassadorial level, for the presence of Dr Ahmad Sidqi al-Dajani of the PLO as one of the co-chairmen of the Arab delegation and for the fact that the Europeans officially used the Troika formula, now so baptized, for negotiating the final communiqué with the Arabs. The decision had been taken by the Ministers of the Nine at their meeting on 3 May, and may be quoted in full in view of the importance the formula later took on in the work of EPC: 'En ce qui concerne la rédaction finale de ce communiqué, elle sera faite, au niveau euro-arabe, selon la formule de participation "troika", c'est-à-dire la Présidence actuelle et le représentant de la Commission, assistés par la Présidence précédente (Italie) et par la Présidence future (Pays-Bas).'

The General Committee held its second meeting in Tunis on 10–12 February 1977. The scenario was the same as in Luxembourg; the Arab side made a statement on political questions, and the Nine made a statement on their own position in response. It should be recalled that, had all gone as planned, the Nine would have made a statement on the Middle East in January 1977 which would have marked an advance on the Declaration of November 1973. On the economic side, decisions were reached on financing joint Dialogue activities. The Arab League had already made budgetary provision the previous year for joint Dialogue activities, and shortly before the Tunis meeting the EC Council had also reached preliminary agreement. The amounts involved were small, but marked an important step forward on the European side in the interaction between EPC and the Community. Political Co-operation did not have a budget; in order to finance actions to secure its political objects, it had to turn to the Community. Indeed, at one stage in the proceedings the Political Committee explicitly gave its support to the Commission's request to the Council for budgetary appropriations.

Building the House (1973–1977)

The third meeting of the General Committee took place in Brussels on 26–9 October 1977, in a very different atmosphere from that of Tunis, since it came after the London Declaration of June 1977 in which the Nine had recognized the need for a homeland for the Palestinian people. While the meeting was in progress, the Nine voted in favour of UN Resolution 126 of 27 October 1977 which called upon Israel to abandon its illegal annexation of Jerusalem. On the economic side, financing was confirmed ($15 million from the Arabs and $3.5 million from the Community) and a costed list of projects and activities was agreed.

From this point on, the course of the Euro-Arab Dialogue was diverted by the Camp David Agreement and the expulsion of Egypt from the Arab League. The achievements so far were by no means negligible, although not what had originally been intended. What had started out as a bold attempt to forge a political and economic *entente* with the Arabs and thus secure stability of oil supplies and a favourable position in a neighbouring part of the world had been diverted by the opposition of the United States and changing appreciations on the part of new European governments into a more modest dialogue with the potential to build up a network of economic co-operation between Western Europe and the Arab world. The inability of the Europeans to move fast enough in response to Arab expectations on political questions and the unforeseen events set in train by President Sadat's visit to Jerusalem in November 1977 ensured that this potential was never realized. The Euro-Arab Dialogue nevertheless left a lasting mark on the way in which the participants organized their affairs. The Arabs were obliged to set up new collective machinery in the Arab League in order to conduct their dialogue with the Community, and the status of the PLO in international diplomacy was strengthened, in spite of European hesitations. On the European side, the Nine's failure to work out a strong political position meant that the economic side had to carry a greater political burden. This embedded the Commission more deeply in Political Co-operation and led EPC to look for new ways of interacting more efficiently with the Community.

The CSCE

The Second Phase in Geneva

The Nine's intensive preparation for the CSCE and their tabling of a series of proposals in January 1973 had largely determined the CSCE's agenda and led to the successful opening of the first stage of the Conference at Helsinki on 3–7 July 1973.

The Conference then moved to Geneva for the second stage, during which detailed work was to be done, beginning in September, on the agenda items which had been agreed at Helsinki. The Nine therefore had to organize themselves to take part in this work. The first decision they had to take concerned how the Commission was to carry out its role for those items which fell within Community competence. The question of Community participation had already been discussed at length in preparation for the Helsinki meeting, but had not been resolved beyond what was necessary for the meeting itself. Now practical arrangements for the Commission's presence in Geneva had to be made. Immediately after the Helsinki meeting, President Ortoli addressed a letter to Political Co-operation raising the problem. The Commission's view was that it should speak on behalf of the Community; it was prepared to accept that its representative should not have a nameplate at table and should be seated next to the Presidency representative.

Mr Andersen's speech at Helsinki had contained a reminder that agenda item II, which came to be known as the second basket, encompassed matters of Community competence, especially regarding commercial exchanges where the Community had a common policy. The Danish Minister drew the attention of participants to the fact that 'depending on the subjects, the Community may become involved according to its own competence and procedures in the future work of the Conference and that the implementation of any possible outcome of negotiations on these subjects will depend on agreement with the Community.' It was accepted by Member States that the Commission had to be represented in the Second Commission dealing with economic questions, and in particular in the Subcommittee on commercial exchanges. Most Member States took the view that this could best be done by the inclusion of a Commission official in the national delegation of the Presidency,

Building the House (1973–1977)

although there was much discussion as to how he should be described. Denmark would have preferred the question to be settled in the Council by strict application of the provisions of Articles 113 and 116 of the EEC Treaty, but did not insist in the face of a clear preference by the others to keep the procedural discussion in Political Co-operation. The matter was decided by the Ministers at their meeting on 10–11 September 1973. The Commission representatives would appear on the list of the Presidency's delegation, and their quality and function as Commission officials would be stated. A corresponding announcement was made by the Presidency at the opening session of the Economic Commission of the CSCE on 18 September in Geneva. Recalling the passage in Mr Andersen's speech quoted above, the Danish representative said:

In order to give expression to Community views in those areas mentioned in the statement by my Foreign Minister, representatives of the Commission of the European Community appear on the list of the Danish delegation. When these representatives intervene in the course of our discussions, they will express the Community view to the extent required by the Community's competence and procedures.

The formula was seen, at least by the Commission, as a stopgap measure; it survived for sixteen years.

This procedural question out of the way, Political Cooperation devoted its attention to the substantive preparation of the second stage of the Conference. Most of the work was done on the spot in Geneva, where the Subcommittee and the *ad hoc* Group were in semi-permanent session. It was only from time to time, and on the more important questions, that the Political Committee or Ministers were called on to arbitrate or to set political guidelines. The general approach to the future of the Conference was clear. The Nine were determined to resist Soviet pressure to set up permanent machinery for the Conference which would have the effect of freezing the status quo and putting a brake on the development of the Community. They therefore rejected the idea put forward by the Czechs of a standing Consultative Committee and put the emphasis instead on practical implementation of commitments. For the future, the Nine were prepared to envisage, after the signing of the Final Act which would close the second stage, an interim period during which the implementation of commitments could be closely watched; thereafter a new meeting could take place to review progress. This presupposed that concrete progress could be made during stage 2 on substantial measures in both the political and the economic sectors.

The technical work involved in preparing positions, papers, and resolutions in the many areas covered was immense, especially in Basket II, given the Nine's preference for substantive achievements rather than general declarations. One of the advantages of Political Co-operation was that this work could be shared out among the partners. In the Commercial Exchanges Subcommittee, for instance, the United Kingdom was responsible for business representation, the marketing of Eastern exports, obstacles to trade, improved facilities and contacts, and information of economic and commercial value. The Commission took on responsibility for the trade obligations to be undertaken by the Eastern countries, as well as the general conception of work in the Subcommittee's area. Belgium was responsible for credits. There was a similar division of labour involving the Federal Republic, the Commission, France, and the Netherlands on industrial co-operation, the environment, and co-operation in other sectors. Outside the Basket II area, Italy was asked to prepare proposals on security and military affairs and Denmark was made responsible for Basket III on human contacts.

Progress during the first half of 1974 was slow, mainly because of Soviet rigidity on Basket III. Work in the Second Commission went ahead more rapidly, however, thanks in part to the activism of the European Commission representatives and the cohesion given by Community discipline, to the extent that care had to be taken not to get out of phase with the other two Baskets. The main points remaining to be settled in Basket II were of course the most difficult ones: most-favoured-nation treatment, liberalization, and the preservation of the Community's position for the bilateral trade negotiations with the state trading countries for which the Council had expressed its readiness on 7 May 1974.

The discussions ground their way forward all through the autumn and the following spring. Two major difficulties arose for the Nine. The Soviet Union attached great importance to the question of the inviolability of existing frontiers. The Nine on

Building the House (1973–1977) 113

the other hand, bearing in mind their commitment to European Union as well as the possible reunification of Germany, did not wish to rule out the possibility of peaceful change. The question was in the end dealt with through drafting acceptable to the West, to which the United States secured Soviet agreement. On the question of most-favoured-nation treatment, however, the Nine feared that the United States might be more flexible in compensation for breaking the US–Soviet trade agreement, whereas it was essential for the Community to secure effective reciprocity from the East. This point remained outstanding until almost the last moment.

At last in June 1975 the Soviet Union began to make its moves. Indeed, the concessions came so fast that there was a danger that some of the Nine's requirements, including the reciprocity question, might be forgotten in the rush to bring stage 2 to a conclusion and set a date for the meeting which would mark stage 3 of the Conference. The cohesion of the Nine began to give way under the strain. The French put forward a proposal in Geneva about the date for a meeting without having first submitted it to EPC co-ordination. A Swiss proposal on the follow-up also split the cohesion of the Nine, the Danes this time being the ones to leave the camp. The breach was healed in the Political Committee in June thanks to Herculean efforts by its Chairman, the Italian Political Director, Mr Ducci, who had played a leading part in Political Co-operation since its inception. Even then it was no easy task to enforce the Political Committee's unitary position on the recalcitrant delegations in Geneva. The fact that this was successfully achieved shows that membership of the EPC club can produce co-operative results beyond what the texts require if they are taken only at face value; it also shows the weight which can be exerted by individuals in the absence of permanent institutions.

The Helsinki Meeting

The Conference duly convened in Helsinki at the end of July 1975 and the Final Act was signed on 1 August. Mr Moro performed this act both as Italian Prime Minister and, as President-in-Office, on behalf of the Community, adding a declaration stating acceptance of the Act by the Community. The manner in which these Acts were to be performed had been the subject of difficult discussions for some months previously. Much to the disgust of the Political Committee, these had taken place mainly in the Council framework. Opposition by the Soviet Union to Community participation as such was reinforced by a threat to demand similar treatment for Comecon. This would not have been to the liking of the Community, which at the time was keeping Comecon at arm's length while attempting to negotiate bilateral agreements with the Comecon member countries. The threat was real, but also served as a convenient pretext for those Member States, especially France, which wished to keep to a minimum the Community's presence in what they saw as an EPC undertaking. The question was solved by each signatory signing as he pleased, with or without the addition of titles and office.

Implementation and the Belgrade Review Meeting

After the strenuous efforts involved in reaching agreement on the Final Act, the Nine showed a marked disinclination to take the same active role in the next phase, that of monitoring the implementation of what had been agreed. Even the need to maintain the EPC structures which had been put in place for Geneva and Helsinki was now questioned by France, although the other Member States wanted close co-ordination to continue. France was persuaded to agree to the replacement of the former Subcommittee and *ad hoc* Group by a CSCE Working Group with a broad mandate, although it successfully opposed including in this mandate a provision that the Commission would regularly take part in the meetings of the Group. In practice, Commission representatives did take part, even though their position was theoretically precarious.

In spite of these hesitations, it was agreed that EPC co-operation on the CSCE should continue in the post-Helsinki phase. For some months the work was confined to lengthy analyses of the Final Act and line-by-line commentaries on it; the Nine's collective approach to the implementation exercise was definitely low key. It was only as the first CSCE Review Meeting—which it had been agreed should be held in Belgrade in 1977—approached, that they were galvanized into a show of activity. Eighteen months after the signing of the Final Act, the Nine were still not clear how they should organize the assessment of implementation. The Basket II issues, including some economic

Building the House (1973–1977) 115

questions concerning the Mediterranean, were entrusted to a Coreper Working Group, which was supposed to include CSCE experts from capitals and to report to both Coreper and the Political Committee. This interesting experiment in merging the preparatory work on the EPC and the Community sides does not seem to have been carried very far, and of course only concerned economic questions.

The Political Committee was not in a position to submit suggestions to Ministers on tactics for Belgrade until May 1977. The reaction to the Brezhnev proposals for specific meetings on energy, transport, and the environment in the framework of the UN Economic Commission for Europe (ECE) was lukewarm, except on a high-level meeting on the environment, on which it was thought the Community had something positive to contribute. The Germans were in favour, the United Kingdom feared that too many new initiatives would distract attention from the implementation of the Helsinki Final Act. For the same reason, the Nine were on the whole not in favour of new proposals at the Belgrade Conference.

When the Conference itself began in September 1977, the Nine were reasonably satisfied. The atmosphere was not confrontational and the study of the implementation of the Final Act was developing on the lines the Nine had suggested. The principal themes which had been identified were being discussed, and the new proposals which had passed muster had been tabled. The cohesion of the Nine had held up and they had succeeded in retaining the initiative. On the other hand, the Soviet Union had attempted to drown the first phase of evaluation of the new proposals by tabling a very large number of their own; by December eighty new proposals had been examined. The Belgrade Review Meeting was not to end until March 1978, when a further Meeting was agreed on, to be held two years later in Madrid.

The Nine had had their usual difficult discussions on how the Community was to be represented at Belgrade. The Commission argued strongly that an advance should be made on the arrangements which had been agreed for the second stage of the Helsinki Conference. This met with little enthusiasm from Member States, who thought that the improvement of the status of the Community was not an end in itself. The discussion, again mainly in Coreper, centred on whether or not the

Community should have a nameplate at table. The idea which found most favour was to have a double nameplate (*double pancarte*). This meant that the Member State which held the Presidency would, in addition to its national nameplate, have a nameplate as the European Community. The *double pancarte* solution was agreed unanimously by Coreper, but met with considerable difficulties in the Political Committee. France was reluctant to advance beyond the Helsinki and Geneva formula, and other countries thought that there would be little chance of securing the agreement of the Yugoslavian hosts to the *double pancarte* solution. All agreed that the *double pancarte* should in any case be used for Basket II discussions only. The matter was put to Foreign Ministers at their informal meeting at Leeds Castle on 21–2 April. They came out broadly in favour of the *double pancarte* but without any clear idea of what they would do if the Yugoslavians, or others, made difficulties.

This in fact is what happened. The Nine contented themselves with making a declaration in protest, a United Kingdom proposal that the Community should put up a makeshift *pancarte* of its own not having been thought seemly. Indeed, enthusiasm for the formula waned during the summer, and at the Review Meeting itself the French idea of a *pancarte orale* was adopted, i.e. a declaration by the country holding the Presidency stating that it was acting in a double capacity. This called forth no violent reaction.

The Nine and the CSCE

The fact that the early years of the CSCE process coincided with the beginnings of Political Co-operation, and that the Six, later Nine, were able to rise to the occasion, gave the infant EPC a head start. The papers tabled jointly in January 1973 were substantial and inventive, and the strength given to them by the cohesion of the Nine ensured that they determined the way the CSCE developed. The statement made on behalf of the Nine and the Community in July 1973 served notice that a new international political actor had come on stage. This cohesion and effectiveness continued during the Geneva phase of preparation for the Helsinki meeting. During this phase, however, most of the co-ordination of the Nine was done in Geneva, given the technical nature of the discussions and the need for permanent co-

Building the House (1973–1977)   117

ordination to prepare for the meetings of the thirty-five participants in the CSCE. The input of the central bodies—Ministers and Political Committee—became less. This may have contributed to the strain which was placed on the system towards the end of the Geneva phase, when pressures mounted to reach agreement rapidly in order to allow the Helsinki meeting to take place. It was to the credit of the system and of those responsible for its management that fissiparous tendencies were mastered. Prime Minister Moro's declaration in Helsinki marked again the unity and responsibility of the Community, but the opportunity was lost to secure a form of representation for it more in conformity with the Treaty. The opposition of the Soviet Union and its allies to the participation of the Community as such was real, as was their threat to seek a similar status for Comecon, but the will was lacking on the part of Member States, by this time bereft of the drive and inspiration of Pompidou, Heath, and Brandt, to test this opposition to the limit. After the achievement of the Helsinki Final Act the Nine's co-operation on CSCE questions became a matter of routine and a *chasse gardée* for technocrats, through the Madrid meeting and beyond. The CSCE was one among many areas in which the Nine co-operated, but no longer the focus of their interest and a testing ground for procedural innovation. This meant that the Nine played a less decisive role in the CSCE after the Final Act was signed than they had in previous years; an internal consequence was that, as the CSCE fell out of the limelight, the promising mechanisms for ensuring consistency between the political and economic aspects of policy did not develop as they might otherwise have done.

Comecon and Eastern Europe

The bulk of EPC's work on East–West relations in this period naturally concerned the CSCE. Some attention was nevertheless also paid to Comecon and the East European countries.

The question of relations with Comecon was topical because of the extension of the Community's common commercial policy to the state trading countries. It will be recalled from Chapter 3 that this was one reason why the Six had decided to co-ordinate their policies on the CSCE in the first place. To the extent that the Soviet Union was prepared to envisage a relationship at all between Eastern Europe and the Community, it was strongly in favour of channelling this through Comecon, which it could control more easily than the individual trade policies of the Comecon members. The standing of Comecon, and thus the influence of the Soviet Union, would be enhanced if it became the recognized partner of the European Community. These trade-policy questions were handled in the Community framework, but the Political Committee sought on a number of occasions to exercise political guidance over Coreper's discussions, with mixed success. An EPC paper on the subject was forwarded to the Council in September 1973; in March 1976 the East European Working Group was asked by the Political Committee to comment on the political aspects of the draft agreement with the Community which had been proposed by Comecon, and the Group's report was subsequently forwarded to Coreper. The Commission had opposed the involvement of EPC in this question, fearing the consequences of dealing with questions of Community competence in an inter-governmental framework, but in the event found that the Group's report confined itself to generalities, reflected (not surprisingly) the political analysis which had been current in Coreper for some time, and had in any case been more or less drafted by Commission representatives.

The Eastern European Working Group had been in existence since the early days of Political Co-operation, but had never been allowed to develop its activities into the operational field because of the determination of France, supported by Denmark, to maintain national bilateral policies towards the Soviet Union and the East European countries and its corresponding reluctance to engage in EPC co-ordination in this area. The work of the East European Working Group was therefore confined to rather academic studies on such topics as the implications of the Conference of European Communist Parties, the attitude of the East European countries towards the developing countries, the place of the Soviet Union and the East European countries in the world economy and the dissident and human-rights movements in those countries. Commission contributions to these studies, even on economic questions, were frequently excluded on principle by France.

Cyprus

The co-ordination of the policy of the Nine on the CSCE and the Middle East was an act of political will. The Member States chose to be active in those areas and they knew what they intended to achieve. They were successful in the case of the CSCE, less so in the Middle East because of the strain put on their cohesion by the October War and the American position. Another main area of EPC policy co-ordination between 1973 and 1977, the Mediterranean, was of a different nature. Here the co-ordination of the Nine was sparked off by crisis. Had it not been for the Sampson coup and the Turkish invasion of Cyprus, the revolution in Portugal, and the executions in Spain, there is no particular reason why the Nine should have had a policy in those areas. These were the first examples of what came to be a dominant feature of Political Co-operation, reaction to events, otherwise known as crisis management.

On 15 July 1974 Nikos Sampson mounted a coup in Nicosia with the support of the Greek Colonels and overthrew Archbishop Makarios, the elected President of the Republic of Cyprus. The French Presidency of EPC took immediate and forceful action to co-ordinate the diplomatic action of the Nine, which resulted in a statement issued the next day. In this statement the Nine reaffirmed their support for the independence and territorial integrity of Cyprus and their opposition to any intervention or interference tending to put it in question. The Presidency was instructed to make this common position known to the governments concerned. The Nine thus condemned the overthrow of the established Cypriot government and at the same time warned off both Greece and Turkey.

The policy lead was given by the United Kingdom, happy to secure multilateral support for its efforts in dealing with an intractable problem. The Wilson government's line was to get the Greeks and the Turks to the negotiating table. Three days after the Nine's declaration the Prime Minister and Mr Callaghan, the Foreign Secretary, flew to Paris, where Callaghan expressed the wish that the Nine should intensify their co-operation. On 20 July Turkish troops landed in north-east Cyprus and rapidly occupied that part of the country. The same day, the Ambassadors of the Nine in Paris were summoned to the Quai d'Orsay where the decision was taken to make renewed *démarches* in Athens and Ankara in support of the British initiative. As fighting continued over the next two days, French diplomacy remained active on behalf of the Nine. The Americans and the UN Security Council, as well as the British bilaterally, were of course equally active and it is not possible to judge the effectiveness of the Nine's diplomacy. Nevertheless, the Nine did succeed in forging an identity in the crisis and their efforts certainly contributed to bringing about the cease-fire which was due to take effect on 22 July.

Ministers met in Brussels the same day, when by good fortune a regular session of the Council of the Community provided the opportunity for them to discuss the Cyprus crisis in Political Co-operation and issue a communiqué. Deploring the failure to observe the cease-fire universally and recalling their three previous *démarches*, the Nine, basing themselves on Security Council Resolution 353, called for an immediate application of the cease-fire, full co-operation with the UN forces, and the re-establishment of the constitutional order. They renewed their support for the United Kingdom initiative and called for the immediate opening of the proposed discussions in Geneva. The Ministers said that they expected the three countries concerned—Cyprus, Greece, and Turkey—all of them associated with the Community, to heed their call. The implication was that the associate status of the countries concerned entitled the Nine to expect that the appeal would be heeded, and this relationship may well have played a part in bringing the first, most explosive, phase of the crisis to an end. However, neither now nor later did the Community resort to freezing the normal functioning of the Association Agreements to compel compliance with their views, although the political situation later led to delays in the passage to the second stage of the Agreement with Cyprus.

The fall of the Colonels on 24 July and the return of Greece to democracy under the government of Caramanlis, together with the collapse on 14 August of the second round of talks in Geneva, brought about a change in the circumstances which had enabled the Nine to play so effective a role in the first weeks of the crisis. The newly democratic Greece immediately announced its intention of seeking membership of the Community,

Building the House (1973–1977)

and its application was welcomed by a number of Member States led by France. The even-handed approach, which had enabled the Nine to carry equal weight in Athens and Ankara, was now less credible to the Turks. The collapse of the Geneva talks, and thus of the British initiative, meant that the Nine no longer had a political basis for their action. Although discussions continued throughout the next year and there were frequent contacts with those directly involved, it proved difficult for the Nine to agree on a new joint position of substance. They came near this in September 1975, when the Ministers in Venice were considering a policy which would have warded off the risk of a unilateral declaration of independence by the Turkish Cypriots through support for a bizonal federal solution combined with an approach to the Greeks to cease opposing the resumption of US aid to Turkey, provided that the Turks accepted the Community's good offices. The chances of success of such a policy were, however, limited by its being leaked to the Greek press. As on other occasions—the publication in the Springer press of the Schumann document on the Middle East is one—the effectiveness of EPC diplomacy was handicapped by the difficulty of maintaining confidentiality once discussions reached the Ministerial level.

Failing action on their own, the Nine supported the efforts of the UN Secretary-General, Dr Waldheim, to encourage progress through intercommunal talks. They were also attracted in the autumn of 1976 by an offer from Dr Kissinger to engage in a co-ordinated US–EPC initiative which would have set out a number of principles and thus provide a new focus for discussions in the face of hardening positions. The principles proposed were rather vague, and the Nine, unlike the Americans, insisted that Cyprus should maintain the right to determine freely its foreign policy, but the possibility was discussed for some time across the Atlantic until the arrival of the Carter Administration at the beginning of 1977 set US foreign policy on a fresh course.

The Community was very little involved in the work of Political Co-operation on the Cyprus question. The Commission, in spite of its repeated requests, did not receive invitations to attend the meetings of the Southern European and Mediterranean Expert Group, the body which prepared the discussions of the Political Committee and Ministers on the Cyprus question. During the period under review, the Community was involved only with aid for the Cypriot refugees and the renewal of the Association Agreement with Cyprus.

The Commission had granted emergency food aid to refugees via the UN High Commissioner for Refugees at the end of August 1974 and had proposed further emergency food aid from the Community. This information was conveyed to the Political Committee in September as a contribution to the Nine's political discussions. A year later, the Nine were again attracted by the idea of bolstering their position by granting Community aid to the refugees. Ministers meeting in Rome on 30 October 1975 took the decision in principle, and instructed Coreper to carry it out. They also suggested there should be co-ordination of the aid given by Member States and by the Commission. Coreper was reluctant to agree to aid on a scale which the Commission and some Member States thought appropriate, and the Commission sought to enlist the support of the Political Committee to ensure that the more generous approach prevailed.

Under the terms of the Association Agreement with Cyprus, the first stage of the Agreement was due to come to an end on 30 June 1977 and negotiations on the second stage were supposed to begin eighteen months before then. The Commission put forward its proposals for the negotiation of the second stage in March 1976. Sir Christopher Soames, who was the Commissioner responsible for Cyprus at the time, took the view that little progress could be expected until the problem of the relations between the two communities had been settled; in any case, there had to be guarantees that both communities would profit from the Community's concessions. The matter dragged on, the delay being caused by the attitude, implicit or explicit, of the Community Institutions, and it was not until Ministers met in London on 31 January 1977 that they instructed the Political Committee to study the political aspects of the future Association Agreement in time for the Council meeting in March. The Working Group duly submitted its report to the Political Committee on 1–2 March, pointing out that to fail to engage in negotiations would be to administer an unnecessary rebuff to the government of Cyprus, and that the Community's legal obligations could not be neglected. However, care should be taken to ensure that the revised arrangements benefited both communities; the Commission would therefore need to have informal contacts with the Turkish Cypriots. The report was duly approved and forwarded to the Council Presidency, after a broadside from the Commission in the Political Committee had succeeded in removing from it two sections on the content of the future agreement which the Working Group had been imprudent enough to insert, thus trespassing on the prerogative of the Commission. The Council gave the Commission the necessary directives on 3 May. The direct intervention of Political Co-operation was unusual.

Portugal

The Nine's dynamic role in the early days of the Cyprus crisis was later impaired by the need to support the emerging democracy in Greece. A similar concern for pluralist democracy was prominent in the response to events in Portugal, although on that occasion it was the Community, not EPC, which took the leading part.

The fall of Caetano on 25 April 1974 did not call forth an immediate response from the Nine. It was not until the EPC Ministerial Meeting on 10 June that the question was raised, under 'topical questions', the catch-all agenda item which in those days enabled Ministers to discuss developments outside their main areas of interest. Speaking to the press afterwards, Mr Genscher said that the Nine had followed with sympathy events since the change of government in Portugal. They welcomed the process which opened the way to a democratic development in Portugal and made it possible to pursue a policy which would lead to the end of the long civil war in Africa and expressed their hope that the development would enable Portugal to develop its relations with the Community.

This first approach was not carried further in Political Co-operation. Indeed, Member States seemed to prefer to hold their fire until the extremely confused situation, both in Portugal and in Africa, became clearer. Instead, the scene of action passed to the Community. Portugal had had a Trade Agreement with the Community since 1973. On the overthrow of the Caetano regime, the new Portuguese government applied for this Agreement to be replaced by a broader economic and financial agreement. The Commission's response was encouraging but non-committal. Given the chaotic political situation in Lisbon, Sir Christopher Soames, the Commissioner for External Relations, was not prepared to be more forthcoming in the absence of concrete Portuguese requests. These were unlikely to be made as provisional governments came and went in rapid succession. Nevertheless, with the approval of the Council, some progress was made in the EEC–Portugal Joint Committee at the end of November, which together with Sir Christopher's subsequent visit to Portugal made it possible for a further meeting of the Joint Committee on 28 May 1975 to recommend the opening of negotiations for a wider-ranging agreement. The Commission duly forwarded the proposal to the Council on 11 June. Exceptional financial assistance was also proposed.

This opening towards a deeper—and more expensive—relationship had been made as a political gesture to the new democratic system. However, as discussions of the Commission's proposal went ahead in the Council, doubts began to grow. Although the moderates had done well in the April 1975 elections, the results were flouted by the Communists, whose occupation of key positions throughout the country gave rise to fears that a hardline Marxist regime might well be installed in Portugal. The Socialist and Democrat Ministers resigned from the government following the Communist occupation of the Socialist press and proposals for a Popular National Assembly which would provide a new forum alongside the traditional parties. As the situation worsened, the European Council of 16–17 July 1975 made it clear that the Community's offer of assistance was conditional: 'The European Council reaffirms that the European Community is prepared to initiate discussions on closer economic and financial co-operation with Portugal. It also points out that, in accordance with its historical and political traditions, the European Community can give support only to a democracy of a pluralist nature.'

The situation in Portugal improved during the summer, especially after the fall of Prime Minister Gonçalves in August and the imprisonment of the populist Carvalho, the Head of the Security Police. After further discussion in the autumn it was agreed at the Council on 7 October that the European Investment Bank should provide a loan of 150 million ecu on

Building the House (1973–1977) 125

favourable terms financed for an additional 30 million ecu by the Community budget; directives were also agreed for the negotiation of a new agreement. The decision on the EIB loan, which rode roughshod over Community procedures, was quite clearly taken for political reasons.

In dealing with events in Portugal, the Community had taken some highly political decisions of great importance for the future. They had made it plain that there was a price to be paid by countries which wished to have good relations. Portugal's catastrophic economic situation made it susceptible to pressure from the Community and strengthened the hand of those political forces inside the country which wished to see a closer relationship with it. The course taken by Portugal was important not only for the future development of Western Europe, but also for the Atlantic Alliance and for a large part of Southern Africa. Yet, curiously enough, these decisions were taken by the Community and not by Political Co-operation. After the first discussion in June 1974, the case of Portugal was discussed by Ministers in EPC only in September 1974 and again in September and October 1975, and then only to take note of, and encourage, the work going forward in the Community. The all-important decision of the European Council in July 1975 was a Community affair.

Why should this have been? On the face of it, the problems which had to be solved were typically ones for Political Co-operation. The most likely explanation is that discussions were so much centred on the use of Community instruments (unlike in the case of Cyprus, where there was deliberate avoidance of bringing Community instruments into play) that it was inevitable that the Community framework should be used for the political discussion as well. The case was proof that the Community did indeed have a political dimension and was capable of using it, regardless of the existence of Political Co-operation.

Spain
Public opinion in the Community was equally concerned with the lack of progress towards democracy in Spain, but the differing attitudes of the Nine to the Franco regime made for a less united approach. The Northern human-rights belt, led by the Netherlands and Denmark, was in favour of forceful

declarations and action. Other countries, especially France, had an eye to the potential future role of Spain in strengthening the Southern camp in the Community. France, like Ireland, was in any case more sympathetic to the Spanish government's difficulties with the Basques.

It was indeed over the Spanish handling of Basque terrorism that Political Co-operation was first obliged to take a public position. In the summer of 1975 five Basque terrorists were tried under the anti-terrorist laws and condemned to death. Although the Netherlands had called for action by the Nine at the Ministerial Meeting in Venice on 11–12 September, there was disagreement on what the Nine should do and how far they should go. It was not until the Political Committee and Ministers moved to New York two weeks later for the opening of the General Assembly Session that agreement was reached on a *démarche* on purely humanitarian grounds to the Spanish government expressing the hope that the executions would not be carried out.

The executions took place three days later, on 27 September. Political Co-operation did not distinguish itself in its subsequent diplomatic action. Although the Italian Presidency tried to co-ordinate the Nine's withdrawal of their Ambassadors from Madrid, the Netherlands did not wait for the results of this and the abrupt departure of the Dutch Ambassador led to the recall in dribs and drabs of most of the others.

Action bearing on the relations with Spain of the Community as such was better co-ordinated and more effective. Spain had been included in the Community's Global Mediterranean Approach and negotiations for the updating of the 1970 preferential trade agreement were about to restart, having been broken off the previous December. Following a call by the European Parliament for the freezing of trade relations with Spain, pending the establishment of a democratic regime, the Commission proposed on 1 October the suspension of negotiations.

Foreign Ministers met to consider the situation in the margins of the Council meeting in Luxembourg on 6–7 October. Their discussions were prepared by the Political Committee. The Ministers deplored the executions and the fact that their *démarche* had been fruitless; they nevertheless hoped that a democratic Spain would find its place among European countries.

Building the House (1973–1977)

As Council, the Ministers took note that at the present stage negotiations with Spain could not be resumed.

The failure of Political Co-operation to respond in a co-ordinated way to the executions is not surprising, given the severe pressure some governments were under domestically to make an early gesture. The comparison with the Sampson coup in Cyprus is instructive. On that occasion, the French Presidency acted through the Ambassadors of the Nine in Paris and had a policy based on the British initiative which attracted general support. The Italian Presidency acted through the Coreu system and was dependent on positive decisions from nine capitals, which had to be taken at short notice to be effective. When it came to the Community, there was the same readiness as in the case of Portugal to manipulate the Community's trade relations with Spain to signify displeasure and as a means of bringing pressure to bear. The initiative was taken by the Commission in the exercise of its treaty powers. Political Co-operation, although it played a greater role than in the case of Portugal, was only involved at the time of the Ministers' decision in October; the possibilities of action of this kind had not previously been raised in the EPC forum.

Southern Africa

In 1974 the Nine did not discuss African questions and there was no Africa Working Group. It was only in March of that year that the Political Committee considered that there might be advantage in extending the activities of EPC to this area. Yet by 1977, African affairs were taking up a large part of the time of Political Directors and Ministers.

As often in Political Co-operation, there was a direct stimulus as well as an underlying cause. The stimulus was the break-up of the Portuguese colonial empire in 1974–5. The Nine saw this as an opportunity to affirm their collective personality by adopting a common position towards the newly independent African States. The underlying cause was concern that the Soviet Union might extend its influence in Southern Africa by exploiting the Marxist liberation movements which had won power through the anti-colonial struggle. This would not only be a reverse in the global ideological conflict, but also threaten the West's investments in that resource-rich part of the world.

The Nine's attempts to adopt common policies in Southern Africa met with mixed success. Political Co-operation was not yet sufficiently developed for co-ordinated action to be perceived as an overriding need, and residual post-colonial interests could lead to the policies of one Member State being given unquestioning support (Rhodesia) or being presented as a *fait accompli* (Zaïre).

In 1977 Member States began to develop a policy towards South Africa. Paradoxically, this was more successful than policy towards neighbouring black States, perhaps because it was more difficult to achieve. The constructive tension between Member States wishing to take a strong line against apartheid and those whose condemnation was tempered by economic considerations led to the adoption of the Code of Conduct, which served a useful political purpose in demonstrating the Nine's collective opposition to apartheid while achieving modest improvements in the working conditions of the African employees of foreign subsidiaries.

Angola and Mozambique

Portuguese colonial rule in Africa began to crumble following the collapse of the Caetano regime in April 1974. It is a measure of the perception of the growing personality of the Nine that they felt it incumbent on them to respond collectively to these events. They had successfully adopted a joint position when Guinea-Bissau became independent in August 1974, although they did not reach agreement on the Federal Republic's proposal to set up a joint Embassy there. Emboldened by this success, it seemed the natural thing for them to attempt a similar operation when Mozambique became independent on 25 June 1975. A declaration was issued setting out the Nine's intention to recognize Mozambique simultaneously on Independence Day, approving the process of decolonization, and expressing their readiness to establish co-operation with Member States as well as with the Europe of the Nine (a reference to the Lomé Convention). A similar Presidency declaration was prepared for the independence of São Tomé and Principe on 12 July; in view of the uncertain situation, action on Cape Verde was left pending. In spite of the joint declaration, the new Frelimo administration in Lourenço Marques invited to the independence celebrations only those Member States (the United Kingdom, the Netherlands, and Denmark) which it felt the need to reward for past policies.

Angola was to become independent on 11 November. The situation there was more confused. The transitional coalition government composed of the three rival liberation movements had collapsed in bitter conflict, fomented by outside intervention. The National Front for the Liberation of Angola (FNLA) received support from the Americans, while the Popular Movement for the Liberation of Angola (MPLA) was given increasing amounts of Soviet aid in the form of supplies and military advisers, both Russian and Cuban. In the south the National Union for the Total Independence of Angola (UNITA) was receiving Western support, and South African forces had struck deep into the country. When independence came, the Nine were at a loss to know which horse to back. The line of least resistance—to support the policy of the Organization of African Unity (OAU)—was not at the time a way out, given the uncertainty as to what that policy was. The same difficulties arose over aid; the Community should grant humanitarian aid, but to whom?

The policy of maintaining neutrality between the liberation movements and working for an African solution involving all three factions became more difficult to sustain as the year drew to a close. US military aid to the pro-Western liberation forces was halted by Congress and the South Africans withdrew to the Namibian border. The Soviet-backed MPLA offensive met with weakened resistance and the MPLA came close to establishing themselves as the *de facto* government. The Nine now came under pressure from the Americans to play a more openly active role. This they were reluctant to do, still preferring to rely on the OAU, which was now seeking a solution based on a tripartite administration and the withdrawal of foreign forces. All the Nine agreed that the decision taken by Ministers in October not to take national initiatives without consultation should be maintained.

The OAU approach became untenable as the MPLA consolidated its position, and the feeling began to grow, especially in London and Paris, that it would be prudent to recognize a *de facto* MPLA government so as not to leave the field free for the Soviet Union and the Cubans. At the same time, Dr Kissinger was urging delay in messages to all nine governments. The EPC machinery was working on this in February 1976 and plans for simultaneous recognition were laid; a declaration to be issued at the Ministerial Meeting on 23 February was suggested. This was pre-empted by France, which in spite of attempts by partners to restrain her, announced on 17 February her intention to recognize Angola, and hence the MPLA government, the same day. The rest of the Nine were left to follow suit in whatever order they could.

French motives were no doubt mixed, ranging from a desire to waste no time in following the shift of opinion in francophone Africa to resistance to being put under pressure once again by the US Secretary of State. The implications of the French action for the process of Political Co-operation were important. An image of discord was created; the partners were embarrassed and resentful; and it was shown that at difficult moments national interests prevailed over the common good.

The image of unity was to some extent restored when the Foreign Ministers issued a declaration as planned on 23 February. After the débâcle of the previous week, it was thought to be too brazen to restrict the declaration to the question of Angola, although the French fought hard against any extension. The Nine therefore took the opportunity to set out their policy towards Southern Africa as a whole. They expressed their readiness to develop co-operative relations, if wished by the Africans, and their opposition to any action by any State to establish a zone of influence in Africa; they asserted their respect for the independence of all African States and their right to define national policies without foreign interference; they confirmed their support for the OAU in its efforts to encourage African co-operation and their endorsement of the right to self-determination and independence of the peoples of Rhodesia and Namibia; and they voiced their condemnation of apartheid. The declaration thus marked the opening up of a new area of interest for Political Co-operation.

Rhodesia, Zaïre, and Namibia

The achievement of a joint overall approach towards the problems of decolonization in Southern Africa did not mean that the Nine were in a position to execute a successful and co-ordinated policy in every case. The Member States which had residual colonial responsibilities tended to act on their own, and those which were members of the Security Council sometimes had a preference for that framework. France in particular looked on francophone Africa as its own domain.

In the case of Rhodesia, the Nine contented themselves with voicing support at regular intervals for the policy of the United Kingdom. In fact, British foreign policy under the Atlanticist guidance of Dr David Owen looked to the United States for a partner rather than to the Europeans. The latter were kept on board by being given regular briefings, both in the Political Committee and in Geneva while the Conference was being held there, but the policy was in no sense formed by discussion in Political Co-operation and even the briefings gave out when it came to the Anglo-US proposals mooted in the summer of 1977.

Nevertheless, support for the United Kingdom was generously given. The United Kingdom thus benefited for the second time, the first being over Cyprus, from one of the more appreciable advantages of Political Co-operation, solidarity with a Member State in difficulties. The European Council meeting in Luxembourg on 1–2 April 1976 issued a statement in which the Nine expressed support for the United Kingdom's objectives and efforts with regard to Rhodesia and appealed to the minority there to move towards a majority system. They confirmed, as they regularly did in declarations on Rhodesia, that they would continue to apply the Security Council decisions. Successive declarations of support for British moves were made over the next year, but Dr Owen's colleagues did not attempt to influence policy. In the summer of 1978, the Anglo-US plans for a settlement founded on a limited period of direct British rule before independence were worked out without the partners even being informed.

The events in Zaïre in April 1977 involved Political Co-operation even less. Following the invasion of Shaba by Katangese ex-gendarmes from Angola, a Moroccan force left for Zaïre in air transport provided by France 'in the name of Europe'. The Nine were barely informed of the French intention before the aircraft left. They issued a declaration at the Ministerial Meeting on 18 April which drew on the general principles of the Africa declaration of the year before, but the reaction to the French initiative was very guarded.

The situation in Namibia was rather different. All the Member States gave their support to efforts by the United Nations to bring Namibia to independence, but there was no agreement on how the Nine might play a part. Some Member States preferred to leave the responsibility to the Contact Group of Five, based on the Western members of the Security Council at the time and thus including Germany as well as the United Kingdom and France, but this exclusion from responsibility, and sometimes even from information, was resented by some of the smaller Member States.

Activity by the Nine consisted largely of a series of *démarches* to the South African government, usually timed to tie in with similar action on the part of the permanent members of the Security Council. A United Kingdom proposal in April 1976 that the Nine should send a fact-finding mission to Namibia met with opposition, particularly from France, and was not taken up, for fear of cutting across work in the Security Council. It was also opposed by the South West Africa People's Organization (SWAPO) as a diversionary tactic.

South Africa

It has always been easy for the Nine to condemn apartheid, and they have not failed to do so at regular intervals. Such a condemnation featured in the Nine's declaration on Africa of 23 February 1976. Similarly, it took no great effort collectively to refuse recognition of Transkei on its 'independence' in October 1976. A more interesting discussion in this respect concerned the economic effects of the closure of the border between Transkei and Lesotho. This question was transferred to the Community, the Commission not failing to point out that its absence from the Africa Working Group made co-ordination difficult.

It was more difficult to agree on a course of action which went beyond declarations. In particular the Netherlands, Denmark, and Ireland pressed for deeds, not words, but the Member States with important interests in South Africa—the United Kingdom, France, and the Federal Republic—were reluctant to advance along that path. For the first time, the Nine found themselves facing the problem of sanctions, and in disarray.

Faced with this difficult problem, the Nine decided not to

Building the House (1973–1977) 133

discuss it. It has always been both a strength and a weakness of Political Co-operation that its agenda can be infinitely adjusted to avoid controversial topics. However, the Nine were not in control of the agenda in other forums, and when the question of an arms embargo against South Africa came up at the General Assembly in autumn 1976, the Danes broke ranks and voted with their Nordic partners against the rest of the Nine. The issue was not so much the embargo as the language used in the resolution, which was highly critical of some Member States. The lack of solidarity caused much resentment, and the Danes had a good deal of explaining to do; the incident showed the sensitivity of the topic.

The Netherlands, however, were determined not to let the matter rest. The Dutch position on apartheid had been hardening over the years, and the area was of particular concern to the Socialist Foreign Minister of the day, Max van der Stoel. The Labour government in the United Kingdom found itself in a cleft stick: it could not remain indifferent to apartheid, and yet action should not be allowed to endanger the country's economic interests. Only the France of Giscard was unsympathetic to action of any kind and tried to keep it to a minimum. No government was able to ignore mounting public concern, especially after the Soweto riots in 1976.

The political juncture was therefore favourable to a move on South Africa, but progress in Political Co-operation was slow. The Working Group was not able to agree on a report until June 1977, and this contained divergencies on the arms embargo and other economic measures which were not resolved at the level of the Political Committee. The issue came to a head at the Ministerial Meeting on 12 July 1977, when the Foreign Ministers could no longer put off adopting a common position. As usual, there was a proximate cause. A United Nations Conference on apartheid was due to be held in Lagos on 22–6 August, and the Nine felt it was politically untenable for them not to take a joint stand. This was to take the form of a declaration to be made by the Belgian Presidency. The preparation for this Conference was the specific question submitted to Ministers at their July meeting.

Ministers went a good deal further. Strongly pressed by Dr Owen and Mr Genscher, they decided in principle to accept a 'Code of Conduct' which would set out guidelines for the subsidiaries of European firms in South Africa on working conditions for their African employees. In the words of Dr Owen, the move was a positive counter to third-world criticisms that the industrialized countries made declarations about apartheid, but took no action; the guidelines should be worked out urgently in time for the Lagos Conference. The idea of a Code of Conduct was welcomed by the Dutch and the Danes, but they wanted to go further, for example by blocking new investments or asking the oil companies to reduce their exports to South Africa. Mr Genscher suggested limiting state guarantees for new private investment. The question of additional measures was not therefore shelved by the decision on the Code of Conduct. M. Simonet, as President, told the press that sanctions had not been ruled out, depending on the effectiveness of the Code, and the Working Group was instructed to examine further possible measures.

The idea of a Code of Conduct was not new. Indeed, as early as April 1976 the United Kingdom and the Netherlands had floated in Political Co-operation the possibility of influencing firms with subsidiaries in South Africa by setting conditions and wages. The response had not been unfavourable, but there had been no further discussion of the idea as the basis for collective action. A Code of Practice had, however, been in force in the United Kingdom since 1974, introduced by the Wilson government to counter growing domestic criticism of British involvement in South Africa. It was a constructive and inventive move to transfer this to the Community level, and the Ministers concluded their meeting on 12 July in an atmosphere of considerable euphoria, caused not least by the feeling that they had taken an important policy decision on their own, without the benefit of preparation by officials. In fact, the British had started laying their plans as early as February, and the surprise manœuvre succeeded because of the strong Anglo-German front.

The euphoria was too good to last. The discussions in the margins of the Council on 26 July, at which the finishing touches were put to the Belgian Presidency's speech in Lagos, were not easy, in particular over the question of whether there should be a reference to an inventory of possible economic measures. At this point, prudence prevailed, and the Nine confined themselves to announcing their readiness actively to examine a range of initiatives to use the Community's collective weight.

The Code itself was drafted with almost indecent haste and no consultation of interested parties. It was adopted by Ministers in the margins of the Council on 20 September, a number of reservations being lifted at the last minute, so that everyone gave up some cherished point. The most important innovation in comparison with the British Code was the provision that firms should publish annual reports on progress in the application of the Code, thus providing a form of surveillance. The Code was nevertheless to be voluntary; no sanctions could be applied if firms chose to ignore it. Apart from publishing the Code, the Commission played no part in the affair, which remained the exclusive business of Political Co-operation from first to last.

The effectiveness of the Code in improving working conditions in South Africa is a matter for economic analysis and debate. Its political value cannot be denied, both as a shield against criticism and as an example of joint action by the Nine, for the first time outside their immediate neighbourhood of Europe and the Mediterranean. The continuing discussion of an inventory of further measures, however, dragged on for some time without any consensus being possible in the face of opposition from the three largest Member States.

Aid

It is perhaps surprising, given the paucity of political instruments, that the Nine should have been as unenterprising as they were in the use of economic instruments. It was of course the case that the Community gave aid to the African countries, whether emergency and humanitarian aid or structural support through the Lomé Convention, but this was never harnessed to a consistent Africa policy in Political Co-operation. The question was discussed in 1976 in the Political Committee, but in general terms, and the Commission had to inject a dose of financial realism to the debate. More specific co-ordination was hampered by the Commission's absence from the Africa Working Group. The Commission itself, moreover, was vigilant to ensure that discussion on aid stayed in the Community framework. It found an unusual ally in France, which was anxious that the financial support whose distribution had been negotiated in the Lomé

Convention should not be disturbed for extraneous political reasons, still less redistributed in favour of countries not party to the Convention.

In the reverse direction, Political Co-operation sometimes tried to halt Community aid to countries which presented political problems. For example, the question of aid to the Uganda of Idi Amin was raised on a number of occasions in 1977, in particular by Dr Owen as a matter of principle regarding the co-ordination of EPC and Community policies.

The United Nations

Co-operation among the Six in New York barely existed in the first years of Political Co-operation, not least because the Federal Republic of Germany did not become a member until 18 September 1973. Thereafter co-operation intensified as the Nine were increasingly recognized as a group capable of acting collectively. Partly no doubt because of their late arrival on the scene, the Germans in particular encouraged this and were at the origin of moves to systematize the co-operation.

Neither the Luxembourg nor the Copenhagen Report contained specific provisions for Political Co-operation at the United Nations. The latter merely gave a general exhortation to the Permanent Representatives of the Member States 'to the major international organizations' to consider matters together and seek common positions. The Document on the European Identity of December 1973 went a step further by announcing the determination of the Nine 'to contribute to international progress, both through their relations with third countries and by adopting common positions whenever possible in international organizations, notably the United Nations and the Specialised Agencies.'

If the Nine were to be coherent, they had no choice but to express collectively in New York the common positions which were being adopted on an increasing number of subjects. The difficulty was that the requirements of debate in the United Nations, particularly in the sessions of the General Assembly, ran ahead of policy-making in Europe. There were the beginnings of a common line on the Middle East, but where were the policies on Cambodia, Korea, the PLO, disarmament, and South Africa? It was left to the Permanent Representatives to make these as best they could, or fail in the attempt. The voting record of the Nine, though by no means discreditable in this period, showed that consistency of voting owed more to luck than good management.

It was the Federal Republic, under the Irish Presidency of the first half of 1975, which took the initiative to introduce improvements designed to raise the success rate. The conjunction of these two Member States was not unimportant. The German interest has been mentioned above; Ireland's main, if not only, foreign-policy guideline before joining the Community had been support for the United Nations and its principles. The German Political Director, Mr van Well, proposed to the Political Committee in January 1975 that it should engage in systematic preparation for the General Assembly and the Special Session. An expert group should be set up to prepare a decision by Ministers, which would assess the situation, identify subjects on which joint positions should be achieved, and prepare draft resolutions of the Nine.

Although the Permanent Representatives had run into difficulties in achieving common positions on typically Political Co-operation questions, the immediate cause for German concern was economic. This was the era of the great North–South debate and the Paris Conference, and the United Nations was an important battleground for the hearts and minds of the third world on the New International Economic Order. Although the Conference and the Seventh Special Session of the General Assembly (1–12 September 1975) were prepared exclusively in the Community framework, the need was felt to have closer co-ordination of the Member States' position in New York, where the European Commission was an even more recent arrival than Germany, the Community having been granted observer status on 11 October 1974. Coreper had set up a special UN group in the Council framework, and there was a degree of rivalry between it and its opposite number in Political Co-operation.

Measures on the lines recommended by the Federal Republic were approved in principle by Ministers in Dublin on 13 February and implemented by them for the first time at their meeting on 26 May. On that occasion the Ministers had before them a report from the Working Group and another from the Permanent Representatives in New York. The Working Group argued that if the Nine were to demonstrate successfully their collective identity in New York, procedures would have to be put in place to ensure that co-ordination worked. The Working Group would itself provide guidance for the operation on all subjects other than those which were of strict Community competence. The Permanent Representatives, in their report, identified the problem areas in which votes tended to diverge, and at the same time drew attention to the role of spokesman which devolved increasingly on the Presidency, making the need for common positions even more pressing. The remedy they proposed was to study the different problem areas as far as possible in advance in capitals, extending the Nine's ambit if necessary (it was thus that the UN-Disarmament Working Group came into being), and keeping the Permanent Representatives more closely informed of the policies which were developed in the capitals and in Brussels.

The recommended approach, which conferred a central strategic role on the UN Working Group, was approved and put into execution. The importance of Political Co-operation in the United Nations was underlined by the European Council in a statement on 17 July, giving support at the highest level to the decisions taken by Ministers. As a final contribution to the exercise, the Political Committee in September approved the idea that when Mr Rumor made his speech to the General Assembly as Foreign Minister of Italy, he should also, as President of the Council, speak on behalf of the Nine on EPC questions and of the Community on economic questions, the two sections being prepared in the respective frameworks.

The theory of Political Co-operation in New York was fine, but the results in practice were disappointing. The Nine were able to engage in a number of useful actions on subjects as diverse as the equating of Zionism and racism, the United States' threat to withdraw from the International Labour Organization (ILO), and human rights in Chile, but on the principal issues their views stayed obstinately apart. Whereas the Nine had succeeded in voting together on 65 per cent of the total in 1975, the percentage had fallen to 53 per cent the next year. The recalcitrance of the problem caused regular concern. From time to time Ministers were called on to approve improvements to the system. For example, in July 1977 an 'early-warning system' was introduced to allow difficult subjects to be identified at an earlier stage, but the problems persisted and the complaints of the Permanent Representatives in their report of 1975 continued to ring down the years without a noticeable echo.

The fault lay partly in the proprietary attitude of Member States to their image in the United Nations. It ought in theory to have been no more difficult to reach a common position in New York than in the capitals. In practice this ignored the high visibility of national positions in the General Assembly, where Member States were often represented by personalities from outside their diplomatic services, in which the principal attachment to Political Co-operation lay. The incentive to co-operate was further reduced when some Member States were thought to be witholding their support on 'singling out' resolutions, in which one or two Member States were attacked. The Danish vote on South Africa sanctions in the autumn of 1976 was an example of this which left traces for a long time. At this period, the principal difficulties came from the Danes and the Dutch, Member States with a long tradition of support for progressive causes in the United Nations, who felt that an abrupt change in the foreign policy of a Member State would tarnish its image. It is a tribute to the powers of attraction and perceived benefits of Political Co-operation that so much time was spent in endeavouring to achieve the highest possible rate of common positions against considerable odds—and a measure of the difficulties that the reward for so much effort should have been so meagre.

REACHING OUT TO UNION

The Paris Summit of December 1974

'Le Sommet européen est mort. Vive le Conseil européen.' With this glad cry President Giscard d'Estaing hailed the decision of the Heads of State and Government in Paris on 10–11 December 1974 to put their meetings on a regular footing and to assume a role of political impetus in the Community. The idea did not spring fully armed from the head of Giscard and of Schmidt, although the leaders of France and Germany played a crucial part in the Community's first institutional advance since the Hague Summit of 1969.

The commitment made at the Paris Summit of 1972, to transform before the end of the decade the whole complex of their relations into a European Union, still stood, and the Community Institutions which had been requested to draw up reports on this question before the end of 1975 were continuing their work. The Foreign Ministers had done their part by adopting the Luxembourg Report in 1973, but EPC was not involved in the preparation of the reports on the wider aspects of European Union, much though the Political Committee regretted this state of affairs.

Some dynamism was given to the process by the events of 1973. France in particular was provoked by the failure of the Nine to respond adequately and in time to the challenge of the October War and to assert European interests which it felt were not on the agenda of the superpowers. This led President Pompidou to call for regular meetings of the Nine at the level of Heads of Government. In his press conference on 27 September 1973, the President said that

> if, for example, one feels that in order for political co-operation to develop more rapidly it must be discussed from time to time, at not too frequent, but still regular, intervals, by the highest authorities among themselves and themselves alone, I for my part am in favour of this and I am ready, not to take the initiative, but to discuss it with our partners. If we do in fact succeed in having a European policy *vis-à-vis* all the others, all third countries, then the road will be clear.

The idea of having Heads of Government meet regularly was in the direct line of Gaullist thinking and had figured in the Fouchet Reports. In spite of this rather suspect origin, it was taken up by both Heath and Brandt in order to give impetus to the development of the Community. The Copenhagen Summit was prepared on this basis, although participation was wider than Pompidou had in mind; under pressure from the smaller Member States, the Foreign Ministers at their EPC meeting on 20–1 November ensured that they themselves, as well as the President of the Commission, took part. The Summit decided that in future 'sessions would be held whenever justified by circumstances and when it appears necessary to provide a stimulus or lay down further guidelines for the construction of a united Europe.'

Building the House (1973–1977)

The implementation of this decision was taken up in Political Co-operation, discussion focusing on the mechanisms for regular meetings at the level of Heads of Government and for consultations in times of crisis. The atmosphere in which the discussions took place was, however, altered in the spring of 1974 by changes in the government of the three biggest Member States. Wilson replaced Heath, Giscard replaced Pompidou, and Schmidt replaced Brandt between March and May 1974. Each one had an interest in distancing himself from the European slogans of his predecessor. Together with Pompidou's European idealism, Giscard was able to drop his Gaullist overtones. Schmidt put greater emphasis than his predecessor on a pragmatic approach to Europe which combined attentiveness to the transatlantic dimension with the reluctance to be paymaster to be expected of a former Minister of Finance. Wilson was tied up with Labour Party policy which led to the renegotiation of British membership and made it convenient for the United Kingdom to follow an inter-governmental line in discussions on the future of Europe.

The shape of the European Council which emerged from the Paris Summit was determined by Giscard and Schmidt, who met on at least two occasions before the Summit to co-ordinate their policy and were frequently in touch by telephone. Encouraged by these contacts, Giscard invited his colleagues at short notice to an informal working dinner in Paris on 14 September 1974, at which the themes were decided for a Summit meeting which duly took place on 11–12 December.

On the institutional side the setting up of the European Council, which put the Summit meetings on a regular basis, was justified by the need to bring together Community and EPC policy. The operational part of the text reads:

2. Recognising the need for an overall approach to the internal problems involved in achieving European unity and the external problems facing Europe, the Heads of Government consider it essential to ensure progress and overall consistency in the activities of the Communities and in the work on political co-operation.

3. The Heads of Government have therefore decided to meet, accompanied by the Ministers of Foreign Affairs, three times a year and, whenever necessary, in the Council of the Communities and in the context of political co-operation. The administrative secretariat will be provided for with due regard to existing practices and procedures.

In order to ensure consistency in Community activities and continuity of work, the Ministers of Foreign Affairs, meeting in the Council of the Community, will act as initiators and co-ordinators. They may hold political co-operation meetings at the same time.

These arrangements do not in any way affect the rules and procedures laid down in the Treaties or the provisions on political co-operation in the Luxembourg and Copenhagen Reports. At the various meetings referred to in the previous paragraphs the Commission will exercise the powers vested in it and play the part assigned to it by the above texts.

The creation of the European Council, with the job of ensuring overall consistency, raised a number of questions, to all of which the text gave ambiguous answers. Was there to be a secretariat? It 'will be provided for in an appropriate manner with due regard for existing practices and procedures.' Were the Foreign Ministers to wear interchangeable hats when acting as initiators and co-ordinators to ensure consistency and continuity? They 'may hold political co-operation meetings at the same time [as the Council].' Does the Foreign Ministers' role as initiator supersede that of the Commission? 'These arrangements do not affect the rules . . . laid down in the Treaties.' Does the Commission acquire powers in EPC? 'These arrangements do not affect the provisions . . . in the Luxembourg and Copenhagen Reports.'

The creation of the European Council was criticized at the time and since as being a departure from Community orthodoxy and as weakening the powers and authority of the supranational Institutions. Why then was it accepted by those Member States which held those causes dear? At one level, it was seen as a way to break the log-jam in which the Community found itself in its search for progress towards political union. As politicians with a superb technical grasp of their dossiers, Giscard and Schmidt had full confidence in their powers to solve problems, however intractable. The regular involvement of the Heads of Government could therefore be a bonus. This consideration also attracted the support of Jean Monnet. At another level, the creation of the European Council was only one part of a package of decisions taken by the Paris Summit, which included setting up a Regional Fund, direct elections to the European Parliament, the abandonment of the Luxembourg compromise, and agreement on a 'corrective mechanism' for the United Kingdom's budgetary contribution to the Community. There was thus something for everyone, even those to whom institutionalized summitry would normally have been anathema.

The Tindemans Report

A further decision taken in Paris to show that the ambitions of the 1972 Paris Summit had not been abandoned was the commission given to Prime Minister Tindemans of Belgium to prepare a report on European Union. The Tindemans Report overtook the various reports drawn up by the Community Institutions in response to the mandate of the 1972 Summit. While drawing largely on them, it deliberately took on a pragmatic, realistic cast designed to be its hallmark. The task given to Tindemans, according to his own account in the letter of transmission to his colleagues, was 'to define what was meant by the term "European Union"'. Tindemans declined the invitation to provide a Constitution for the future Union; instead, he proposed measures which, while remaining part of a continuous process, would make a significant leap forward.

Although the Report covered all areas of current concern including economic and monetary policy, sectoral policies, and social and regional policies, its thrust was founded on a vision of Europe in the world and thus directly affected the way in which foreign policy was decided. Of the six components of European Union identified by Tindemans, the first concerned the Union's external personality:

> European Union implies that we present a united front to the outside world. We must tend to act in common in all the main fields of our external relations whether in foreign policy, security, economic relations or development aid. Our action is aimed at defending our interests but also at using our collective strength in support of law and justice in world discussions.

The convergence of the two factors of vulnerability and relative impotence was given as one of the main reasons why the European Union should have an external policy. To make progress towards this objective, Tindemans proposed three decisions to be taken by the European Council. First, the distinction between EPC and Community meetings at Ministerial level should be abolished. Second, all problems relevant to European interests could be discussed, including security aspects and without the distinction between political and economic, industrial, financial, and commercial questions which made increasingly less sense in the modern world.

These two decisions taken together would set up a single decision-making centre, so that different aspects of problems could be dealt with together, at least at Ministerial level, by the same people and in the same place. Given this single centre, Tindemans proposed a radical change in the nature of Political Co-operation. The political commitment was to be replaced by a legal obligation. In technical terms, it was suggested to amend paragraph 11 of the Copenhagen Report. The implications were far-reaching. Tindemans, proceeding from the logic that Political Co-operation incorporated within its structure the possibility of failure by the pursuit of different policies whenever co-ordination had not been achieved and that the European identity would not be accepted by the outside world so long as the European States appeared sometimes united, sometimes disunited, drew the conclusion that there should be an obligation to reach a common point of view. This meant that the minority must rally to the views of the majority at the conclusion of the debate.

Tindemans went on to make specific proposals for reaching a common policy in four areas which reflected the concerns of the day. These were the new world economic order, relations between Europe and the United States, security, and the crises occurring within Europe's immediate geographical surroundings. The events Tindemans had in mind were the Conference on International Economic Co-operation, the Year of Europe, the CSCE, and crises in the Middle East, Portugal, and Cyprus. The specific proposals made are of less interest today than the method adopted, which was to identify problems on which there seemed a fair chance that the Nine would be able to act in a way which corresponded with Tindemans's conclusions of principle, and which were not politically insignificant.

The approach was to fail. The Report was discussed by the European Council on a number of occasions throughout 1976, only to be buried with faint praise at The Hague in November of that year. It was agreed that the Foreign Ministers and the Commission should present to the European Council annual reports on progress towards European Union. This rapidly became a bureaucratic chore and then an irrelevancy, with the result that on at least one occasion it was totally forgotten without anyone noticing until after the event.

What went wrong? Partly, domestic politics were once again to blame. In all four big Member States the leaders were too concerned with national issues to be able to expend political capital on progress on European integration. Perhaps more significant was the climate of the times. In 1975 economic growth was faltering under the oil shock, and the era of Euro-pessimism, which was to last a decade and more, was beginning to set in. There was no longer any confidence that the Community was a forward-looking and dynamic enterprise with the potential for solving national problems. And the specific proposals of Tindemans on the foreign-policy side, let alone his ideas for internal progress in the Community, involved a loss of sovereignty which Member States were not prepared to contemplate in a period of political and economic retrenchment.

Institutional Innovations

Failure to agree on the great leap forward proposed in the Tindemans Report did not prevent the Nine from continuing to make pragmatic improvements in the functioning of Political Co-operation. In addition to setting up the European Council, the Paris Summit had taken two decisions strengthening the role of the Presidency and granting a limited role to the European Parliament. Paragraph 4 of the Paris text reads:

With a view to progress towards European unity, the Heads of Government reaffirm their determination gradually to adopt common positions and co-ordinate their diplomatic action in all areas of international affairs which affect the interests of the European Community. The President-in-Office will be the spokesman for the Nine and will set out their views in international diplomacy. He will ensure that the necessary concertation always takes place in good time. In view of the increasing role of political co-operation in the construction of Europe, the European Assembly must be more closely associated with the work of the Presidency, for example through replies to questions on political co-operation put to him by its Members.

Strengthening the role of the Presidency reflected what was already a fact of life. The growing profile of the Nine had attracted interest from third countries, particularly at the United Nations, and this, combined with the various *démarches* which were increasingly entrusted to the Presidency, meant that it was an easy matter to formalize the arrangement. Of course, the Presidency exercised its role as spokesman in third countries as well as in its capital. This meant that rules had to be worked out to decide who held the Presidency, since the Presidency-in-Office did not always have a diplomatic representative in the third country concerned. The problem was brought to the attention of the Political Committee in March 1975, in the aftermath of the Paris Summit, but the rules were worked out in the Community framework, which was facing the same problem as that of EPC as the Presidency took on an increasing role in the Community's external relations, and EPC contented itself with endorsing the Council's formula in October 1977.

The implementation of the decision on the European Parliament, on the other hand, required more reflection, as it was the first time EPC had been required to expose itself in this way. The procedures were worked out by the Correspondents with the assistance of a representative of the Commission, since it was thought to be logical for Political Co-operation to model itself on Community practice. The results were approved by Ministers at their meeting in Dublin on 13 February 1975. It was decided that in the first instance the exercise would be limited to written questions; to reply to oral questions at question time was thought to be too difficult, given the need to approve all replies by consensus. The questions would be sent in advance by Parliament to the Presidency of EPC, which would forward copies to the Council and the Commission so that a check could be made that questions of Community or mixed competence were not being addressed to the wrong forum. In fact this procedure was soon abandoned, and for practical reasons questions were sent directly to the Council Presidency which forwarded them to EPC. A draft reply was prepared by the Presidency and circulated for approval by Coreu, the Correspondents acting as a co-ordinating body in case of difficulties. The procedure worked moderately well, except that Parliament had to be reminded to keep questions to matters on which EPC could reply and not to use the procedure as a way of questioning Member States on matters of national policy.

Building the House (1973–1977)

One of the decisions of the Copenhagen Summit concerned crisis management, following the failure of the Nine to respond adequately to the challenge of the October War. After the Summit, Political Co-operation attempted to put into place procedures which would improve their capability in this respect. A report was studied in October 1974 which drew largely on the experience gained in the Nine's initial success over Cyprus. The key to the procedure was the convening by the Presidency, if a Member State thought there was a crisis, of the Ambassadors of partners in the capital of the Presidency. This group would discuss whether an emergency meeting of the Nine was necessary. The need for preparedness and a system of rapid and confidential communications were recognized as being necessary to make this procedure work.

It was also recognized that potential crisis situations had to be detected in advance. This implied medium- and long-term reflection rather than reaction. It was proposed that the Political Committee should identify specific subjects which lent themselves to this sort of treatment and entrust them either to existing Working Groups or to a special group of analysis and research. The proposal hung fire, and was not taken up again until the United Kingdom Presidency of the first half of 1977. A Presidency paper proposing setting up a planning facility met, however, with an unenthusiastic reaction, and the conclusion reached was that the Working Groups were sufficient, which was manifestly not the case. The creation of a Group of Planners had to wait until the German Presidency of 1983, and a crisis procedure was only agreed in 1981, after the Ten's failure to be seen to be coping in time with the Soviet invasion of Afghanistan.

The same dynamic British Presidency of 1977 introduced the *recueil*, or collection of EPC texts adopted in each Presidency, following the previous Belgian Presidency's inauguration of the *coutumier*, or collection of procedural texts. It also encouraged the co-operation of the Nine in third countries which had been growing up spontaneously over the years. A discussion paper was tabled in December 1976 and discussed by the European Correspondents in the following months. The discussion revealed a general readiness to consider further areas for practical co-operation. Although formal directives were not to be adopted until much later, Embassies in third countries came increasingly to realize the sort of co-operation which EPC could offer and thus help develop an *esprit de corps*.

SELECTED READING

The attempt by the Europeans to forge a personality during the Year of Europe is described in Köhler (1982), Kissinger (1982), and Pierre (1974).

In addition to Ifestos (1987) and Greilsammer (1981), the Middle East in this period is covered by de la Serre (1974), van Well (1976), Lieber (1976), and Maull (1976). The two last are particularly instructive on the interplay between politics and economics during the energy crisis.

There are many works on the Euro-Arab Dialogue. Allen (1982), Maull (1980), Bourrinet (1979), and Al-Mani' (1983) among them give a balanced view.

For a view of co-operation at the United Nations at this period, see Hansen (1975).

The beginnings of the European Council can be traced in Bulmer and Wessels (1987) and Moreau Defarges (1988).

5
European Political Co-operation Comes of Age (1978–1981)

ARGUMENT

EPC was now to go through a period of stagnation. For two years it became little more than a forum for the exchange of diplomatic information. The Nine were shaken out of their complacency by the Soviet invasion of Afghanistan. Their embarrassing failure to deal collectively with the crisis provoked them into rethinking their working methods, as well as taking a more active approach to the Arab-Israeli conflict. The Venice Declaration which resulted from this activity petered out, however, in the face of external difficulties and the Nine's own uncertainties, while the policy they eventually worked out on Afghanistan had no greater success. At the same time, other areas continued to be dealt with barely less superficially than in the previous two years. At the end of the period, however, faced with the challenge of enlargement as well as the recollection of Afghanistan, the Nine strengthened their working methods by adopting the London Report, and the movement which was to lead to the Stuttgart Solemn Declaration was under way.

MEETING THE CHALLENGE

It is commonly held that by the end of 1977 EPC had reached a plateau—the Nine could continue more or less with what they were already doing, but it was difficult to do much more on the basis of existing data and structures. This assessment, by participants at the time, may have been too optimistic: EPC had difficulty in maintaining even the level of activity it had previously attained. Throughout 1978 and 1979 Member States' delegations met to exchange information, but few suggested taking an initiative and those who did met with little enthusiasm. Ministerial Meetings, for example that scheduled for 22 November 1978, were cancelled for lack of matter. Partly a cause of this, partly a result, Member States turned to other, more effective, forums for their foreign-policy initiatives—the Contact Group of Five for Namibia, NATO for the CSCE after the Belgrade meeting, even the Western Economic Summits, although these were not designed to deal with foreign-policy questions—or preferred bilateral approaches to diplomacy, like the Anglo-US efforts on Rhodesia.

The reasons for this stagnation are various and hard to pin down. It was partly because, since Political Co-operation had no institutional underpinning, its successful functioning depended more than most on a climate of optimism among the officials who took part in it. If this was lacking, the steam went out of the operation. This climate was certainly affected for the worse by the morosity prevalent in the Community, then suffering from the second oil shock and about to enter the long period of introspection during which attention was concentrated on the British budget problem. These difficulties were compounded by a number of problems peculiar to EPC. After a period of rapid growth, the system was well on the way to becoming bureaucratic. Its working methods and the structure of the Working Groups were well established; an easy routine was not shaken by any calls to innovate. There had been a change in the leading personalities; the Political Directors who had created the system had been replaced by others who found a machine apparently in good working order and were neither aware of the struggles which had gone into its making nor personally so committed to its success. The situation could perhaps have been remedied if a dynamic Presidency had chosen to stimulate the Nine, but this did not occur.

The absence of internal dynamism within the system meant that the Nine failed to discuss the most crucial question of the day, that of East–West relations in Europe. Détente was in decline, the Soviet Union's human-rights record was causing increasing concern, and the stationing of Cruise and Pershing II missiles in Europe was the major topic of public debate. The divisiveness of the issue and its military nature disqualified EPC from acting as a forum for discussion, even though a thorough common analysis of the fundamentals of East–West relations could have underpinned the Nine's position in the debate. The problem was too difficult for EPC; throughout the period there was practically no discussion of East–West relations in Europe, except in relation to the CSCE. The Eastern Europe Working

Group, which could have provided the material for this work, continued to be confined to studies of purely academic interest, mainly on the insistence of France.

Political Co-operation was ill served during the first years of the period by a lack of international crises to which it would have been obliged to react. The Soviet invasion of Afghanistan at the end of 1979 furnished just such an opportunity. The Nine's failure to seize it provided the stimulus which was necessary for them to reassess their co-operation and led directly to the London Report; it also encouraged them to take a bolder line on the Middle East. But EPC's activity on these two questions masked the fact that between the invasion of Afghanistan and the adoption of the London Report the Nine's activities in other areas showed little improvement in quality over the preceding period. EPC's tardy and reluctant decision to impose sanctions, following the taking of the US hostages in Iran, lost credibility because of problems in implementation.

The final and most important reason for the quiescence of EPC can be found in the attitude of France. Under Pompidou France had taken a proprietary interest in Political Co-operation. This enthusiasm now seemed to have waned. Giscard's officials consistently took a restrictive line on all the most important subjects, whether it was the Euro-Arab Dialogue, the strengthening of the Code of Conduct, the improvement of the working methods of EPC, or the CSCE. The French proposal for a conference on disarmament in Europe was launched outside the framework of the Nine. The fact that France held the Presidency during the first six months of 1979, and was reluctant to encourage discussion on questions like the Middle East and Iran, contributed to the general disillusionment with Political Co-operation. The French attitude is hard to understand, given Giscard's more relaxed approach to Europe, and may be attributable to some key officials in the Quai d'Orsay, whose traditionally Gaullist line was given free rein by the diminished interest Giscard and his Ministers showed in EPC as a process. Giscard himself was more concerned with launching the Summit of the Four (at Guadeloupe in 1979).

The small change of diplomatic commerce continued to be handled in EPC, which now counted a dozen or so Working Groups covering subjects ranging from the Middle East, Asia, and Africa to the United Nations and UN-Disarmament. The

Nine followed developments in Cyprus, and intervened from time to time to encourage the UN Secretary-General to press for progress in the intercommunal talks. They decided how to handle the question of the Cambodian seat in the United Nations after the fall of the Pol Pot regime, and were active in promoting the Geneva Conference on the question of the Vietnamese boat people. From time to time *démarches* were made on human-rights cases, whether executions in Ghana or imprisonments in South Korea. The Nine were informed by France of Libya's intervention in Chad, and later of its withdrawal.

EPC was regularly informed by France, Germany, or the United Kingdom of the work of the Contact Group on Namibia, but was content to leave action to that body. Similarly, it was kept fully informed by the United Kingdom, under both the Labour and Conservative governments, of efforts to bring about a settlement in Rhodesia, but limited itself to expressing sympathy, support, and, in the closing stages, congratulations. No progress was made on South Africa. The adoption of the Code of Conduct in 1977 was seen by some Member States as only the first step towards a much firmer policy, culminating in the imposition of sanctions. It had been agreed at the time that 'further possible measures' would continue to be examined, and this exercise continued first as a ritual and then as a farce as successive reports by the Working Group were regularly sent back to it for updating. Meanwhile the Netherlands Parliament was making the Dutch Minister's life difficult by calls for an oil embargo. Nor was the Code itself functioning as had been intended. The United Kingdom's partners took their time in producing their national assessments based on the reports of their firms, some being as much as two years behind, and the British proposal to draw up and publish a joint assessment was long resisted by the French.

The Nine continued their co-ordination on CSCE questions and the machinery which had been set up to deal with the Helsinki Conference remained in existence and was used. Complaints were heard, however, about the quality of the co-ordination at the various meetings which had been agreed on in Belgrade, in particular the Valetta meeting on the Mediterranean. At the next full meeting in Madrid in 1980 EPC co-ordination played a useful part in working out the 'new

EPC Comes of Age (1978–1981)

proposals' which were to be tabled in the name of the Nine and in ensuring that adequate time was made available for reviewing the implementation of the Helsinki Final Act, i.e. the human-rights record of the Soviet Union and the East European countries. Times had changed since Helsinki, however. Détente was no longer so much in favour, the argument was raging over the stationing in Europe of Cruise and Pershing II missiles, and Soviet actions such as the arrest of Sakharov aroused public opinion. The invasion of Afghanistan at one moment endangered the CSCE process. In the circumstances, the United States took a greater interest in the CSCE, as a forum in which to challenge the Soviet Union, than had previously been the case. This led to greater attention being given to co-ordination in NATO rather than in EPC even in the earlier stages of the Madrid meeting, which created difficulties for Ireland as well as for the Commission. The Commission would have been quite happy to take part in NATO co-ordination whenever invited, but this met with objections from the Irish.

The tendency to co-ordinate in NATO was reinforced in the later stages of the Madrid meeting which were largely concerned with the military questions involved in framing the mandate for a Conference on Disarmament in Europe. This had originally been a French initiative, launched in May 1978 outside the EPC framework in order to get the French back into the debate on disarmament from which they had excluded themselves by their refusal to take part in the MBFR talks in Vienna. The idea met with a lukewarm reception from France's partners in the Nine, who feared that the hiving off of security questions from Basket 1 of the Helsinki Final Act, as the French plan originally implied, would lead to an imbalance in the Final Act which would be damaging to the CSCE process as a whole. It was not until their meeting on 20 November 1979 that Ministers gave the support of the Nine to 'an approach aiming at the adoption at Madrid of a mandate establishing the conditions for negotiations with the objective of agreeing by common accord on meaningful confidence building measures in the military field', and even this was subordinated to prior discussion in NATO. Naturally enough, the military aspects of the negotiations, in particular the all-important question of the geographical coverage of the Conference, were co-ordinated in NATO rather than in EPC.

The period was not without some modest progress, however,

in new areas like the Association of South East Asian Nations (ASEAN), Latin America, and judicial co-operation, the latter a new departure for EPC.

Afghanistan

The Soviet invasion of Afghanistan on 26 December 1979 caught Political Co-operation off balance. The Presidency was due to pass from Ireland to Italy at the end of the year, and the Irish Presidency had already packed its bags in anticipation of the handover. The timing, between the Christmas and the New Year holidays, was the worst possible one for EPC to be able to act. The Soviet Ambassadors in the capitals of the Nine made *démarches* to explain their government's move in the period 27–9 December. Member States reacted by issuing national statements. Although many would have preferred the cover of a statement by the Nine, it proved to be too difficult to agree on a text by Coreu. Nor was it possible to reach consensus early in the New Year on the question of whether or not to withdraw Ambassadors from Moscow, following the American example.

The Italian Presidency was slow off the mark when it took over the reins on 1 January. Rome saw no need to call an emergency meeting of the Political Committee, and was content to allow discussion to take place at the meeting of the Asia Working Group already scheduled for 10–11 January. The Italians were even doubtful about organizing a meeting of Ministers in the margins of the General Affairs Council on 15 January, but finally agreed to do this. The Working Group produced a draft declaration to be submitted to Ministers. In the meanwhile there had been intense diplomatic activity in New York. A Security Council Resolution had been vetoed by the Soviet Union and the General Assembly had adopted a Resolution. The Italian Presidency in New York had secured agreement to make a statement in the General Assembly on 10 January on behalf of the Nine, but otherwise Member States had acted on a national basis. The inaction of EPC contrasted with the intensive discussions going on at this time in NATO.

Meetings in both NATO and EPC took place in Brussels on 15 January. However, the NATO Council met at the level of officials, while the Foreign Ministers foregathered for the first time ever in both the EPC and Community frameworks, and were accompanied by their Political Directors as well as by their Permanent Representatives. They adopted, with only minor changes, the draft declaration submitted by the Working Group. In this the Nine took the view that 'the Soviet intervention constitutes a flagrant interference in the internal affairs of a non-aligned country belonging to the Islamic World and constitutes furthermore a threat to peace, security and stability in the region.' They were 'convinced that détente is indivisible and has a global dimension' and urged the Soviet Union to withdraw its troops and allow the Afghan people to determine their own future without foreign interference.

The larger part of the Ministers' discussions was devoted to questions of Community competence. Acting as Council, they confirmed the cancellation of the 1979 food aid programme for Afghanistan which had already been provisionally suspended by the Commission on 9 January. The Council also undertook to decide rapidly on proposals the Commission would make for emergency aid for the Afghan refugees and took steps designed to prevent undercutting of the measures taken by the United States on the export of agricultural produce, especially grain, to the Soviet Union. These had already been discussed in some detail in talks between the Commission and the United States. The Council also ordered further study of the question of export credits.

Ministers returned to the subject in the margins of the General Affairs Council on 5 February, the day on which President Giscard and Chancellor Schmidt issued a not particularly tough joint declaration on Afghanistan in Paris. The Ministers were sufficiently encouraged by an apparent narrowing in the gap between their national positions to instruct the Political Committee to draft a declaration for them to make at their next meeting. Political Directors were not clear whether their instructions were limited to preparing a declaration or went wider than this. The United Kingdom tabled a paper setting out a wide-ranging diplomatic strategy, but France contested that this fell within the Ministerial mandate and in the event discussion concentrated on the draft declaration. The French aim was to seek Soviet withdrawal by diplomatic means, exploring with the Soviet Union the conditions, including guarantees, on which this might be achieved, while the United Kingdom, pointing to the position taken by the third world and more receptive to the firmer American view, wanted withdrawal to be unconditional. Germany, intent on preserving as far as possible its policy of openness towards the Soviet Union, was more inclined to the French position. The same difference of approach prevented consensus on the question of participation in the Olympic Games in Moscow. Subsequently France opposed any idea of a new declaration.

In these unpromising circumstances the Foreign Ministers met in Rome on 19 February and succeeded in producing an inventive declaration which, had it been issued before the January meeting of the Security Council and the 26–9 January emergency meeting of the Islamic Conference, might have had a greater influence on the course of events. They still failed to reach consensus on participation in the Olympic Games.

The initiative came from Lord Carrington, who proposed that the Nine should put forward the idea of a neutral status for Afghanistan, guaranteeing the Soviet Union that the withdrawal of its troops would not lead to a change of camp in Kabul. The British Foreign Secretary drew inspiration for his proposal from the policy of neutralization which the government of India had attempted to apply to Afghanistan at intervals throughout the nineteenth century. This approach rapidly commended itself to Ministers, some of whom had been consulted before the meeting. It was agreed that the Nine should not give the impression of imposing neutrality on the Afghan people against their will. In less than an hour Ministers had agreed on press guidelines in which the Nine, having recalled their previous position, took the view that

> the crisis could be overcome constructively through an arrangement which allows a neutral Afghanistan to be outside competition among the powers. Accordingly, they have decided . . . to concert their position on the subject with all allied and friendly countries and with all countries having an interest in the equilibrium and stability of the region.

The response to this approach was generally favourable, especially from the third world. The Secretary-General of the Islamic Conference said that he thought it was the best way of achieving a solution and offered his full support for implementa-

EPC Comes of Age (1978–1981)   157

tion. The Canadians had apparently been discussing something on similar lines with the Americans. Only the Soviet Union (which, however, was officially unaware of the Nine's text, since there was no consensus to bring it to their attention) and its allies took a negative line. The guidelines of 19 February remained the basis of the Nine's approach and of their diplomatic activity for the next year.

It was not until over a year later, in June 1981, that the Ten decided to take their initiative a stage further. The United Kingdom Presidency was due to begin in July, and Lord Carrington, so closely associated with the February 1980 guidelines, was anxious to find a constructive role for Political Co-operation. There now seemed a better prospect of reaching consensus in the Ten, following the elections in France in May 1981 and the victory of President Mitterrand.

Lord Carrington therefore floated the new initiative in great secrecy at the Ministerial meeting on 22 June in Luxembourg, and it was endorsed by the European Council on 29–30 June. The idea was that there should be a two-stage conference, to be held early in the autumn. The purpose of the first stage would be to work out international arrangements designed to bring about the cessation of external intervention and safeguards to prevent it in the future and thus to create conditions in which Afghanistan's independence and non-alignment could be assured. The participants would include the permanent members of the Security Council and countries of the region as well as the Secretaries-General of the United Nations and the Islamic Conference. The second stage would also include the representatives of the Afghan people and its purpose would be to reach agreement on the implementation of the international arrangements worked out in stage 1.

The United Kingdom transmitted this proposal to the Soviet Union on 23 June, immediately after the Ministerial meeting, and Lord Carrington himself went to Moscow and discussed the question with Mr Gromyko on 6 July. The response was not encouraging. Mr Gromyko described the idea as 'unrealistic', and when the official Soviet reply to the British *aide-mémoire* arrived on 22 July, the position had hardened: the idea was now 'unacceptable'. Lord Carrington drew what crumbs of comfort he could from Mr Gromyko's response. The Soviet Foreign Minister had made no difficulty about dealing with him as spokesman for the Ten, and the prospect of a further meeting in New York in September had been held out.

The meeting in New York duly took place, but there was no change in the Soviet position. The Ten's initiative had failed in its object of bringing about a settlement of the Afghan problem, perhaps not surprisingly, since it was based on the political premiss which the Soviet Union had rejected the previous year, even though the European Council had been careful to refer to 'non-alignment' rather than to 'neutrality'. Nevertheless the fact that the Ten had been able to take this initiative, together with the Venice Declaration and the move to improve the working methods of Political Co-operation which led to the London Report, all to a marked degree attributable to Lord Carrington's interest in EPC as a process, showed that the Ten had taken the charge of stagnation to heart. The Afghanistan initiative also heightened their profile in world affairs, especially in the third world and with the countries of the Islamic Conference, and provided a firm area of agreement for the political discussions with the ASEAN countries which took place in October 1981, thus helping to cement that relationship.

The Venice Declaration

President Sadat's bold and glamorous journey to Jerusalem in November 1977 could not fail to strike the imagination. It would have been difficult for the Nine to withold approbation of what appeared to be a brave new initiative for peace, and they did not attempt to do so. The French initially had doubts, both because of the unpopularity of the move in the Arab world and because of its unfavourable implications for French policy, for which after many years' diplomatic toil they had achieved a large measure of endorsement by the Nine. However, in the end they bowed to the popular mood and joined with the Germans in putting forward a draft which served as the basis for the declaration the Nine made on 22 November. There was also thought to have been American pressure for the Nine to come out in public support of the Sadat initiative.

The declaration expressed support for the 'bold initiative of President Sadat' and the 'unprecedented dialogue begun in Jerusalem'. It also repeated the cardinal points of the Nine's policy. The Nine expressed the hope that the Israeli-Egyptian dialogue 'would open the way to a comprehensive negotiation leading to a just and lasting overall settlement taking account of the rights and concerns of all parties involved', and pointed out that 'it is a matter of urgency that genuine peace at last be achieved for all the peoples in the area, including the Palestinian people, on the basis of principles recognized by the international community and embodied in particular in the declaration of the European Council of 29 June 1977.' The Nine expressed 'the hope that it will be possible in the near future to convene the Geneva conference'. With hindsight, this language has been interpreted as covertly sapping the Sadat initiative while paying it lip-service. It should not be too harshly judged. At the time of President Sadat's visit to Jerusalem, it was not a foregone conclusion that the method chosen was not one way among others of achieving a global settlement, on lines consistent with the London Declaration of the Nine. This was revealed only in the course of time.

In fact, the initiative had changed the rules for policy-making on the Middle East. The Nine's London Declaration of 29 June 1977 had been based on the premiss of an international community united in its efforts to bring about a negotiated global peace, with a homeland for the Palestinians as a key element and the Geneva Conference as the ultimate forum. The Carter Administration had appeared to share this broad approach and had joined with the Soviet Union in a joint statement on 1 October 1977 in which the two co-chairmen undertook to work for a resumption of the Geneva Conference not later than December of that year. Now all this was changed. The Arab world was split. The most important country in it was prepared to do business with Israel, negotiating a step-by-step approach in which the Palestinian question was reduced to one of local autonomy. The United States backed this approach, closing the door to wider international involvement. Most important of all for the Europeans, the Sadat initiative consecrated the United States' role as exclusive arbiter in the Arab–Israeli conflict. There was no more talk of the Geneva Conference; as long as the Sadat approach was being followed, the Europeans had to content themselves with the role of political observers.

The Nine kept a low profile for as long as the Camp David process continued with any chance of success. They were put under pressure, in different directions, by both Egypt and the other Arab countries. President Sadat twice pressed the Nine in the early part of 1978 to ease the pressure on him by playing a more active role, bringing out in particular the question of a Palestinian homeland and the application of Resolution 242. It was in response to this that following the European Council on 7–8 April the Presidency indicated to the press that Resolution 242 should be 'applied in all its parts and on all fronts'. That apart, the Nine made no effort to revise the position taken in the London Declaration, preferring to await the outcome of the Camp David discussions.

Their silence was broken on the conclusion of the Camp David agreements on 17 September 1978. Two days later, the Nine issued a bald statement of support, congratulating President Carter on his successful conclusion of the Camp David meeting and expressing their appreciation for the efforts of President Sadat and Prime Minister Begin. They recalled, however, that their welcome for the Sadat initiative had been based on the position set out in the London Declaration and in expressing their hope that the 'outcome of the Camp David Conference will be a further major step on the path to a just, comprehensive and lasting peace, and that all parties concerned will find it possible to join in the process to contribute to that end' did not commit themselves as to the likelihood of their hope being fulfilled.

The Nine's judgement of the future course of the Camp David process was going to depend on the extent to which it kept open the way to a global settlement. The Peace Treaty between Egypt and Israel, signed on 26 March 1979, was not thought to be encouraging in this respect. The Nine had a declaration ready, which had been worked out at a restricted meeting of the Political Committee three days previously during which widely differing points of view, in particular between the United Kingdom and France, had been brought together only with difficulty. France took the view that the Treaty had removed a lever on Israel, whereas the others thought that it might be a step in the right direction, provided that Israel did not harden its position towards the other Arabs. The resulting statement gave only qualified and lukewarm approval to the Treaty, which, it considered, 'constitutes a correct application of the principles of that resolution (242) to Egyptian-Israeli relations.' The Nine renewed their call for 'a comprehensive settlement translating into fact the right of the Palestinian people to a homeland'. The Nine concluded with a reference to the Israeli policy of settlements in the occupied territories as impeding the search for peace.

Ever since the Sadat visit to Jerusalem, the Nine had confined their comments on the Arab-Israeli conflict to those occasions when it could not be avoided, whether it be a meeting of the European Council or some external event like the signing of the Camp David agreements or the Egypt–Israel Treaty. This public silence was accompanied by a dearth of internal discussion. One reason why the London Declaration was a point of reference in the comments that were made was because it would have been extremely difficult to agree on anything else. France was determined to maintain the policy expressed in the Declaration, which broadly represented its own views. The Netherlands and Denmark took a line traditionally closer to Israel. The United Kingdom of Mr Callaghan and Dr Owen and the Federal Republic of Chancellor Schmidt were inclined to give more weight to relations with the United States, which looked to the Europeans to give their support to the Camp David process, but otherwise to keep out of the kitchen. It is a measure of the low ebb Political Co-operation had reached that little attempt was made to face these differences squarely. Indeed, during the first few months of 1979, the impression was gained that the French Presidency was deliberately keeping the Middle East off the EPC agenda.

The repercussions of the Egypt–Israel Treaty in the Arab world obliged the Nine, however unwillingly, to engage in further reflection. Egyptian membership of the Arab League was suspended and the League's secretariat was moved from Cairo to Tunis. Hitherto moderate Arab countries joined the countries of the Steadfastness Front in wholehearted opposition to the Camp David process. The Arabs took the initiative of suspending the Euro-Arab Dialogue. France therefore launched a fresh round of consultations involving Ministers at their Gymnich-type meeting at the Château de Mercues and a special restricted meeting of the Political Committee, which led to the Declaration adopted by the Nine in Paris on 18 June.

The statement's imbalance against Israel was intentional. The Nine summarized their position with references to the declarations of 29 June 1977 and 25 March 1979. This summary traditionally led off with a reference to the 'inadmissibility of the acquisition of territory by force' and the 'need for Israel to end the territorial occupation which it has maintained since the conflict of 1967'. The Nine quoted the 'Israeli claim to permanent sovereignty over the occupied territories' and 'the policy of settlements pursued by the Israeli government in the occupied territories' as being examples of attitudes 'such as to create obstacles in the search for . . . a comprehensive settlement.' They concluded with an indirect reference to the activities of Israel in the south of Lebanon and the difficulties encountered by the United Nations Interim Force in the Lebanon (UNIFIL). This forthright condemnation was categorically rejected by Israel; it received only moderate praise from the Arabs, who thought that the Nine should have gone further.

This leap towards the Arab position proved, however, to be a flash in the pan. Under the Irish Presidency, which began on 1 July, the Nine relapsed into their previous attitude of waiting to see what the Camp David process, now embarked on the discussion of autonomy for the Palestinians in the Gaza strip and Cisjordan, would bring forth. The sole exception to this was the speech which the Irish President-in-Office gave to the General Assembly of the United Nations on 26 September 1979. Mr O'Kennedy, referring to the legitimate rights of the Palestinian people, said that 'these include the right to a homeland and the right, through its representatives, to play its full part in the negotiation of a comprehensive settlement.' He added that it was necessary for Resolutions 242 and 338 'to be accepted by all those involved—including the Palestine Liberation Organization —as the basis for negotiation'. It required an expert to detect that this represented a step forward in the Nine's position. The phrasing on Palestinian participation in the negotiations was more forthcoming and the PLO was mentioned for the first time in a text of the Nine, although the ambiguity of the reference was such that its favourable reception by the PLO was in doubt. In another advance on their previous position, the Nine also declared that they did not accept any unilateral moves claiming to change the status of Jerusalem. In votes in the General Assembly they showed their move towards the Arabs and away from Israel by abstaining where previously some of them would have voted against.

EPC Comes of Age (1978–1981)

It was against a background of disillusionment with the Camp David process, now increasingly unlikely to produce results in the autonomy talks, that the Nine began in the early part of 1980 to consider whether they should attempt to resume the role in the Middle East which they had been forced to lay to one side over two years earlier. If the attempt was to succeed, fresh thought would have to be given to the Nine's position on the Palestinian question, for the Arabs had left the world in no doubt that this was now the key to the solution of the Arab-Israeli conflict. In reality, this move had already begun the previous autumn, when the French, who had long taken this point of view, were joined by the British. Following Mrs Thatcher's victory in the May 1979 elections, the installation of a new team at the Foreign Office with long experience of the Middle East had made it possible to take a fresh look at policy in the area. Lord Carrington told the UN General Assembly in September that Resolution 242 was incomplete in the handling of Palestinian rights, and the adoption of a new Security Council Resolution to remedy that flaw became in the following months an objective of British foreign policy. In February 1980 he was openly declaring that, as the Camp David process had come to a halt, a European initiative had become a necessity. President Giscard took a similar line following his visit in March to the Gulf and Jordan, during which he had called for Palestinian self-determination and indicated that all interested parties 'must be included in the negotiations, notably the Palestinian people, which implies the participation of the PLO.'

The Nine were also stimulated into a more active approach by the débâcle over Afghanistan at the turn of the year, which had given rise to much criticism of Political Co-operation as a process on the part of those Europeans who were attached to its success. No doubt the Nine would have reviewed their policy on the Middle East in any case, but the knowledge that EPC was in dire need of more substance acted as an additional spur. The possibility of a new initiative was discussed by the Political Committee and by Ministers in March, and the idea was agreed in principle, it being understood that nothing should be attempted until after the expected failure of the Camp David autonomy talks on the expiry of the deadline on 26 May. At the same time, the Euro-Arab Dialogue was to be resumed on a wider basis, to include a political dimension. The Luxembourg

European Council, 'conscious that Europe may in due course have a role to play', announced on 28 April 1980 that it had instructed Foreign Ministers to submit a report on the problem on the occasion of its June session in Venice.

The political guidelines were set by Foreign Ministers at their Gymnich-type meeting in Naples on 17–18 May. The analysis of the situation was not contested. The situation in the Middle East was deteriorating; the risk of the oil weapon was not excluded; the initiative could fill a dangerous political gap between the presumed collapse of the autonomy talks on 26 May and the US Presidential elections in November; any implication that Camp David was finished would nevertheless be avoided; and the Nine would see how best to act in the United Nations, whether through the Security Council or the General Assembly. Elements of a possible Security Council Resolution could be studied.

The United States, Israel, and Egypt now launched a full-scale campaign to deter the Nine from pursuing their intentions. In the month which followed, the Member States were put under relentless diplomatic pressure. The most blunt statement of the United States' position was made by President Carter in an interview with Cable News Network on 31 May, which had a telling effect in the capitals of the Nine. President Carter said

I don't believe that the Europeans will make any move within the next couple of weeks;

We are encouraging the European allies not to intervene in the negotiations as long as we are meeting and are making progress toward a Mideast peace settlement;

... even if they do come in, we will not permit the United Nations any action that would destroy the sanctity of the present form of UN 242;

... we have a veto power that we can exercise ... to prevent this Camp David process from being destroyed or subverted, and I would not hesitate to use it if necessary.

These pressures were effective. At the beginning of June the Italian Foreign Minister visited Washington to explain to Secretary of State Muskie that the Europeans did not want to oppose Camp David, and only wanted to be constructive. The idea of promoting a successor to Resolution 242 was abandoned in the face of the threatened US veto, the references to the Palestinians were heavily toned down and the relaunch of the

Euro-Arab dialogue, which Egypt did not want to have a political dimension in its absence, was dissociated from the European initiative on the Arab-Israeli conflict. The declaration made by the European Council in Venice on 13 June 1980 was striking enough, but it was modest in comparison with what had originally been envisaged. After referring to growing tensions affecting the region, the Nine claimed a special role which required them to work in a more concrete way towards peace. They recalled the bases of their policy so far and the two guiding principles of 'the right to existence and security of all the States in the region, including Israel, and justice for all the peoples, which implies the recognition of the legitimate rights of the Palestinian people'. The declaration went further than previous statements on the question of the Palestinians. The right to self-determination was expressly recognized ('The Palestinian people, which is conscious of existing as such, must be placed in a position, by an appropriate process defined within the framework of the comprehensive peace settlement, to exercise fully its right to self-determination'), and it was acknowledged that the PLO had a role to play ('These principles must be respected by all the parties concerned, and thus by the Palestinian people, and by the PLO, which will have to be associated with the negotiations'—a position which had been foreshadowed in the O'Kennedy speech and by President Giscard's March visit to the Gulf). As regards the procedure, the Nine announced that they had decided 'to make the necessary contacts with all the parties concerned . . . and, in the light of the results of this consultation process, to determine the form which an initiative on their part could take.'

The Israeli reaction was predictably vehement: 'Nothing will remain of the Venice decision but a bitter memory.' In one of Prime Minister Begin's favourite historical images, the Declaration was likened to 'a Munich surrender . . . to totalitarian blackmail'. That of the PLO leadership was equally negative: ' . . . it ignores the fundamental factors for the establishment of a just peace'; '. . . the Europeans have yielded to US blackmail.' This disappointment came from the fact that the Palestinians' expectations had been raised very high and in the event had not been satisfied. There had been no rejection of the Camp David process; no move to revise Resolution 242; and no recognition of the PLO as sole representative. No wonder that the PLO executive committee claimed on 16 June that the statement 'is largely a clear response to the US will and pressures.' The reaction from moderate Arab countries like Jordan and Saudi Arabia was however more constructive and recognized that the Europeans had taken an important step forward. The United States put a brave face on it. Secretary Muskie said that he did not 'see anything on the face of it which directly challenges the Camp David process' and implied that American pressure had succeeded in moderating the language used on the PLO ('association' instead of 'participation').

The Nine now had to decide how to follow up the Venice Declaration and in particular how to organize their contacts with all interested parties. The European Council had given no guidance on this question. The problem was a difficult one. The Nine found themselves in a tactical position not of their choosing. The original idea, of promoting an update of Resolution 242, was ruled out by the American attitude. The fallback position, of organizing soundings with those concerned, was likely to run up against the difficulty that the content of the Venice Declaration left the Nine in a weak position with both Israel and the PLO. They might have some chance of bringing influence to bear on the United States, but this was an inglorious ambition compared with the European initiative which had been bruited before Venice.

It was in these daunting conditions that Gaston Thorn, in his capacity as the Luxembourg Presidency Foreign Minister from 1 July, began a series of visits throughout the summer to Washington and the countries of the Middle East. The mission was in itself an institutional innovation in Political Co-operation. It was the first time that a President-in-Office had been allowed to take on a task of such wide-ranging diplomatic importance without detailed instructions from his colleagues about what he was to say. M. Thorn chose to be assisted by one or two Luxembourg diplomats, although the idea had been mooted that he might be accompanied by diplomats from other Member States. The Troika concept was not yet firmly established; at a later date the Presidency Foreign Minister would certainly not have been allowed to go alone.

The round of visits revealed two sets of difficulties which the Nine attempted to address throughout the autumn. The first was uncertainty about the nature of their role. Were the Nine to influence those with influence, or to take an initiative of their own? And was the initiative of the Nine still to come, or was the Venice Declaration their initiative? Secondly, what did the Venice Declaration mean? Some notions contained in the Declaration such as 'self-determination' or 'putting an end to territorial occupation', were given widely differing interpretations by the interested parties. The closer definition of these notions occupied the Nine for much of the period up to the European Council in December.

The effort proved to be in vain. There was not even agreement to publish the documents which had been prepared, although they were later comprehensively leaked. Whereas in the spring the Nine had wished to fill the gap between 26 May and the US presidential elections, in the autumn they preferred to delay a decision on what to do next until the new US Administration had had a chance to work out its position. This was particularly the case after 4 November when President Carter failed to secure re-election. In a volte-face reflecting the fact that the Thatcher government felt more comfortable with Reagan than with Carter, Lord Carrington said on 14 November that the United Kingdom wanted to wait and, for the time being, restrain European efforts in the Middle East. This brought forth a stinging rebuke from the French. The convergence between the British and the French positions, which had proved indispensable for the Venice Declaration, was in danger. The European Council on 2 December could do no more than ask the incoming Netherlands Presidency to begin a fresh round of contacts.

Given the traditional position of the Netherlands and the criticism to which it had been subjected by Israel, it was scarcely to be expected that Mr van der Klaauw would approach his task with much enthusiasm. The Presidency's natural reticence was reinforced by the tougher approach taken by the new Reagan Administration, which not only continued to exclude talks with the PLO as long as it refused to accept Resolution 242, but also placed greater emphasis on stemming Soviet influence in the area than on resolving the Arab-Israeli conflict. The United States remained unalterably opposed to a European initiative outside the Camp David process. This stage of the Venice initiative was finally exhausted when the arrival of President

Mitterrand at the Élysée in May 1981 brought about a shift in French policy to one more favourable to Israel and the Camp David process and the rejection of the procedure, though not the principles, of the Venice Declaration. In the view of France, explicitly confirmed later in the year by the Foreign Minister, Claude Cheysson, there would be no European initiative. Henceforth national diplomacy on the Middle East again came to the fore. The efforts of the Ten concentrated on exploring the possibilities of practical confidence-building measures.

The Venice Declaration remained the point of reference for the Ten in their subsequent statements on the Middle East. It had served a useful purpose in bringing Member States closer to the Arab position. It had provided a striking example of EPC's capability to produce a bold initiative, at a time when such a demonstration was sorely needed. It had failed to open a new way towards a settlement of the Arab-Israeli conflict. That result might have been achieved if the Nine had unambiguously offered to hold the stakes between Israel and the PLO. This was in fact what President Sadat proposed in his speech to the European Parliament in February 1981 when he spoke of the Europeans helping to persuade both Israelis and Palestinians to accept a 'formula of mutual and simultaneous recognition'. That they did not succeed was not entirely the fault of the Nine, given the traditional differences among Member States and the strains to which they were subjected by outside pressure. It was, however, a weakness of Political Co-operation that it had no mechanism to throw up a bold initiative transcending national differences, and it was a weakness that, six years after the Gymnich arrangement, the nature of the Nine's relationship with the United States remained unresolved.

The Iran Hostage Crisis

Although the Nine had kept an eye on the situation in Iran throughout 1978, this had not led to any concerted action beyond close co-ordination among Embassies in Tehran on matters like possible evacuation. This changed as a result of the seizure by student revolutionaries of the US Embassy in Tehran on 4 November 1979 when sixty-three Americans and others were taken hostage. The United States reacted by putting an embargo on the import of oil from Iran on 12 November and by freezing Iranian assets in the United States on 14 November. Joining in the international condemnation, the Nine issued on 20 November a statement rejecting the violation of international law and calling for the release of the hostages. This was backed up by a joint *démarche* in Iran. The statement was reaffirmed by the European Council on 29–30 November. In addition to these public declarations, useful work was done by the Ambassadors of the Nine in Tehran, of which the United States was kept fully informed. The Political Committee was happy to allow the Ambassadors to use their collective judgement about what would be the most helpful action on the spot.

At first the United States tried to mobilize the pressure of international public opinion to force the Iranian government to release the hostages. As the year drew to a close and these tactics seemed less and less likely to succeed, the US Administration turned its attention to securing support for economic sanctions. On 4 December the Security Council called for the release of the hostages and a peaceful settlement and expressed support for the Secretary-General's mission of good offices, but went no further at that stage. A further resolution imposing sanctions was vetoed by the Soviet Union on 13 January, a fortnight after the invasion of Afghanistan. The United States thereupon announced unilateral action and started to apply pressure on its allies to line up behind it.

The prospect caused some disquiet among the Member States, none of which was unreservedly in favour of sanctions. It was thought that they could even be counter-productive, making the position of the moderates in Tehran more difficult and driving Iran into the arms of the Soviet Union. It was therefore with some relief that the Nine noted a relaxation of American pressure as negotiations with the Iranians continued and seemed to have some chance of success. These hopes were, however, disappointed at the beginning of April in circumstances of maximum embarrassment to President Carter, who had announced on the morning of the Wisconsin primary that the hostages were about to be released. On 9 April, therefore, the United States appealed to its allies to join in the sanctions and to strengthen them. Military action against Iran was threatened if the allies failed to respond.

By chance the Foreign Ministers of the Nine were all in Lisbon on 10 April for a meeting of the Committee of Ministers of the Council of Europe. They took the opportunity to discuss how to respond. Although the question of Community sanctions was under consideration, no one thought to invite the Commission, which was not even informed of the outcome. A decision was put off. The Ministers announced that they would decide on their position after having made a further *démarche* in Tehran.

The *démarche* was fruitless, but the Nine still did not lose hope that the threat of sanctions, rather than their reality, might have some effect. After preparation in both Coreper and the Political Committee, the Ministers resumed their discussions in the margins of the Council meeting on 22 April in Luxembourg. Community sanctions had been ruled out in the preparatory discussions as a result of the opposition of France and Denmark. The Ministers therefore announced that, in view of the fact that the persistence of the situation imperilled international peace and security, they had decided to seek immediate legislation where necessary in their national Parliaments to impose sanctions on the lines of those which would have been mandatory had the Security Council draft resolution not been vetoed. These legislative processes should be completed before the Ministers' next informal meeting due to take place on 17–18 May in Naples. If no decisive progress had been made by then, the Nine would proceed immediately to the common application of the sanctions.

This decision apparently succeeded in its immediate objective. The White House let it be known that any military action would as a result be delayed until the summer. The Nine did not know at the time that, on the very day they had been meeting in Luxembourg, President Carter had taken the decision to go ahead with the hostage-rescue operation on 24 April. The embarrassing failure of this operation was tactfully ignored, but enabled the European Council on 28 April to place itself on a higher level of generality also covering the situation in Afghanistan and the Middle East.

The Naples meeting confirmed the sanctions decision. The Ministers decided on the immediate implementation of the Security Council's January draft measures in jointly fixed conditions and modalities. All contracts concluded after 4 November 1979 were to be covered by the embargo. A drawback in the decision to prefer national to Community measures soon showed itself. The United Kingdom proved unable to deliver. There was a rebellion in Parliament both by Labour and by many Conservatives, and it was only with difficulty, on 29 May, that the United Kingdom was able to announce its decision to implement sanctions, and then not retroactively.

The episode marked a serious decline in the confidence of the Nine in President Carter's ability to steer a steady course and a worsening in relations between the Nine and the United States. At the same time the perceived shortcomings of Washington emboldened the Nine to strike out for themselves in both the Middle East and Afghanistan and to hesitate long before responding to the call for sanctions over the Iran hostages. The attitude taken by the Nine was not without influence in the world, thus showing the extent to which EPC positions had come to be a respectable point of reference for third countries anxious not to commit themselves without being sure of company. In the case of the Iran hostages, Japan took care to align itself on the position of the Nine. The Japanese Foreign Minister, Mr Okita, even took the trouble to go to Luxembourg on 21 April and to meet five of the Foreign Ministers and the President of the Commission before the 22 April Council meeting. The Japanese had been similarly concerned to know the Nine's position before taking their own decision about participation in the Moscow Olympic Games. Under similar pressure from the United States, the Japanese found a convenient refuge in the position of the Nine.

Enlargement

In the first part of 1978 Member States had to tackle the problem of how to absorb a new member into Political Co-operation. Negotiations for the accession of Greece to the Community were proceeding apace, and Portugal and Spain were not far behind. The question arose of what parallel moves should be made in EPC. It was assumed that membership of the Community entailed membership of Political Co-operation; the possibility of one without the other was not seriously envisaged.

This was in fact the first time that Member States had had to give thought to the question. Although Political Co-operation had been in existence for three years when the first enlargement took place, its creation had been so bound up with the accession of the United Kingdom, Denmark, and Ireland that those countries had been closely involved from the start. In the eight years of its existence Political Co-operation had developed an inheritance of collective experience which a new member would have to accept. How this was to be done, together with the procedures for the progressive association of Greece before actual accession, was the subject of long and difficult discussions among the Nine.

Two additional questions had to be addressed. The United Kingdom insisted that the opportunity should be taken to review the adequacy of the existing arrangements of EPC. The ideas for change centred on providing more support for an increasingly burdened Presidency as foreseen in the Copenhagen Report. In 1977 Belgium had borrowed a staff member from the outgoing British Presidency for this purpose and had in its turn lent one to the Danish Presidency in the first half of 1978; Ireland and Italy made a similar exchange in 1979 and 1980. The practice was found to be useful and reappeared in strengthened form in the Troika Secretariat established by the London Report of 1981.

Although there was some support for the idea of strengthening EPC procedures, there was no consensus. France in particular took the view that the existing procedures were adequate to cope with enlargement to Ten, or even Twelve, and should be kept flexible, and other Member States like the Netherlands may have thought that minor changes of the sort being discussed would reduce the pressure for the more radical changes which they favoured. In any event, no one wanted to insist on change to the extent of blocking a decision on the immediate issue of Greek accession, and so the question was dropped for the time being.

The second question concerned the way in which Turkey should be treated as Greece became associated with, and later joined, EPC. It was clear that the arrival of Greece would complicate the discussion of Eastern Mediterranean issues, namely Cyprus, and a formula for involving Turkey at least in those discussions had to be found. Membership of EPC was excluded as long as Turkey was not a member of the Com-

EPC Comes of Age (1978–1981)

munity, but in view of Turkey's entitlement, alone among third countries, to ultimate membership of the Community as well as because of its membership of NATO, some form of external, but special, relationship was required. The nature of that relationship was hotly contested. The United Kingdom was strongly in favour of formal consultations on East Mediterranean affairs, while France was opposed to any formula which gave the impression of *de facto* membership. Germany and Belgium leaned to the British view, and the Netherlands and Ireland to the French. The compromise which was reached ruled out consultation meetings with all the Nine and provided instead for reciprocal information meetings with the Presidency accompanied by representatives of the past and future Presidencies. This mechanism, which was copied from the Troika familiar in the Euro-Arab Dialogue, was designed to cope with the situation which would arise under a Greek Presidency. In fact, the proposals were found to be inadequate by the Ecevit government and were only agreed under the Demirel government in early 1981.

The Nine having agreed on how to deal with Turkey, the way was clear to invite Greece to accept the *acquis* of EPC. This was done on the occasion of the Ministerial Meeting held with Greece as part of the enlargement negotiations on 26 June 1978. By *acquis* was meant the corpus of procedures which EPC had accumulated over the years. The documents transmitted were the Luxembourg and Copenhagen Reports, the Document on the European Identity, and a collection of procedural texts. The Presidency indicated in a letter addressed to the Greek Minister that the Nine expected Greece, at the time of the signature of the Accession Treaty, to give an undertaking to take part in EPC with all its attendant rights and obligations. The Greek acknowledgement of the Presidency's letter was the official act by which Greece signified its readiness to accede to Political Co-operation as well as to the Community. It was not until the following September that the Presidency transmitted to Greece a collection of the most important statements of EPC. These were not part of the *acquis*, and acceptance of them was not required. Indeed, it was problematic whether all the Member States would still have been able to subscribe to every word of them, not surprisingly, given the shifting nature of international and domestic politics.

In this respect the common inheritance of Political Co-operation was different from that of the Community, founded in immutable legal texts.

The need to prepare the collections of rules of procedure and of the most important documents led the Nine to codify two practices which had already grown up informally. The Germans had first put together a collection of the disparate texts, adopted piecemeal as the need arose, by which the Nine managed their affairs. This was now put into order by the European Correspondents, and became known as the *coutumier*. Responsibility for keeping it up to date lay with the Presidency, but until the advent of the Secretariat Belgium traditionally produced and circulated to partners successive editions. The basis for the collection of most important documents was a practice begun by Belgium whereby each Presidency produced and sent to partners a bound collection of the most important EPC documents during its term of office. These collections became known as the *recueil* and were the only official archives of Political Co-operation.

In addition to the communication to Greece, the Nine decided on the procedures whereby Greece would gradually be associated with Political Co-operation before accession. It was not thought appropriate to repeat the practice of the first enlargement, when the candidate countries had participated fully in EPC from the signature of the Accession Treaty. Bearing in mind the experience with Norway, which had had to be excluded from association with the Six following the referendum decision rejecting accession to the Community, the Nine preferred now to provide for Greek association in stages. After signature of the Accession Treaty in May 1979 the Nine moved from the stage of information to consultation. The Presidency communicated Political Committee agendas to Greece in advance and circulated Greek comments to partners, and the Greek Political Director was invited to meet his colleagues of the Nine in the margins of the European Council meetings in Strasbourg and Luxembourg in June 1979 and April 1980. Although the Accession Treaty was ratified on 25 June 1980, Greece's participation as an observer did not begin until the Ministerial Meeting on 4 November and the Political Committee on 4–5 December. Greece participated fully in EPC as from accession on 1 January 1981.

THE LONDON REPORT

The attempt in the early part of 1978 to use the opportunity afforded by enlargement to strengthen the working methods of Political Co-operation had not been persisted in. The question nevertheless surfaced from time to time. Towards the end of the year the Political Committee decided to hold a special session in March 1979 to discuss the evolution and possible improvement of EPC. The discussions duly took place and were apparently not unfruitful, but no record was made by the French Presidency and when the European Correspondents came to put something down on paper later in the year the apparent prospects for progress had disappeared.

The failure of EPC to react immediately after the Soviet invasion of Afghanistan in December 1979 gave the stimulus required to set discussion in motion again, this time reinforced by the consciousness of the Ministers themselves that the shortcomings of their foreign-policy co-ordination had been embarrassingly exposed. Lord Carrington was particularly acerbic in his criticisms of EPC, the force of his strictures reflecting the value he attached to the process. At the Ministerial Meetings in February 1980 he criticized the slow and unco-ordinated action of the Nine and proposed that an automatic mechanism for crisis consultations should be introduced. To the press he was even more outspoken, later describing the imbroglio as 'frankly . . . a bit of a mess'.

The lesson was not immediately taken to heart. True, Political Co-operation had its plate full with the Afghanistan problem itself as well as with the American hostages in Iran and the preparation of the Venice Declaration. But it took two speeches by the Foreign Office Minister Douglas Hurd, one in the House of Commons on 31 July and another to the Conservative Summer School at Oxford, which drew some attention from the United Kingdom's partners in the Community, before Political Co-operation got down to considering the possibility of improving the machinery. The British approach focused on the need for rapid decision-making, a strengthened commitment to EPC, and possibly a permanent staff for the Presidency. As Mr Hurd said to the House, 'These are limited but practical suggestions for improving what is clearly one of the success stories of the Community.'

Lord Carrington explained his ideas to his colleagues at the Gymnich-type meeting at Echternach on 25 October and later set them out publicly in a speech to the Übersee Club in Hamburg on 17 November. As part of a visionary programme for the Europe of the 1980s, he made three concrete proposals on EPC. First, the Ten should re-examine their political commitment to EPC and should try to find ways of co-operating more closely and committing a greater part of their national diplomatic efforts to the furthering of Europe's common objectives. Secondly, Political Co-operation should have the support of an experienced foreign-policy staff, perhaps seconded temporarily from Member States, which would enable it to give a stronger lead to the Community. This staff would not need to be large in number, but would need to be of high quality. Finally, Lord Carrington suggested a procedure for convening meetings automatically within forty-eight hours if any three of the Ten believed that there was a crisis which required rapid consultations.

The proposals which were discussed by the Correspondents and the Political Committee during the ensuing Dutch Presidency naturally did not stop there. Other suggestions flooded in. The German Delegation in particular was aware that their Minister had made a speech in Stuttgart in January calling for a much more radical approach to Political Co-operation, and indeed to European Union, which was to lead later in the year to the Genscher–Colombo proposals and ultimately to the Stuttgart Solemn Declaration. Among Mr Genscher's proposals was one to extend Political Co-operation's ambit to include security questions, which found support from Lord Carrington. The mood in the Political Committee, however, was to keep ambition within modest limits and eliminate any 'unrealistic' suggestions. This approach was confirmed by Foreign Ministers when they met informally at Venlo on 9–10 May 1981, and it was on that basis that a draft report was prepared. There was little evolution on the strengthening of the 'commitment to EPC' (the obligation to accept common disciplines), the least adventurous option in place of a permanent secretariat had the preference of the majority, little advance was made on relations with the European Parliament, the Commission was still not to be

EPC Comes of Age (1978–1981)

admitted to all EPC meetings, and Ireland together with other Member States opposed any new role for EPC on security questions.

The coming to power of President Mitterrand in May 1981, and in particular the appointment of a former Member of the Commission, Claude Cheysson, as French Foreign Minister meant that progress could now be made on at least some of these points. At their Gymnich-type meeting at Brocket Hall on 5–6 September there was agreement on a support team of three diplomats for the Presidency, on a slightly more forthcoming approach to Parliament, and on the crisis procedure. Above all, France withdrew its objection to the Commission's full association with Political Co-operation at all levels. On the other hand, Ireland continued its opposition to any advance on security questions.

The Report incorporating these changes was adopted by the Foreign Ministers at their meeting on 13 October 1981 and became the London Report, the third in the series, after the Luxembourg and Copenhagen Reports, which laid down the guidelines for Political Co-operation until the adoption of the Single European Act. If it broke less new ground than its predecessors, it nevertheless provided a useful compilation of procedures introduced over the eight years since the last Report and a signal that Political Co-operation was institutionally on the move again after a long period of stagnation. Two of its innovations were of direct operational significance, the Troika Secretariat and the full association of the Commission and the emphasis given to the role of the Presidency, particularly for contacts with third countries, reflected an important new trend in EPC.

Part I of the Report has the form of a preamble in which the merits of Political Co-operation are extolled and the need for it justified, especially in a period of increased world tension and uncertainty. Amidst the verbiage three concepts stand out. It is stated that 'Political Co-operation . . . has developed to become a central element in the foreign policies of all member states.' This assertion, although not strictly accurate, would have been inconceivable only a few years before. It is, if nothing else, a measure of how large EPC now loomed in the consciousness of its practitioners.

Secondly, security was for the first time mentioned as a legitimate concern of EPC:

As regards the scope of European Political Co-operation, and having regard to the different situations of the member states, the Foreign Ministers agree to maintain the flexible and pragmatic approach which has made it possible to discuss in Political Co-operation certain important foreign policy questions bearing on the political aspects of security.

This was as far as the Irish were prepared to go, and they maintained that it was no further than EPC had already gone. Lord Carrington confirmed at the press conference after the Ministerial Meeting that the arrangement 'had to be *ad hoc* more than anything else but it's certainly not going to impinge on defence or embarrass the Irish.' In fact, the London Report allowed the Ten to discuss the sort of things they had been discussing in the CSCE since 1970, but on a strict interpretation would prevent them from discussing the confidence-building aspects of the forthcoming Conference on Disarmament in Europe (CDE). It was not what Mr Genscher had been looking for when he launched his initiative at Stuttgart.

On the 'commitment to EPC', the precise terms of which had been under discussion up until the last minute, the Foreign Ministers emphasized 'their commitment to consult partners before adopting final positions or launching national initiatives on all important questions of foreign policy which are of concern to the Ten as a whole'. The sentiment was admirable, but the text seemed scarcely to justify the time and effort that had been spent on it. At best the text represents a display of goodwill, but as so often in the basic texts on Political Co-operation, general language over which infinite pains are taken risks becoming insignificant through the lack of any enforcement mechanism.

Part II of the Report set out certain practical improvements in the machinery and procedures of Political Co-operation. Many of these are of minor importance and little more than good bureaucratic practice, such as the instruction that Working Groups' reports should include a summary drawing the attention of the Political Committee to points requiring decision, but others are more substantial.

The Report foresaw that third countries would increasingly express the desire to enter into more or less regular contact with the Ten. The responsibility for maintaining these contacts was conferred on the Presidency in a significant strengthening of its role, and the Report specified certain ways in which the Presidency could carry out its function. These included the generalization of the Troika formula: 'If necessary, and if the Ten so agree, the Presidency, accompanied by representatives of the preceding and succeeding Presidencies, may meet with representatives of third countries.' The Report also gave a place to the increasing co-operation among Missions of the Ten in third countries.

Given the increasing workload on the Presidency in its role as spokesman in the European Parliament and in contacts with third countries,

. . . it has become desirable to strengthen the organisation and assure the continuity of Political Co-operation and to provide operational support for the Presidency without, however, reducing the direct contact, pragmatism and economy which are among the chief virtues of the present arrangements. Henceforth the Presidency will be assisted by a small team of officials seconded from preceding and succeeding Presidencies. These officials will remain in the employment of their national Foreign Ministries, and will be on the staff of their Embassy in the Presidency capital. They will be at the disposition of the Presidency and will work under its direction.

The Troika Secretariat (not to be confused with the Troika formation of diplomats from capitals used for certain contacts with third countries) was a highly successful experiment whose innovative potential was not pushed far enough. The degree to which the mechanism genuinely assisted the functioning of Political Co-operation depended on the personal qualities of the members of the Troika and the extent to which the Presidency was prepared to make use of them and to open to them national facilities; this varied according to the Presidency. The impact of foreign diplomats working within the portals of Foreign Ministries was, however, considerable and beneficial both to the host Ministry and to the seconded officials. Had the experiment continued (the omission of the definite article before 'preceding and succeeding Presidencies' was designed to leave the door open for subsequent expansion to five members), it might have led to interesting results in the interpenetration of national diplomatic services, but it was replaced as a result of the Single European Act by the permanent Secretariat in Brussels.

The Commission was finally admitted to full participation in Political Co-operation: 'Within the framework of the established procedures the Ten attach importance to the Commission of the European Communities being fully associated with Political Co-operation at all levels.' This convoluted and rather grudging phraseology reflected the need, particularly of Denmark, to ensure that the Commission thereby acquired no institutional competence in Political Co-operation. The modalities of the Commission's full association were remitted to the Political Committee and, in spite of some rearguard actions from the more old-fashioned Member States, were settled by the end of the year, after the Commission had given strict undertakings about the way in which it would organize its participation, in particular as regards confidentiality.

Finally, the Report introduced the crisis procedure for which Lord Carrington had called nearly two years earlier: 'The Political Committee or, if necessary, a Ministerial meeting will convene within 48 hours at the request of three member states.' Ironically, the mechanism was no sooner introduced than it spectacularly failed to function. In the case of Poland, only three months later, the Ministerial Meeting the Presidency had convened during the Christmas holidays could only be held at the beginning of January and the Political Directors who met in their place could only do so on an informal basis. It was not until the invasion of Lebanon in June 1982 that the mechanism was formally brought into play.

SELECTED READING

The prevailing state of mind as EPC moved into the 1980s is well reflected in de Schoutheete (1979) and Carrington (1981–2).

For the Venice Declaration, see Moisi (1980) in addition to the general works on the Middle East (Ifestos, 1987, and Greilsammer and Weiler, 1984).

For the Iran hostages, see Smith (1984–5) and Tanaka (1984).

The antecedents of the London Report are explained in Hurd (1981), Hill (1982), and da Fonseca Wollheim (1981), then

European Correspondent of the Commission. The French and Irish positions are described in de la Serre (1982) and Salmon (1982) respectively.

6

A Bridge Too Far (1982–1986)

ARGUMENT

The London Report of October 1981 had newly codified Political Co-operation, provided the beginnings of a Secretariat and ended the last restrictions on the full association of the Commission. It owed this success to its pragmatic and low-key approach, limited to EPC. A more ambitious plan for further progress towards European Union, launched at the same time by Foreign Ministers Genscher and Colombo, proved to have aimed too high. The Solemn Declaration of Stuttgart, the result of two years' discussions of the Genscher–Colombo initiative, did little more than reveal the split between Member States in their vision of Europe.

The years following the London Report were marked by the Europeans' increasing unease with the policies followed by the Reagan Administration, particularly on East-West relations. This had a noticeable effect on the discussions in Political Co-operation, where the Ten were torn between giving support to their ally and maintaining the policies they believed to be right. This showed in their policy on Poland, the CSCE, and what could no longer be called détente, but also on the Middle East, where attempts to carry forward the movement which had been begun in the Venice Declaration ran into the sand.

During this period the Ten had to deal with a number of international problems. The way they did so showed that they were now ready, if only as a matter of expediency, to consider using Community instruments to implement policies decided in Political Co-operation. Sanctions following the imposition of martial law in Poland and those applied to Argentina after the invasion of the Falkland Islands, the new relationship with the countries of Central America, and finally the Ten's policy on South Africa, in which Community restrictive and positive measures were combined, constituted a series in which, as the experience of working together accumulated, the institutional sensitivities of the past became less acute. These developments were assisted by the presence of the Commission in EPC following the London Report.

THE GENSCHER–COLOMBO INITIATIVE AND THE STUTTGART SOLEMN DECLARATION

The London Report of October 1981 had its origin in the sustained pressure for a strengthening of EPC exerted by the United Kingdom since 1978. The approach adopted by the British was pragmatic, looking for improvements through tightening procedure, although their proposals for a reinforced commitment to EPC and for setting up an EPC Secretariat could have had far-reaching effects. The discussions throughout 1981 showed, however, that only modest procedural improvements could find consensus. Bolder ambitions, for example on security, ran up against a veto.

The procedural approach did not appeal to some of Britain's European partners, and in particular to the Federal German Foreign Minister, Hans-Dietrich Genscher. Two months after Lord Carrington's speech in Hamburg, Genscher as leader of the German Liberals seized the opportunity of the traditional Epiphany meeting of the Free Democratic Party (FDP) on 6 January 1981 in Stuttgart to make a speech in which he called for further progress towards European Union. If Europe wanted to have an effective foreign policy and, together with the United States, exert an influence on East–West dialogue and disarmament, then it had to demonstrate its willingness and capacity to help ensure transatlantic defence.

The philosophy behind the Genscher initiative was explained in an article published in May that year by Dr Niels Hansen, who was Head of the Planning Staff of the Federal Foreign Ministry at the time. There was a fear in Bonn that international economic and political developments had made the building of Europe more difficult. The energies of the Community were perforce directed to finding practical solutions for the problems presented by the oil crisis, the enlargement of the Community, and economic difficulties at home. The political goal of European Union had receded into the background; this was a danger for the internal cohesion of the Community. A political prospect was necessary if in the long run the peoples of Europe were not to lose their commitment to the Community and if political compromises were not to be increasingly difficult to come by.

It was perhaps significant that the initiative should have been launched before a domestic political audience in Germany. This was the era of the British budget problem. Genscher saw that the Community was in danger of becoming in the eyes of the public, and particularly the German public, no more than a place where people argued about money, with Germany being expected to foot the bill. A strong tendency in the Social Democratic Party (SDP), with whom the Liberals were in partnership in government, increasingly took this view. In order to counter this development, Genscher saw the need to provide a Community more striking to the imagination and one which ordinary people could perceive as relevant to their interests. He therefore put the question whether the time had not come for a Treaty on European Union, whose objects would be the development of a common European foreign policy; building up Community policies in all areas covered by the Treaties; branching out to include security policy; co-operating more closely on cultural matters; and engaging in legal harmonization.

This was to be done by drawing together in a Treaty the existing components of the Community, namely the *acquis communautaire*, the inter-governmental co-operation of EPC, and the European Council. The approach was deliberately inter-governmental. In a speech made in August, Genscher described his initiative as 'a combination of federal and confederal elements in a construction similar to that of a modified Fouchet Plan'. The result would form the basis for future expansion. It would also provide some immediate advantages. There would be more effective interaction between EPC and the Community. A security-policy capability would give the Ten the weight they required, particularly in their relations with the United States. Already on 4 June 1980—at the height of the difficulties with the United States over the forthcoming Venice Declaration—Genscher had said: 'Perhaps Europe's voice would be better heard in Washington if this Europe of ours spoke more with one voice and acted together more decisively.' It might also be better heard in Jerusalem—the Federal government had been criticized for having launched out on the Venice Declaration without a European military capability to back it up. Cultural co-operation was important to build a Community-wide sense of belonging together. In this perspective, the Genscher proposals formed a coherent whole designed to meet a political need.

A Bridge too Far (1982–1986)

The initiative was launched by Genscher as Foreign Minister and party leader rather than by the Federal government as a whole. He therefore looked for support abroad. Germany's natural ally in promoting the development of the Community would have been France, as happened three years later at the European Council in Milan when the movement leading to the Single European Act was launched. It was by no means certain, however, that President Giscard was thinking on the same lines as Genscher. Indeed, in an interview in *Le Monde* on 27 January, Giscard took a non-committal position towards the initiative and instead launched the idea that, since EPC was outside the Treaties, it could be carried on by whichever of the partners wished to join in, and should not be held back by the weakest and the slowest. Furthermore, as was already evident in Giscard's attitude in the previous period, Europe's voice would be better heard if the Big Four co-operated more closely for action on the world stage. This resurrection of the *directoire* approach was not at all what Genscher had in mind.

Rather than Paris, Genscher chose to go to Rome, where on 21 January he found a sympathetic reception for his ideas from Foreign Minister Colombo. A week later Colombo made a speech in Florence in which he took a similar line. There was the same call to go further along the road to Union, to develop a European cultural policy, to strengthen political co-operation by going beyond day-to-day management, and to look towards a common security policy. Unlike Genscher, however, Colombo gave first priority to exploiting fully the existing Treaties and to finding effective ways of coping with the regional disparities in a Community soon to be enlarged to twelve.

These differences of emphasis reflected differences about substance which could only with difficulty be resolved in a series of meetings between the Political Directors of the two Foreign Ministries. Whereas the Germans were more concerned with the political aspects, the Italians argued that equal emphasis had to be placed on economic integration for which they demanded an action programme. This was of particular concern to them, as traditional beneficiaries of Community economic policies, at a time when the future of the Community budget was being discussed following the 'mandate of 30 May 1980'. Conversely, it was an aspect the Germans would have preferred to play down, as they would no doubt be expected to meet the extra cost of such policies—and the reluctance of the Federal government to do so was precisely the problem with which Genscher was trying to deal. There was also a difference between the two sides on form. The Germans wanted a Treaty or other similar legal act, while the Italians preferred a political declaration, knowing full well that to insist on binding legal obligations would sharply reduce the chances of getting agreement from the other Member States.

These differences, combined with the fact that the Federal Foreign Ministry needed time to put into concrete form Genscher's broad approach, meant that it was not until the autumn, after the adoption of the London Report, that the two Foreign Ministers were able to make a joint proposal to their colleagues. This they did on 12 November 1981. There was a discussion in the Council on 17 November and in the European Parliament two days later, at which both Ministers spoke. In his speech Colombo stressed the need to advance with 'realistico gradualismo' as the only way to avoid divisive quarrels over European unity, and both Ministers believed that they were adopting a cautious method of proceeding, which would lead only in the fullness of time to European Union. The unenthusiastic response of the other Member States showed that this was over optimistic.

The Genscher–Colombo proposals were curiously unbalanced in structure, reflecting the diversity of their origin and the compromises which had gone into their drafting. There were two separate documents. The first was entitled 'Draft European Act' and, although it was couched in the form of a declaration attributed to 'The Heads of State or Government of the Ten Member States of the European Communities, meeting within the European Council', was a mixture of political declaration and quasi-legal text. It contained a section on principles which included the aims of enabling 'Member States, through a common foreign policy, to act in concert in world affairs' and of 'the co-ordination of security policy and the adoption of common European positions in this sphere'. Some loosely worded measures to further the development of EPC were included, but these barely went beyond what had already been agreed in the London Report except for that concerning 'greater respect for resolutions of the European Parliament when the Ten come to decisions'.

A Bridge too Far (1982–1986) 187

The second section covered the Institutions. The European Council was to be given formal status as the source of political guidance for both EPC and the Community, and the central importance of the European Parliament was to be recognized by improvements in its status, including the right to debate EPC matters. A Council (foreign affairs) was to 'be responsible for European political co-operation', and there was to be co-operation in matters of security. For the latter, 'the Council may convene in a different composition (i.e. Ministers of Defence) if there is a need to deal with matters of common interest in more detail.' Other Councils were to be set up to deal with the new areas of co-operation like culture and legal questions. The European Council and these new councils in the fields of foreign policy, security policy, and cultural co-operation would be assisted by 'an expandable Secretariat of European political co-operation', except in areas covered by the treaties, for which the Council Secretariat would retain its functions. The remainder of this section was devoted to the fate of the 'Luxembourg compromise' or the national veto in the Community.

The final section of the Draft European Act looked to the future. It provided that the Act should be reviewed after five years with a view to incorporating progress achieved in European unification in a Treaty on European Union.

The Draft Act ran to ten pages. The second document in the Genscher–Colombo proposals, which was a draft statement on questions of economic integration included on the insistence of Italy, was a mere six paragraphs, but included commitments to bring the common market to completion and, looking ahead to economic and monetary union, to aim at a closer co-ordination of economic policies, not least with a view to the further development of the European Monetary System.

The proposals were given a grudging reception. The reaction from the traditional supporters of the Community approach was one of outright hostility, not surprisingly, since development of the Community on integrationist lines was to be confined for the future to those areas already covered by the Treaties. Any other development was to be on lines of inter-governmental co-operation, with a strengthening of the role of the pre-eminently inter-governmental European Council and the setting up of an EPC Secretariat responsible not just for foreign policy, but for all the new areas of co-operation as well.

Nor were the proposals attractive to those who were far from being integrationists. The Irish were against co-operation on security questions, as were the Danes and the Greeks; the latter were also against cultural co-operation, together with the British. France and the new Member States were attached to the Luxembourg compromise. Most Member States failed to see the sense in diverting precious time to the discussion of institutional questions when the budget problem remained to be solved. The Parliament was guardedly welcoming, but primarily interested in strengthening its own position and in any case already embarked on the reflections which led to the much more revolutionary Draft Treaty on European Union which it adopted in February 1984. In the circumstances it was not surprising that work on the Genscher–Colombo proposals progressed slowly.

The first question to be decided was who was going to do the work. To entrust it to either the Political Committee or Coreper might already prejudge the type of approach, integrationist or inter-governmental. An intermediate solution was adopted. An *ad hoc* Group was set up under the chairmanship of Philippe de Schoutheete, the Belgian Ambassador in Madrid (Belgium had the Presidency from 1 January 1982 and Ambassador de Schoutheete had extensive experience of EPC and of Community institutional questions). The Foreign Ministers chose their own personal representatives to sit on the Group, which met in Brussels.

Although the discussions were difficult, much of the detailed work of preparation was finished by the end of the Belgian Presidency. It was not possible to come to a final agreement, however, because of difficulties over some remaining points, of which the most important was the voting procedure in the Council. When Denmark took over the Presidency on 1 July, Ambassador Riberholdt succeeded to the chair of the *ad hoc* Group. It was scarcely to be expected that much progress could be made for the next six months, given Denmark's difficulties over so many parts of the Draft. It was not until Germany took over the Presidency at the beginning of 1983 that, under pressure from Mr Genscher, a determined effort was made to reach agreement. This was achieved at the price of verbal acrobatics which left the problems of substance unresolved, and of a large number of Danish and Greek reservations and

A Bridge too Far (1982–1986)

declarations which peppered the final text. The European Act, now transmogrified into a Solemn Declaration to erase any impression that it had legal force, was signed by the Heads of Government at the European Council in Stuttgart on 19 June 1983.

Much of the debate, and much of the Solemn Declaration as finally agreed, was concerned with the Community of the Treaties rather than with Political Co-operation. The long discussions throughout 1981 culminating in the adoption of the London Report had already established how far Member States were prepared to go on EPC, and the results were not likely to be revised so soon afterwards. There were one or two minor innovations at Stuttgart and some reassertions of principle, but for the most part EPC mutton was dressed up as lamb.

The importance of greater coherence and close co-ordination between the existing structures of the Communities and EPC was emphasized. However, the Declaration merely states:

Matters within the scope of the European Communities are governed by provisions and procedures laid down in or pursuant to the Treaties of Paris and Rome and in agreements supplementing them. In matters of Political Co-operation, procedures which were agreed on in the Luxembourg (1970), Copenhagen (1973) and London (1981) reports will apply, together with other procedures to be agreed on if necessary.

This blinding statement of the obvious was another way of saying that there was no consensus to make any progress in EPC procedures or to merge the process with that of the Community. The European Council 'issues general political guidelines for the European Communities and European Political Co-operation' and 'solemnly expresses the common position in questions of external relations'. Each President of the European Council presents a report to the European Parliament which also covers Political Co-operation.

Little remained of the proposal that a council (foreign affairs) should be set up with a view to moving towards a common foreign policy.

With a view to bringing the institutional apparatus of the Community and that of Political Co-operation closer together, the Council deals with matters for which it is competent under the Treaties in accordance with the procedure laid down by the latter, and its members will deal also, in accordance with the appropriate procedures, with all other areas of European Union, particularly matters coming within the scope of Political Co-operation.

This astute wording left the door open to a blurring of distinctions between items on the agenda of the Council and of the EPC Ministerial Meetings and the gradual bringing together of the two forums. This development did indeed occur, but only at the end of the decade and as a result of circumstance, not of the wording of the Solemn Declaration.

It was recognized that the European Parliament debates matters relating to Political Co-operation. The Parliament had of course always done so, but some Member States had in the past contested that right. This was no longer the case. The 'members of the Council', that is the Member States in Political Co-operation, undertook to respond to oral or written questions (a confirmation of existing practice), but also to 'resolutions concerning matters of major importance and general concern, on which Parliament seeks their comments'. This provided Parliament with a tool for extracting comment from EPC and for engaging it in dialogue, but curiously the possibility was for many years left unexploited. The practice of keeping the Parliament's Political Affairs Committee informed of foreign-policy subjects examined in EPC was maintained, and the Presidency undertook to report once a year in plenary session on progress in EPC.

The 'commitment to EPC' was reformulated drawing largely on language from previous texts including the London Report. An innovation was the language now agreed on security. The London Report had only gone as far as co-ordination on the political aspects of security. The Stuttgart Declaration added the economic aspects, in order to make some advance, there being no agreement to include the military aspects. This caused agitation in the Commission, which took the view that economic aspects of security could already be discussed in the Community framework and a declaration to the minutes was made, endorsed by Member States, to preserve this possibility. The debate was about language: discussions in EPC were not noticeably widened as a result of the new provision.

A Bridge too Far (1982–1986)

The Solemn Declaration had little effect on the course of Community life and did not achieve the political objectives Mr. Genscher had in mind. Genscher's political analysis was no doubt correct, and the problems he discerned had to be tackled again later. Perhaps the approach was too ambitious, or ill timed. After all, the initiative which led to the decision of the Milan European Council in June 1985, only two years after Stuttgart, and thus to the Single European Act, had similar objectives, but was much more successful in gathering support. It is true that the budget question had been settled by then, but it is also the case that the 1985 initiative was a Franco-German, not a Franco-Italian one, and that France kept a low profile throughout the discussions on the Genscher–Colombo initiative, being mainly concerned with defending the Luxembourg compromise. It is tempting to draw the conclusion that, for an initiative on institutional reform of the Community to succeed, it must have the support of both France and Germany.

The Solemn Declaration of Stuttgart did have one immediate effect, albeit unlooked for. It convinced those Member States which wanted to go ahead with security co-operation that no progress could be looked for in an organization of which Ireland, Denmark, and Greece were members. The calculation was an easy one: all the members of the Community but those three were members of the Western European Union. The failure on security co-operation at Stuttgart thus led directly to an attempt to revive the WEU as a forum for working out a stronger European position on defence, as the only way to respond to what was felt, in the face of US policy, as a pressing need.

THE FORMATION OF POLICY

East–West Relations

East–West Relations and Relations with the United States

The transatlantic relationship was dominated by a difference of approach throughout the Reagan years. The Carter Administration had been disliked because of its unpredictability and wishy-washy foreign policy. The Reagan Administration was the reverse, and pleased the Europeans no better. Summoned to subscribe to an 'Evil Empire' doctrine, the European countries swung between maintaining good transatlantic relations and preserving what remained of the advantages of détente. EPC policy towards the Soviet Union and Eastern Europe during this period is marked by Western Europe's relationship with the United States.

Although the Ten rarely touched on military questions in EPC, the defence debate was at the back of everyone's mind. The NATO 'double-track' decision of December 1979, whereby the Allies, in the face of the Warsaw Pact's heavy build up of medium range nuclear missiles, indicated their desire for negotiation and their willingness, by deploying Pershing and Cruise missiles, to achieve a more equal basis for them, was never directly referred to in EPC. However, the approach of the different Member States to the question of East–West relations was determined to a significant extent by the missile question and there are frequent coded references in EPC declarations to current debates in NATO.

It would have been inconceivable for the Ten in Political Cooperation to have taken up a position inconsistent with NATO, and yet the existence of the EPC mechanism gave them the possibility of expressing publicly shades of opinion indicative of a separate West European personality. Whereas the United States and the Soviet Union took up extreme positions, the Europeans were more inclined to look for dialogue and the middle way. The invasion of Afghanistan in 1979, the imposition of martial law in Poland in 1981 and 1982, the shooting down of a Korean airliner in 1983, the Soviet withdrawal from the disarmament talks in 1983–4, and their boycotting in April 1984 of the Los Angeles Olympic Games all heightened the tension. The American response was equally hard. Their restrictive line on East–West trade was a particularly sensitive question for the European allies, from the NATO meeting at La Sapinière in the autumn of 1982, at which basic principles for trade were agreed, to the tightening of the Co-ordinating Committee (COCOM) rules in July 1984.

The Europeans tried as far as possible to follow a policy of 'openness but firmness': openness towards dialogue with the Soviet Union, but firmness in not making concessions simply in order to have a dialogue. The position was best expressed in the Foreign Ministers' declaration of 27 March 1984: 'The Ten . . . appeal to the Soviet Union to co-operate in progress towards

A Bridge too Far (1982–1986)

genuine détente . . . they will pursue their efforts aimed at conducting a constructive dialogue with the Soviet Union and its allies in central and eastern Europe. They hope to develop cooperation with each of them . . .' Significantly, the initiative for this declaration came from the Federal Republic, Mr Genscher believing it to be essential that the Ten should keep the initiative *vis-à-vis* the Soviet Union by expressing public readiness for dialogue. This was of particular importance in the Federal Republic, where public opinion, knowing that Germany would be the future nuclear battle zone, was likely to be responsive to any apparently conciliatory moves on the Soviet side.

This search for a middle way made relations with the United States difficult. In the eyes of Washington, the European response to the invasion of Afghanistan and the imposition of martial law in Poland, which will be discussed in the next section, had been inadequate. Relations were made more tense by two incidents which were important for the development of EPC as well as in the wider context. Following the Ottawa Summit of July 1981 at which the United States put the question of East–West trade on the table, pressure was exerted on the European allies, particularly the Federal Republic, to give up their participation in the construction of a pipeline to transport natural gas to Western Europe from the Soviet Union. The Americans were concerned that this involvement, and the long-term contracts for the supply of natural gas which some Community countries had concluded, would make the Europeans too dependent on the Soviet Union for energy supplies; moreover, the hard currency earned would only go to strengthen the Soviet military machine. The United States' sanctions against the Soviet Union following the imposition of martial law in Poland included an embargo on the export of oil and gas equipment to the Soviet Union, a move designed to slow down the implementation of these contracts. The export ban was extended on 18 June 1982 to US-controlled firms in Europe and to equipment produced by European firms under US licence. The Europeans contested the extraterritoriality of the US measures on legal grounds as well as because of their retroactive nature and the lack of consultation. Member States chose to treat the question as a matter of trade policy and therefore one for the Community. This was wise, as to treat the affair as a political one might have exposed serious divisions among the Ten. The question was not raised at all in Political Co-operation, except for one informal discussion at a Political Directors' dinner when it was feared that some Member States were planning bilateral contacts with the United States.

The other incident which this time did fall within the remit of EPC was the shooting down of a Korean civilian airliner by the Soviet Air Force in the early days of September 1983. This caused a further deterioration in East–West relations and cast a shadow over the closing weeks of the CSCE meeting in Madrid. The attack was strongly condemned by the United States and it was commonly expected that the Ten would condemn it too. That they did not was because of the opposition of Greece.

The first Greek Presidency of EPC began on 1 July 1983. The Greek Foreign Minister, Mr Haralambopoulos, taking perhaps a shade too literally the new possibilities provided by the Solemn Declaration signed in Stuttgart only a few weeks before, which enabled the Ten to discuss the 'political and economic aspects of security', put the question of disarmament on the agenda of the first Ministerial Meeting of the Greek Presidency. This caused considerable embarrassment to Ireland and no formal discussion took place, much to the relief of the other Member States who feared that it would not be easy to accommodate within the consensus of the Ten the more forthcoming approach of Mr Papandreou's Socialist government towards relations with the Soviet Union and the East European countries.

These fears were confirmed at the next Ministerial Meeting on 12 September, when Greece refused to countenance any declaration on the shooting down of the Korean airliner which contained a condemnation of the part played by the Soviet Union. The Ten therefore had to confine themselves to reiterating their 'deep distress' at the destruction of the KAL airliner and the loss of human life; they also called for action in the International Civil Aviation Organization (ICAO). For the rest, the public was referred back to national declarations. The failure of the Ten to make a convincing statement was keenly felt by the other Ministers and adversely commented on by the United States. Only a fortnight later Mr Haralambopoulos declared in his speech on behalf of the Ten to the United Nations that 'a further cause of aggravation' in relations between East and West had been the downing of the Korean airliner, a formula which might have saved the day at the Ministerial Meeting, but came too late to repair the damage which had been done.

While not seriously affecting the middle of the road position of the Ten on East–West relations, the attitude of Greece on occasions like this, which attracted attention from the press, was an additional irritant in relations with the United States and made the Ten's overall position less credible. It was, however, inherent in the ground rules of EPC that as long as the Ten adhered to the principle of consensus, they were at the mercy of the maverick. Affairs like that of the Korean airliner did not cause Member States so much embarrassment that they seriously envisaged abandoning the consensus principle, which would have been one way of dealing with the problem.

The year 1984 was a period of inertia in East–West relations. President Reagan was coming to the end of his first term of office, and the Soviet Union was experiencing a procession of lack-lustre successors to Brezhnev. The West European countries individually attempted to fill the gap by maintaining contacts with the Soviet Union and the East European countries. The coming to power of Gorbachev and the re-election of President Reagan in November 1984 brought this period of inertia to an end. If they did not immediately transform East–West relations, these events at least provided a new start which required the Ten to review their position. In a joint declaration on 8 January 1985 the United States and the Soviet Union declared their readiness to resume disarmament negotiations in Geneva. This move was welcomed by the Ten in a statement made at the Ministerial Meeting in Rome on 12 February, in which the objectives of the US–Soviet negotiations were endorsed, thus moving the Ten into the defence field. A note of self-congratulation found its way into the text: 'they emphasize that these negotiations fall within the more general framework of East–West relations. They are pleased that, for their part, they have contributed by their actions, either as the Ten or otherwise, to the resumption of dialogue, of which the negotiations clearly constitute an essential element.' Indeed, the Ten believed that the Ministerial and other level contacts they had had with first the East European countries then the Soviet Union throughout 1984 had played an important part in bringing the superpowers back to the negotiating table. Whether or not this was the case, it can scarcely be called an EPC policy as such. No decision to that effect was taken in Political Co-operation; rather EPC provided a forum, in which some Member States took more advanced positions than others, for a climate of opinion to be established in which national initiatives for contacts seemed not too risky.

Having by their own account brought the superpowers together again, the Ten now found themselves without a mission and in danger of being excluded from discussions at the top table. It would have made sense for them to have worked out a European position on at least the broad aspects of the disarmament negotiations which began in Geneva on 12 March 1985. They were debarred from doing this by Ireland's commitment to neutrality, although this had not stopped the Ten at the London European Council in November 1981 from welcoming 'the commitment of the United States . . . to the goal of major disarmament by means of mutual reductions in nuclear and conventional forces and confidence building measures' and looking forward to the Intermediate-range Nuclear Forces (INF) negotiations. But in addition to Irish neutrality, disagreement among Member States about the line to be followed, and in particular about whether that line should be worked out in EPC or NATO, also precluded a common position on disarmament.

This disagreement meant that in practice the Ten's position on the CDE which began in Stockholm in January 1984 owed more to NATO co-ordination than to EPC. It also meant that President Reagan's Strategic Defence Initiative, launched in March 1985, was scarcely discussed in Political Co-operation. Political Directors had an impromptu discussion shortly after the news broke, in the relaxed atmosphere of dinner during the Brussels European Council on 29 March 1985, all the more valuable for being unprepared, but the question was not taken further in that forum. The French initiative which led to the setting up of the Eureka programme of civilian research projects was briefly presented to the Political Committee a month later, but discussion of it took place either on the Community side or in an *ad hoc* framework. SDI itself continued to be discussed in the WEU, but without reaching a common view. Indeed, the differences of opinion which in the end led to the United Kingdom and Germany taking part in the initiative, but the

A Bridge too Far (1982–1986)

other allies not, would probably have prevented the emergence of consensus in any forum.

If the Ten could not discuss defence questions, they could at least achieve a common political analysis of the new Soviet regime. This to begin with was extremely prudent. The Ten believed that the Gorbachev style and tone were new, but that the substance of Soviet foreign policy had not changed. The initiatives taken in the course of the year, including the Soviet moratorium on nuclear testing and various initiatives in the United Nations for nuclear-free space, were seen as propaganda or diversionary tactics. The Ten's response should be a more sophisticated approach, in order not to appear negative. Above all, they had by a show of solidarity to resist Soviet attempts to drive a wedge between the European allies and the United States.

And yet some cracks were beginning to appear in the polar ice-cap of Soviet policy towards the Community. When Prime Minister Craxi of Italy visited Moscow in May 1985 he was told by Mr Gorbachev in a luncheon speech on 20 May that 'inasmuch as the EEC countries act as a political entity, the Soviet authorities are ready to look together with them for a common language including on specific international questions.' The same message was given by Gorbachev to French parliamentarians when he visited Paris on 3 October, this time with the additional possibility of dialogue with members of the European Parliament. The Ten's reaction was cautious, and consistent with their general political analysis. For several years, the question of a political dialogue with the Soviet Union hung on whether Mr Shevardnadze would invite the Ambassadors of the Ten to lunch. It has to be said that Gorbachev's opening did not immediately translate itself into concrete terms in the various forums in which the Soviet Union was at odds with the Community.

The Craxi visit to Moscow also opened up the prospect of a relationship between the CMEA (Comecon) and the Community. There had already been some indications the previous year that Comecon was moving in this direction; the new element in the Gorbachev speech, referred to above, was the recognition of the Community as a 'political entity' through EPC. The following month Comecon reopened discussions by proposing to the

Commission a joint EC–Comecon declaration. The response proposed by the Commission was made up of four elements: the normalization of relations, parallelism of relations with Comecon on the one hand and its European Member States on the other, differentiation among the European Member States, and a 'territorial clause' safeguarding the status of Berlin. This line was approved by the Council and eventually accepted by Comecon. EPC kept a benevolent eye on the proceedings to ensure that the Community's line was consistent with the Ten's political approach.

It was not for another year, about the time of President Mitterrand's visit to Moscow in June 1986, that the Ten observed a new readiness in Soviet diplomacy to query long-established doctrines. This came after a spring during which there had been further disenchantment with American policies, including the decision to renew stocks of chemical weapons and to cease to observe *de facto* the unratified SALT II Treaty. On top of this came the bombshell of the Reykjavik Summit on 11–12 October 1986, at which Reagan and Gorbachev came close to an agreement to eliminate the Euromissiles over the heads of the European allies whose support for their deployment by the United States had cost them politically dear.

The views of the Member States on this issue were strong and relatively united. They were prevented from giving them expression in EPC by the opposition of Ireland, at this time in the throes of domestic debate over the ratification of the Single European Act precisely because of the new security dimension which it was thought the Act conferred on the Community. The United Kingdom Presidency did its best to secure a common position of the Ten at the Ministerial Meeting in London on 10 November, but failed. The discussion was transferred to the WEU Council meeting a few days later, and Mrs Thatcher met President Reagan on 15 November to discuss 'the way forward on arms control after Reykjavik' in her national capacity and representing the views of some of the European allies, not as President of the European Council. This was the final proof that the Ten could not have a credible position on East–West relations in the 1980s, nor a credible relationship with the United States, so long as they were unable to achieve a common stand on defence questions.

Poland

The tension in transatlantic relations and US pressure on its allies dominated the response of Political Co-operation to the imposition of martial law in Poland in December 1981 and brought about a change in the policy previously adopted.

In the months after August 1980 Solidarity had increasingly become a national force which had to be taken into account in Polish political life. Political Co-operation was slow to respond to this development. Mr Genscher took the lead in drawing attention to the implications for the West, but discussion in EPC went little further than exchanges of views and analyses. And yet the Nine needed to prepare their position thoroughly. Although hopes were rising of a more liberal and democratic regime, the risk of Soviet intervention, political and military, could not be excluded. Member States could not afford to be taken unawares by a repetition of Prague 1968.

In fact the response came not from Political Co-operation, but from the Community. Following a request by the Polish authorities, the Council decided in December 1980 to grant food aid to Poland at prices subsidized by the Community budget. Since Poland was in dire financial straits, it needed hard currency for purchases even at these subsidized prices. This came not from the Community, but from credits provided by the Member States. The national decisions on credit were beset with difficulties and delays, and information available in the Community framework was frequently inadequate. The inability of the Community to co-ordinate adequately the two types of decision impaired the political effectiveness of the action. In the course of 1981 two further instalments of food aid were decided, and in November the European Parliament voted an additional 10 million ecu, which it was decided should be used to supply 8,000 tonnes of beef as a gift.

Political backing and the rationale for these measures were given by the European Council in December 1980 and March 1981. On both occasions the Heads of Government gave a thinly veiled warning to the Soviet Union not to interfere in the developing political situation in Poland: 'Poland has shown that she is capable of facing her internal problems herself in a spirit of reason and responsibility. It is in the interest of the Polish people that Poland should continue to do so in a peaceful manner and without outside interference. It is also in the interest of the stability of Europe.' This line was justified by the obligations entered into by the signatories to the Helsinki Final Act; it was thought necessary because of ostentatious and sustained Warsaw Pact manœuvres, accompanied by references to the indivisibility of the socialist countries more in keeping with the Brezhnev doctrine than with the spirit of Helsinki. Western economic aid, on which the European Council took only a cautious commitment, was designed to buy time for the Poles to implement plans for economic stabilization and reform.

Throughout the autumn of 1981 the economic situation of Poland became increasingly desperate and energy shortages and the virtual collapse of food-supply arrangements during the coming winter were widely predicted. The political outlook was gloomy too, as opinion in both Solidarity and the Communist Party hardened further, but hope had not been abandoned that a trilateral power-sharing arrangement involving Solidarity, the Party, and the Church might yet be worked out.

These hopes were dashed when on 13 December General Jaruzelski proclaimed martial law and arrested some 7,000 people, mostly Solidarity activists. The Nine's reaction was immediate, but prudent. It was perhaps unfortunate that they were compelled by the timing of the EPC calendar to make a public statement before full analysis of the events was possible. The Political Committee had a scheduled meeting in London on 14–15 December and used it to prepare a statement for Ministers to issue on 15 December which did little more than express sympathy with the Polish people, repeat the European Council's previous warnings, and agree to remain in close consultation. The Ministers also decided that the existing Community aid should be continued, for humanitarian reasons, but that channels should be found to ensure non-discriminatory distribution. Decisions on further aid for 1982 were postponed. The Ministers' conclusions were announced by Lord Carrington at a press conference. He declined to comment on the United States' decision to suspend all new food aid to Poland.

The question of sanctions, on which the United States looked to their allies to line up behind the US position, became a delicate and divisive one. It soon became obvious that the decisions Foreign Ministers had taken on 15 December were inadequate as a response both to the situation and to the increasing American pressure. NATO contingency planning had been built on a Soviet military intervention. The unexpected imposition of martial law by the Polish authorities themselves found the allies at odds over the appropriate level of response. Many of the Twelve, but in particular the Germans, were anxious to preserve as far as possible the hard-won gains of détente.

The Twelve were torn between the American and the German positions. An attempt was made to convene a Ministerial meeting during the Christmas holidays. A number of Ministers found this inconvenient, and consensus was eventually reached on an informal meeting in London of Political Directors accompanied by economic advisers. The meeting did not take place until 30 December, although efforts had been made to hold it earlier; so much for the crisis mechanism instituted barely three months previously in the London Report. As in the case of Afghanistan, there seemed no point in meeting merely to disagree.

The previous day, President Reagan had announced without prior consultation a number of measures including the suspension of Aeroflot flights to the United States, the suspension of export licences for certain high technology and oil and gas equipment, the postponement of negotiations on a new long-term grain agreement, and a review of all US–Soviet exchange agreements. The Political Directors discussed these measures, as well as the events in Poland, and finalized arrangements for a Ministerial Meeting to be held in Brussels on 4 January.

Poland was the first of several crises to befall Belgium during the six months of its Presidency, putting a severe strain on its resources and proving the value of the Troika support team set up in the London Report. It so happened that in the Poland crisis, as well as the Falklands crisis three months later, solutions were found whereby Political Co-operation had recourse to Community instruments, setting important precedents for the future. This development is attributable in part to chance, in part to the predisposition of the Belgian Presidency to look for Community solutions, and in part to the convenience of having EPC and EC meetings in the same city.

At the Ministerial Meeting of 4 January an attempt was made to respond in an adequate manner to the savage curtailment of civil liberties while salvaging as much as possible of the achievements of détente. In the eyes of most Ministers, the course of action would have to be sufficiently firm to come up to American expectations and thus prevent a further deterioration in transatlantic relations. The result was a strong political statement which called for the end of martial law, the release of those arrested, and the restoration of a genuine dialogue with the Church and Solidarity. These came to be the three criteria by which the Ten subsequently judged their relations with Poland. At the same time, they issued a solemn warning against any open intervention by the Warsaw Pact. Direct humanitarian aid to the Polish people was to be continued.

The key passages regarding sanctions, carefully described as economic measures, are found in paragraphs 7 and 10 of the declaration.

The Ten have taken note of the economic measures taken by the United States Government with regard to the USSR. The Ten will undertake in this context close and positive consultations with the United States Government and with the Governments of other Western States in order to define what decisions will best serve their common objectives and to avoid any step which could undermine their respective actions.

Other measures will be considered in the light of developments of the situation in Poland, in particular measures concerning credit and economic assistance to Poland, and measures concerning the Community's commercial policy with regard to the USSR. In addition the Ten will examine the question of further food aid to Poland.

At no time were sanctions against Poland contemplated on a Community basis. Some Member States decided in the NATO context not to give new credits other than for food and not to reschedule Polish debts, but the discussion in the Community turned on measures against the Soviet Union.

Although the declaration was agreed by consensus, the Greek government subsequently withdrew its agreement to much of the text, including the above paragraphs. Indeed the unfortunate Greek Minister who had taken part in the meeting found himself dismissed while still in the air returning to Athens. Greece was not able to agree to any part of the text which implied sanctions against the Soviet Union. Much of the effort over the next few weeks was devoted to solving this problem. The discussions were conducted against a background of continuing pressure by the United States in the NATO framework for its allies to adopt tough measures; at the same time the Europeans were becoming increasingly nervous that the Americans would extend to European companies the ban on the supply of oil-pipeline equipment to the Soviet Union which formed part of the US package.

The first step was for the Council to announce on 26 January that it had instructed Coreper, in conjunction with the Commission, to see what trade-policy measures relating to imports would be open to be taken *vis-à-vis* the USSR, and that it had further requested Coreper and the Commission to conduct an exchange of information and an analysis of the economic measures taken by the United States in respect of the Soviet Union. In the light of this study, the Council would be called upon to decide the necessary action to respect the commitment made in paragraph 10 of the declaration of 4 January. Greece adopted a negative position on these decisions.

The Commission examined the possibilities and found that, in the absence of Community export-control mechanisms, the only alternative was import restrictions. On 23 February the Council noted that a very large majority was in favour of a reduction in the Community's imports from the Soviet Union, to be carried out on the basis of Article 113 of the Treaty. Greece maintained its negative position on the substance and Denmark had reservations of a legal nature on the use of Article 113. The next day the Commission agreed a proposal to reduce quotas for certain Soviet products covering some 8 per cent of imports. Greece was excluded from the application of these provisions. After the Commission's proposal had been amended by the Council to reduce the trade impact, the final regulation adopted on 15 March limited the cuts to sixty products covering 1.4 per cent of imports. A separate regulation, adopted at the same time, suspended the application of the first regulation to Greece. Both regulations were to run until the end of the year. The Commission was asked to inform in particular the United States, Canada, Australia, and Japan of the measures.

This, the first occasion on which recourse was had to a Community legal act to give effect to a foreign-policy orientation decided in Political Co-operation, came about more as the result of circumstance than by an act of will. The rejection by Greece of the operational sections of the 4 January declaration ruled out any possibility of reaching consensus in EPC on measures against the Soviet Union. Failure to act and the uncoordinated measures which would thereafter have been taken by Member States would have sent the wrong political signal to both the United States and the Soviet Union. Both Greece and its partners had been taken prisoner by the EPC consensus rule. It was therefore fortunate that they could be delivered from their plight by the more flexible procedures of the Community. It was Lord Carrington who first pointed out in the Council that the application of Community regulations could be differentiated and that Greece could be exempted from applying sanctions. The Greek representative leapt at the chance and dragged Denmark in his wake, since the Danes could not oppose the use of Article 113 when that was the only way out of the impasse.

It has been pointed out that the measures taken were not punitive in scope, and have indeed been caricatured as applying principally to caviar. It is true that there was some in-fighting in the preparation of the Council regulations as commercial interests came to the fore. However, no Community measure was likely to bring the Soviet Union to its knees, and the symbolic value of the restrictions was appreciable, regardless of their scope. Thanks to circumstance and procedural inventiveness, EPC and the Community managed to survive the Poland crisis and by developing a new instrument of policy set a precedent which was to prove invaluable when a few weeks later General Galtieri invaded the Falkland Islands.

As so often when sanctions have been applied, there was uncertainty about what to do next. Although the situation in Poland got no better, as time went by some of the Member States began to doubt whether it was enough to stand pat on the decision of 4 January without making an effort to work out a new and more imaginative policy towards Poland. It was argued that the situation in the other Eastern European countries was just as bad, without calling forth the same reaction from the Ten. Against this it was pointed out that expectations had been higher in Poland and that discontent was correspondingly greater. In July 1983 martial law was lifted and many political

A Bridge too Far (1982–1986)

prisoners were released, but the mass rallies at the end of August on the anniversary of the Gdansk agreements showed that the population was not yet reconciled to the regime. The Ten were nevertheless put in a difficult position. The conditions they had laid down in their 'sanctions' decision had been largely fulfilled, and yet there had been no improvement in the situation to justify a relaxation of their attitude. In the event the Community measures against the Soviet Union, having been renewed once, were quietly allowed to lapse at the end of 1983, and little by little contacts with Poland were resumed, avoiding any spectacular move which would have given legitimacy to the regime.

In their search for an alternative policy towards Poland, the Ten once again turned to the instruments available in the Community framework. Humanitarian aid to the Polish people was continued in spite of budgetary difficulties, the Parliament showing itself more generous than the Council in voting the necessary funds. This was relatively uncontroversial, since the aid was distributed by non-governmental organizations; a more ambitious scheme to assist agriculture directly was to be the subject of difficult discussions over several years.

The Polish Church had worked up a scheme to assist private agriculture and small private businesses by channelling foreign donations in hard currency through a Foundation which, although recognized by the government, would be administered by the Church. To begin with both the Commission and Member States were sceptical about the viability of the scheme. It was thought that the negotiation of the operating conditions of the Foundation would be fraught with difficulties, as indeed proved to be the case, and that in the end the aid, being structural in nature, would benefit the government as much as the private sector. Nevertheless, the plan had strong backing from the German government, which was anxious to find positive ways of developing its relationship with Eastern Europe and Poland in particular, and Mr Genscher was able to convince his colleagues at the Ministerial Meeting on 12 September 1983 to give their support to the scheme. By this time the United States, where the Polish Church had been engaged in effective lobbying, had also promised its support. The Commission indicated its readiness to look at possible assistance, provided that the Foundation became a reality, but pointed to the lack of available funds.

The Commission took its time over this, partly because of continuing doubts among Member States about the practicability and desirability of the scheme, but also because of delays in securing the appropriate legal basis in Poland. The authorities put innumerable difficulties in the way, including the tax status of the Foundation and its ability to handle hard-currency donations direct. The attitude of the Member States was ambivalent. Without German pressure, the Ten would never have given serious consideration to the scheme. The French at first were against, but later changed their minds as the traditionally strong Polish lobby in Paris brought its influence to bear. The British were in favour in principle, but opposed to the provision of Community finance, which in accordance with Treasury practice would have been offset against the Foreign Office's own budget.

Finance was a recurrent problem whenever Member States in EPC sought to make use of the Community budget for foreign-policy ends. It was rarely the case that the current budget had sufficient flexibility to meet unforeseen foreign-policy expenditure, and the Member States' representatives in the Council were usually reluctant to follow the lead of their EPC colleagues and make the necessary addition to the Community budget. So it proved in this case. In the end it was the European Parliament which added 2 million ecu to the budget for the Polish Church scheme in both 1985 and 1986.

These efforts were in vain. Moves to set up the Foundation continued to be obstructed, and the Church reluctantly decided to abandon the scheme in September 1986. The outcome was scarcely surprising. The Polish authorities could not be expected to acquiesce in the financing by the West of a system which would strengthen the authority of the Church, remove from state control the handling of scarce hard-currency resources, and promote the interests of the private over the state sector. The hesitancy shown by the Ten demonstrated that they were not yet ready to face the implications of Western economic intervention in the affairs of a member of the Warsaw Pact and that, even if the political will had been there, the budgetary machinery was lacking to give expression to it. A policy towards

The Falkland Islands

At midnight on the night of 1–2 April 1982 Argentinian commandos and frogmen seized port installations in Port Stanley. The invasion force was in place by dawn and in the early morning Government House was surrounded. The Governor and seventy Royal Marines were deported to Uruguay.

The same day the Foreign Ministers of the Ten issued a declaration condemning the armed intervention and appealing urgently to the government of Argentina to withdraw its forces. The speed of the reaction was proof that the machinery of EPC was in better working order. Gone were the hesitations which had followed the invasion of Afghanistan and, more recently, the imposition of martial law in Poland. On this occasion the decision was admittedly easier. There was genuine indignation at the Argentinian action, and a willingness to show solidarity with a Member State which had been directly attacked. Indeed, the Community had in a sense been attacked itself. As the Commission's declaration on 6 April pointed out, the Falkland Islands were 'a British territory linked to the Community', being listed as one of the overseas countries and territories to which the provisions of Part IV of the Treaty of Rome applied. Unlike in the case of Afghanistan, Iran and Poland there was no outside pressure on the Community to apply sanctions. Indeed the United States, far from pressing action on its European partners, was reluctant to go as far as they did. The fact that the Ten were acting *motu proprio* not only made decisions easier, but marked a new stage in their search for a common external identity.

The British government launched an intensive diplomatic campaign to gather support, the first fruits of which were Security Council Resolution 502, adopted on 3 April. This Resolution played an important part in underpinning the action later taken by the Community. It demanded an immediate cessation of hostilities and an immediate withdrawal of all Argentine forces from the Falkland Islands and called on the two governments to seek a diplomatic solution.

Although the United Kingdom's first concern was to secure its position at the United Nations and in Washington, it also rapidly brought its European partners into play. The Ten's political support having been given, the next move was to solicit an arms embargo and trade sanctions. France, Germany, Italy, and the Netherlands all very rapidly imposed national arms embargoes, and the Community was asked to prohibit the import of all goods from Argentina in support of the national measure which the British announced on 6 April. Quite apart from the political significance of such an act by the Community, something had to be done to prevent the British ban from being circumvented by Argentinian goods circulating freely in the Community according to the principles of the EEC Treaty. Derogations from the principle of free circulation were permitted under Article 224 'in the event of . . . serious international tension constituting a threat of war', and it was to this Article that the United Kingdom referred in introducing to Coreper its request for action by the Member States to ban imports from Argentina and the export of arms to that country, as well as to suspend export credits. The United Kingdom had at the same time seized the Political Committee of the general question, but was raising the trade measures in the Community framework only.

Member States were thus faced with two questions, which intensive discussions over the next few days showed to be closely linked. Should sanctions be adopted, and if so, should they be adopted by Member States individually or by the Community as a whole? The view of the Commission was that the Community should act collectively on the basis of Article 113 of the Treaty, governing trade policy. This was both on grounds of principle, with a view to safeguarding Community competence, and in order to avoid the chaos which would ensue if the Member States adopted their own separate measures, which were bound to differ in significant detail. This view was supported by Member States like Germany and Belgium. Denmark, on the other hand, while anxious to show solidarity with the United Kingdom and willing to adopt an embargo, was opposed to doing so by a Community act, mindful of the battering it had received over Poland from domestic political

A Bridge too Far (1982–1986)

forces determined to preserve the purely economic nature of the Community. Other countries like Ireland and Italy had difficulties with an embargo as such and found it easier to accept a Community measure than a purely national one, since they were thus able to find some shelter from domestic pressure behind the screen of Community action.

Intensive consultations and a shuttling of texts backwards and forwards between the Political Committee and Coreper made it possible to come to a decision on 10 April which took these various positions into account. The fact that Belgium had the Presidency meant that the Political Committee met in the Palais d'Egmont, the Belgian Foreign Ministry's conference centre, while Coreper met a few minutes away in the EC Council's building, the Charlemagne. This greatly facilitated co-ordination, especially for the Commission, responsible for making any formal proposals, whose representative was the only one to sit in both bodies. The solution found was that the political basis for measures by the Ten should be provided by a text produced by the Political Committee, which was duly issued by the Belgian Presidency on 10 April. In this the Ten stated that they had decided to adopt a series of measures against Argentina which should be implemented as soon as possible. After recalling that an arms embargo had already been imposed by national action, the statement continued, in a passage provided by Coreper: 'They [the Ten] will also take the measures needed to prohibit all imports into the Community from Argentina.' It was explained that since these were economic measures, they would be taken in accordance with the relevant provisions of the Community Treaties.

This Sibylline phrase masked the fact that Denmark was still opposed to the use of Article 113. Their acceptance of this four days later marked a considerable effort on the part of the Danish authorities, and was achieved at the cost of a number of precautions in the text of the Regulation which the Council adopted on 16 April, valid for one month. The recitals of the Regulation included references to 'discussions in the context of European Political Co-operation which have led in particular to the decision that economic measures will be taken with regard to Argentina in accordance with the relevant provisions of the Community Treaties' and to consultations among Member

States pursuant to Article 224 of the Treaty, following measures taken by the United Kingdom. The order of the recitals made it plain that the discussions in EPC were a prerequisite for Community action.

The Ten had good reason to congratulate themselves on their achievement. Although the discussions had been difficult, this had not appeared to the outside world, which in any case would have had scant interest in the esoteric institutional question mainly responsible for the difficulty. Argentina certainly was disagreeably surprised by the Ten's rapid and decisive action, as was shown by the diplomatic campaign it and other Latin American countries conducted against it. Although the sanctions did not apply to contracts concluded before the Regulation was adopted and were not in force long enough for it to be seen whether or not they had an effect on trade, their political impact was considerable and they were reported to have influenced the view taken by the banks of their Argentinian creditors. As time went by, however, the credibility of the Community sanctions was impaired by increasing doubts among the partners about the policy followed by the British government.

The sanctions were due to expire on 17 May. No doubt it was expected that by then a diplomatic solution would have been found, and indeed the Ten placed a good deal of trust in the peace-making efforts of the Americans. At an informal meeting on 20 April at which the new British Foreign Secretary, Francis Pym, brought his colleagues up to date on the situation, the Foreign Ministers of the Ten 'wishing for a peaceful settlement to this crisis in accordance with the Security Council Resolution, welcome and support the efforts made by Mr. Haig, the American Secretary of State, to encourage a peaceful settlement.' It was not to be. The Argentinians did not move, and meanwhile the British task force was approaching the South Atlantic. Fears began to be expressed about the dangers of escalation. These were sharply reinforced when South Georgia was retaken on 25 April and when Secretary Haig announced on 30 April the collapse of the US peace initiative and the end of US neutrality. However, the event which more than any other contributed to the breakup in the hitherto solid Community front was the sinking of the battle-cruiser *General Belgrano* by a British submarine on 2 May with the presumed loss of 368 lives.

The situation was sufficiently serious for the Political Committee to hold a special meeting on 4 May at which the British Political Director came under heavy pressure from his colleagues to give diplomacy another chance. The most extreme position was taken by the Irish. Immediately after the sinking of the *General Belgrano* the Taoiseach, Mr Haughey, had declared that he was 'appalled by what amounts to open war between Argentina and Great Britain in the South Atlantic' and announced that 'the Irish Government regards the application of economic sanctions as no longer appropriate and will therefore be seeking the withdrawal of those sanctions by the Community.' Although this categorical approach was later toned down, it was clear that the renewal of sanctions would run into considerable difficulties.

The Council was not due to meet until 24 May, while the sanctions were due to expire a week earlier. Had consensus been reached in the Political Committee and Coreper, this would not have presented a difficulty, as the Council could have adopted the extension by written procedure. But consensus could not be reached at the level of officials, and so Ministers were hastily assembled in the evening of Sunday 16 May in Luxembourg, where they were due to meet the next day on regular NATO business. They could do no more than adopt a temporizing measure, extending the sanctions for one week until the Council met. Even so, Ireland and Italy took advantage of the escape clause provided by Article 224 of the EEC Treaty to withdraw from the sanctions, while undertaking not to allow the measures still in force in the other Member States to be undermined, and Denmark stated that it too would withdraw from the Community system as soon as it had enacted identical national measures. This was also the basis on which the Council extended the sanctions, without this time fixing an expiry date, when it came to discuss the matter again on 24 May.

The position taken by Ireland has to be seen in the context of Anglo-Irish relations. Since his re-election in March, Mr Haughey had taken a tougher line on Northern Ireland and his relations with Mrs Thatcher had deteriorated. A crucial by-election was coming up in May, and the sinking of the *Belgrano*, in addition to genuine shock over the loss of life, called forth caustic comparisons with the sinking of an Irish trawler by a British submarine the previous month.

Italy's opposition to the renewal of sanctions stemmed from the fact that large numbers of Argentinians were of Italian origin and the ties between the two countries were close. Even more germane was the fact that a bill was in preparation to allow all Italians living abroad to vote in Italian elections, which would have had the effect of enfranchising over a million Argentinians of Italian extraction. This was an ideal situation to exploit, and the Italian politicians did not forgo the opportunity. The position taken by the Italian representatives in Brussels was forced upon them by domestic politics.

With two members of the Community abandoning the consensus, Denmark could no longer hold the line as it had done the previous month. It was therefore obliged to revert to its classical theory of the separation of political and economic functions in the Community.

Although only these three countries ceased to apply the Community measures, the United Kingdom's remaining partners were by no means happy with the situation in which they found themselves. It has been suggested that their support for sanctions waned as a result of the British intransigence over the annual agricultural-price negotiations, which were reaching a crucial point just at this time. The United Kingdom, in a bid to cut agricultural expenditure, was holding out against the emerging consensus in the Agriculture Council and was in fact outvoted on 18 May, its attempt to veto the proceedings by invoking the Luxembourg compromise being overruled. It is going too far to suggest that a link between the price decisions and the Falklands sanctions was ever established, but it is certainly the case that the climate of sympathy for the United Kingdom which had been created by the Argentinian invasion was in the process of being dissipated by the feeling that in the eyes of Whitehall Community solidarity was a one-way street.

Perhaps more significant, especially in the Political Committee, was the feeling that once the United Kingdom had secured the support of the Community, it ceased to pay any more attention to it and concentrated on other matters. In the eyes of many the price of support should have been a greater readiness on the part of the British to take their partners into their confidence and consult them on the political approach to be adopted. The Member States felt that they were being taken for granted, and resented it.

A Bridge too Far (1982–1986) 213

Yet with all its imperfections, Political Co-operation came well out of the Falklands affair. The impact of rapid Community action at the beginning was far greater than that of the crumbling of consensus in the later stages. One great advantage, as in the case of the earlier sanctions over Poland, was that the use of the Community mechanism made the differentiated application of measures possible. Even though Ireland, Italy, and Denmark withdrew, Community sanctions remained in place until abrogated on the cessation of hostilities. Political Co-operation and the Community were drawing more closely together, and in the process strengthening their international profile. Nationally, the support given to the United Kingdom by its European partners proved to the British public that there was more to the EEC than quarrels about beef mountains and wine lakes and gave the Community a much needed shot in the arm.

On the other hand, success was only possible because of two circumstances which could not be guaranteed for the future. Had Spain already been a Member of the Community, the Ten could not have taken the action which they did. Secondly, had the Belgians not held the Presidency and the Political Committee therefore not been meeting in Brussels, the close coordination with Coreper, which was indispensable for agreement on the terms for Community sanctions, would not have been possible. The coincidence masked the need for joint meetings of the two bodies which was to become evident again only eight years later when the Community had to deal with the collapse of the Communist regimes in Eastern Europe.

The Middle East

The Ten were unable to press home the advantage they had gained by the adoption of the Venice Declaration in June 1980. Faced with the opposition of the United States and the downright hostility of Israel, the Ten's cohesion began to fray, and the missions to the region of Mr Thorn and Mr van der Klaauw suffered from a lack of conviction about the proper role of EPC. President Mitterrand's election in May 1981 not only brought about a radical change in French policy towards the Middle East but also, for the first time since Political Co-operation began in 1970, meant that French diplomacy concentrated on national action regardless of the European position rather than making certain that EPC policy corresponded to that of France. In these unpromising circumstances, Political Co-operation had to respond to two challenges, the setting up of a Multinational Force in Sinai and the Israeli invasion of Lebanon.

The Multinational Force and Observers in Sinai

The Egyptian–Israeli Peace Treaty which formed part of the Camp David process provided for the withdrawal of Israeli forces from Sinai. This was to be monitored by a United Nations force, according to the Treaty, or, failing that, by a multinational force. The latter had the preference of Israel, mindful of the withdrawal of the UN force which had made possible the attack by Nasser in June 1967. The United States also was wary of the UN framework because the Soviet Union was certain to make difficulties in the Security Council, as indeed occurred. The Americans had been working on the assumption that they would have the responsibility for organizing a multinational force, and this was finalized in a Protocol concluded by Egypt and Israel on 3 August 1981 and witnessed by the United States.

This development did not square with the policy of the Ten. The MFO was widely seen, particularly by the Arabs, as a symbol of the continued existence of the Camp David approach. The new US Secretary of State, Alexander Haig, wanted to push Camp David through to its conclusion in the form of a Palestinian autonomy agreement excluding both Palestinian self-determination and the participation of the PLO. Determined to forestall any new initiative by the Europeans based on the Venice Declaration, he was doubly anxious to involve them in the MFO. Their presence would provide a guarantee that the Force was not part of a grand strategic design on the part of the United States, and would tie the Europeans into the logic of the Camp David approach. The Secretary did not approach the Ten as a group, but only the British, French, Italians, and (later) the Dutch—after the Australians had said that their participation would depend on that of the Europeans. The Germans were left out because of constitutional restrictions on the deployment of German forces.

The reaction was not over-enthusiastic. Lord Carrington hoped to use the British Presidency in the second part of 1981 to

A Bridge too Far (1982–1986)

take the Venice process a stage further. He planned to visit Saudi Arabia in November to see whether the 'eight points' which Crown Prince Fahd had launched on 8 August could contribute to finding a solution, particularly through the provision that the right of all the countries of the region to live at peace should be affirmed. If all went well, the European Council later that month could make a new declaration. British participation in a Camp David mechanism would fit awkwardly into this scenario. Lord Carrington's opposition to European participation was the subject of an angry exchange with Secretary Haig at President Sadat's funeral on 10 October.

The position of France was less clear. President Mitterrand supported the step-by-step approach of Camp David and wished to improve relations with Israel which had fallen into disrepair under his predecessors, but also recognized the need for Palestinian statehood and the involvement of the PLO, a position which went well beyond the Venice consensus.

The question of European participation was discussed by the Ten for the first time in the margins of the EPC Ministerial Meeting in London on 13 October. The countries approached were left to consider their positions separately. It soon became clear that the response would be positive. Thwarted by Lord Carrington, Secretary Haig secured the agreement of Mrs Thatcher and, after an appeal at the Yorktown Summit on 16–19 October, of President Mitterrand. The Italians and Dutch were soon to follow suit. A joint declaration by the four was to make it clear that the peace agreement between Israel and Egypt was a first step towards a comprehensive peace settlement and the arrangements for the Israeli withdrawal from Sinai distinct from the rest of the Camp David process. The decision of the four was to be taken 'in consultation and agreement' with their partners of the Ten, who discussed the question at lunch in Luxembourg on 26 October, following which French Foreign Minister Cheysson announced somewhat prematurely that the four were considering participation.

The disadvantages of Ministerial discussions at lunch, with no officials to take note, rapidly became apparent. Ireland denied that consensus had been reached, pointing out that a limited number of Member States could not act on behalf of the Ten and objecting to the drafting of the declaration. They were joined in this by Greece. Greek opposition was mainly to participation as such, in view of the hostile reaction of the Arabs to the idea. Ireland shared this view, but its position was complicated by the military aspect. The Irish claimed that Ireland could only be associated with a military operation if it derived from a decision of the UN Security Council, like the UNIFIL in South Lebanon in which an Irish contingent was serving, and that this taboo extended to any military action which purported to be taken on behalf of the Ten.

Agreement was reached *in extremis* on 4 November, just before Lord Carrington left for Saudi Arabia, on a declaration of the Ten which would have brought out even more clearly the principles of the Venice Declaration and the distinction between the arrangements for the withdrawal from Sinai and the Camp David process. Both these points were unacceptable to Israel. The Presidency therefore worked out with the United States a tortuous procedure for getting round the difficulty. The four countries would address a letter to the governments of the United States, Egypt, and Israel which would contain a factual and neutral announcement of their decision to participate, while the statement of the Ten would be amended to make it more acceptable. Intensive diplomacy ensued to secure agreement especially by Greece, where the matter had by now reached the level of the Prime Minister. Success was achieved on 21 November, the messages of the four despatched over the next two days, and both sets of texts published on 23 November. The statement by the Ten was terse in the extreme:

The Ten consider that the decision of France, Italy, the Netherlands and the United Kingdom to participate in the multinational Force in Sinai meets the wish frequently expressed by Members of the Community to facilitate any progress in the direction of a comprehensive peace settlement in the Middle East on the basis of the mutual acceptance of the right to existence and security of all the States in the area and the need for the Palestinian people to exercise fully its right to self-determination.

In spite of the fact that neither the national messages nor the statement by the Ten mentioned the Venice Declaration, Israel found them unacceptable and was preparing to reject them, threatening at the same time not to withdraw the remaining

A Bridge too Far (1982–1986)

Israeli troops from Sinai if the MFO was not established. The four were induced to state in writing on 26 November that 'they have attached no political conditions, linked to Venice or otherwise, to their participation' in the MFO. Thus armed, the United States persuaded an Israel ever suspicious of European motives to join it in subscribing on 3 December to a joint declaration noting this and reiterating the two countries' commitment to the Camp David accords as the only viable and ongoing negotiating process. After further diplomatic exchanges conducted by the four alone Israel accepted their participation and the contingents of the four countries duly took their place in the MFO.

The experience was not a happy one for Political Co-operation. It had been made abundantly clear that the United States and Israel would block any move on the part of the Ten to attempt to make progress on the lines of the Venice Declaration. Under pressure from those countries, the Ten had done violence to their principles, engaged in internal quarrels damaging to their cohesion, and disappointed the Arabs who still hoped for a European move to help resolve the problem of the Arab–Israeli conflict. But the pressure could not have been resisted without causing damage to the transatlantic relationship. Moreover, there was a risk that without the Europeans the MFO would not have existed and the Israelis would not have completed their withdrawal from Sinai. It was a risk the four could not afford to take. As so often before on Middle East questions, the limits to independent action in Political Co-operation were there for all to see.

Even more significant was the failure of the Ten to seize the opportunity to demonstrate that the machinery of EPC was sufficiently flexible to allow military action, if only of a peace-keeping nature, by some of its members in support of a political aim endorsed by the Ten as a whole. The political conditions were not right, but setting that aside, the strong opposition of the Irish to the concept of action by some members of the Ten on behalf of the Ten as a whole and their rejection of the association of EPC with independent military action were factors which henceforth had an inhibiting affect on what might have been a promising line of development.

But for this, things might have been different on at least two subsequent occasions. When the Multinational Force was deployed in Beirut in August 1982 to oversee the evacuation of the Palestinians, French and Italian participation was decided without reference to the Ten or political cover from them. Years later, when some of the Ten took part in the international effort to keep the sea lanes clear in the Gulf in the later stages of the Iran–Iraq war, the exercise, including the beginnings of operational co-ordination, was centred not on EPC, but on the WEU.

The Israeli Invasion of Lebanon

Any lingering hopes that the Ten might still have a constructive part to play in the Middle East were dissipated in the first part of 1982. Foreign Minister Tindemans of Belgium, which now had the Presidency, toured the region in the spring, but in the absence of a mandate from EPC, he had no new ideas to put forward. The Arabs were disappointed. A general willingness to be helpful was not enough, and was in any case overtaken by events on the ground.

On 6 June 1982 the Israelis launched a full-scale invasion of Lebanon. Operation 'Peace in Galilee' took as its pretext the shooting on 3 June of the Israeli Ambassador in London, but its declared purpose was to eliminate the military threat presented to Israel's northern settlements by the PLO, which had turned southern Lebanon into a state within a state. Prime Minister Begin explained that the Israeli army had been instructed to push back the terrorists to a distance of 40 kilometres to the north, but it soon became clear that this was the long-term aim, to secure which much deeper penetration into Lebanese territory was envisaged. By 14 June the Israeli army had surrounded Beirut, with the presumed intention of rooting out the Palestinian forces there.

The invasion coincided with the Economic Summit meeting at Versailles. Although the Seven succeeded in expressing their 'deep shock', the reaction was not impressive and co-ordination among the Ten was non-existent. This was scarcely surprising. Belgium as Presidency was only present at Versailles on sufferance. The Commission's position was more secure, but it could not take the initiative for EPC co-ordination when its own association with Political Co-operation had so recently been

A Bridge too Far (1982–1986) 219

admitted in the London Report. Moreover, with only five of the Ten present and no Coreu link readily available, the mechanics were lacking.

Although EPC could not organize itself on the spot at Versailles, it nevertheless took up a position with commendable speed thereafter. The Political Committee held a special meeting in Brussels on 8 June to prepare a draft declaration, and at the formal request of Greece and France the Foreign Ministers met on 9 June in Bonn where most of them were attending the NATO Summit the next day. This was the first time the crisis mechanism of the London Report had been successfully activated, following the débâcle of the Poland meetings the previous Christmas.

The Ministers did not find it easy to agree on a text and success was only assured by their need to arrive on time for dinner with the Federal Chancellor properly accoutred in dinner jackets. Discussion turned on the balance of the text and the question of sanctions. By 'balance' was meant the tempering of the condemnation of Israel by a reference to the provocation it had suffered. The solution was to mention 'the bombardments which preceded [the invasion] and which caused intolerably high loss of human life', but not the attack on the Israeli Ambassador, as some delegations had wished. The question of concrete action by the Ten, should Israel refuse to comply with the Security Council Resolutions calling for withdrawal, was more difficult. According to Greece, the Ten should state that in the case of refusal they would examine the possibility of future action, including economic or other measures. France could have accepted a less specific reference to measures, with the precedents of Community action against the Soviet Union and Argentina in mind. Other Member States were opposed to any mention of measures. The formulation in the declaration—'should Israel continue to refuse compliance with the above resolutions the Ten will examine the possibilities for future action'—was agreed under pressure of time after the United Kingdom had pointed out that the UN Resolution had referred to the possibility of examining practical measures consistent with the UN Charter.

The Ten had not done badly. In spite of sympathies divided between the Israelis and the Arabs, the Member States had achieved a reasonable position in a short space of time. They now had to build on this. On the political side, the Ten approached Israel for assurances on ten points ranging from admission for international humanitarian-aid organizations to observance of a cease-fire. The approach was rejected as unacceptable.

The Community drew its conclusions as regards relations with Israel. Having consulted the President of Coreper, the Commission decided not to sign the new Financial Protocol with Israel, and to submit to the Council the question of whether to postpone the meeting of the Joint Co-operation Council scheduled for July. The Council on 21 June confirmed the decision to put off signing the Financial Protocol and decided to postpone the Co-operation Council meeting. This was confirmed by the European Council on 29 June. No further measures were taken, however, although the Commission was under pressure from some Member States to propose them. The Commission was obliged to point out that, short of denouncing the Agreement with Israel which would not take effect for twelve months, any measure of restraint on trade would be contrary to the Agreement and therefore in breach of international law. The Ten were thus debarred from action against a third country they wished to penalize, always supposing consensus could have been reached, by the fact that the Community had, for excellent economic and political reasons, a contractual relationship with the country concerned.

The Ten Resigned

The June European Council was the last occasion on which the Ten made a serious attempt to go a step further in order to have a contribution to make towards resolving the Arab–Israeli conflict. President Mitterrand sought to extend the Ten's position to include a recognition of the PLO as an 'essential interlocutor' and a mention of the Palestinians' right to a state structure of their choice. There was no consensus on this. The most that could be achieved was the reiteration of the hallowed phrase 'the Palestinian people, who should have the opportunity to exercise their right to self-determination' with the Sibylline addition 'with all that this implies'. What this did imply was

A Bridge too Far (1982–1986)

carefully not spelt out. For some it implied a Palestinian State; for others it was a truism which added nothing of significance. The phrase took its place on the shelf with the collection of verbal trophies which the Ten's position on the Arab–Israeli conflict had come increasingly to resemble.

France was now alone among the European countries in actively promoting a Middle East policy. It did this relying on its position as a permanent member of the Security Council and in alliance with Egypt. A Franco-Egyptian draft Security Council Resolution designed both to deal with the crisis in the Lebanon and to bring Resolution 242 up to date by facing squarely the problem of the Palestinians was actively promoted by French diplomacy, but not in meetings of the Ten. Discussion in EPC of what France and the United Kingdom did as permanent members of the Security Council was still out of bounds.

Political Co-operation could do no more than note and endeavour to reconcile the various initiatives which followed in rapid succession, from the Reagan Plan of 1 September 1982 to the Fez proposals of 9 September to the Hussein–Arafat agreement of 11 February 1985. One of the ideas put forward in this agreement was that of an international peace conference for the Middle East. This became for two years a matter of hot debate among the by then Twelve, who did not publicly endorse the idea until it had long lost its power to inflame passions.

The failure of the Ten to play the role in the Middle East which in the period before the Venice Declaration they had correctly identified as a political necessity can be ascribed to a number of reasons. The withdrawal of France from its traditional position as the architect of the Middle East policy of EPC left no one to arbitrate the shifting divisions among the Ten between pro-Israelis and pro-Arabs. No one stepped forward to take France's place. British officials, with their long tradition of Middle East expertise, were fertile in putting forward schemes. However, after the departure of Lord Carrington and the greater involvement in foreign policy of Mrs Thatcher, more responsive to American views, more sympathetic to Israel, and more allergic to the PLO, they lacked political support. The radical positions put forward by Greece had the effect of crystallizing opinion in EPC and making impossible what a few years previously might have been achievable by compromise. Above all, the Middle

Central America

The Ten had been curiously neglectful of their relations with Latin America. For the first ten years or so the Latin America Working Group met only once in each Presidency, and rarely sent up items for the Political Committee's agenda. The one discussion the Political Committee did have was at the height of French disinterest in EPC in 1979, and there was no agreement on whether Political Co-operation should be more active in the area. From time to time individual subjects were dealt with—the EEC Agreement with the Andean Pact, the coup in Bolivia, or the Sandinista revolution in Nicaragua. The Nine's response to the latter was to begin with fairly favourable, in order not to commit the same mistake as had been made with Cuba and drive the new regime into the arms of the Soviet Union.

The coming to power of President Mitterrand in May 1981 changed French, and with it European, policy towards Central America. Régis Debray was an adviser in the Élysée and Claude Cheysson was Foreign Minister. As European Commissioner, Cheysson had tried to develop the North–South dialogue. From his new vantage point he was able to advance the idea that the Community should contribute to stability in Central America by assisting in the economic development of the region. The French argument, which came to be the foundation of the policy of the Ten, was that instability was caused by economic and social backwardness. Cheysson also held that engaging the Central American countries together in political dialogue would oblige them to develop regional structures. Finally, the involvement of Europe would provide a 'third way' for Central America, between Cuba on the one hand and on the other a United States which under the new Reagan Administration saw Central America primarily as a facet of the East–West conflict.

Responding to the discussions in Political Co-operation, the Commission sent to the Council on 4 December 1981 suggestions for an aid programme for Central America as a whole. The Presidency was asked to co-ordinate discussion in the Community and in EPC. While in favour of the French policy, the

Commission was concerned about the shortage of funds in the budget and the absence of a regional interlocutor. Unless overall funds were increased, additional aid for Central America could only be provided at the expense of other countries, and there was a notable absence of unity among the Central American countries themselves. On the part of the Member States, there was some unease about likely policy divergencies with the United States, as a result of which, as well as of concern about the financial implications, the Political Committee hesitated to give EPC backing to the suggestions for increased aid put forward by the Commission.

Pressed by President Mitterrand, the European Council on 30 March 1982 issued a statement 'noting that the tensions and conflicts ravaging Central America frequently stemmed from the grave economic problems and social inequalities which had been aggravated by world economic conditions to the detriment of the poorest countries.' It 'agreed that the aid given by the Member States of the Community and by the Community itself for development in Central America and the Caribbean should be co-ordinated and increased within the limits of their possibilities' and 'instructed the Foreign Ministers to work out detailed arrangements for the provision of Community aid on the basis of proposals by the Commission.'

The Commission responded to this orientation by proposing a 'special action' for 1982 directed to agrarian-reform projects and to strengthening the import capacity of the countries concerned. The necessary finance would be found within the existing budget. A decision by the Council on this proposal was held up until the autumn by the problem of 'globality', in other words whether all the eligible countries should benefit from the special action, including Nicaragua, or whether there should be a degree of differentiation. The United Kingdom firmly opposed the inclusion of Nicaragua, whose Sandinista regime was becoming more Marxist and authoritarian. The Council agreed on 22 November to increase the allocation for Central America by 30 million ecu, less than half what the Commission had proposed. A formula was found avoiding specific mention of Nicaragua, while allowing it to benefit in practice.

It was the Ten's contention that Central America should be allowed to solve its problems by itself without outside interference. At no time therefore did they themselves consider launching an initiative, but supported whatever indigenous proposals seemed most likely to be effective. In March 1982 the European Council welcomed the initiative of the Nassau Four (Canada, Mexico, Venezuela, and the United States) for economic support to the region (later to develop into the US Caribbean Basin Initiative). A more hopeful development was the peace initiative of Contadora, support for which formed the basis of the policy of the Ten for the next few years.

On 5 January 1983 the Foreign Ministers of Mexico, Venezuela, Panama, and Colombia, meeting on the island of Contadora in the Gulf of Panama, called on the countries involved in the Central American conflict to institute multilateral negotiations, on neighbouring countries to help them with economic initiatives, and on all foreign powers to withdraw their advisers. Like the Europeans and unlike the Americans, the Contadora Group viewed the origins of the problems of Central America in terms of economic, social, and political inequalities rather than of the East–West conflict. After a further meeting in April attended by the Central American countries, an agenda for negotiations was drawn up.

Confused by the plethora of initiatives—there had been at least eight in the previous two years—and by no means certain of the ultimate success of Contadora, the Ten hesitated to respond immediately to appeals for support, the more so as it was known that a declaration by them would be unwelcome to the Americans, who under Reagan were shifting to a more hardline position against Communism wherever it appeared. However, as the initiative gained ground, they came round to it. The Foreign Ministers emphasized the importance of efforts made in the region to begin a dialogue, particularly by the Contadora Group, at their Gymnich-type meeting on 14–15 May, and this position was confirmed by the European Council in Stuttgart on 17–19 June in a statement which laid down the future policy of the Ten.

The Heads of Government were

> convinced that the problems of Central America cannot be solved by military means, but only by a political solution springing from the region itself and respecting the principles of non-interference and inviolability of frontiers. They, therefore, fully support the current

A Bridge too Far (1982–1986)

initiative of the Contadora Group. They underlined the need for the establishment of democratic conditions and for the strict observance of human rights throughout the region. They are ready to continue contributing to the further development in the area, in order to promote progress towards stability.

President Reagan took a different view. Speaking on the same day, he said: 'We must not listen to those who would disarm our friends and allow Central America to be turned into a string of anti-American Marxist dictatorships.' The different appreciation of the situation by the United States—and the Americans' readiness to counter the feared developments by military means—became an inhibiting factor in the formation of EPC policy and created internal difficulties, but on this occasion the Ten succeeded in holding to their position without excessively diluting the consensus.

Political Co-operation now had to follow up the policy orientation given by the European Council. On the political side, it was decided to hold a Ministerial-level Troika meeting with the Contadora Group, as a gesture of support. This duly took place in New York on 29 September. On the economic side, the Commission explained that increased Community aid was not possible. A special effort had been made in 1982–3 because there had been some slack in the Community budget, but this would not be the case in future years. If Foreign Ministers wanted to increase aid to Central America, they would have to persuade the Finance Ministers to make the funds available.

In spite of these difficulties, the Ministers decided on 22 November to study carefully the possibilities of increased co-operation with Central America, and the Council had a first discussion of the economic aspects a week later. The decision followed pressure for a significant increase in financial assistance to the area from both the Contadora Group at the Troika meeting in September and President Betancur of Colombia on his tour of Europe on behalf of Contadora in November. It owed much to the interest of Mr Genscher, who had returned from a meeting at the end of September in Costa Rica with the German Ambassadors in Central America convinced that the Community should conclude a co-operation agreement with the countries of the region, on the lines of the agreement with ASEAN in the conclusion of which he had played an important part. German policy was influenced by the links of the party Foundations with Latin America, especially in the case of the Christian Democrat Konrad Adenauer Stiftung. Similarly, the presence of many Irish religious orders in the region guaranteed interest on the part of Dublin.

The Commission presented its thoughts on this question to the Council in February 1984. It supported the idea of an agreement for political reasons, but stressed that it would need to be concluded with all countries in the region and provide for a significant increase in aid. An agreement without substance would only be a source of frustration.

Conscious of the difficulties to which the Commission's provisos were bound to give rise, the Council was in no hurry to come to a decision. The debate was accelerated by an initiative of President Monge of Costa Rica, the only neutral Central American country and one whose democratic credentials were in no doubt. On a visit to Europe in June he extended an invitation to a conference of EC and Central American Foreign Ministers to be held in Costa Rica at the end of September. The initiative came as no surprise, since at President Monge's request Germany had announced it to the Ten in advance. A conference would, it was thought, be a visible expression of political solidarity and could be followed up by meetings of senior officials for which the EC–Central American Co-operation Agreement would provide an exclusive framework. Annual meetings at the level of Foreign Ministers were foreseen. According to this approach, the political aspects of the proposed arrangement would be more important than the economic one.

The Ten accepted President Monge's invitation, once it had been made clear that all Central American countries would take part. Indeed, participation was extended to the Contadora Group as well as Spain and Portugal. The Conference, held on 28–9 September in San José de Costa Rica, issued a communiqué covering both political and economic questions which had been discussed at great length in advance. On the European side, the positions had been prepared separately in the EPC and Community frameworks. In order to prepare their own positions, the Central Americans had been constrained to come together for the first time in a series of meetings before the Conference began.

A Bridge too Far (1982–1986)

The importance of the process as a guarantee of independence was brought out in several of the speeches. Mr Genscher made the point that only a political dialogue can open the way to co-operation among countries. A dialogue with the Community was only possible when the partner was a regional unit; the formation of a Community in Central America would open the way to political and economic independence. Mr Genscher went on to set out the political conditions for dialogue: free elections, pluralist democracy, and respect for human rights. This warning balanced the offer of support for the diversification of the foreign relations of the Central American countries.

M. Pisani, who represented the Commission, put across the same message:

The presence of Twelve European Ministers and a European Commissioner will take on its true significance only if the countries of Central America adopt clearly and irrevocably a pact of the same type and spirit, and with the same democratic basis, as that adopted by the European countries themselves. For there can be no doubt that it is only if this Central American solidarity asserts and organizes itself that the danger of external intervention feared by all can really be removed.

The concrete outcome of the Conference was to continue the dialogue.

A comprehensive discussion took place between the Ministers of the Ten Member States of the European Community and those of the Central European countries on the political, economic and cultural relations between them . . . They have agreed that further meetings in this dialogue should take place at regular intervals. The level of such meetings, whether at ministerial or official level, will be determined in the light of circumstances.

It was also decided to negotiate an agreement with the Community. 'The Ministers of the European Community and those of Central America . . . declared themselves ready to start discussions as soon as possible with a view to negotiating an interregional framework agreement.' The Community would have had difficulty in taking this decision had it not been for the political pressure.

The Ten now had to follow this up. On the political side, views on whether the dialogue should take place at ministerial or official level and whether the Ten should be represented by the Troika or all take part depended on the degree of enthusiasm with which individual Member States regarded the Contadora process, in which Nicaragua and the other Central American countries seemed farther apart than ever. The Ten were careful not to identify themselves with successive versions of the draft Act which was under negotiation, and made it plain in a message issued on 12 February 1985 that the dialogue between Europe and Central America would be conditioned by progress in the Contadora process.

On the Community side, preparations for the negotiation of an agreement were put in hand, and an additional 20 million ecu was written into the 1985 budget. From the beginning of 1985 the negotiations were the responsibility of M. Cheysson, who had returned to the Commission with responsibility for Latin America. The ideas of a Community agreement making no distinction between political and economic aspects was thought likely to raise too many difficulties with Member States and was abandoned. The proposal which the Commission sent to the Council on 15 May 1985 was for an agreement consisting of two interdependent parts, machinery for a regular, structured political dialogue based on provisions to be adopted by EPC procedures and economic measures in accordance with the usual Community rules, including a substantial increase in aid.

The previous month, the Ten extended an invitation to a second Ministerial meeting in Europe before the end of the year. The political situation subsequently became more difficult, however. The United States introduced a trade embargo against Nicaragua on 1 May. Fortunately they did not ask the Community to support the American measures or introduce sanctions of its own. The result was none the less to increase the pressure on the Commission and the Council to expedite work on the Agreement, which now appeared likely to be the centre-piece of the Ministerial meeting.

The form of the Agreement gave rise to discussion in both the Community and Political Co-operation. The Commission's proposal for an Agreement with interdependent political and economic sections was supported by a number of Member States, including the United Kingdom, which argued that a global agreement would be a useful precedent for strengthening the link between the Community and EPC (and the inclusion of a political element would help mask any shortfall in generosity on the economic side). The Federal Republic and Denmark, however, both feared difficulties in national parliamentary ratification of a mixed agreement, which would not be necessary in the case of a traditional agreement concluded by the Community. Their doubts were shared by Greece. At least in the case of Denmark and Greece, one may wonder whether the underlying concern was not to preserve the institutional purity of EPC. These difficulties were solved on 22 July by the Council giving directives to the Commission to negotiate a classical framework co-operation agreement, while at the same time Ministers in EPC agreed that the political part of the dialogue would be enshrined in a Final Act to be concluded at the San José II Conference. The text of this would be negotiated by EPC.

This was the structure approved by the Conference, which met in Luxembourg on 11–12 November. The Co-operation Agreement was a traditional Community agreement negotiated by the Commission in accordance with the Council's directives. It laid special emphasis on regional integration in the area, the Community's intention being to give priority assistance to regional projects. It also referred to the objective of contributing to stability, especially by implementing operations aimed at improving social and economic conditions, and to human rights. These three elements were all important from the political point of view, and were also referred to in the Final Act and the political communiqué.

The Final Act set out the objectives of the political and economic dialogues and described how they were to be organized. The economic dialogue would be carried out through the Co-operation Agreement. The political dialogue 'should be institutionalised, in particular by the holding of annual meetings, in principle at Ministerial level.'

Both the economic and the political dialogues served their purpose in encouraging regional integration. On the economic side, the increased aid was devoted as far as possible to regional projects. On the political side, the very fact that meetings with the Twelve were held at regular intervals obliged the Central Americans themselves to meet beforehand to agree on a line to present to the Europeans. While the Europeans carefully refrained from putting forward initiatives themselves, the general political interest they showed provided the countries of the region with a respectable point of reference between the United States and the Soviet Union and gave the Contadora process a lifeline without which it might not have survived. The Central American policy of the Ten was unwelcome from the start to the US Administration and sometimes contested by it, but unlike in the case of Poland the United States chose not to make a public issue of it. In spite of national differences, the Ten were able to develop and maintain a coherent position. This fact, together with the bringing together of the political and economic parts of the relationship, marked a further step in the development of Political Co-operation.

South Africa

The adoption of the Code of Conduct in 1977 was designed to dispense Member States from having to contemplate more drastic ways of opposing apartheid. Although in theory the question of 'other measures' stayed on EPC's agenda, the Netherlands in time gave up pressing the point and Political Co-operation won seven years' respite from facing a difficult issue. This position became increasingly uncomfortable from 1984 on, as trouble flared in South Africa. At their meeting in Dublin on 11 September 1984 the Ten 'considered that the recent violence and rioting in black townships . . . reflected . . . the frustration of black South Africans at their deliberate exclusion from South Africa's political life and at the denial of adequate political means to express their grievances.' They were not, however, able to go further than recalling their traditional opposition to apartheid.

The situation had not changed the following April, when the Ten declared that 'the measures recently announced do not match the reality or scale of the problem. Only the abolition of discriminatory practices and of the system of apartheid, together with recognition of the civil and political rights of the black population, are capable of ensuring the peaceful evolution of South African society.' Although the language used was stronger than ever before it was recognized that there was no point in discussing sanctions, given the absence of consensus. The Ministers did, however, agree to study the possibility of revising the Code of Conduct.

This attitude was not tenable for much longer. The US Congress was taking a hard line and pressure for sanctions was growing particularly in the Scandinavian countries and the Netherlands. The European Parliament echoed these moves, a matter of supreme indifference to the Member States, but one which caused considerable concern to the Commission, which was under pressure to use its Treaty powers to propose Community sanctions. This explains the unusually active and public role the Commission took in the sanctions debate in EPC, which attracted criticism from the Member States.

The turning-point came with the declaration of a state of emergency by the South African government on 22 July 1985. The Ten condemned the action, but in the face of British opposition could not agree to examine possible measures as proposed by France. The French Socialist government lost no time in taking national measures. On 25 July it recalled its Ambassador and banned new investments in South Africa, a measure already taken by Denmark in May. It so happened that the ten Foreign Ministers were all in Helsinki on 31 July for a meeting to commemorate the tenth anniversary of the signing of the Helsinki Final Act. They took the opportunity to have a discussion on South Africa. The Ministers decided to send their Troika colleagues to Pretoria, with a Member of the Commission, 'to discuss the recent serious developments in South Africa in the light of the concern expressed by the Ten in their recent statements.' This mission would be prepared by a special meeting of the Political Committee with the participation of Ambassadors from Pretoria. All Member States were thus able to recall their Ambassadors without having to state whether this was a political gesture. In addition to establishing an inventory of national measures, the Political Committee was to discuss 'measures to take in order to contribute to the abolition of apartheid'.

As so often with Ministerial Meetings when the accredited EPC scribes are not present, there was some doubt later about the scope of the Ministers' decision. Although the Political Committee on 22–3 August adopted a mandate for the Troika couched in fairly firm language, the question of whether future measures should be announced was not resolved: 'In the absence of any appreciable progress within a reasonable period, [the Ten] reserve their right to reconsider their attitude.' The firm language was the more necessary as the Troika mission was strongly criticized by African groupings, who saw it as a means of diverting attention from the real issue of sanctions.

The Troika visited South Africa from 29 August to 2 September. It was widely criticized in the media, the main reason being the inability of the Ten to come out in favour of sanctions. This was therefore the main topic of discussion at the Ministerial Meeting on 10 September in Luxembourg.

The Ministers spent much of the time, with a short break for lunch served in the meeting-room, in drafting a paper divided into three parts: a general declaration setting out the views of the Ten; a list of restrictive measures on which their attitudes were to be harmonized; and a list of positive measures to help the black population. This followed the strategy advocated by Mr Genscher at the Helsinki meeting of combining 'restrictive' with 'positive' measures, and was worked out on the basis of proposals for a 'common core' of measures put forward by the Luxembourg Presidency. French proposals for more wide-ranging economic sanctions were not accepted. The British Minister had taken part in the drafting exercise, which led partners to believe that the United Kingdom was prepared to compromise. However, at the end of the drafting session Mr Rifkind was obliged to refer back the proposal to recall military attachés, on which some of the partners were insisting. This caused a delay of some three hours while officials tracked down the Prime Minister, believed to be visiting some of the more remote Highland distilleries. When the reply came, it cast doubt on the usefulness of the whole section on restrictive measures. By now it was too late to negotiate a different text. The Chairman, Mr Poos, had no option but to release the text agreed by nine Member States with a British footnote which read: 'The United Kingdom is able to support the general statement and the positive measures but wishes to give further consideration to the other measures proposed and believes it premature to come to a decision today on these matters.' The situation was reminiscent of the Greek reservation on the Ten's declaration on Poland three years earlier, except that on this occasion the Ten were aware before the meeting ended of the absence of consensus, but saw no way, given the late hour and the hordes of press waiting outside, of doing anything about it.

The restrictive measures on which the nine Member States agreed to harmonize their attitudes were an arms embargo, military co-operation, the recall of military attachés, the discouraging of cultural and scientific agreements and freezing of sporting and security contacts, the cessation of oil exports to South Africa and of sensitive equipment for the police and armed forces, and the prohibition of new collaboration in the nuclear sector. Positive measures included the adaptation of the Code of Conduct, programmes of assistance to non-violent anti-apartheid organizations and for the education of the non-white community, and programmes to assist the Southern African Development Co-ordination Conference (the economic grouping of neighbouring countries) and the Front Line States. Ministers also asked for the possibility of increasing social and educational assistance from the Community to the non-white population and to political refugees to be examined.

The United Kingdom was able to announce on 25 September that, in the spirit of Community solidarity, it was able to lift its reservation on the restrictive measures. The counterpart for this was that they were to be implemented on an exclusively national basis. The Commission tabled proposals based on the EEC Treaty, but implementation in the Community framework was opposed by the United Kingdom, Germany, and Denmark. In order to preserve a united political front, the question was not pressed. National implementation was supposed to be monitored by the Commission, but in the absence of a uniform interpretation of what had been decided, this proved difficult in practice.

A revised version of the Code of Conduct was adopted by Ministers on 19 November. Apart from that, the implementation of the positive measures depended largely on action by the Community. A special programme funded from the Community budget was set up to assist the victims of apartheid. The question of distribution was a difficult one. The Commission had no Delegation in South Africa, and it would have been inappropriate in any case to go through government channels. The problem was solved by administering the programme at one remove via four non-governmental channels, the Protestant and Catholic Church organizations, the trade unions, and a body called the Kagiso Trust specially set up to cover non-church and non-union recipients. The Trust became a controversial matter with the Member States, especially the United Kingdom, because of the exclusion of Inkatha owing to the opposition of the other African groupings.

Aid was granted by the Commission according to a set of guidelines which it drew up. The lack of consultation with Member States attracted criticism. The Commission felt that it was important, however, that the aid should be seen to have no political conditions attached, something which the involvement of EPC might have cast into doubt. Certainly the Community was one of the few donors which found an effective way of getting help to those in need. Its example was imitated by others, the Japanese also using the Kagiso Trust as a vehicle for its donations. The Commission was also reluctant to provide details of individual beneficiaries to Member States or indeed to anyone else, for fear of reprisals by the South African authorities. This secrecy was resented by the Member States and in particular by the Embassies in South Africa. These various considerations made it necessary for a particularly complicated machinery for the management of the aid programme to be set up. The end result was satisfactory, the Community's programme being reputed to have had a definite political effect on South Africa.

The Twelve had now little room left to carry their policy forward and were obliged to exploit to the maximum their position of 10 September. In order to retain the diplomatic initiative, they decided to hold a meeting at Ministerial level in Lusaka on 3–4 February with the Front Line States, the first there had been between the two groups. Although few full Ministers attended, the meeting had a positive effect. It was agreed that, if the measures announced by the Community, the Commonwealth, the Nordic countries and the United States failed to achieve the desired results, 'further measures should be considered.'

The Netherlands had taken over the Presidency on 1 January 1986 and were anxious to achieve a toughening in the policy of the Twelve. They were unable to pursue this actively in the first part of the year, however, as the diplomatic initiative now lay with the Commonwealth Group of Eminent Persons. It was only reasonable for the Twelve to await the results of this before reviewing their own position. By June the Group had presented its Report, concluding that South African policy for the time being excluded negotiations as a way forward and suggesting a number of international 'measures'. At the same time the South African government on 12 June reimposed a state of emergency and arrested opposition leaders. The Presidency therefore took up the Group's idea of 'measures', beginning with import restrictions on fruit, vegetables, and wine. Both the Netherlands and Ireland had announced their intention of introducing a national ban on these products, even though they were covered by the common agricultural policy. It was intended that the European Council in The Hague on 27 June should take a decision.

The European Council had before it a package consisting of strengthened positive measures and a number of restrictive measures including import bans on coal, iron, steel, and gold coins, as well as the agricultural products previously mentioned. It was not possible to come to an agreement on this. The United Kingdom and Germany, supported by Portugal, were opposed and France under the new Chirac government, while prepared to go along with anything all the Twelve decided, put more emphasis on the positive measures. The Twelve gave themselves another breathing space. The European Council agreed that 'in the next three months the Community will enter into consultations with the other industrialised countries on further measures which might be needed covering in particular a ban on new investments and on the import of coal, iron, steel and gold coins from South Africa.' Fruit, vegetables, and wine were dropped in order to facilitate agreement and were replaced by a ban on investments, mirroring moves in the United States. The European Council also asked Sir Geoffrey Howe, representing the incoming British Presidency, to visit Southern Africa 'in a further effort to establish conditions in which the necessary dialogue can commence.'

As Foreign Secretary of the country known to have been principally responsible for the failure to adopt sanctions at The Hague, Sir Geoffrey had a difficult time. In addition to holding the Presidency of EPC, Sir Geoffrey was also engaged in defending the isolated British position in the Commonwealth, an additional reason for making him an unwelcome visitor in Southern Africa. The African National Congress refused to meet him and Prime Minister Mugabe of Zimbabwe described his mission as 'reprehensible, futile and useless'. Nor was Sir Geoffrey able to persuade the South African government to adopt the measures the Twelve thought essential. Acceptance by all the Member States of the package worked out at The Hague was beginning to seem inevitable as the end of the three months' grace period approached. The prospects for this were improved by the Commonwealth mini-Summit at the beginning of August which agreed on a set of measures, each Member being free to decide on their imposition. The United Kingdom thereupon made it known that it would not stand in the way of a consensus among the Twelve on the imposition of the restrictive measures which had been listed in the European Council's statement at The Hague.

The decision was finally taken by the Ministers meeting in Brussels on 15–16 September. The points which caused difficulty were whether or not coal should be included and how the measures were to be implemented. The change in the British position had left Germany and Portugal isolated in their opposition to sanctions. As the price of agreeing to a package, Mr Genscher successfully insisted on the exclusion of coal (one-third of South Africa's coal exports went to the Federal Republic). The exclusion was strongly resisted, with the result that, exceptionally for Political Co-operation, the Twelve's statement noted the majority position: 'Most partners were also willing to implement a ban on the import of coal from South Africa if a consensus on this could be achieved.' Subsequent efforts to implement the package of The Hague in its entirety also failed.

The second point concerned the implementation of the measures. The ban on iron and steel was implemented immediately by the representatives of the Member States following normal ECSC procedure. As regards gold coins and new investments, however, several Member States argued that the decisions should be implemented by Community measures. Belgium made acceptance by its partners of Community implementation a condition for its acceptance of the substance of the measures. The United Kingdom and France were opposed. The problem was not resolved for another month and required much detailed discussion by the Community experts. This resulted in

A Bridge too Far (1982–1986)

the ban on the import of gold coins being implemented through a Council Regulation on 27 October, and that on new investments through a Decision of the same type as the ECSC iron-and-steel ban.

The difficulties the Ten, later Twelve, experienced in reaching agreement on sanctions detracted from the considerable achievement of their South Africa policy. The positions of the Member States were wide apart, and yet EPC provided a mechanism which resulted in a substantial European position. The position was less advanced than the Dutch, for example, would have wished, but more so than the British or the Germans ever intended. Political Co-operation produced a position which was the median, not the lowest common denominator, of the different national positions. It has to be admitted that the decisive move came in a forum outside EPC, the Commonwealth mini-Summit, but this in turn through EPC had a direct effect on German and Portuguese policy. The position of the Twelve, established with such difficulty and perhaps for this reason, became a point of reference for countries like Japan.

The implementation of sanctions through measures of a broadly Community nature and the programme of aid to the victims of apartheid took the Twelve a step further in the practical bringing together of EPC and the Community. Objections to the use of Community instruments to implement EPC policies were less on grounds of principle, as they had been in the past, than for reasons of substance, in order not to give too high a profile to the measures. When the Twelve next came to apply sanctions, against Iraq four years later, the appropriateness of action through the Community was no longer in doubt.

SELECTED READING

There are two accounts of the Genscher–Colombo inititative and the Stuttgart Solemn Declaration by participants in the negotiations. These are Lay (1983), European Correspondent of Italy, and Neville-Jones (1983), then seconded to the Secretariat-General of the Commission. Other studies include Bonvincini (1987), Hansen (1981), Weiler (1983), and Rummel and Wessels (1983).

On East–West relations, see the two surveys by Maslen (1984 and 1987), who was Head of Division for Eastern Europe in the EC Commission.

For the EPC aspects of the Falklands crisis, see Edwards (1984).

The Middle East in the period 1982–6 is best covered by Greilsammer and Weiler (1987), Pijpers (1984) on the Sinai force, Sicherman (1985), and Legros (1982) on the invasion of Lebanon.

For Central America, see Gräbendorff (1990).

7
The Single European Act (1987)

ARGUMENT

That EPC made such a tardy entrance on the scene in 1970 was the result of quarrels about its place in the Community institutional order. Since then it had had fifteen years of productive existence by steering clear of these difficulties, building up an effective machine as a pragmatic response to successive challenges. It had no legal basis, relying entirely on a handful of documents agreed informally by Foreign Ministers without reference to national parliamentary authority and on a sizeable body of procedure and precedent which remained confidential. It was now to abandon this comfortable state for one which gave it a personality in international law and for the first time associated it with the Community legal order. This came about as a by-product of a wider movement towards Community reform.

THE EUROPEAN PARLIAMENT'S DRAFT TREATY ON
EUROPEAN UNION

The movement began in the European Parliament. Directly elected for the first time in June 1979, it saw itself as having a responsibility to forward the cause of European integration. The instigator and orchestrator of this movement was Altiero Spinelli, a lifelong federalist who in this his last battle trimmed his sails to considerable effect in order to secure for his vision of a European Union a broad measure of parliamentary support transcending national and party divisions.

Spinelli saw that federalist efforts over thirty years had been brought to nothing because negotiations had ended up in the hands of governments. His aim was therefore to secure the adoption by Parliament of a draft Treaty on European Union which could be exploited by a direct appeal to public opinion and national Parliaments over the Heads of Governments. His tactics were to accept compromise even if this meant falling short of the ideal, and to recognize that it would not be possible for the transfer of responsibilities from the national to the

European level to take place simultaneously in all domains. The draft Treaty on European Union which emerged from the European Parliament's Institutional Committee, of which Spinelli was co-ordinating rapporteur, distinguished between exclusive competences reserved to the Union, concurrent competences shared between the Union and the Member States, and co-operation for matters which remained in the inter-governmental mode. International relations fell into the last category. The inter-governmental character of EPC was thus preserved for as long as governments wished, but could be transformed into concurrent or exclusive competence in the future.

It took nearly the whole of the five-year life of the Parliament to achieve this result. During this time the Genscher-Colombo initiative had been launched with disappointing results, there was dissatisfaction with the capacity of Political Co-operation to speak with a single voice, and the Community itself, the British budget problem still unsolved, seemed incapable of rising to the mounting technological challenge of the United States and Japan. These factors, combined with Spinelli's persuasiveness, ensured that the draft Treaty establishing the European Union was adopted by Parliament on 14 February 1984 by 237 votes to 32 with 34 abstentions.

THE *AD HOC* COMMITTEE ON INSTITUTIONAL AFFAIRS

Spinelli's hopes of appealing to public opinion and national Parliaments over the Heads of Governments were disappointed. The European elections of June 1984 were fought largely on national issues, not on the future of the Community, and only the Italian Parliament rapidly approved the draft Treaty. President Mitterrand of France, however, saw in the Parliament's initiative a springboard for his own European policy and gave it his support, albeit in characteristically guarded and ambiguous terms. Speaking to the European Parliament on 23 May as President of the European Council, Mitterrand said:

. . . here is the House encouraging us to go further along this path by proposing a draft Treaty on European Union . . . Those of us who are interested will observe that the same old method is being used. The new situation calls for a new Treaty . . . which must not, of course, be a substitute for existing Treaties, but an extension of them to fields they do not currently cover. This is the case of the European political community. France . . . is available for such an enterprise. I, on its behalf, state its willingness to examine and defend your project, the inspiration behind which it approves. I therefore suggest that preparatory consultations, perhaps leading to a conference of the Member States concerned, be started up. The project of a European Union and the solemn declaration of Stuttgart will be a basis for this.

No one could doubt President Mitterrand's sincere attachment to the European cause. He recalled it himself in the same speech: 'I am . . . speaking to you as a French European whose personal commitment has been in evidence at every stage of the emergence of Europe. When, in May 1948, just three years after the war, the European idea took shape at the congress in The Hague, I was there and I believed in it.' Equally, no one could be sure what sort of Europe Mitterrand wanted. On the one hand, he had himself said to the European Parliament that a new Treaty should extend the fields covered by the existing Treaties. This was not, then, a new attempt *à la* Fouchet to subsume the existing Communities in a European political community whose institutions remained to be defined. On the other hand, Mitterrand raised once again the spectre of a political secretariat. In a different part of the 23 May speech he said 'Let us give the Council of Ministers back its means of implementing the policies of which the European Council lays down the guidelines. Let us give the European Council a permanent secretariat for political co-operation.' The idea of a permanent political secretariat had already been aired in a speech Mitterrand made in The Hague on 7 February, a week before the vote in the European Parliament. It was not calculated to reassure the original Six, who were entitled to wonder whether France was reverting once again to the proposals they had already had to fight off in the Fouchet negotiations and again before the Paris Summit of 1972. Although much water had flowed under the bridge since then and integrationist ardour had cooled, the prospect of a secretariat deriving its authority from the Heads of Government and unconnected with the Community institutions was bound to cause concern to partisans of the Community method.

President Mitterrand presented his initiative at the European Council at Fontainebleau on 25–6 June 1984. The circumstances were propitious. After five years of debilitating wrangling a solution was about to be found to the British budget problem and thus to the financing of the Community. Little time was left after dealing with these questions for discussions on the future of the Community. A French text which would have set up a political secretariat there and then was not given consideration. Instead, it was agreed to set up an *ad hoc* committee of personal representatives of Heads of State and Government 'to make suggestions for the improvement of the operation of European co-operation in both the Community field and that of political, or any other, co-operation.'

The analogy between the *ad hoc* Committee and the Spaak Committee which laid the groundwork for the Treaties of Rome was freely drawn, but was imperfect. Unlike its predecessor, the *ad hoc* Committee was not composed of outstanding personalities who could impose a vision of Europe on reluctant governments. It was chaired by Senator Dooge, a former Foreign Minister of Ireland, simply because Ireland was in the chair of the Council from 1 July on. Its members, with some notable exceptions, not only represented their Heads of Government, but acted as the mouthpiece for national positions. It was decided at an early stage that the Committee would not be a slave to consensus, and that differing views could be expressed. This had the advantage of bringing out clearly the different points under discussion, and equally clearly the lack of agreement among Member States. An interim report was presented to the European Council in Dublin in December 1984 and a final report in Brussels in March 1985.

The Dooge Report started from the premiss that the Community was in a state of crisis, unable to achieve a growth rate sufficient to reduce the level of unemployment and exposed to both industrial and technological challenge and threats to its political independence. The Committee concluded that at the end of the day the common political will of the Member States 'must be expressed by the formulation of a genuine political entity among European States: i.e. a European Union.' The Committee was flexible about the means to achieve this aim: the union should have the power to take decisions 'according to procedures which could vary depending on whether the framework is that of intergovernmental co-operation, the Community Treaties, or new instruments yet to be agreed.'

The Single European Act (1987)

Most of the report was concerned with the internal development of the Community. One section was devoted to 'the search for an external identity'. This preserved the distinction between the Community and EPC, but pressed for them to be brought more closely together:

> Europe's external identity can be achieved only gradually within the framework of common action and European political cooperation (EPC) in accordance with the rules applicable to each of these. It is increasingly evident that interaction between these two frameworks is both necessary and useful. They must therefore be more closely aligned.

The question of security was handled in general terms, reserving the position of the Atlantic Alliance and the nuclear powers. The Committee proposed strengthened consultations on security in political co-operation, including weapons technology and strategic doctrines, and common standards and joint development of military equipment.

The Committee's practical proposals on EPC were limited. Its structures were to be strengthened by

> the creation of a permanent political cooperation secretariat to enable successive presidencies to ensure greater continuity and cohesiveness of action; the secretariat would to a large extent use the back-up facilities of the Council and should help to strengthen the cohesion between political cooperation and the external policies of the Community [and by] the regular organization of EPC working meetings at the Community's places of work, while meetings of ministers should also be arranged in the Member States' capitals.

There was thus to be a permanent secretariat, but its role was one of support to the Presidency and limited to EPC questions, on the lines of the one the British had proposed in the years before the London Report, not a political secretariat responsible to the European Council, as suggested by Mitterrand.

EPC was to be improved through the formalization of commitments to prior consultation, by 'seeking a consensus in keeping with the majority opinion with a view to the prompt adoption of common positions and to facilitating joint measures', by adopting common positions particularly at the United Nations, possibly by common representation of Member States and the Community at international institutions and in countries where only a few Member States were represented, and by the codification of EPC rules and practices.

The final report was peppered with reservations and comments from the members of the Committee, including the section on an external identity. The Danish representative had a reservation on the whole section. He 'considered that, instead of structural changes, it is necessary to have a new pragmatic development of European political cooperation on the existing base . . . Particularly in relation to security, it should be confined to political and economic aspects.' The Greek representative entered a number of reservations designed to block any diluting of the consensus principle and to distance EPC from the Atlantic Alliance. Senator Dooge himself on behalf of Ireland did not agree to the inclusion of the section on security and defence. The British, on the other hand, aligned themselves with the original Six on the external section and the Prime Minister's representative, Mr Rifkind, took an active part in the discussion of it.

The Twelve therefore found themselves in exactly the same position on these issues as they had during the discussion of the Genscher–Colombo proposals three years earlier. As to procedure, the Committee had proposed the convening of a conference of Member States to negotiate a draft European Union Treaty based on the *acquis communautaire*, its own Report, and the Stuttgart Declaration 'and guided by the spirit and method of the draft Treaty voted by the European Parliament'. The European Council meeting in March 1985 could not agree on this. It 'expressed its warm appreciation of the Committee's excellent work', always a sign of imminent burial, and put off further consideration until the June meeting in Milan.

THE MILAN EUROPEAN COUNCIL

The Italian Presidency began a round of contacts to prepare the discussion, and President Mitterrand was reputed to be meditating a 'surprise'. On 21 May the Presidency submitted a draft brief for the inter-governmental conference which involved negotiating a Treaty for the gradual completion of European Union. In response to this initiative, the Netherlands proposed that the main aim of the conference should be to revise the EEC

The Single European Act (1987)

Treaty in accordance with Article 236 and to draw up a protocol to the Treaty to consolidate and institutionalize political co-operation. In order to ward off revision of the EEC Treaty, which would require ratification by national Parliaments, Sir Geoffrey Howe circulated to his colleagues at the Gymnich-type meeting of Foreign Ministers in Stresa on 8–9 June a draft agreement on Political Co-operation, which had the form, although not the title, of a Treaty.

The United Kingdom felt uncomfortable in its position of relative isolation which the work of the Dooge Committee had shown up. Although Mr Rifkind had managed by the time of the final report to whittle down the number of footnotes he was obliged to put his name to, the Foreign Office felt dangerously exposed on some Community issues, particularly decision-making. They were also aware that a significant number of Conservative Members of the European Parliament had voted in favour of the Spinelli draft Treaty and that an even more significant number of Labour Members had voted against it. Sir Geoffrey Howe therefore launched a two-pronged operation at Stresa, combining a sophisticated, and in intention more open, reformulation of the Luxembourg compromise with the Political Co-operation text referred to above.

The latter was a minor miracle of scissors-and-paste drafting. Composed of a preamble, nine Articles, and three Annexes, it looked like a Treaty, but was not one. Indeed, the British authorities took the view that it would not require parliamentary ratification, although this would not have been the case in the other members of the Community. It was made up almost entirely of snippets of existing texts or recognized EPC practice, cleverly assembled to present a coherent picture and clad in legal form. The exception was the Article on security, which drew its inspiration from the work of the Dooge Committee. Apart from this, it would have been difficult for anyone to object to any one sentence, since each was either unexceptional or relied on authority disinterred from the dusty archives of EPC, and yet the whole was more than the sum of its parts.

The overall effect was inevitably static. There was no attempt to deal with the problems caused by the rule of consensus, no enforcement of the obligation to consult and more emphasis on cohesion between EPC and the Community than on bringing the two closer together. 'The Member States shall ensure maximum coherence between the external policies of the Communities and the policies agreed in European Political Co-operation.' In one respect the draft was retrograde: whereas the full association of the Commission with EPC had been admitted since the London Report, the British text provided for the Commission to be invited to all meetings 'unless in any particular case all Member States agree to the contrary'. In addition, a secretariat was to be set up on traditional British and Dooge lines: 'The Presidency shall be assisted by a small Secretariat based in the main place of work of the Communities. The office space and services shall be provided by arrangement with the Council Secretariat. The Head of the Secretariat shall be appointed by agreement among the Member States.' The functions of the secretariat included in the first place to 'advise the Presidency as necessary on the conduct of Political Co-operation, in particular on maintaining coherence between the external policies of the Communities and the policies agreed in European Political Co-operation.' This was not the all-embracing political secretariat of the Fouchet Plans, the Pompidou initiative of the early 1970s, or even the more limited Mitterrand initiative of the previous year.

The British had struck too soon. The day before the European Council began, France and Germany jointly presented a counter-draft, entitled 'draft Treaty on European Union'. There were two significant differences in comparison with the British draft. The latter had been confined to Political Co-operation, but the Franco-German draft, while in fact only dealing with the same matters, purported to 'transform without delay the whole of the relations among their States into a European Union' based on the Communities operating in accordance with their own rules and on Political Co-operation operating under eleven Articles set out in the text. These were closely modelled on the nine British Articles, but couched in more elevated language and with some changes of detail. The British restrictions on the presence of the Commission were dropped and the provisions on security were more prudent.

The second significant difference was in the nature of the Secretariat. On the lines foreshadowed by President Mitterrand, this was to be a 'Secretariat General of the Council of the

The Single European Act (1987)

European Union [the new body into which the European Council would be transformed] permanently installed in the main place of work of the Community', under the direction of 'the Secretary-General of the European Union, in charge of Political Co-operation, who will be appointed by the Council of the European Union for a period of four years'. The other members of the Secretariat-General would be appointed by the Foreign Ministers for a period of two years. Their status would be governed by the arrangements applying to European Community officials, while the Secretary-General would enjoy the privileges and immunities of the Vienna Convention.

The Franco-German draft was regarded with suspicion on a number of counts. Italy and the Benelux countries were opposed to applying the 'European Union' label to a codification of Political Co-operation which brought no advances on the Community side. They were joined by the United Kingdom, Greece, and Denmark in their distrust of a high-level Secretary-General for the European Council. The dramatic way in which the draft had been tabled aroused old fears of a Franco-German coalition. The divisions which had crippled the Genscher–Colombo and Dooge discussions seemed as strong as ever. The omens for a successful European Council in Milan were not good.

Yet the European Council not only took the decision to convene a conference on European Union, but confirmed the objective of a single market and gave its support for the French Eureka project. These decisions formed a triptych. They meant that the Community was launched on a course of genuine development, the success of which was ensured by the dynamism of the single-market process; they also meant that future discussions were not confined to political-co-operation aspects. The conference was to work out 'with a view to achieving concrete progress on European Union: (i) a Treaty on a common foreign and security policy on the basis of the Franco-German and United Kingdom drafts' and (ii) amendments to the EEC Treaty mainly on decision-making and the extension to new spheres of activity. The success was largely the work of Prime Minister Craxi, who forced the decision through against the firm opposition of the United Kingdom, Denmark, and Greece and the prudent attitude of other delegations including France and Germany.

The European Council's decision was put into legal form by the General Affairs Council on 22 July. The Conference to examine proposals for the revision of the EEC Treaty was formally convened at the level of Ministers of Foreign Affairs and its first meeting fixed for 9 September. The preparatory work was given to two groups. That on the revision of the Treaty was chaired by Ambassador Dondelinger, the Secretary-General of the Luxembourg Foreign Ministry (Luxembourg had taken over the Presidency on 1 July), and met for the most part in Brussels. The work on the Political Co-operation side was entrusted to the Political Committee:

> The Ministers for Foreign Affairs instruct the Political Committee to draw up by 15 October 1985 the text of a draft Treaty on the basis in particular of the Franco-German and United Kingdom drafts concerning political co-operation with a view to a common foreign and security policy. This draft will be considered by the Ministers for Foreign Affairs meeting for the purpose within the Conference convened under 2 above.

The decision that work on EPC and the Community should proceed in a single framework was an important one, paving the way ultimately to a single Treaty. It was far from being a foregone conclusion. Voices had been raised for the negotiation of the EPC Treaty to be a separate exercise, in the classic form of an international diplomatic conference, with no link to the Community. But as a result of the decision, even though the preparatory work was done in different bodies, no distinction was made at the ministerial level of the Conference proper. On the other hand, it was still assumed at this stage that there would be a separate EPC Treaty, as was indicated by the language of the Milan European Council. Indeed the Council succeeded by sleight of hand in watering down that commitment. Whereas the European Council had envisaged a conference 'to work out . . . a Treaty on a common foreign and security policy', the Foreign Ministers called for 'a draft Treaty . . . concerning political co-operation with a view to a common foreign and security policy'. The change was deliberate, and designed to help those countries which foresaw difficulties about strengthening the common commitment to EPC.

In addition to the Franco-German and British drafts, which were formally part of the Conference's remit, the Netherlands and Italy both presented proposals before the summer holidays designed to bring Political Co-operation closer to the Community. The Netherlands draft attempted to bridge the gap between the British and the Franco-German drafts. The Italian draft drew more on the Dooge Report. While preserving Political Co-operation as the second pillar, it aimed at a common external policy qualitatively different from that followed hitherto in EPC. In pursuit of this objective, the Italians proposed that consensus should be built around the majority view and that a single Ministerial Council should deal with both EPC and Community matters. On security, there were to be close links with WEU. Finally, there was to be a revision clause.

Work began in September on the basis of a draft prepared by the Luxembourg Presidency which tried to take into account all four contributions on the table. The Presidency set a cracking pace. Compared with the Dondelinger Group, the Political Committee had an easy time of it. In only three meetings, it succeeded in producing a text on which there was a broad measure of agreement, leaving to Ministers at dinner discussions on security and the secretariat and in plenary session only the semantic dispute about the object of EPC. Was this to be a common foreign policy? An external policy? The Ministers decided that the Parties 'should endeavour jointly to formulate and implement a European foreign policy.' These three words require exegesis. It was to be 'a' policy because there might be others, it was to be 'European' because there was no agreement that it should be 'common', and it was to be 'foreign' because if it had been 'external', that might have implied that EPC with its inter-governmental procedures also governed the external relations of the Community.

The broad measure of agreement in the Political Committee was achieved at the cost of abandoning the bolder ideas put forward by the Netherlands and Italy. On most points, the 'codification' approach on which the British draft had been based won the day. This was most noticeably the case in the debate on security, the part of the discussion which was the most sensitive and took up the most time. The determined opposition, for different motives, of Ireland and Greece meant that no progress could be made, even on the prudent lines of the Franco-German draft. The end result was no more than a reiteration of the Stuttgart commitment to co-ordinate more closely national positions on the political and economic aspects of security, to maintain the technological and industrial conditions necessary for their security 'both at national level and, where appropriate, within the framework of the competent institutions and bodies' (the latter phrase deliberately ambiguous so as not to exclude the Community, a more direct reference being ruled out by French attachment to the inter-governmental framework of Eureka), and the grudging admission that 'nothing in this Title shall impede closer co-operation . . . between certain of the High Contracting Parties within the framework of the Western European Union or the Atlantic Alliance.'

Throughout its discussions the Political Committee had avoided two issues which it felt would be better settled at a higher level. These were the question of the secretariat and that of whether the text on Political Co-operation would be separate or linked with the amendments to the Treaty of Rome. The two went together, in the sense that the Franco-German draft presented before Milan saw the Secretary-General of a revamped European Council as an integral part of a Union with both political and economic components.

The Commission had from the start argued in favour of combining the political and economic aspects of the inter-governmental Conference, whereas, it will be recalled, the opposite approach was implicit in the conclusions of the European Council in Milan. In the opinion it gave on 22 July in accordance with Article 236 of the EEC Treaty, the Commission stated that 'it is necessary, in the general context of transition to European Union, to make fresh progress not only on economic and social integration but also on foreign policy. Indeed, the fact that the two form an indivisible whole should be recognized by incorporating the proposed new provisions in a single framework.' Again,

> Efforts to consolidate, strengthen and widen cooperation between the Member States on common foreign and security policy . . . must draw on the experience of fifteen years of political cooperation. If there is a genuine desire to move towards European Union, it is imperative that the two areas of activity be combined. Otherwise fresh obstacles will be created, multiplying possible sources of conflict and weakening the potential and dynamism of the Community . . . Realistic conditions for

The Single European Act (1987)

osmosis between economic, social, financial, and monetary affairs on the one hand and foreign policy on the other must be established. At the end of the day only unified institutions—one Council, one Parliament, one Commission—will prove effective and speed progress towards European Union.

If Community and political cooperation activities are to remain within a single institutional framework, it is essential that a single conference deal with both.

The Commission pursued its overall approach by tabling a paper on the structure of the texts which the Conference would produce at the first meeting of the Political Committee on 3–4 September 1985. The Commission explained that it was not intended to alter the intrinsic nature of political co-operation. There was to be no change in the principle of consensus nor in the role of the Community institutions. At the same time, the objectives set out in the Commission's Opinion had to be borne in mind. This could be done through an Act with the following structure: a preamble and short common section affirming the common goal, followed by two separate Titles, one dealing with amendments to the EEC Treaty, the other with Political Co-operation, which would have the status conferred on it by traditional public international law, and final provisions for an ultimate *rapprochement* between the Community and Political Co-operation.

By common consent the discussion was postponed, but as time went on, the Commission's ideas began to make some headway. Matters were precipitated by France, which at the Ministerial session of the Conference on 19 November tabled a draft 'Act of European Union' structured on the lines proposed by the Commission without the last section on ultimate *rapprochement*, but also resurrecting the ideas of the Franco-German draft: a Council of the Union to replace the European Council and to be assisted as necessary by a secretariat placed under the authority of the Presidency.

The Luxembourg Presidency wisely did not burden the European Council which met on 2–3 December with questions of structure. Twenty-eight hours of discussion were barely enough for the Heads of Government to reach agreement on a substantial package, which took the form of separate texts on each of the chapters including Political Co-operation. How these were to be put together was left to the Foreign Ministers meeting in Brussels on 16–17 December. Agreement was reached on a proposal by the Presidency, which circulated a text based as to structure on the French draft, but omitting controversial points like the Council of the Union and its secretariat. The Single European Act thus came into being, 'single' because it covered both the Community and EPC in one legal text.

The decision on the structure of the Act was one of the most important taken by the Conference. Had the EPC text not been brought within the ambit of a legal instrument shared with the Communities, the way towards a *rapprochement* of the two would have been barred. As it was, the door was left open for a future move towards greater integration. Article 30.12 provided that 'five years after the entry into force of this Act the High Contracting Parties shall examine whether any revision of Title III [on EPC] is required.' The fact that the deadline thus fixed coincided with the completion of the single market in 1992 was no accident. However, it proved impossible, contrary to what some had hoped, to provide in this Article that revision should be with a view to strengthening links between EPC and the Community.

The single nature of the Act is expressed in the preamble and in Title I—common provisions. The preamble sets out the finality of the European endeavour, to transform relations as a whole among the States into a European Union, and lays down the principles on which this is based. The principles which apply to Political Co-operation are, by acting with consistency and solidarity, to protect more effectively Europe's common interests and independence; to display the principles of democracy and compliance with the law and human rights; and to contribute to the preservation of international peace and security in accordance with undertakings under the UN Charter. In Title I, the Communities and EPC are stated to have as their objective to contribute together to making concrete progress towards European unity ('Union européenne' in the French text). The same article provides that EPC shall be governed by the provisions of Title III.

Title III, which in a concession to those who would have preferred a separate EPC Treaty is described as containing 'Treaty provisions on European co-operation in the sphere of

The Single European Act (1987)

foreign policy', should be read in conjunction with a separate Decision adopted by Foreign Ministers on 28 February 1986. This provides further technical details on relations between EPC and the European Parliament, co-operation of Member States' missions and Commission Delegations in third countries and international organizations, the EPC Secretariat: responsibilities and organization, the venues for EPC meetings, and the use of languages in EPC. The advantage of this procedure was that minor details could in the future be altered by Ministerial decision without having to amend the Act itself.

Reference to the text of Title III will show the many similarities with previous EPC texts and practice. Three features deserve special attention, the degree of commitment, consistency with the Community, and the Secretariat. As regards the degree of commitment, the obligations assumed by the Member States are set out in Article 30.1 and 2. The scope of EPC is given as 'any foreign policy matters of general interest' (compare 'important foreign policy matters of interest to the Ten as a whole' in the London Report) and the determination of common positions 'shall constitute a point of reference for the policies of the High Contracting Parties.' Not too much should be read into the precise wording, which reflects a series of verbal compromises between those who wished to strengthen the existing commitments and those who did not. The fact remains that in general the commitment, unusually in a legal instrument, was to endeavour, but not necessarily to succeed.

The same caution was shown on the decision-making procedure. In spite of efforts by some delegations, the consensus principle remained sacrosanct. Article 30.3 provided that 'the High Contracting Parties shall, as far as possible, refrain from impeding the formation of a consensus and the joint action which this could produce.' This was but a faint shadow of the Dooge Committee's recommendation of 'seeking a consensus in keeping with the majority opinion'. Although it is doubtful whether there is any meaningful stage between that and the type of consensus-forming actually practised in EPC, the inability to agree on a more binding formulation was seen as a victory for the inter-governmentalists.

Arguments over the details of wording were of little moment, given that no provision was made for enforcement. The Political Committee made sure (Article 31) that the jurisdiction of the

European Court of Justice would not extend to Title III or the Preamble. Member States were not to be held to account if they chanced not to observe their commitments; national delegations may also have feared that the Court would, if given the opportunity, deliver the sort of interpretative judgments on Political Co-operation which had proved such a potent force in extending the Community's competence in external relations. Above all, the impression had to be avoided that EPC was being assimilated to the Community.

The same concern prevented any significant moves towards a bringing together of EPC and the Community, like the merging of the agendas of the Ministerial Meetings and the General Affairs Council. Article 30.3 merely affirms that 'the Ministers for Foreign Affairs . . . may also discuss foreign policy matters within the framework of Political Co-operation on the occasion of meetings of the Council of the European Communities', a possibility which had been open to them since the Paris Summit in 1974.

On the other hand, great interest was shown in maintaining 'consistency'. Article 30.5 stated that 'the external policies of the European Community and the policies agreed in European Political Co-operation must be consistent. The Presidency and the Commission, each within its own sphere of competence, shall have special responsibility for ensuring that such consistency is sought and maintained.' The question of the relationship between EPC and the Community had been a difficult one from the beginnings of EPC. The Copenhagen Report provided that the organs of EPC should conduct their activities bearing in mind the implications and effects in the field of international policy of Community policies being worked out. Respect for this obligation was ensured by the Commission's giving its opinion and the Presidency's transmitting to the Council any EPC conclusions of interest to the Community. Both the British and the Franco-German drafts, while repeating the obligation of consistency, placed responsibility for ensuring it on the Member States themselves. This was thought to be insufficiently operational, and the opportunity was taken to share this function between the Presidency and the Commission, the involvement of the latter being one of the rare elements of rapprochement between EPC and the Community in the text. The stipulation that these institutions would operate each within its own sphere of competence was nevertheless designed to make it clear that the Commission did not thereby acquire any new institutional role.

Article 30.10 provides for the setting up of a Secretariat. It baldly states that 'a Secretariat based in Brussels shall assist the Presidency in preparing and implementing the activities of European Political Co-operation and in administrative matters. It shall carry out its duties under the authority of the Presidency.' For further information, one has to refer to the complementary decision of 28 February 1986, Section III. In addition to the duties laid upon it in the Act itself, the Secretariat is there given the responsibility of 'assisting the Presidency in ensuring the continuity of European Political Co-operation and its consistency with Community positions'. Attempts to have this task, which figured prominently in the British draft, confirmed in the Act itself were resisted by those who feared that this would detract from the role of the Commission.

Apart from this, the Secretariat was given essentially administrative tasks. It was not to prepare papers on its own initiative ('assist the Presidency in the organization of European Political Co-operation meetings, including the preparation and circulation of documents and the drawing up of minutes'), nor to act as spokesman for the Twelve ('assist the Presidency, where appropriate, in contacts with third countries'). It was to be composed of seconded national diplomats on the 'enlarged support team' principle, the Troika set up in the London Report being enlarged to five and moved permanently to Brussels.

RATIFICATION AND IMPLEMENTATION

The Single European Act was signed by nine Member States on 17 February 1986 and by Denmark, Greece, and Italy on 28 February. The delay was caused by Denmark. Having failed to win a majority in the Folketing because of the attitude of the Social Democrats, who were divided on Danish membership of the Community, Prime Minister Schluter took the bold step of putting the Single European Act to a referendum. This was fought on the question of continued Danish membership, and resulted in an unexpectedly comfortable majority for those in favour.

The case was different in Ireland. Plans had been made for ratification in time for the instrument to be deposited before the end of the year. The government took the view that Title III did not require to be enacted into domestic law; indeed in the explanatory guide it had published it stated that 'it is not considered that the provisions of Title III give rise to any constitutional difficulty.' A Bill was duly submitted to Parliament covering those parts of the SEA which dealt with the Community, passed all stages of the procedure by 17 December, and was signed by the President on 24 December.

On the same day a private citizen, Mr Raymond Crotty, sought an interlocutory injunction restraining the government from depositing the instrument of ratification. This was granted, thus preventing the Single European Act from entering into force on 1 January 1987 as had been foreseen. The substantive claim was dismissed in the High Court, but Mr Crotty appealed. His argument was that ratification went beyond the margin of authority conferred by the Irish people in the 1972 referendum on accession to the Community and could not therefore take place until approval had been given in a new referendum. There was also the feeling that Title III was in some way a threat to Irish neutrality, a point which came out very strongly in the subsequent referendum campaign.

The Supreme Court gave judgment on 9 April. By upholding the constitutionality of the European Communities (Amendment) Act 1986, it upheld all but Title III of the SEA, which the government had chosen not to submit to approval by Parliament. In a three-to-two majority judgment, the Court held that Title III could only be ratified if an appropriate constitutional amendment was made. The amendment was duly approved by referendum in May and the instrument of ratification deposited in time to enable the SEA to come into force on 1 July 1987. In view of the discussion of Title III in the referendum campaign, and in particular of the security aspects, the government issued a declaration to be made on depositing the instrument of ratification. The part concerning neutrality read:

The Government of Ireland note that the provisions of Title III do not affect Ireland's long-established policy of military neutrality and that co-ordination of positions on the political and economic aspects of security does not include the military aspects of security or procure-

The Single European Act (1987)

ment for military purposes and does not affect Ireland's right to act or refrain from acting in any way which might affect Ireland's international status of military neutrality.

As the only judicial interpretation of Title III which exists or is likely to, the judgments of the Irish Supreme Court repay some attention. The Court preferred an extensive interpretation of Title III, particularly as regards national sovereignty, which was certainly not the intention of the authors of the Act. That intention is reflected in the minority view, as expressed by Chief Justice Finlay:

> [the provisions] do not impose any obligations to cede any national interest in the sphere of foreign policy. They do not give to other High Contracting Parties any right to override or veto the ultimate decision of the State on any issue of foreign policy. They impose an obligation to listen and consult and grant a right to be heard and consulted.

The majority view, as expressed by Justice Henchy, was that

> ... commitments expressed in s 30 make manifest that, although the approach to the ultimate aim of European Union is to be reached by a pathway of gradualism, each Member State will immediately cede a portion of its sovereignty and freedom of action in matters of foreign policy. National objectives and ideological positions must defer to the aims and decisions of an institution known as European Political Co-operation, which is to work in tandem with the European Communities. A purely national approach to foreign policy is incompatible with accession to this Treaty.

Apart from its implications for Ireland's future approach towards Political Co-operation, the point is likely to remain an academic one. The fact that Member States took the postponement of the entry into force of the Single European Act in their stride and simply acted as though the delay had not occurred is itself sufficient indication that the Act was not considered to introduce any novelty in the practice of EPC. Even the Secretariat, which formally did not exist until 1 July 1987, was in full operation in Brussels from 1 January.

The preparations for setting it up had taken most of the previous year. The summary indications of the Act and the accompanying decision needed some fleshing out. The first point to be settled was the question of the Head of the Secretariat. A Secretary-General with political weight on the lines of the French proposal had been ruled out, but there was still disagreement about whether the Head of the Secretariat should be specially appointed or whether the member of the Secretariat from the country of the Presidency should act as Head for the six months of the Presidency and then give way to his successor. Political Directors were torn between ensuring a minimum of efficiency and taking care not to create a rival to themselves. Foreign Ministers decided on 21 July 1986 to appoint Ambassador Jannuzzi, the Italian Deputy Political Director, for a period of two and a half years without prejudice to future decisions. Mr Jannuzzi's term of office was later extended.

The material conditions for setting up the Secretariat were worked out by a restricted group of European Correspondents. Again, the choice lay between efficiency and making sure that the Secretariat was not sucked into the Community apparatus. The question was whether the Secretariat should be in a building physically separate from the Council Secretariat and have its own budget or whether it should be in the Charlemagne building of the Council and be financed essentially from the Community budget. Efficiency won the day, assisted by the reluctance of Member States to engage in additional recurrent expenditure. The Secretariat was installed in its own wing of the Charlemagne and a meeting room for Working Groups provided on its premises. Financial responsibility was divided among the Presidency for the costs which it had traditionally met, the Member States for capital costs in a once only payment, contributions for which were calculated using the Community budget key, and the Secretariat of the Council for recurrent administrative costs against payment of a symbolic ecu by each Presidency. The salaries and allowances of the Members of the Secretariat were met by their home administrations.

The transformation brought about by the Single European Act applied to the Community's decision-making procedure and relied on the dynamism of the move towards the Single Market of 1992. The provisions relating to EPC were included almost by accident, a combination of an attempt by the United Kingdom to divert the discussion into channels more convenient to it, the resurrection by France in alliance with the Federal Republic of old French ideas about the primacy of the Heads of Govern-

The Single European Act (1987)

ment, and the determination of the other countries, especially Italy, to salvage something from the Dooge Report as a further move towards European Union. It can be argued that Title III was of little moment, being no more than a codification of existing practice, Certainly, the reformulated undertakings in Article 30 had little effect and indeed were merrily broken by Member States within weeks of the Act's coming into force. Nevertheless, the fact that Political Co-operation acquired a legal personality as the second pillar of the Community, on a par with the Community of the Treaties, but following intergovernmental procedures, was significant in itself. The establishment of the Secretariat brought about an important change in the ethos of EPC, which became more bureaucratic as it became more efficient. The increased efficiency was indispensable, as EPC faced a rising tide of work caused by its increasing attraction to third countries. The growing weight of the EEC internationally as the Single Market was consolidated led to increased interest in the Community as a political entity, to which EPC had to respond.

SELECTED READING

Several Officials involved in the negotiation of the Single European Act have published studies of it. These include De Ruyt (1987), Krenzler (1986), Mischo (1987), and Nuttall (1986). The Act's origins in the European Parliament's draft Treaty are described in Burgess (1986) and Schmuck (1987). The work of the Dooge Committee is discussed in Meenan (1985), and in Keatinge and Murphy (1987). Other general studies include Corbett (1987), 'Istevene Gaius' (1986)—the *nom de plume* of a participant—and Wessels (1986).

Among more specialized aspects of the Act, Mitterrand's approach is analysed in Moreau Defarges (1985), and the genesis of the Secretariat described in Lay (1986). Temple Lang (1987) discusses the Crotty case before the Irish courts, and other legal aspects of the Act are examined by Dehousse and Weiler (1990) and Freestone and Davidson (1986).

8
European Political Co-operation and the Community

The only way to become a Member of Political Co-operation is to accede to the Community. This was made clear by the Single European Act, but has not been in doubt since the beginnings of EPC. It would be logical to suppose that the policies followed in the two forums should be complementary. That this has not always been accepted is the result of the circumstances in which Political Co-operation was set up.

EPC was designed to operate in such a way as to guarantee that national sovereignty in the conduct of foreign policy should not be diminished by contamination with the Community system. In the early years, not only was the Commission excluded from many of EPC's activities, but Member States were reluctant to make use of Community instruments to implement the policies of EPC. Countries like France, and later Denmark and Greece, anxious to keep the inter-governmental nature of Political Co-operation unsullied, were reticent, but so also were countries like the Netherlands which did not wish the methods of EPC to be imported into the Community. Over the years sensitivity regarding the use of Community instruments declined under the pressure of events. Faced with some international crisis, the Member States needed to adopt a course of action which was seen to be effective, even if this lay beyond the bounds of EPC. Progress was not regular, and there were setbacks as well as successes, but over two decades a point was reached in which the use of Community instruments became normal. The events which carried this process forward have been described in previous chapters from the viewpoint of the policy of the Twelve. They will now be reviewed as examples of interaction between EPC and the Community.

SANCTIONS

The most eye-catching example of the use of Community

EPC and the Community

instruments to pursue EPC policies is the application of sanctions. The decision to apply sanctions is taken as a matter of political judgement in Political Co-operation, and the corresponding Community measure, usually a Council Regulation, is then adopted by the Community. For many years Member States hesitated to do this, not just because of the relationship between EPC and the Community but also because of legal doubts as to whether the instruments of the Community's common commercial policy under Article 113 of the EEC Treaty could be applied to political ends.

To begin with, there was no question of such a procedure being adopted. When the Security Council voted for mandatory sanctions against Rhodesia, they were applied through national, not Community, measures. In 1975 the Council gave a definition of the common commercial policy from which the conclusion was drawn that the measures concerning Rhodesia, taken for the purpose of maintaining peace and international security, did not fall within the scope of Article 113 and that the Community as such was not responsible for applying the Security Council's decisions. In the Council's view, the case was covered by Article 224 (the 'reserve of sovereignty' Article of the EEC Treaty). Although following broadly the same line, the Commission added a nuance. It recognized that Article 224 left Member States free to take action to discharge obligations accepted in the interests of peace and national security, and had been invoked on this occasion, but did not exclude Security Council decisions impinging on areas within the Community's jurisdiction.

The divergency in views on the legitimate use of Article 113 depends on whether the criterion applied is the nature of the instrument or the objective pursued. If the former view is held, Article 113 can be used to apply sanctions, even though they pursue a political aim falling outside the overtly commercial objective of the Article. The partisans of this instrumental approach found some comfort in the Opinion delivered by the Court of Justice in October 1979 on the International Agreement on Natural Rubber. Although not concerned with the specific issue of sanctions, the Court took a non-restrictive view of Article 113 which was taken to support the broad interpretation in other cases.

When in April 1980 the Ten came to discuss the question of sanctions against Iran as a result of the American-hostage crisis, the climate of opinion had begun to change. Germany was anxious that a Community instrument should be used, and the Commission played its part by providing technical guidance on how this might be done. Agreement was not possible because of the opposition of France and Denmark. The Ten therefore decided to introduce national measures, but recognized that steps would be taken in the Community to avoid obstructing the proper functioning of the Common Market. The need for this arose almost immediately, since the United Kingdom was unable to apply the measures in the same conditions as the other Member States. The obvious conclusion was that these difficulties could have been avoided and the measures would have had a greater impact had they been applied uniformly through a Community measure.

The leap forward was made in February 1982 when sanctions were applied to the Soviet Union following the imposition of martial law in Poland. For a number of reasons, including relations with the United States, action was essential. Because of the opposition of Greece, there was no consensus in EPC, and without consensus a collective decision to impose national measures was not possible. It was the British who pointed out that the Community framework allowed a partial application of the measures, and two Council Regulations were adopted, the second one exempting Greece from the first.

The Danes had strong institutional objections to this procedure, but reluctantly had to accept it. They could not afford to be accused of having blocked for institutional reasons a measure which was a political necessity. The decision nevertheless caused considerable difficulties in the Danish Parliament, which adopted on 14 April a Resolution preventing the government in the future from having recourse to Article 113 for sanctions motivated by political reasons or in general in the area of foreign policy, a decision which explains why subsequent Regulations applying sanctions include a recital referring to deliberations in EPC.

The sanctions against the Soviet Union provided a useful precedent when, two months later in April 1982, Argentina invaded the Falkland Islands. The United Kingdom's request for a ban on imports from Argentina was originally made in the Community framework to prevent circumvention of the British national ban, but readily agreed to by the Member States as a gesture of political solidarity. The Commission, supported by Germany and Belgium, was anxious to avoid the confusion which would ensue if national measures were introduced, each differing slightly from the others. Ireland and Italy found it easier for political reasons to accept a Community measure than to enact a national one. Denmark wanted to show solidarity with the United Kingdom, but had its hands tied by the Folketing over the use of Article 113. In order to secure Danish agreement, a structure for the Council Regulation was devised which has since served as a model, whereby the recitals refer to 'discussions in the context of European Political Co-operation' in an order which implies that these discussions provide the necessary grounds for the Community decision.

The question arose again over the implementation of sanctions against South Africa. The first set of restrictive measures adopted in September 1985 was implemented by national action as the price for British acceptance of the package. When the second package was adopted a year later, the pressure for Community implementation was much greater. There was a need for the stronger political signal which Community implementation would give, and the experience of the previous twelve months had shown that national measures gave uneven results. Belgium went so far as to make its acceptance of the package conditional on Community implementation. The United Kingdom resisted this, but in the end accepted a range of Community or Community-like measures which varied according to the matter dealt with.

The ban on the import of certain iron and steel products took the form of a Decision of the Governments of the Member States meeting within the Council, in the classic form for dealing with questions of ECSC external relations. It followed the model of the decision banning the import of ECSC products from Argentina, but added a recital referring to discussions in EPC.

The ban on the import of gold coins and on new investments proved more complicated. Gold coins figured in the Common Customs Tariff, and the Commission tabled a proposal based on Article 113. The Council adopted a Regulation without a reference to any particular Article of the Treaty, but with the by now traditional mention of discussions in EPC, which, it was stated, had led to a consensus (rather than a decision) to suspend the import of gold coins.

A similar procedure was followed with regard to new investments. The Commission tabled a proposal based on Article 235, which provides for action to attain one of the objectives of the Community for which the Treaty has not provided the necessary powers. The measure adopted took the form of a Decision of the Representatives of the governments of the Member States, meeting within the Council. There was no reference to the Treaty at all, but after a mention of discussions in EPC leading to a consensus, a recital was added which read: 'Whereas it is necessary that Member States take harmonised measures with a view to such a suspension.' Further national action was therefore required for the Decision to have effect, and this was stipulated in the text. No provision was made for the circumstances in which the Decision would cease to have validity.

The tortuous procedure adopted reflected lingering disagreement on institutional questions, but much more the United Kingdom government's dislike of the substance of the measures. The British wanted to keep implementation in their own hands (and later unilaterally lifted the ban on new investments without waiting for consensus). Member States which took the contrary view were at least in part motivated by the need to secure European cover for potentially unpopular national decisions.

The speed with which the Community introduced sanctions following the invasion of Kuwait in August 1990 showed that the use of Community trade-policy instruments for EPC purposes had by then come to be regarded as normal procedure. It helped that there was a genuine consensus among the Member States on the need for sanctions, and that the Commission took care not to exploit the situation to extend the generally accepted range of Article 113, but nevertheless the fact that the complicated Community procedure had been completed and sanctions were in place within a few days of the invasion was impressive.

The Iraqi troops of Saddam Hussein invaded Kuwait in the early hours of 2 August. The same day, Political Co-operation issued a statement condemning the invasion, and this was followed up by a second statement on 4 August in which the Twelve announced their decision to impose an embargo on oil imports from Iraq and Kuwait and (for the first time for political reasons) to suspend the application to those countries of the Generalized System of Preferences (GSP). By 6 August the

Commission had prepared the necessary draft Community legislation to implement these measures. In fact, the Commission was ahead of events. The draft had to be revised following the Security Council's Resolution 661 of 6 August which imposed a more wide-ranging embargo including a ban on imports of all commodities and products originating in Iraq or Kuwait. The Council imposed sanctions on 8 August, which took the legal form of a Council Regulation and a corresponding ECSC Decision.

The Regulation referred to the Security Council Resolutions and to the 4 August EPC declaration. The fourth recital noted that 'the Community and its Member States have agreed to have recourse to a Community instrument in order to ensure uniform implementation, throughout the Community, of the measures concerning trade with Iraq and Kuwait decided upon by the United Nations Security Council.' The same language was used in the ECSC Decision.

The situation became more complicated when it was later wished to extend the Community embargo to cover all non-financial services. The decision in principle was taken by the Foreign Ministers at their extraordinary meeting in Rome on 7 September and confirmed at the General Affairs Council ten days later. The corresponding proposal, based on Article 113, was forwarded by the Commission immediately afterwards. A discussion ensued as to whether Article 113 covered services as well as goods, or whether the Regulation should be based on Article 84 for services in the transport sector and on Article 235 for all others. The question was far from being an academic one. Quite apart from the precedent which would be set for trade policy if services were admitted to fall under Article 113, both Articles 84 and 235 required unanimity and Article 235 required the European Parliament to be consulted as well. Indeed the Parliament voted for Article 235 instead of Article 113, preferring to increase its own powers rather than assert the principle of majority voting in the Council. Behind this discussion lay the more fundamental question of how to entrench consensus, and therefore national sovereignty, for questions with EPC implications which could under the Treaty be decided by qualified majority. In the end Article 235 was chosen as the legal base, in spite of the Commission's protests.

FAILURES AND FRICTIONS

The process of *rapprochement* of EPC and the Community was momentarily halted in 1984 by the affair of the precursors of chemical weapons. The question of chemical weapons was discussed by Ministers in EPC following the publication of a United Nations report confirming allegations of their use in the Iran–Iraq war. At their meeting on 9 April 1984 Ministers decided to compare national arrangements for the supply of chemicals and the products covered. Coreper was asked to consider the question, in particular with regard to the Community aspects.

Ministers took the view that it was necessary to control the export of certain chemicals which might be supplied to belligerents. The Commission made a proposal to the Council based on Article 113, which was supported by some Member States, but opposed by others. At the end of the discussion there was no majority for the Commission's proposal for Community implementation, although there had been consensus in Political Co-operation on the substance. The affair was returned to the EPC framework, where an *ad hoc* group identified the core products which would be covered by national measures. The technique of implementation and the destinations covered differed widely, however.

The failure to agree on Community measures can be laid mainly at the door of France, which held the Presidency. It was largely because of the nature of the products covered. The precursors of chemical weapons, although all but a small number were dual-use products, were too close in nature to weapons to be allowed to fall within the Community framework. The French feared, too, that an opening here might give the Community, and therefore the Commission, entrance by the back door to the negotiations on chemical weapons taking place at the UN-Disarmament Conference in Geneva, an area of pre-eminently EPC interest.

The question was revived when in January 1989 the US Air Force shot down two Libyan MIGs, an action linked by many to growing suspicions that a Libyan factory at Rabta was in fact manufacturing chemical weapons. The affair caused intense political embarrassment to Germany because of charges that German firms had been involved in construction of the factory.

Mr Genscher therefore called for the Commission's proposal to be resuscitated. It became clear in discussion in both the Community and EPC that the Member States which had opposed Community implementation in 1984 would no longer do so, provided that the leading role of EPC was brought out. A Council Regulation was therefore adopted on 20 February after some hard bargaining over a text which emphasized the role of EPC more strongly than ever before and preserved the prerogatives of Member States for the future. Initiatives for the revision of product coverage are supposed to come, not from the Commission, but from the EPC *ad hoc* Group.

A question related to sanctions concerns the political control of development aid. This has been a permanent source of friction between EPC and the Commission. The difficulty arose from a difference of approach to development-aid policy which can be found in national capitals as well as in the Community. Those responsible for the conduct of foreign policy believe on the whole that political considerations should be taken into account in administering aid policy, while the development experts think that aid should be given for developmental purposes only. Within the Member States there are disagreements between Foreign Ministries and Development Ministries which can if necessary be arbitrated at Cabinet level. In the Community the Commission, as the executor of policy and responsible to the Development Council, finds itself representing the developmental school of thought and is therefore at odds with the political school represented by the Foreign Ministry officials meeting in Political Co-operation. Unlike in national governments, there is no machinery for arbitration, and cases have tended to be settled on an *ad hoc* basis, depending on the political issues at stake.

The apolitical nature of the Community's aid has itself been an important element in the political relationship between the Community and the beneficiary countries. The principle applies equally to African, Caribbean and Pacific (ACP) countries and to others, but the question is a particularly sensitive one with the former because of the contractual nature of the relationship through the Lomé Convention. When the third Lomé Convention was being negotiated there was a hostile reaction to the Community's suggestion that there should be a dialogue on policies. This was misinterpreted as an attempt to impose a 'policy dialogue' in the sense of a discussion on the non-developmental policies followed by the governments concerned, whereas what the Community had in mind was a discussion between equal partners of development policies. An even more delicate question is that of human rights. References to human rights have been strengthened in the fourth Lomé Convention, but still do not provide a justification for altering unilaterally the contractual relationship guaranteed by it.

Exceptions from this policy have from time to time been admitted, especially when there have been persistent and aggravated violations of human rights. For example, the Council decided on 21 June 1977 'to take measures in the framework of its relations with Uganda in order to ensure that any assistance to Uganda by the Community by virtue of the Lomé Convention should on no account lead, with respect to the people of that country, to an increase in or prolongation of their being deprived of basic rights.' This followed discussion in EPC at the initiative of Dr Owen, British Foreign Secretary at the time, who raised as a matter of principle the relationship between EPC and Community aid policies.

Sometimes the distinction between human rights and political considerations has been less clear. Commission decisions to grant even emergency and humanitarian aid to Vietnam were often criticized by delegations in the Political Committee as inappropriate, given the Vietnamese occupation of Cambodia. The difficulty was one of procedure as well as of substance. The Commission insisted on exercising its powers to execute the Community budget without obtaining the prior agreement of Member States. Information procedures were set up, but Member States would have liked a greater share in taking the decisions whenever there were political implications.

Ethiopia was a particularly difficult example. The need to help an impoverished and starving population had to be balanced against public disapproval of the policies followed by the authorities, particularly concerning resettlement and collectivization. These policies were economically disastrous, but it was their Marxist origins which made them ineligible in the eyes of some Member States. Should the European Development Fund be used to obtain a change in these policies? EPC did not find it easy to reach a common position. The statement on Ethiopia and the Horn of Africa adopted by Ministers on 21 July 1986 contains a passage in which a reference to Community aid is followed by the announcement that the Twelve would continue to pay careful attention to the human consequences of resettlement and villagization programmes. The conditionality is not explicit, the reader being left to induce it from the sequence if he or she so chooses.

At the same time, EPC was trying, under pressure from the Dutch Presidency, to formulate its general approach to human-rights questions. This of necessity also had to deal with how Community aid would take human-rights considerations into account, and therefore had to be prepared in co-ordination with the Community. A text was prepared by the Political Committee for the EPC sections and in the Council framework for Community matters and was adopted at the EPC Ministerial Meeting on 21 July by 'the Foreign Ministers of the European Community, meeting in the framework of European Political Co-operation and of the Council'. The relevant passage read: 'the Foreign Ministers affirm that in the development of their relations with non-member States as well as in the administration of aid the European Community and the Member States will continue to promote fundamental rights so that individuals and peoples will actually enjoy to the full their economic, social and cultural rights and their civil and political rights.'

The trend is towards a greater concern for human rights and political conditionality in both EPC and Community policies. Following the killings on Tienanmen Square, the European Council in Madrid on 27 June 1989 decided among other measures 'the postponement by the Community and its Member States of new co-operation projects and the reduction of programmes of cultural, scientific and technical co-operation to only those activities that might maintain a meaning in the present circumstances'. Similarly, an element of conditionality has been introduced into the Community's approach towards the events in Central and Eastern Europe.

ECONOMIC ASSISTANCE

The Community has a budget, Political Co-operation does not. In theory it should be possible for the Member States to pool, or at least co-ordinate, their programmes of economic assistance in order to provide an instrument of collective support for EPC policies, but this has never proved effective. Central America and South Africa are cases in point. In practice, the only option for Political Co-operation is to turn to the Community.

The fact that the Community has economic ties with third countries can itself have a political effect without EPC necessarily playing a part in shaping Community policy. The Community's Agreement with ASEAN is a peg on which the political dialogue is hung, but EPC and the Community only converge when there is a need to put together the economic and political parts of the Presidency's speech at the EC-ASEAN Ministerial Conferences. Similarly, the economic relationship with the ACP countries is an important political fact, but EPC does not normally intervene in the operation of the Lomé Convention.

Economic assistance from the Community can be provided in accordance with a political assessment made in Political Cooperation without resulting directly from it. The economic aid given by the Community to Poland before the period of martial law and the humanitarian assistance afterwards fitted in very well with EPC's analysis of political requirements and was welcomed on that account but would have been given in any case. The same applies to the Community's aid programmes and other economic actions for the benefit of the Occupied Territories. These and other Community policies had an important political dimension, but the existence of EPC was not a necessary condition for their adoption.

This was not the case in other areas. The Ten's approach to Central America was based on the premiss that 'the tensions and conflicts ravaging Central America frequently stem from . . . grave economic problems and social inequalities.' Member States were led by the logic of their position to accept the case for deploying the resources of the Community to help remedy this, and the Commission exploited the situation to secure approval of a special action programme in 1982 which the Council would not have agreed to otherwise. The European Council in Stuttgart expressed readiness to continue contributing

EPC and the Community

to further development of the area, in order to promote progress towards stability, but when the Foreign Ministers met three months later in September 1983, they noted that the Community was not in a position to envisage a significant increase in its economic aid to Central America. The additional funds made available in the 1985 budget would probably not have been found without the stimulus provided by the conclusion, for political reasons, of the EC–Central America Agreement in Luxembourg that year.

The fact that funds are tight and that Foreign Ministries are not well placed to intervene in the budgetary process puts a brake on the use of the Community budget as a means of implementing EPC policies. It can even happen that the necessary funds are voted by the European Parliament drawing on its own margin, as in the case of the Polish Church's Agricultural Foundation. Parliament also came to the rescue of EPC over the question of positive measures with regard to South Africa. It added 10 million ecu to the 1986 budget for the Community's programme of aid for the victims of apartheid and doubled that amount in the 1987 budget.

The arrangements for the implementation of the programme of positive measures were complicated, specific to the case, and not supposed to create a precedent. The Commission, in line with the position customarily taken by the European Parliament, claimed sole responsibility for the execution of the budget. Member States insisted on being closely involved in decisions which were likely to be politically sensitive. A compromise was struck in Coreper whereby an *ad hoc* consultative group of national officials under the chairmanship of the Commission was set up to give advice, but not take decisions, on projects submitted. The system worked well at the technical level, comments being well founded and taken into account. The same officials also met under the chairmanship of the Presidency to co-ordinate national assistance programmes, an operation which soon became perfunctory.

Although the *ad hoc* group forwarded its reports to EPC, this procedure in effect excluded Political Co-operation from the management of the programme. This was resented by the Africa Working Group and in particular by the Ambassadors in Pretoria. Experience showed, however, that complete secrecy was necessary for the successful conduct of the operation as well as confidence on the part of the beneficiaries that there would be no 'political interference' on the part of the Member States. The principle that the Commission should remain responsible for the execution of Community policies, even when these had been adopted in response to EPC requirements, with any necessary consultation with Member States taking place in the Council framework, was therefore maintained.

A similar situation arose with regard to the Community's activities in the Occupied Territories. The Commission knew from its presence in Political Co-operation that the proposals it put forward to the Council in July 1986 on aid and trade relations with the Occupied Territories were likely to be favourably received. Measures were adopted by the Council on 27 October which foresaw financial assistance primarily for small job-creating and training projects and for improving the operation of local Palestinian institutions. These projects were discussed with Member States in the Council framework following an *ad hoc* procedure modelled on that used for aid projects for the non-associated developing countries. Under pressure from the Consuls-General in Jerusalem, who considered themselves to be best placed to advise on the choice of projects, the Middle East Working Group of EPC claimed a share in the decision-making procedure, but again the principle of Commission responsibility for executing Community policies was upheld.

A further example concerns the provision of aid to Afghanistan following the withdrawal of Soviet troops. The agreement on Soviet withdrawal signed in Geneva on 14 April 1988 included an agreement between Pakistan and Afghanistan to encourage the voluntary return of refugees. The response of the Twelve and the Community had already been discussed in EPC. Two requirements had been identified: aid for the return and resettlement of refugees and longer-term reconstruction aid. On 14 April the Twelve stated that they would be 'ready to contribute, in close co-ordination with the international organizations concerned and other States prepared to act similarly, to the repatriation of Afghan refugees'.

On 25 April, following an analysis of the situation presented by the Commission, Ministers decided to set up an *ad hoc* EPC

EPC and the Community

Group to prepare guidelines for submission to the Political Committee. Meanwhile, the Commission forwarded to the Council a communication on the co-ordination of Community and Member State aid and itself set up an *ad hoc* Group on Community aid measures. The EPC orientations were adopted on 13 June. They set out the political environment for the grant of aid by the Community and the Member States, while providing that existing Community procedures for the management of aid should be respected. The EPC *ad hoc* Group would continue to meet as required to examine the political aspects, in close co-ordination with the competent bodies of the Community.

This new approach to co-ordination is different from the procedures set up for the aid programme for the victims of apartheid in that a specific body in EPC is given responsibility for looking after the political aspects of aid for the Afghan refugees. This signifies a shift in the balance towards EPC, with the Commission executing the Community budget in direct implementation of EPC policies.

The effectiveness of turning to the Community budget for the implementation of EPC policies is limited by the preallocation of budget resources and the deliberately complicated procedures for increasing them. This is shown by the Twelve's attempts in 1990 to provide assistance to countries affected by the Iraqi invasion of Kuwait.

It became clear soon after the invasion and the imposition of sanctions that the economies of Iraq's neighbours were going to be badly hit. The transit trade through Turkey and Jordan was cut off, and Egypt was deprived of the remittances from its citizens working in Iraq and Kuwait, most of whom had fled. The Commission was able very rapidly to provide financial assistance to speed the flow of refugees through Jordan, but an effort to solve the medium-term economic problem required bigger sums than were available in the budget. The Commission, therefore, in a memorandum presented to the special meeting of Foreign Ministers in Rome on 7 September 1990, put forward ideas for a package of assistance to which the Community and the Member States would contribute in co-operation with other countries. The ideas were welcomed, and the Commission was invited to flesh them out in time for the General Affairs Council ten days later.

Although the Member States 'reaffirmed their willingness to provide significant short-term assistance to those countries particularly affected by the strict implementation of the embargo, particularly Egypt, Jordan and Turkey', they were not prepared to take an immediate decision on the 1.5 billion ecu package proposed by the Commission, divided in equal shares between the Community budget and the Member States. There was disagreement about how the amount should be divided up, the United Kingdom in particular believing that its contribution was already being made, and handsomely, in the military field. Agreement was only reached when the Foreign Ministers met again in the margins of a CSCE meeting in Paris on 2 October. The Commission's figure of 1.5 billion ecu was accepted, but the balance was changed, only 500 million coming from the Community budget, while the rest came from the contributions of Member States. A decision on the breakdown of national contributions was postponed.

The Council decided that the Regulation which translated this agreement into legal terms should be based on Article 235 of the EEC Treaty, which meant that the decision had to be unanimous and that the European Parliament had to be consulted and give a favourable opinion. The consultation of the Parliament was also obligatory because the additional sums required breached the guidelines for budgetary expenditure. The delays caused by this procedure, and Parliament's not unnatural desire to bring its influence to bear when for once the Member States were obliged to listen to its views, meant that the final decision was not taken until 4 December. The three months' delay between the political decision in principle and the adoption of the Community measures weakened their impact and correspondingly diminished the Twelve's presence on the diplomatic scene. It also demonstrated the limits of the Community budget in providing more than a token response to foreign-policy requirements.

A UNIQUE CASE—EASTERN EUROPE

The signature of the EC–Comecon Joint Declaration on 25 June 1988 in Luxembourg marked the end of an era rather than the beginning of a new one. Although it was a result of diplomatic negotiations extending over several years, the premisses on which it was founded were to disappear during the *annus mirabilis* of 1989. The status of Berlin, so long a sticking-point in the negotiations, was no longer an issue as first the Berlin Wall came down and then Germany was reunited. The collapse of Soviet hegemony over the countries of Central and Eastern Europe and the move towards democratic pluralism and a market economy not only obliged Political Co-operation to rethink its East European policy, but also altered the framework in which it had operated hitherto. The relationship with the United States, which had underlain all the Twelve's important policy decisions, could not remain static as the Iron Curtain came down, and the very assumptions about membership of the Community on which the Twelve's policy had been built were now beginning to seem uncertain.

The challenge was as much a domestic as a foreign one, so it is perhaps not surprising that the response came in substance more from the Community than the Political Co-operation side. The need to work together, however, gave rise to some interesting procedural innovations.

The rationale of the Community's approach to the European members of Comecon at first remained the pragmatic and flexible development of relations, taking into account the special features of each individual case. It was on this basis that a trade and economic co-operation agreement with Hungary was signed on 26 September 1988, reflecting the fact that Hungary was a member of the General Agreement on Tariffs and Trade (GATT) and that its economic system had already moved away from the socialist model. The same approach was adopted by the European Council in Rhodes in December of that year, as part of a Declaration on the international role of the Community which had been finalized on the spot in joint meetings of the Political Directors and the Permanent Representatives. In itself, the Declaration did not break new ground. No more prescient than others, the Heads of State and Government had not yet realized the changes in store and the need for a fresh policy, even though at the Gymnich-type meeting in Joannina a few months previously Foreign Minister Tindemans of Belgium had drawn the attention of his colleagues to the need for stronger cohesion between the Community and EPC precisely in view of the developing situation in Eastern Europe.

This need soon became abundantly clear. The General Affairs Council on 24 April 1989 called on the Community and its Member States to react constructively to the political and economic reforms being undertaken in Eastern Europe. It stated that the co-operation which the Community was in the process of establishing with the countries concerned had to be complementary to that of the Member States, and that greater consistency had to be sought between Community policies and those agreed in the framework of EPC. This quotation from the Single European Act did not signify that there was inconsistency between the two sides of the Community, but that a greater effort had to be made to combine their potential. This line was strengthened by the European Council at Madrid on 26–7 June 1989:

The European Council has reaffirmed the full validity of the comprehensive approach integrating political, economic and co-operation aspects which the European Community and its Member States follow in their relations with the USSR and with Central European and East European countries. It has assessed positively the concrete steps which the Community and its Member States, following the Rhodes Declaration, have taken in these fields.

The Community, for its part, had been busy. A trade agreement covering industrial goods had been signed with Czechoslovakia on 19 December 1988, and negotiating directives had been adopted for trade and co-operation agreements with Poland, Bulgaria, and the Soviet Union. EPC discussions with Hungary and Poland were beginning, but the substance of the relationship depended on the content of the economic agreements being negotiated by the Commission.

This kaleidoscope pattern of discussions and negotiations was given a decisive shake when the Heads of State and Government of the seven most advanced industrial nations meeting in Paris on 14–16 July 1989 decided to entrust the Commission with the task of co-ordinating international assistance efforts to Poland and Hungary. This was the 'Summit of the Arche', called after the nearest landmark, which in particular welcomed the reform process under way in Poland and Hungary and affirmed the readiness of the Seven 'to support this process with co-ordinated economic aid aimed at transforming and opening up their economies in a durable manner.' The establishment in those countries of political and economic systems based on democratic values was at stake. It was the responsibility of the industrialized world to ensure that the experiment did not fail.

The initial dismay of the already hard-pressed Commission officials on hearing of the new task laid upon them quickly gave way to a determination to rise to the challenge. Fact-finding missions to Poland and Hungary were launched and the first co-ordination meeting of representatives of twenty-four donor countries, all members of the Organization for Economic Co-operation and Development (OECD), took place in Brussels on 1 August 1989 under the chairmanship of the Commission. This was the beginning of what came to be known as G24, which has succeeded in achieving a satisfactory level of co-ordination in the international aid effort, but above all in maintaining a coherent political line. Succumbing to the Commission's passion for acronyms, the aid operation itself was dubbed PHARE (assistance with economic recovery in Poland and Hungary). The Commission proceeded to draw up an action plan for co-ordinated measures reflecting the main priorities, which was intended both as a framework for action by the Community itself and as an incentive to the other members of the G24 to take similar and co-ordinated initiatives. It was broadly welcomed by the G24 at a second meeting on 26 September and endorsed by the Council on 3 October.

The speed of events had been such that the Community, and indeed the Commission, had so far been in the driving seat. Political Co-operation had issued general statements of policy, but these had not been an essential precondition for Community action. Nevertheless, the co-ordination between the two sides of the Community had worked well, assisted by a new procedural device whereby the Chairmen of the responsible Working Groups in EPC and the Council had attended the meetings of each other's groups and reported on developments. In an attempt to ensure that co-ordinated directives at the highest political level were injected into the Community's policy-making process, the French Presidency of the second half of 1989 convened a working dinner of Heads of State and Government in Paris on 18 November which was billed as 'an important step in the development of the Community since the Single Act, and in particular in integrating political co-operation and Community activities: guidelines for Community action were drawn up on the basis of a common analysis.' The Troika, with the Commission, was bidden to prepare for the Strasbourg European Council on 8–9 December proposals for a development-and-modernization bank for Eastern Europe, a European Training Foundation, and the extension of youth-exchange programmes. In fact the work on the European bank, later the European Bank for Reconstruction and Development (BERD), was mainly done in Paris, since it was an initiative taken by France in its national rather than its Presidency capacity, while the papers on the other two questions were produced by the Commission.

The Strasbourg European Council was less successful in achieving consistency. It adopted two texts on Central and European Europe, one from Political Co-operation and one from the Community side. The two were not inconsistent in substance, since one dealt with the broad political framework and the other with concrete activity, but the failure to set up a joint drafting body, as had been done at Rhodes a year before, was a setback.

This failure induced the incoming Irish Presidency to organize in Dublin in the early months of 1990 two meetings of Foreign Ministers to discuss developments in Central and Eastern Europe wearing both Council and Political Co-operation hats simultaneously, and with both Permanent Representatives and Political Directors present. The idea of the joint format, known as 'informal Councils', was suggested by the Commission at its traditional meeting with the Presidency on 6 January.

The first meeting took place on 20 January. In addition to endorsing current activities, the Ministers showed interest in the Commission's idea of a new generation of association agreements with the Central and East European countries and gave their approval to a CSCE summit meeting in the course of the year. The question of human rights and democracy was raised in terms which prefigured the conditionality always latent in the Twelve's approach, but not so far formally expressed. It was made explicit by the General Affairs Council on 5 February, which had before it a new action programme from the Commission. In confirming the Community's readiness to extend PHARE assistance to other countries besides Poland and Hungary, the Council stated that

EPC and the Community

Co-ordinated assistance should be provided on the basis of commitments from the countries concerned to political and economic reform. In addition, the programme of assistance should be adapted to each country's own situation, specific requirements and absorption capacity. The ideas set out in the Commission's communication concerning these two aspects had been favourably received and these matters would be followed up within the framework of the Group of 24.

The missions to the so-called 'extension countries' to receive the necessary commitments were carried out by the Commission. The pre-eminently political task of establishing and verifying conditionality was thus carried out on the Community side.

The second 'informal Council' was held in Dublin on 21 April in order to prepare for an extraordinary meeting of the European Council a week later. It discussed the questions of German reunification and the future association agreements, which should contain an element of conditionality. Both discussions were introduced by the Commission. The European Council endorsed the Commission's three-stage approach for the integration of the German Democratic Republic into a unified Germany, and hence into the Community, and also the question of association agreements. These, according to the European Council, should include an institutional framework for political dialogue; furthermore, 'The Community will work to complete association negotiations with these countries as soon as possible on the understanding that the basic conditions with regard to democratic principles and transition towards a market economy are fulfilled.'

The Twelve's policy with regard to relations on the continent of Europe was not confined to the Community's own relations with the Eastern and Central European countries and the Soviet Union. The second pillar, equally important, was support for the CSCE, whose existing pan-European role was to take on a new character corresponding to the changed circumstances. The institutionalization of the CSCE, long resisted by the West, was now seen to be an urgent necessity, in order to involve directly in the future development of Europe not only the members of the moribund Warsaw Pact, but also the United States and Canada, whose continued interest in the affairs of the continent had to be assured.

If primacy in dealing with the Community's bilateral relations with the East European countries lay with the Council and the

Commission, the future role of the CSCE remained first and foremost a Political Co-operation subject. The key statement of principles was made by the EPC Ministerial Meeting in Dublin on 20 February 1990, and was repeated in the guidelines on the CSCE adopted by the European Council on 28 April. The substance of the Community's position with regard to the CSCE was clear; the procedures for its association gave rise to the traditional difficulties. The CSCE Conference on economic co-operation held in Bonn from 19 March to 11 April 1990 was a Basket II affair and hence prepared in the Community framework. The question of how the Community was to be represented was eventually settled by reviving the old idea of a *double pancarte*, whereby the nameplate of the Member State holding the Presidency mentioned both the country and the Community. The Commission was included in the Presidency delegation. The same system was followed at the CSCE Summit Conference later in the year.

The compromise underlined a significant difference in approach. Whereas the Community conducted its policies towards Central and Eastern Europe in its capacity as a regional body, and was all the more attractive to the countries concerned on that account, the CSCE operated on the old principle of state sovereignty, which did not fit comfortably with the Community's institutional set-up. The rapprochement between Political Co-operation and the Community had not progressed sufficiently for the Twelve to have found an easy solution to this problem.

The course of events in Eastern Europe in 1989 and 1990 had a profound influence on the way in which Political Co-operation and the Community worked together and provided the necessary stimulus for making a reality of the consistency provisions of the Single European Act. There is no guarantee, however, that circumstances will repeat themselves, or that the procedural gains will be permanent. Certainly, the Member States were obliged to think in an integrated way. The speed of developments and the enormity of the challenge were such that the classic progression of deliberations in EPC followed by action in the Community was no longer realistic. Everything had to be done by everybody, all at once. The intrinsically economic nature of the problem gave the lead role to the Commission, which did not muff its lines, and was backed up in its rapid and

EPC and the Community

integrated action by the Member States. On the other hand, the experiment of informal Councils with the presence of officials from EPC as well as from the Community has not been repeated. What is likely to remain is the disappearance of the last shreds of toleration for the idea that, at the level of Ministers, there is any sense in dividing discussions into EPC and EC compartments.

SELECTED READING

The interaction between EPC and the Community is discussed by Nuttall (1988 and 1989) and by Louis (1983). The question of sanctions is addressed by Kuyper (1982 and 1991).

9
Talking with the World

Political Co-operation has often seemed introspective. The Member States have given the impression of being more intent on the process of reaching a common position from the starting-point of divergent national positions than on projecting the common position, once it has been reached. This is partly because of the absence of a permanent spokesman with an institutional responsibility for conveying EPC positions and policies to public opinion and to third countries. The task is carried out by the Presidency, and the rotation in this office of the Member States can lead to confusion as inevitably the style, emphasis, and choice of priorities vary from one Presidency to the next. Member States still hesitate to entrust regular diplomatic contacts to the Secretariat.

This lacuna causes the Twelve considerable organizational difficulties. There is a great demand on the part of third countries both to know what the Twelve are thinking and to be seen to be in a formal dialogue with EPC. This has not always been the case. The institutional nature of the co-operation of the Six was not immediately apparent in the early days. It was only when EPC began notching up achievements that the corporate personality of the Member States began to appear. There was at the time no philosophy about how to organize relations with third countries. Member States invented whatever procedures seemed most appropriate as each case arose, in the first instance with the United States and Turkey.

This *ad hoc* approach continued as the trickle of requests for dialogue came in over the years. After the London Report of 1981 the trickle became a flood, and Member States were in two minds about how to respond. On the one hand, the interest shown in EPC was encouraging and it was to the Ten's advantage to seize the opportunities which arose. On the other hand, the rapid increase in the number of dialogue partners laid a heavy burden on the Presidency, which led the Ten to prefer the lightest possible procedures. For the same reason, attempts were made to rationalize arrangements by the introduction of a hierarchy of formulas for dialogue, ranging from meetings with all the Foreign Ministers, believed to be particularly appropriate for dialogues with regional groupings, through the Troika to the Presidency alone. A further distinction could be made by placing the dialogue at the lower level of Political Director. The difficulty was that the concept of descending levels for dialogue would not work unless corresponding decisions were made about the relative importance of the dialogue partners. This Ministers were reluctant to do. There was always a good reason for giving favourable treatment to a new applicant, and in any case the strict application of hierarchical principles would have involved an unacceptable downgrading of some partners who had been awarded too high a place in the past. The pattern of dialogue remains therefore a confusing patchwork, and presents one of the greatest organizational problems EPC has to face.

TURKEY AND UNITED STATES

It was natural that the Six should first of all give their attention to those countries which could expect in the near future to become members of the Community, and almost from the beginning the four candidate countries were closely associated with EPC. The arrangements lapsed on enlargement, and in the case of Norway even before then, following the referendum rejecting membership of the Community. Norway attempted on a number of occasions to seek a special relationship with EPC, but the Member States remained deaf to advances from a country which could, if it chose, become a full member. It was not until 1982 that contacts with the Presidency at the level of Political Directors were begun, and that without the benefit of a formal decision by the Ten.

The other countries which were formally recognized as potential members of the Community were Turkey and Greece. If at that time there was no question of political discussions with the Greece of the Colonels, the case was different with Turkey, a fellow member of NATO and occupying a vital strategic position on the Allies' Eastern flank. Arrangements were made in 1972 for the Presidency to inform the Turkish Foreign Minister of developments in Political Co-operation. The twice yearly meetings of the EEC–Turkey Association Council were a convenient opportunity for doing this. We have seen that EPC's relationship with Turkey was a matter of hot political debate before the accession of Greece to the Community, and that the formula of meetings with the Troika of Political Directors was brought into play as a result.

The first occasion on which policies, rather than proximity, obliged the Nine to give thought to the form of their dialogue with a foreign country was in 1973–4, when Kissinger's 'Year of Europe' speech, followed by the war in the Middle East and the oil crisis, revealed the ambiguity of the relationship between the new European grouping and the United States. Secretary Kissinger's claim that when he wanted to speak to Europe he did not know what number to call was disingenuous; the arrival on the scene of a foreign-policy bloc apparently restive under American dominance made it imperative for the United States to ensure that its concerns would be taken into account at an early stage of European policy-making. Kissinger's determined efforts to bring this about threw the Europeans into disarray. The Gymnich formula of April 1974 brought the crisis to a close, but failed to put the relationship with the United States on a transparent footing. The formula itself was vaguely worded, did not provide for regular contacts and did not even mention the United States by name. Nevertheless it governed the relationship between Political Co-operation and the Europeans' closest ally for more than ten years.

In fact the system worked well, both sides preferring effective communication to formal dialogue. Regardless of the terms of the Gymnich formula, the practice which grew up was that the US Ambassador in the capital of the Presidency was given advance notice of the subjects likely to be discussed at meetings of the Political Committee or of Ministers and in due course forwarded to the Presidency the State Department's views. He was then debriefed after the meetings, separately from the other 'like-minded' countries who had to be content with a collective briefing. The use EPC made of the American input depended on the Presidency; circulation of the US papers as documentation was thought to be in poor taste.

The United States' interest in EPC grew over the years. From 1985 the State Department has posted an additional official to the US Mission to the EC in Brussels in order to follow EPC full time, and US meetings in preparation for each new Presidency, covering both EPC and Community questions, take place with officials from the US Embassies in the Troika countries. The initiative to put the Gymnich arrangement on a more solid footing came, however, from the Europeans, concerned about the apparent breakdown in communications in the Reagan years.

There had been irregular meetings of the Political Directors in the Troika format since the latter part of 1982, arranged as and when the diaries of the participants allowed. This was not often. One meeting had to be held between two flights in Frankfurt airport, others were squeezed into busy schedules during the first week of the General Assembly in New York. At the initiative of Germany, the Foreign Ministers decided at their Gymnich-type meeting in Heemskerk in June 1986 that the political dialogue with the United States had to be strengthened. Trade relations were worsening, there was a widening gap in views on East–West relations, and the Europeans had had for the sake of Atlantic solidarity to gloss over incidents, such as the invasion of Grenada and the attack on Libya, of which they basically disapproved. As incoming Presidency, the United Kingdom took up the running. The following September, Sir Geoffrey Howe was able to agree for the first time a regular structure for contacts with the Americans. Without any formal authorization, the practice had grown up of the Foreign Minister of the Presidency going to Washington during his term of office; this practice was confirmed. The Troika meetings of Political Directors were also confirmed and put on a half-yearly basis, and it was agreed that there should be regular contacts in Washington with the Embassies of the Twelve. The Twelve did not, however, agree to a pressing request from the Americans for contacts at the level of Working Groups, some Member States still fearing American pressure exerted on them collectively at a stage before EPC positions had been finally decided.

The new arrangements worked well, aided by the relaxation in tension between the United States and the Twelve. Other mechanisms were added; from 1987 the Foreign Ministers have had dinner with the US Secretary of State during their New York week at the end of September. But even this improved structure of dialogue was seen to be inadequate in the face of events in the Soviet Union and Eastern Europe in 1989–90. The Americans realized very early that the return to democratic forms of government in the countries of Central and Eastern Europe, the absorption of the Soviet Union in its domestic affairs, and the effective collapse of the Warsaw Pact required the United States and Europe to evolve a new relationship to put alongside NATO. This was reflected in the speech made by Secretary Baker in Berlin in the autumn of 1989, followed up by pressure from the Bush Administration and the President himself to put EC–US relations on a new institutional footing. As a result of these developments, new arrangements were agreed between the Irish Presidency and the United States in February 1990. According to these, the biannual meetings between the President of the European Council and the President of the United States were formalized, there were to be two meetings a year between the Foreign Ministers and the US Secretary of State instead of one, and there was at last agreement on contacts at Working Group level in the Troika format.

These arrangements were taken over and given formal expression in the transatlantic declaration issued on 23 November 1990 after the CSCE Summit meeting in Paris. The declaration set up a new institutional framework for consultation which combined the previously existing dialogues on the EPC and Community sides and raised them to a higher level. There were to be biannual consultations between, on the one side, the President of the European Council and the President of the Commission, and on the other side, the President of the United States. There were also to be biannual consultations between the Community Foreign Ministers (with the Commission) and the US Secretary of State, alternately on either side of the Atlantic, and *ad hoc* consultations between the Presidency Foreign Minister or the Troika and the US Secretary of State. The existing consultations between the Commission and the US government at Cabinet level would become biannual, and Presidency briefings on EPC meetings at Ministerial level would continue. In practice, the briefings extended to meetings at all levels.

The institutional arrangements in the transatlantic declaration reflect not only the changes in Central and Eastern Europe, but

Talking with the World

also new ways of representing EPC and the Community in relations with third countries. It is a sign of the way EPC and the Community have moved closer together after the Single European Act.

THE LONDON REPORT AND AFTER

The London Report of 1981 held that

> As European Political Co-operation intensifies and broadens the Ten as such will appear as significant interlocutors. Third countries will increasingly express the desire to enter into more or less regular contact with them. It is important that the Ten should be able to respond effectively to these demands, in particular vis-à-vis countries of special interest to them, and that they should speak with one voice in dealings with them.

The responsibility for conducting these contacts was placed squarely on the Presidency, with the possibility of recourse to the Troika if the Ten so agreed.

Third countries, already interested in Political Co-operation, rapidly responded to the implicit invitation to seek regular contacts with it. In the years which followed, in addition to requests by many countries for contacts through diplomatic channels, Norway, New Zealand, Canada, Japan, China, and India all sought a formal dialogue. In March 1983 a dialogue was instituted with Japan, based on twice yearly Troika Ministerial meetings, one in the spring on the occasion of the OECD Council meeting in Paris and one in the autumn during the General Assembly week in New York. Since 1984 there have also been twice yearly Troika meetings of Political Directors, which take place between Ministerial meetings, alternately in Tokyo and in the capital of the Presidency.

China followed in April 1983, beginning with a twice yearly meeting between the Political Director of the Presidency and the Ambassador in the Presidency capital. From 1986 on, there have been in principle annual meetings between the Chinese Foreign Minister and the EPC Troika, held during the New York week. Since 1985, a dialogue has been sporadically conducted with India according to the 'light Troika' formula, whereby the Foreign Minister of the Presidency is accompanied not by Ministers, but by the local Ambassadors of the Troika partners.

Also during this period the practice grew up of discussing political questions informally on the occasion of meetings of the Association Councils established with the countries, mostly the Arab countries of the southern and eastern Mediterranean as well as Yugoslavia, with which the Community had Association Agreements. The discussions took place at lunch or dinner, and were the more appreciated because they provided a richer fare than the arid and formalized agenda of the Councils themselves.

REGIONAL DIALOGUE

Dialogues with individual third countries have been started either to solve a political problem or at the request of the countries themselves. When it comes to dialogues with regional groupings, the initiative has been taken by the Twelve. This is in part a response to international developments, as in the case of Central America and the Front Line States, but also because the Twelve have seen themselves as particularly suited to regional dialogue. Since the Community is itself a regional organization, the argument goes, its dialogues with other regional organizations and groupings are enhanced by shared institutional experience, which gives the relationship a quality lacking in contacts between Nation States.

The first attempt at regional dialogue was with the Arab countries in 1973, at their request, but in furtherance of policy aims in the Middle East strongly promoted by France. In spite of the fact that the structures of the Euro-Arab Dialogue are the most complicated of all in which the Twelve are engaged, it has never satisfactorily served the purposes for which it was intended and yet has obstinately refused to wither away. The Dialogue's comparative failure can be attributed mainly to the difficulties encountered by EPC policy on the Middle East, but the lack of a strong structure on the Arab side has been a contributory factor. The formal interlocutor is the Arab League, together with its Member States, but that body has not been able to sow the seeds of integration in the Arab world which would have allowed it to act as a valid regional spokesman. Unlike in other areas, such as ASEAN and Central America, the Twelve are not sufficiently weighty, and their Middle East policy is not sufficiently cohesive, for them to be able to provide an effective stimulus towards regional integration in the Arab world.

Talking with the World

The dialogue with ASEAN had a mixed parentage. The initiative came on the economic side. Contacts with the Community were begun by ASEAN in 1972, and discussion proceeded in the following years as ASEAN's own institutions developed. The breakthrough came following the ASEAN Summit in Bali in 1976, when the ASEAN countries sought to broaden their contacts with both the Community institutions and the Member States. The idea of a joint Ministerial Meeting was put forward by Mr Genscher on his visit to the region in 1977 and such a meeting eventually took place in November 1978, giving rise to a Co-operation Agreement concluded in March 1980. The Agreement dealt exclusively with economic matters and there was no separate agreement dealing with political dialogue, but the practice has grown up of Ministerial Meetings at approximately eighteen-month intervals at which both political and economic questions are discussed. In addition, the Presidency Minister and the Troika partners take part in ASEAN's annual meetings with its 'dialogue partners' (the Pacific OECD members and the Community).

Although the Agreement would not have been concluded had the Community not calculated that it was in its economic interest to do so, there was also a feeling that ASEAN was itself a factor of stability in the region and therefore of political interest to the Europeans. The point was made in Mr Genscher's speech to the ASEAN Ministers in Brussels in November 1978: 'ASEAN thus contributes to increasing stability in the whole region and to improving conditions for a lasting peace. We know that tensions and armed conflicts in other parts of the world risk damaging our own security interests.' Two days later the President of the Commission, Roy Jenkins, brought out the special contribution the Community could make:

The Community has always been in favour of regional cooperation because we firmly believe that such cooperation does not only contribute significantly to the economic development of the individual countries of the grouping but is an important factor for political stability and peace. From the formation of ASEAN we in the Community have always sought to treat with ASEAN as a region since we from our own experience have learnt that an external stimulus can often support internal cooperation.

The political dialogue with ASEAN was the brainchild of Mr Genscher, who has been the consistent advocate of regional dialogue for the contribution it can make to increased stability. He used the occasion of the Presidency speech to the United Nations in 1978 to set out his philosophy: 'The European Community . . . can . . . serve as an example of the countries of a region forming an association and combining their efforts so as to accomplish the task at hand and to strengthen the independence, the political stability and the economic growth of that region.' In line with this philosophy, Genscher provided essential support for the idea of a political dialogue with Central America, and made the decisive move towards a relationship with the Gulf Co-operation Council.

The events which led to the setting up of a political dialogue with Central America have already been described. It was following a visit by Mr Genscher to the region that President Monge of Costa Rica launched the series of San José Ministerial meetings. The agreements with Central America concluded at Luxembourg in November 1985 marked a new stage in the institutional development of EPC and the Community, the political dialogue being connected with, but separate from, the economic Co-operation Agreement.

In addition to the dialogue with Central America, the Twelve have begun a dialogue with the Latin American countries which make up the Group of Rio. The dialogue was at first conducted on an informal basis through regular meetings which brought together the Foreign Ministers of all the participants on both sides. The first meeting was held in September 1987 in New York, following the Conclusions adopted on 22 June 1987 by the Council and the representatives of the Governments of the Member States concerning relations with Latin America. This was the first joint declaration ever issued by EPC and the Community, in which the Twelve declared they were 'following with special interest the attempts of certain Latin American countries to set up political cooperation bodies, for example the Rio Group, with a view to giving positive consideration to any possibilities there might be for contacts between the Twelve and such representative groups.' Although the Twelve's contacts with the countries concerned had begun on the political side, in their capacity as members of the Contadora and support group which at one stage played an important role in developments in Central America, they continued mainly on the economic side, focusing on questions like debt, trade questions, and drugs. The dialogue was formalized on a six-monthly basis in the Rome Declaration of December 1990.

While to all appearances economic, the dialogue with the Gulf Co-operation Council has strong political undertones and would not have seen the light of day without a political dialogue. The initiative came from the Community for economic reasons to do with market-access conditions for petroleum products from the Gulf. The primary impulse, however, was of political and strategic origin, resulting from the second oil shock and the outbreak of the Iran–Iraq war. Since the Euro-Arab Dialogue was stalled, the Community saw that greater stability of oil supplies depended on placing EC–Gulf relations on a more direct and positive basis. The Iran–Iraq war encouraged the setting up of the Gulf Co-operation Council and thus provided the Twelve with an interlocutor. Under pressure from Mr Genscher, negotiating directives were adopted, and a draft Co-operation Agreement was initialled on 24 March 1988.

The texts did not include a reference to political dialogue. However, the Commission had already circulated in Political Co-operation a draft declaration on this to be made by the Member States at the time of the signature of the Agreement. The draft reproduced the terms used in the Council's negotiating directives and was based on the arrangements made with Central America. After extensive redrafting in EPC, the text was issued on 15 June 1988 as a joint declaration of the European Community and its Member States and the Co-operation Council for the Arab States of the Gulf and its Member States. It stated that

in accordance with the provisions of the Agreement [there are no specific provisions concerning political dialogue; the reference is to Article 14] they decided to hold one annual meeting with the participation of the Member States of the Community and the Commission on the one hand, and the Member States of GCC and the Secretariat General of the GCC on the other hand.

The political dialogue meetings are held in tandem with the annual meetings of the Joint Council set up under Article 14 of the Agreement. In addition, Ministers continue their custom of meeting for lunch in New York and Troika meetings have been held.

THE SINGLE EUROPEAN ACT AND AFTER

Article 30.8 of the Single European Act provides that 'The High Contracting Parties shall organize a political dialogue with third countries and regional groupings whenever they deem it necessary.' Like the London Report previously, this gave rise to a number of requests for formal dialogue as a result of which Australia, Austria, Canada, Cyprus, Malta, Norway, New Zealand, and Yugoslavia were added to the dialogue partners of longer standing.

Most notable, however, has been the development of political dialogue with the Soviet Union and the countries of Eastern and Central Europe. For many years the Twelve's contacts with the Soviet Union were regulated by guidelines which went back to 1985. In spite of the growing Soviet interest in the Community as a result of the policy of *perestroika*, the Foreign Minister seemed disinclined to take what the Twelve had indicated should be the first step, namely to accept an invitation to lunch with their Ambassadors in Moscow. There were sporadic contacts between the Foreign Ministry and the Presidency, but no moves towards a deeper political relationship. This changed as the Soviet Union relaxed its grip on the countries of Eastern and Central Europe and the Iron Curtain was dismantled in 1989 and 1990. The first signs of a breakthrough came in January 1989, when there was a meeting in Vienna between the Foreign Ministers of the Soviet Union and the Spanish Presidency. This was followed up by a lunch with all the Twelve in New York in September of that year, on the same lines as the Twelve's dinner with the US Secretary of State, which is set to become an annual event. The Political Directors meet every six months in the Troika format, alternately in Moscow and the capital of the Presidency.

The countries of Central and Eastern Europe naturally looked to the Community for support in affirming their new-found independence. They sought not only co-operation agreements which would strengthen their economic and trading position, but also the political cachet which a dialogue with Political Co-operation would bring. While anxious to respond positively, the Twelve began to show some nervousness about the administrative burdens of proliferating dialogue. A new formula was therefore invented for contacts with Hungary, Poland, and Czechoslovakia. Beginning in 1990, there have been meetings once each Presidency, in the capital of the Presidency, between the Political Director of the country concerned and his opposite numbers in the Presidency and the Commission. The heavy machinery of the Troika, which it requires considerable effort on the part of the Presidency and Secretariat to put into motion, is thus abandoned, and the Presidency and the Commission are able to carry out the duty of ensuring consistency imposed on them jointly by the Single European Act in an area in which it is particularly necessary.

Following the decision taken by the European Council in Dublin in April 1990, the new generation of 'European Agreements' with the countries of Eastern and Central Europe will include a clause establishing political dialogue both in the Association Council and, at the level of officials, with the Presidency and the Commission. This establishes a significant procedural innovation compared with the previous agreements with Central America and the Gulf Co-operation Council.

SELECTED READING

A full survey of EPC's contacts with third countries at the time is given by Regelsberger (1985). For an overall appreciation see von Jagow (1990), the European Correspondent of Germany.

10
The Grey Area

Member States have found it convenient to use the intergovernmental machinery of EPC for other areas of co-operation besides foreign policy. This applies primarily to judicial co-operation, which brings together representatives of the Ministries of Justice of the Member States. The object is to move towards a single European judicial area. Achievements have been few, however, partly because of the inherent difficulty of bringing together legal systems with long national traditions, partly because of the anomaly of a situation whereby the Political Committee is responsible for supervising the work, but has no authority over the representatives of the Ministries of Justice who do it.

Co-operation among the police and security authorities of the Member States takes place in a separate framework, known as Trevi. The weak co-ordination between Trevi and Political Co-operation is frequently criticized by the latter. In recent years the foreign-policy aspects of the fight against international terrorism have taken on more importance, as a result of which EPC has its own Working Group on Terrorism.

JUDICIAL CO-OPERATION

The origins of co-operation on judicial questions are to be found in the spread of international terrorism during the 1970s. It was thought that the extradition of terrorists from one Member State of the Community to another should be easier than it was. In December 1975 and again in July 1976 the European Council called for co-operation in the prosecution or extradition of terrorists, particularly when hostages had been taken, and called on the Ministers of Justice to work out an appropriate Convention. A legal instrument designed to achieve precisely this, the European Convention on the Suppression of Terrorism, was already in an advanced stage of preparation under the auspices of the Council of Europe and was opened for signature in January 1977. This Convention was based on the principle that a State either had to extradite alleged terrorists or try them itself, and was designed to limit the number of criminal offences regarded as political offences for which extradition could be refused.

The sensitivity of the concept of the political offence in some countries, especially Ireland and France, was such that few States ratified the European Convention. Belgium therefore put forward the idea that the Member States of the Community should agree to apply the Convention among themselves without reservation, even though many of them had not yet ratified it, on the grounds that limitation to a narrower circle would diminish the political sensitivity. An *ad hoc* Group of legal experts, mainly from Foreign Ministries, was set up to look into the matter.

This work was already under way when President Giscard d'Estaing took a much bolder initiative, which for a time monopolized the attention of the Nine and delayed progress on the Belgian proposal. This was the proposal, made at the European Council in December 1977, to set up a European Legal Space. Care was taken not to detract from the striking force of this concept by encumbering it with unnecessary detail, but it was clear that something radical was intended, to take into account the free circulation of persons and goods within the Community and the fact that internal frontiers were doomed to disappear. The French had tabled in the *ad hoc* Group an alternative text on extradition which went beyond the immediate question of terrorism addressed in the Belgian draft, but it became plain that the Giscard Plan was more radical than this, covering both civil and criminal law, and that the French wanted it discussed among Ministers of Justice, not Foreign Ministers.

This presented a difficulty. Whereas the work on extradition had fallen halfway between the responsibilities of Foreign Ministries and Ministries of Justice, and was an obvious candidate for inter-governmental procedures in the absence of any Community responsibility, the same could not be said for co-operation on civil law. Article 220 of the EEC Treaty provides for negotiations among Member States on a number of civil-law questions, including the reciprocal recognition and enforcement of judgments. Although these provisions are inter-governmental in character, as a matter of convenience the work had been done in the Community framework, usually on the basis of drafts supplied by the Commission and with the benefit of the Community's multilingual legal expertise. The supporters of the integrationist method did not want to see these activities and others like them taken over by an extraneous body.

A compromise was reached by holding a combined meeting of first the Council (Ministers of Justice) and then of the Ministers of Justice in an inter-governmental framework. This took place in Luxembourg on 10 October 1978. Substantive progress was slow. The draft Agreement on the application of the Council of Europe Convention on terrorism was ready, but signature was delayed because of the need to reconcile it with the more wide-ranging French ideas on extradition. Work on these had begun, but agreement was not in sight. There were also doubts as to whether a corresponding exercise on civil questions was appropriate, both because of worries over the powers of the Community and also because of British fears that the common law would be exposed to inroads from the Napoleonic system. The setting up of a separate group to deal with civil-law questions was opposed, and the work for the time being abandoned.

The result was that the Agreement on extradition was not opened for signature until the Dublin European Council on 4 December 1979 (hence known as the 'Dublin Agreement'). Subsequently work proceeded on the wider French draft for co-operation on criminal law, resulting in a draft Convention which was due to be submitted to a meeting of the Ministers of Justice in Rome in June 1980. The Netherlands announced their inability to sign this, ostensibly on the grounds of its limited usefulness and possible negative effects on Conventions worked out in other bodies like the Council of Europe, but also because the Dutch government was unlikely to command in Parliament the support it would need for ratification. As a result, the Convention was not opened for signature. France thereupon refused to ratify the Dublin Agreement, partly in retaliation, but also because of opposition in its own public opinion and National Assembly to any weakening of the traditional right of political asylum. Other Member States followed suit, and the Dublin Agreement did not therefore enter into force.

The situation remained unchanged until President Mitterrand came to power in France in May 1981. The question of European co-operation in the judicial field was, however, not one of the new government's immediate priorities, and it was not until October 1982 that the Minister of Justice, M. Badinter, presented some new ideas about penal and civil co-operation. These had to be seen as different from those of the previous government; above all, the terminology 'European Legal Space' became taboo. M. Badinter's initiative was not followed through. As a result of the Genscher–Colombo proposals, the question of legal co-operation among the Nine was indeed discussed, but only in a theoretical and institutional way. This led to a cautious and elliptic reference in the Stuttgart Solemn Declaration of June 1983, but not to any practical examples of co-operation.

The French had to wait until their Presidency in the first half of 1984 before being able to get discussion moving again, and even so it was not until a year later that the *ad hoc* Group on Judicial Co-operation was reconstituted in two formations, one dealing with civil, and one with criminal, law. On the civil-law side the group worked on the enforcement of custody decisions and child abduction, the abolition of the certifying of legal acts, and administrative co-operation for the implementation of the Brussels Convention, concluded under Article 220 of the EEC Treaty, on the recovery of alimony. A network of Correspondents was set up among Ministries of Justice to act as contact points for practical co-operation. On the criminal–law side the Group looked into the possibility of saving something from the fiasco of the Dublin Agreement, and other possibilities for penal co-operation were also to be examined.

The fruits of this work were gathered on 25 May 1987, when three international instruments were opened for signature: the Agreement on the application between the Member States of the Community of the Council of Europe Convention on the transfer of sentenced persons, the Convention between the Member States of the Community on double jeopardy, and the Convention abolishing the legalization of documents in the Member States of the Community. These Conventions were the first steps towards a single Community law-enforcement area, to set beside the handful of Conventions drawn up in accordance with Article 220 of the EEC Treaty. The fact that two of them concerned co-operation on civil-law matters, so hotly contested at the time of the Giscard initiative, is a measure of the progress which had been made. They are of course far from being a harmonization of European law, nor were they intended to be. Each in its own way reduces the duplication of legal process resulting from the continued existence of national barriers in the field of law, or otherwise eases the lot of the citizen affected by those barriers. There are some drawbacks, however. Not all the Member States signed all the Conventions. Greece and Germany failed to sign the first Convention; Ireland, Spain, Greece, France, and Germany the second; and Ireland, Spain, Greece, and France the third. The effectiveness of the single European law-enforcement area was thereby impaired, and indeed the reason for the refusal of some Member States to sign was that not all were in a position to do so. The second drawback is the length of time it takes to achieve even meagre results when following the classical method of international legal negotiation. Judicial co-operation, while using the EPC framework for reasons of convenience, does not benefit from such elements of dynamism as Political Co-operation possesses. It is under no pressure of time, and the legal officials in the Member States on whom in the last resort the decision depends are not directly involved in the process and so are not subject to the personal pressures under which the Political Committee operates. Political Co-operation only really works when the Foreign Ministries are in control of the subject matter.

Progress on criminal-law co-operation has been even slower. Desultory discussions on the possibility of applying the Dublin Agreement continued for some time, but by 1987 all the Twelve had become contracting parties to the Council of Europe Convention and it was recognized that this deprived the Dublin Agreement of much of its usefulness. The questions which remained were whether the Twelve could lift among themselves the reservations they had declared when adhering to the Council of Europe Convention and whether Greece, Spain, and Portugal should accede to an Agreement which had been concluded before they had joined the Community.

TREVI AND THE *AD HOC* GROUP ON IMMIGRATION

Like judicial co-operation, which it predates, co-operation among Ministries of the Interior (or of Justice, depending on the Member State) had its origin in the increase in acts of terrorism in the early 1970s. Not only did the organization of terrorist groups spread across national frontiers, there were also signs that otherwise unconnected groups were in contact with each other. Domestic terrorism had become an international phenomenon which could not be successfully resisted in the absence of international co-operation.

The situation was exceptionally grave in 1975. In the course of the year over 200 people died in Northern Ireland as a result of terrorist action, the Chairman of the Berlin Christian Democratic Union (CDU), Peter Lorenz, was kidnapped in February, and the German Embassy in Stockholm was destroyed by terrorists in April. It was at the prompting of the United Kingdom that work began on organizing co-operation in this area, and the fact that the Community now had a new overarching organ in the European Council enabled the necessary directives to be given. The European Council decided in Rome in December 1975 that the Ministers of the Interior of the Member States should meet to discuss matters for which they were responsible. The first meeting took place in June 1976 in Luxembourg, a few days after the Entebbe hijacking had once again concentrated public attention on the terrorist threat. The process of co-operation came to be known as Trevi, after Mr Fonteyn, the Director-General of the Dutch State Police, who chaired the first meeting of the senior officials group.

The Trevi machinery brought together the professionals in anti-terrorist operations from the Member States. The work is supervised by a steering group of senior officials from Ministries of the Interior meeting at approximately six-month intervals, and is carried out at the operational level by a series of Working Groups, also meeting twice a year. There were at first two of these, Trevi Group 1 dealing with the exchange of information on terrorist plans and activities and with mutual assistance in specific cases, and Trevi Group 2 which exchanges technical information with a view to combating terrorism and disturbance of public order. Trevi Group 3 deals with internationally organized crime, and was added in 1985. There is also a new group on drugs, and a group known as Trevi 1992 was set up in 1989 to deal with the police and security aspects of the abolition of frontiers. The meetings at Ministerial level were at first irregular, but since the Italian Presidency in 1985 have tended to take place once during each Presidency, with extraordinary meetings when required, for example at the beginning of the Gulf war.

The activities of Trevi are for obvious reasons conducted in great secrecy and on an even more informal basis than Political Co-operation. It is only recently that a separate confidential-communications network similar to the Coreu network has been installed. Proposals to set up a Trevi Secretariat after prolonged resistance are only now beginning to be taken seriously. Needless to say, the Commission was for many years not allowed to take part in Trevi meetings, although it supplied the simultaneous interpretation, and has only just been admitted to the Trevi 1992 group.

Unlike judicial co-operation, Trevi does not form part of the EPC machinery and is in no way under the control of Foreign Ministries, which sometimes leads to problems of co-ordination. In addition to specific occasions on which the Foreign Ministers would have preferred to reserve to their own judgement the foreign-policy implications of terrorist acts, there is potential rivalry because Trevi from time to time has collective contacts with its opposite numbers in third countries, either through the Presidency or in the Troika format. Furthermore, Trevi is less sensitive than EPC to the need for participation in inter-governmental activity to be limited to members of the Community, which has led, for example, to Trevi's adopting its own timing for the association of candidate countries, as in the case of Spain.

Omne ignotum pro magnifico est. It is hard to appreciate the worth of activities which are hidden behind such an impenetrable veil. The participants are very happy with their work, but this is not necessarily a valid indication, and may have less to do with operational efficiency than with the need for even Ministries of the Interior, security services, and police forces to have their European credentials. It is reasonable to expect that effective co-operation in the fight against terrorism will depend more on bilateral contacts than on collective deliberation. The club atmosphere created by participation in Trevi eases bilateral contacts when these are necessary.

The *ad hoc* Group on Immigration, at one time misleadingly known as Trevi Group 4, was set up by the Ministers of the Interior in London in October 1986 to deal with difficulties arising from the abolition of frontiers inside the Community which the establishment of the Single Internal Market would require. This represented an important turning-point in the Member States' approach. Whereas previously it had been maintained that the abolition of frontiers was, for reasons of public security, out of the question and the Single Market would therefore have to remain incomplete in this respect, it was now recognized that the Single Market had to be fully implemented and that the Member States, and in particular the Ministries of the Interior, had better get together to work out how to deal with any problems which stood in the way.

The *ad hoc* Group's mandate was later defined as the coordination of Member States' visa regulations (at the risk of duplicating similar work being done in EPC at the behest of Foreign Ministers), the definition of common rules governing controls at external Community frontiers and strengthened cooperation against the use of false travel documents. The 'adoption of a number of measures to combat the abuse of the right of asylum' was also recommended in order to fix rules to establish which Member States would be responsible in any given set of circumstances for the examination of applications for asylum. This was considered essential both because of fears that refugees might transit through those Member States which are generous in the grant of asylum to those with more attractive social-security schemes, and because it would put a stop to the sorry spectacle of asylum seekers being pushed from pillar to post while governments argued about responsibility for examining their cases.

Ministers decided in London that the Commission would be invited to attend the meetings of the *ad hoc* Group in order to ensure consistency with work in the Community framework, and the responsibility for organizing the meetings (although the Ministers may not have realized that they were deciding this) was awarded to the Secretariat-General of the Council.

TERRORISM AND EPC

The Member States' co-operation against terrorism continued among the Ministries of the Interior for ten years before the rise in the mid 1980s of 'state-sponsored terrorism' obliged the Foreign Ministries to devote attention to the problem in the framework of Political Co-operation. The new dimension came about because Member States had evidence, or believed that they had evidence, that the governments of foreign countries were behind terrorist attacks perpetrated on their territory. There had to be a reaction to this, which had consequences for foreign policy. The third countries concerned were Libya and Syria, and the Member State concerned usually the United Kingdom. The British could normally have expected from their European partners a display of solidarity such as they had enjoyed over the Falklands. The situation was complicated, however, by the Twelve's wish to maintain a balanced policy towards the Middle East. Action against Libya and Syria would upset the balance, and was moreover liable to be interpreted as giving in to American pressure with the negative effects on Arab opinion that entailed. The measures taken by the Twelve were therefore muted, causing disappointment in the United Kingdom as well as in the United States. A procedural consequence was that the Twelve acquired a permanent Working Group on terrorism, which added a new dimension to their co-operation.

In April 1984 a shot from a window of the Libyan People's Bureau in London killed Policewoman Fletcher, on duty outside in St James's Square. This act of diplomatic folly enraged the British people, and the United Kingdom broke off diplomatic relations. Apart from other considerations, there had been a clear abuse of diplomatic immunity; this was the aspect which the British raised in EPC. An *ad hoc* Group on terrorism and diplomatic immunity was set up to examine what recourse was open in such cases to signatories of the Vienna Convention. It proved more difficult than expected to reach agreement on a declaration, which was not finally adopted until the Ministers met in Dublin on 11 September 1984. This merely confirmed the Ten's guiding principle to make no concessions under duress and announced that a set of measures had been agreed to strengthen existing co-operation. The Ten also declared their readiness to consider common action if one of their number were to suffer a serious terrorist attack involving abuse of diplomatic immunity. Although subjected to heavy pressure at the press conference after the meeting, the Irish Presidency declined to reveal what that common action might involve. This was the price of agreement on the substance.

The Ten's activities in this area thereupon subsided for a while. Mrs Thatcher wanted to raise the question of terrorism, especially hijacking, at the European Council in Milan, but there was no time and the Heads of Government were more concerned with European Union. The initiative did, however, lead to a statement on 22 July in which Foreign Ministers declared their intention to look at the possibilities of strengthened international standards for airline and airport security. The implementation of this decision presented problems. The mandate of the *ad hoc* Group was expanded and its composition was enlarged, but the difficulty of bringing together the large number of different Ministries involved in the question in the Member States meant that progress was practically impossible.

The quickening pace of international events brooked no further delay. Following terrorist attacks at Rome and Vienna airports in December 1985 Italy demanded a discussion by Ministers on 27 January 1986 at which the Twelve issued a statement strongly condemning the attacks and reviewing the measures already taken to combat international terrorism. Co-operation was now to be strengthened in areas including security at airports, control of persons entering and circulating in the Community, visa policies, and the abuse of diplomatic immunity. It was also decided to set up a new Working Group on Co-operation to Combat International Terrorism.

More significant was what the Ten failed to do, which was to respond to increasing American pressure for economic sanctions against Libya, or indeed even to name Libya as responsible for acts of international terrorism. Ever since 1981 the Reagan Administration had been engaged in a campaign to isolate Libya and the Gaddafi regime, and looked to their allies to close down the People's Bureaus and introduce sanctions. There were heavy hints that, failing this, military action was a distinct possibility. US pressure reached a climax in the spring of 1986. Following the bombing of the La Belle discothèque in Berlin, in which US servicemen as well as others were killed, and for which Colonel Gaddafi was held responsible at the time, the Twelve held an extraordinary Ministerial Meeting in The Hague on 14 April, convened at the request of Spain and Italy using the emergency procedure introduced in the London Report. They issued a statement in which they considered 'that States clearly implicated in supporting terrorism should be induced to renounce such support and to respect the rules of international law. They call upon Libya to act accordingly.' The staff of Libyan diplomatic and consular missions was reduced and the movements of those who remained were restricted, and visa requirements were made stricter, but there were no economic sanctions as the Americans wanted, and to balance their identification of Libya, the Twelve added a final paragraph: '... in order to enable the achievement of a political solution, avoiding further escalation of military tension in the region with all the inherent dangers, the Twelve underline the need for restraint on both sides.'

The Twelve hoped they had done enough to satisfy the Americans and to deter them from military action. The question was not put to the test, as the Twelve's decision had come too late. Final approval of a plan and targets was given in Washington the day before, and the United States carried out a bombing raid on Tripoli on 14 April, the ink scarcely dry on the declaration of the Twelve. The raid was bitterly resented by the Foreign Ministers, who felt they had been deceived by the Americans into believing that no final decision had been taken and that time would be allowed in Washington to assess the measures announced by the Twelve. The Netherlands Presidency described the raid as a slap in the face for the Europeans.

The situation was made worse by the fact that the F–111 fighter-bombers which carried out the raid had taken off from American bases in the United Kingdom with the authorization of the British government. The conclusion was inescapable that either Sir Geoffrey Howe had known about this at the time of the EPC Meeting in The Hague and had said nothing to his colleagues, or that he had not known about it, in which case the Prime Minister, and not the Foreign Secretary, was in charge of British policy. Neither conclusion was flattering for the man concerned, but the relative tenderness with which his colleagues later treated Sir Geoffrey showed that they inclined to the latter hypothesis.

The situation required immediate discussion among the Twelve, and once again the emergency procedure was brought into play. At the request of Spain and Greece, the Presidency convened a meeting in Paris on 17 April, taking advantage of the Foreign Ministers' presence there for a meeting of the OECD. The tone, set by Mr Genscher, indicated a serious and reasonable approach, and a desire to be effective, to avoid recriminations, and to maintain European solidarity. No new statement was issued; the Twelve reaffirmed their belief in a political solution and their desire to avoid any escalation. On 21 April they went over the ground again, tightening up and extending the diplomatic measures against Libya, but still declining to introduce economic sanctions to break off diplomatic relations.

The events surrounding the raid on Tripoli are often quoted as one of Political Co-operation's more spectacular failures. Admittedly, the Twelve failed to act in time to dissuade the United States from taking military action, but this was not their only objective. They also had to maintain as far as possible relations with the Arab world, and their collective judgement that to go as far as the Americans asked would have endangered these may well have been correct. It was scarcely glorious, however, that this position was reached not by concordance of opinion among the Member States, but by diversity. The Twelve failed to act because they failed to reach consensus. Furthermore, whatever the truth about the authorization given to the Americans by the British government, the incident showed that EPC only works well when Foreign Ministries are in charge. At least the EPC machinery functioned properly: the Foreign Ministers met three times within a week and succeeded in maintaining public cohesion in trying circumstances. The procrastination which had attended the Afghanistan and Polish crises was a thing of the past.

Only three days after the raid on Libya, the train was laid for yet another crisis which strained relations between the United Kingdom and its European partners and exposed the underlying contradiction between the need to respond to acts of terrorism and the wider requirements of Middle East policy. On

17 April 1986 a bomb was discovered in the luggage of a passenger bound for Tel Aviv from Heathrow Airport on an El-Al flight. The suspicion was that it had been put there, without the passenger's knowledge, by her boyfriend Nezar Hindawi; there were indications of Syrian official involvement. No action could be taken as long as the case was *sub judice*, but as soon as judgment was given against Hindawi, the United Kingdom broke off diplomatic relations with Syria, tightened security measures applied to Syrianair flights, and reviewed visa requirements for Syrians.

The British government would have liked support in EPC for these measures and evidence of solidarity from its partners. Unfortunately the Hindawi judgment was given at the worst possible moment. The jury delivered its verdict on 24 October, towards the end of the Political Committee which was meeting under British Presidency in London. Only three days later there was a meeting of the General Affairs Council, which put the British under pressure to secure an early statement of support from the Twelve. Not only was there insufficient time for the careful diplomatic preparation which would normally have preceded such an approach, but the United Kingdom was inhibited by the fact that it held the Presidency and was therefore expected to assist the search for consensus rather than press its own concerns.

In spite of these difficulties, consensus was almost achieved. Sir Geoffrey Howe was able to announce after the Council meeting that all Member States except Greece had agreed to six guidelines, which included agreement that Syrian diplomats expelled from the United Kingdom in connection with the Hindawi case would not be accepted as diplomats by any other partner and that the Ambassadors in Damascus would present to the Syrian government the evidence of what had taken place and report back to an extraordinary meeting of the Political Committee.

This took place on 6 November in Vienna, where many of the Political Directors happened to be attending a CSCE Review Meeting. The basis was laid for a decision by Ministers at their next regular meeting on 10 November in London. As was announced to the press, there was agreement that further joint action was essential, and that a clear message should be sent to

Syria that what had happened was unacceptable. In addition to the measures already taken, it was agreed that new arms sales to Syria would not be authorized, that high-level visits would be suspended, that the activities of Syrian diplomatic and consular missions would be reviewed, and that security precautions surrounding the operations of Syrianair would be tightened. Of more significance to the Syrians, the United Kingdom proceeded to block the Community's new Financial Protocol or aid package for Syria which was under discussion in the Council, although this was not part of the measures decided by the Ministers in Political Co-operation.

Once again Greece dissociated itself from the text, since it felt that the Syrian authorities should not be publicly held responsible. However, Mr Pangalos, the Greek Minister, said that Greece was in no way inconvenienced by the four specific measures decided on, which it already applied in practice.

As in the case of the Tripoli raid, it can be debated whether EPC was a success or a failure. Certainly from the point of view of the British, who wanted clear-cut condemnation of Syria and significant measures to back it up, it was a failure. From the wider point of view of Middle East policy, given the important position of Syria, it can perhaps be considered a success. But if so, it was once again a success by accident. The Twelve did not come to the rational view that the wider interest required a moderate approach; the moderate approach was all that they could manage in the face of differing national positions. A more remarkable fact was that the objections of Greece, which should normally have prevented consensus, were simply brushed aside. One may speculate that this was done with the connivance of the Greek representatives; certainly Greece was able to agree to a statement by the Twelve on 29 November concerning another case of involvement of Syrian officials with an act of terrorism, this time the explosion in March 1986 at the German-Arab Society in Berlin. As on previous occasions, Greece initially blocked the consensus and then discreetly joined it when the dust had settled.

SELECTED READING

De Schoutheete (1986) contains informative sections on judicial co-operation and terrorism. Terrorism is also covered by Freestone (1985) and Hill (1988). For the US raid on Tripoli, see Pardalis (1987).

11
Can Political Co-operation Survive?

DIFFERING APPROACHES

It is a vain endeavour to assess whether Political Co-operation is a success or a failure. The answer will depend on the yardstick selected. There are those who believe that a common foreign policy is an essential attribute of political union, see Political Co-operation as the best way of achieving this, and therefore judge it by the progress it has made down this road. Let us call them the unionists. Others believe that EPC should develop through changes which enable it to contribute more effectively to solving practical problems, rather than embody institutional progress. These belong to the pragmatist school. Their yardstick is infinitely accommodating. Success does not depend upon progress, but is guaranteed whenever current ambitions are achieved. Difficulties only arise when EPC does not meet the standards it has set for itself.

The main distinction between the two schools lies in the definition of objectives. The unionists have no problems over this; for them, a common European foreign policy is an objective in itself. The pragmatists, when faced with the question, have to take refuge in ambiguity in order to avoid admitting that EPC is only a means to an end, which in some cases is the pursuit of national foreign policy. The attitudes of the larger and the smaller Member States differ in this respect. The larger Member States, like the United Kingdom and France, continue to conduct national foreign policies on a global scale and would do so whether EPC existed or not. There is therefore a temptation for them to regard EPC as a convenient extension of national policy. The smaller Member States are aware that they count for more as members of the Twelve than they would acting separately.

The Federal Republic of Germany and Italy occupy an intermediate position. For historical reasons, Germany has so far preferred to exercise its global power through the European Community, and Italy, because of its relatively recent state tradition and the ambiguity of its relations with the United States, has not yet decided whether it wishes to be a world or a regional power. Spain has emerged too recently from a long period of isolation to be other than a fervent unionist.

This categorization does not, however, provide a sure indication of a country's readiness or otherwise to transfer to the European level national powers over foreign policy. Although counting as smaller States and anxious to secure the foreign-policy benefits of belonging to a wider grouping, countries like Ireland, Denmark, and Greece are no more disposed than the larger States to abandon national sovereignty. They are, however, less likely in practice, whatever footnotes they may insert in the official texts, to seek to oppose the formation of consensus.

A further complicating factor is that even the larger Member States sometimes go along with a policy worked out in EPC in order to justify a change in national policy which is thought to be desirable. This is the 'alibi' dividend of Political Co-operation. An often quoted example is the shift in German policy towards the Middle East, although this could well have happened without EPC. At least EPC can make the shift easier. It is certainly the case that participants in EPC are able to play the European card in support of their own positions when discussing policy nationally.

These underlying differences of approach—a common foreign policy or practical co-operation, a policy representing the European interest or a prolongation of national policy—not only influence the way in which EPC will develop in the future, but also affect the assessment of how it has performed in the past. The unionists are inclined to be pessimistic, the pragmatists to be optimistic. Both are wrong. Contrary to the views of the unionists, Political Co-operation has already made a real contribution towards a common foreign policy, and its practical achievements have not always been what its encomists claim.

THE OPTIMISTS' ASSESSMENT

The optimists claim that whereas before EPC was set up, co-ordination of national foreign policies barely existed and was in any case restricted to bilateral diplomatic channels, now the Twelve produce common positions on a wide range of issues, based on shared information. These have a cumulative effect on world affairs.

It is certainly advantageous for countries which do not have extensive diplomatic resources of their own to have access to the information and analyses provided by those which do. But the advantages should not be exaggerated. The increasing press and television coverage of world events means that the man in the street is often as well informed as many Foreign Ministries about what is happening, and the level of information exchanged in the Working Groups rarely adds much to what is publicly available. One may doubt whether the larger Member States reveal all their secrets; in at least one of them, EPC is not considered to warrant a higher security classification than 'restricted'. This is not to deny the usefulness of exchanging information as part of the collective process of reaching a common position.

A more serious defect in the EPC co-ordination process is its relatively narrow coverage. Not all topics are covered (nor all modes of action, the most serious omission being the activities of Member States in the Security Council). This is because Political Co-operation is in the hands of Foreign Ministries, and Foreign Ministries no longer control all the constituent parts of foreign policy. Financial policy, economic policy, trade policy, and development-aid policy all have important implications for external relations and in most Member States are determined outside the Foreign Ministry. EPC reflects the traditional foreign-policy activities of Foreign Ministries which are gradually becoming marginalized. Indeed, in some cases Foreign Ministries attempt to use EPC to increase their influence on areas of national policy in which without the European dimension they would carry less weight.

A great deal can be said, on both sides of the question, about whether the Twelve should have a common security policy. The interest of such a move is clear on the unionist approach, less so on that of the pragmatists. However, even the latter must admit that the failure to achieve such a policy so far is also a procedural failure, since this is an area for which, in all Member States, Foreign Ministries retain their responsibility. The difficulties mentioned in the previous paragraph do not therefore apply in this case.

A further defect in the EPC co-ordination process lies in the limited degree of penetration it achieves within national administrations. Once more this is a result of the fact that Political Co-operation is confined to Foreign Ministries. By and large, the common positions agreed in EPC are held to as long as control over national actions remains with those who helped to form the positions. Accidents can occur when national positions are set out by those, even within Foreign Ministries, who have not been involved in the co-ordination process. This is very often a problem of information. The problem becomes more serious when Heads of Government intervene, as they increasingly do, in foreign-policy questions. Unless an EPC position has been discussed by the European Council, a Prime Minister may not know about it and may not consider him- or herself bound by a position which has been determined at a level lower than his own. Mrs Thatcher's authorization of the use of US bases in the United Kingdom to mount a raid on Libya and President Mitterrand's convening of a Ministerial Meeting of the Euro-Arab Dialogue in autumn 1989, both on the face of it in breach of agreed European policy, can be ascribed to this phenomenon.

The second great success claimed for Political Co-operation is the phenomenon of 'socialization'. This is the automatic reflex of consultation brought about by frequent personal contacts with opposite numbers from the other Member States of the Community. There is no doubt that the phenomenon is real, and has become an effective substitute for traditional bilateral diplomacy among the Twelve. It is also the case that the experience of working together is durable, and that as time goes by there will be an increasing number of diplomats who have attended meetings of the Twelve, whether in Europe or posted in third countries, and thus feel bound to each other by family ties. The same feeling of solidarity is generated in the diplomatic corps, especially in countries where living conditions are difficult. It is beneficial to European policy that this *esprit de corps* should be felt in a higher degree among the emissaries of the Twelve.

But the extent of the phenomenon should not be exaggerated. Much depends on numbers. At any one time, between twenty-five and forty officials of a Member State will be directly engaged in central EPC activities (the Political Director and the European Correspondent, and one to two representatives in each of the twenty-odd Working Groups). The weight that this has depends on the proportion of those officials to the total number of Foreign Ministry officials. The proportion will be higher, and the weight correspondingly greater, in the smaller countries than in the larger.

This arithmetical proportion is distorted by the fact that the club spirit is at its strongest among Political Directors and Correspondents, because they meet each other most frequently and engage in extra-curricular activities like lunches, dinners, and excursions. In Foreign Ministries in which the Political Director has a dominant position the club spirit will have a greater effect on policy-making than in those in which he does not.

We are also invited by the theory of socialization to assume that participation in Political Co-operation predisposes the participant towards the process. This is often, but not necessarily always, the case. It can occur that a participant is antipathetic to the ethos of EPC or, more likely, that he or she is disillusioned by the absence of easy success, especially if they are unionists in the first place. It also happens that on emergence from several years' experience of EPC the participants find that their release from that somewhat enclosed atmosphere causes them to cast doubt on its overall value in the scheme of things.

Above all, the theory of socialization places EPC in the intergovernmental, diplomatic mode. To advance policy through good personal contacts is the epitome of traditional diplomatic practice. It compensates for the absence of institutions, and is therefore a favourite theme of reflection for the pragmatists.

The pragmatists' preference for remaining within the intergovernmental mode has also led to the perpetuation of the two main features of Political Co-operation, the rule of consensus and the preponderant role of the Presidency. These features are essential for preserving confidence that the system will not develop into an effective competitor with the participants in it, but at the same time they stand in the way of that greater efficiency which is the immediate aim of these same pragmatists.

The consensus rule does not, as some claim, reduce the policy of the Twelve to the lowest common denominator; rather it tends to encourage a median line. The reason for this is the dynamism of discussion in the Political Committee and to a lesser extent in Ministerial Meetings. A lowest common denominator would only result if the procedure followed were that all the national positions were put on the table and whatever coincided became the European position without more ado. This is not what happens. Instead, the first round of national statements, themselves often adapted to what the Member State representatives who have already spoken have said, form the basis for further discussions which usually reach a compromise on the median position between the two extremes. This is not surprising, given the club atmosphere and the predisposition of diplomats to regard a failure to agree as the worst of outcomes. When the Dooge Report recommended 'seeking a consensus in keeping with the majority opinion', it was doing no more than describing how the process actually works.

An exception to the above is if either the United Kingdom or France decides that its national position is too important to be compromised, the reason being that these are the countries which view EPC as being primarily an extension of their own diplomacy.

Two important consequences flow from the fact that EPC policies follow the median line, not the lowest common denominator. The first is that they rarely change abruptly. Suppose that there is a change of government in one Member State, bringing about a radical change in national policy. If the lowest-common-denominator theory applied, there could well be an abrupt swing in EPC policy. Since the median principle applies, the Member State in question simply takes up a different position in the gamut of opinions, and the effect on EPC policy is limited. This provides an element of stability on which third countries can depend, and is a valuable card in the Twelve's hand.

The second favourable consequence is that, whatever other difficulties enlargement may present to EPC, consensus-forming is not one of them. A newly joined country merely places itself at some point along the range of opinion, not necessarily beyond the existing extremes, and does not thereby significantly affect the median. This is what happened over Middle East policy when Spain joined the Community. It placed itself close to the extreme already occupied by Greece, and the Middle East policy of the Twelve did not shift noticeably as a result. Of course enlargement on a wide scale presents other problems, which will be discussed later.

The consensus rule has one major disadvantage (setting aside the criticism that it is not how an integrationist foreign policy ought to be decided). That is that it only works when EPC is in charge of the agenda and the timing. The Twelve like to be able to decide for themselves the areas which their policy positions should cover, thus leaving maximum scope for compromise. This presents no problem when the means of action is autonomous, such as making a statement on a given subject. But the system risks breaking down when the Twelve have to take a position on someone else's agenda. We have seen that this explains their relative lack of success in voting together on Resolutions of the United Nations, and why they are trying to take the initiative in New York to shape draft Resolutions in a form convenient to them.

Similar considerations apply over questions of timing. International events do not wait upon the convenience of the Twelve, who therefore find themselves short of time for the necessary process of consensus-forming. The result of failure to do so under time pressure is that the initiative reverts to the Member States individually or, paradoxically, passes to the Commission.

The second main feature of Political Co-operation, the preponderant role of the Presidency, while protecting the intergovernmental character of EPC, has some operational drawbacks. The obvious shortcomings, such as the lack of continuity in external representation, are probably not too serious, and the argument that the smaller Member States are not equipped to run the Presidency has been disproved by experience. But there is nevertheless a sense in which the difference between the smaller and the larger Member States can be deleterious to the efficient functioning of Political Co-operation.

A Member State sometimes has difficulty in being credible as spokesman of the Twelve. Even when a larger Member State has the Presidency, there can be confusion, sometimes deliberately created, between what is being said in a national capacity and what on behalf of Political Co-operation. The Troika format can help guard against confusion of this kind. Smaller Member States on the other hand have difficulty during their Presidency in running a national policy which is not that of the Twelve, even when the national interest would require a differentiated approach.

In addition, the smaller countries may be over-zealous during their Presidency. This is their opportunity, which only comes round once every six years, to shine on the international stage. They may therefore be tempted to launch initiatives and force through courses of action, when masterly inactivity or Fabian tactics might be the better policy for the relatively short term of six months. The temptation is less strong in the case of the larger Member States, which have the opportunity denied to their partners of making themselves heard through national action.

The main drawback of exclusive reliance on a rotating Presidency as the organ of management of EPC is the total absence of any planning function, for which institutional continuity is required, and the consequent criticism that EPC can only react to outside events. There has been a Working Group of Policy Planners since 1983, but it was not meant to fill this role, and in any case functions imperfectly because many Foreign Ministries do not have Policy Planners and those that do give priority to co-operation in other configurations, whether NATO or bilateral. The EPC Secretariat was implicitly forbidden by the Ministers' decision of 28 February 1986 from performing a planning role, which in any case it does not have the information resources to carry out. The Commission has so far not been called into play because of historical prejudices against its full participation in EPC.

It is of course the case that planning to be effective also needs to be able to rely on a fixed panoply of instruments, which EPC does not yet have.

THE PESSIMISTS' ASSESSMENT

Those who plead for a common foreign policy for reasons of institutional orthodoxy rather than of efficiency have no difficulty

Can Political Co-operation Survive? 317

in finding aspects of Political Co-operation to criticize. However, unless they believe that Political Union can be achieved in one bound, they should recognize that EPC has already made a significant contribution towards the objective they seek. If nothing else, it has introduced a new dimension into the national foreign-policy-making process. A Foreign Ministry can dislike the conclusions reached in EPC, and even decide not to abide by them, but it can no longer ignore them.

Whatever criticisms can be made of the internal procedure, the output is considerable in volume and is closely monitored by third countries. Indeed, the reaction to EPC from outside is the best gauge of its interest and value. An increasing number of countries seek not only information about EPC policies, but also the accolade of formal dialogue. If EPC had treaty-making powers, there would be requests to conclude with it what in a previous age were called Treaties of Friendship and Navigation. Not all those countries can be wrong in their judgement; for such interest to be generated, EPC must have succeeded in creating a foreign-policy identity. Nor is this just a matter of perception; in an increasing number of areas, of which Eastern Europe is the foremost, the Twelve count. In other areas, like South Africa or China, what the Twelve say carries weight, if not with the country concerned, then with other countries.

The criticism that Political Co-operation is limited to declaratory diplomacy is also no longer apposite. A declaration can be an action, as the case of Central America demonstrates. Apart from this, EPC engages increasingly in *démarches* designed to use the collective weight of the Twelve to secure an appropriate response, and, as we have seen, makes ever more frequent use of the instruments available in the Community.

This is an important new feature. It was Political Co-operation which released the political potential of the Economic Community. Of course the Community always had the possibility of doing what EPC enabled it to do, but the fact remains that it had not turned that potential into reality, both because of the opposition of Member States like France and because of structural deficiencies. Whether it would have succeeded in releasing that potential on its own is one of the hypothetical questions of history. As things were, Political Co-operation in the form it took at the end of the 1960s was the only way to do this at the time. If the Princess needed to be kissed, what matter if her suitor were a frog?

The development was made possible because Political Co-operation gave national administrations a stake—indeed the decisive role—in the foreign policy of the Community. In functional terms, this meant that diplomats responsible for national policy-making were guaranteed involvement in the process of forming European foreign policies. This was an important reinforcement of their bureaucratic position in their home administrations, where they had been losing out to their colleagues in other Ministries who had been more directly involved with the Community machine in Brussels.

The close involvement of diplomats in European foreign-policy forming not only is significant in national terms, but also provides an element of strength for a future political union which the unionists should not neglect. Hesitations about the transfer of sovereignty are often caused by the fear of losing control. The mechanisms of Political Co-operation, which go more in the direction of a pooling of sovereignty than a transfer of it, are reassuring, even if they are less efficient than the integrationist procedures believed to be the hallmark of the Community. The participation of national actors in the EPC process reduces the alienation effect—the feeling that it is 'them' in Brussels who are in charge and not 'us'—and needs to be preserved in the future development of Political Co-operation, even by those who wish to diminish the inter-governmental character of EPC.

Another trap into which the unionists, and sometimes also the pragmatists, fall is to judge EPC policy by its resemblance to national policy. It does not follow that Political Co-operation is successful when it achieves the policy that a Member State would achieve in the same circumstances. On the contrary, the Community may most usefully perform an international role when it does something that a Nation State would not do. We have seen the advantages of the long-term stability of Community policy; similar considerations can be adduced in favour of a role for the Community as 'civilian power' or as regional grouping, which would be beyond the capacity of any of its Member States. However, Political Co-operation's current inability to set other than short-term objectives increases the risk that its policies will be nothing more than national policies writ large.

There is a danger in this approach. Put at its crudest, it makes it easier for a Member State to adopt one policy collectively at the European level and follow another nationally, possibly incompatible with the first. This is perceived as an advantage by some Member States. It is most likely to happen when the choice is between a moral and a *realpolitik* approach to a question, particularly one involving human rights. Moral attitudes can be struck at the European level, under cover of which more self-interested policies can be pursued nationally. This is the exutory function of Political Co-operation, which is of advantage, neither to the pragmatist nor the unionist, but only to the cynic.

THE OPTIMISTS AND PESSIMISTS CONVERGE

The distinction made here between unionists and pragmatists is an artificial one, designed to represent ways of thought rather than to describe the positions actually adopted by governments or individuals. Few participants in EPC, and no Member State, fall wholly into one or the other camp, and whether unionist or pragmatic considerations prevail all look for greater effectiveness. Both schools, after all, pursue the objective of making the European voice heard more clearly in the world. The dilemma lies in the degree of effectiveness which can be obtained with the existing machinery.

It is for this reason that increasing weight has been attached in recent years to the concept of 'consistency', a term of art for the interaction between EPC and the Community.

In the early years of Political Co-operation, the primary concern was to prevent contamination of either side by the other. Political Co-operation was not to be allowed to do things which the Community could legitimately do, and the Community, and especially the Commission, was certainly not to play a part in EPC. The rule did not square with reality, and was broken in a limited number of cases of which the CSCE and the Euro-Arab Dialogue were the most important, but in general, Political Co-operation for the first decade of its existence remained a diplomatic enclave.

This began to change during the 1980s, and 'consistency' was laid down as a principle in the Single European Act. The concept was not defined, and has been variously interpreted. In its most literal sense, it is unexceptionable. Of course the policies in EPC and the Community must be consistent, in the sense that they must not cancel each other out, pursue divergent objectives, or give the impression that the right hand does not know what the left hand is doing. It is unlikely that this would be the case, and examples are few and far between. But there is another sense of 'consistency', whereby Political Co-operation dictates the political framework within which the Community subsequently operates. Finally, there is the sense in which the potential of EPC and the Community is merged through the use of Community instruments to achieve foreign-policy objectives.

The coming into force of the Single European Act in 1987 confirmed the trend of interaction between EPC and the Community, whether in the form of sanctions, aid programmes, or joint representation. The ambiguity of the concept of 'consistency' has, however, given rise to disagreements about both decision-making and the execution of policy. If a decision can be decided by majority in the Community, should it be made subject to unanimity in EPC because it has political implications? If a Community policy would normally be implemented by the Commission, should a different procedure be followed because there are political implications? Formulas can be worked out to deal with the latter problem, but in answer to the former a straight yes or no is required and has not so far been given.

Together with the absence of permanent institutions and consequent lack of a planning capacity, the unclear relationship with the Community is an obstacle in the way of the more efficient functioning of Political Co-operation. This is a problem which will have to be solved by pragmatists and unionists alike.

ENLARGEMENT

For the time being the Twelve are under no compulsion to change their ways. Improvements to the system will certainly be made, enough to keep the unionists' faith alive and not too much to shock the pragmatists. There will be a limited increase in effectiveness. A theoretical debate about the transfer of sovereignty would, in the interest of the process, be better avoided.

Political Co-operation will be seriously at risk, however, if the Community accepts a significant number of new members, bringing the total up from twelve to twenty or so. The effect will be less serious for the substance of policy—we have seen that the median-line approach provides some protection here—than for the mechanics of policy-formation and implementation. Some banal examples will serve to prove the point. If each delegate speaks for 10 minutes, it will take 3 hours and 20 minutes to complete a first *tour de table*. This is approximately half the total time available for a meeting of the Political Committee. In 1970, a Member State's turn at the Presidency came round every three years. Scarcely had one ended than the preparations for the next had begun. Now the cycle is six years. It is already difficult to recapture the techniques of Presidency after such a long interval. With twenty members, the turn would come round only every ten years. This is a complete generation in diplomatic terms, and the memory of the last Presidency would be lost before the next one arrived.

An even more serious difficulty will be caused by the relatively low degree of formal commitment to EPC policies which is inherent in the present system. This was of less concern when the range of opinions was fairly limited. The original Six broadly held to the same world vision, and this position was only slightly diluted by the first three enlargements. Further enlargements to include EFTA, Central and Eastern European, and Mediterranean countries would alter this perspective. The effect would be disruptive of EPC discipline. We have already seen that the arrival of Greece caused countries like Ireland and Denmark to be less respectful of Community discipline at the United Nations, for excellent domestic reasons. This would happen on a much larger scale if future enlargements significantly widened the cultural basis of the Community, and changes were not made in the basic procedures of EPC. These changes would involve the introduction of external control of the respect for commitments rather than the self-policing which exists at present.

In the case of substantial enlargement, the system will regress if unreformed. Inter-governmental co-operation is not an effective way of bringing together the foreign policies of a relatively large number of partners. In the long run, the institutionalization of

EPC cannot be avoided. This implies the creation of a stronger Treaty basis, a role for the Court of Justice, and the setting up of permanent institutions. Failing this, Political Co-operation will ultimately wither. Whether that matters, provided that the Community remains strong, is for the reader to judge.

SELECTED READING

For reflective studies on the achievements of EPC and its prospects for the future, see de Schoutheete (1979), Hill (1987), Jannuzzi (1990), and Allen (1978).

BIBLIOGRAPHY

SOURCES

Most EPC declarations and public documents from 1970 on can be found in the monthly *Bulletin of the European Communities*, edited by the Commission and published by the Office for Official Publications of the EC.

All public EPC texts—declarations, documents, speeches, and replies to parliamentary questions—from 1985 on are contained in the biannual *European Political Cooperation Documentation Bulletin* edited by the European Policy Unit at the European University Institute (Florence) and the Institut für Europäische Politik (Bonn). This Bulletin is also published by the Office for Official Publications of the EC. It contains a cumulative index which is comprehensive, but recalcitrant.

The German Foreign Ministry from time to time publishes collections in German, French, and English of selected EPC texts. The most recent English edition was published in 1988. Since the selection is continually being revised, it may be useful on occasion to consult earlier editions.

WORKS ON EPC

The classic work on EPC is Philippe de Schoutheete's 'La Coopération politique européenne' (2nd edn., Paris and Brussels, 1986). Ambassador de Schoutheete gives a clear and penetrating account of EPC illustrated with carefully chosen examples and the key texts. The book is invaluable for its insight into how EPC functions.

The only work in English by a single author devoted solely to EPC is Panayiotis Ifestos's *European Political Cooperation* (Aldershot, 1987), which contains in particular a useful case study of EPC policy in the Middle East. It also investigates the place of EPC in international relations theory, a topic the present author has eschewed. For further studies on this question see J. Weiler and J. Wessels, 'EPC and the challenge of theory', in *European Political Cooperation in the 1980s* A. Pijpers, E. Regelsberger, and W. Wessels (eds.), (Dordrecht, 1988), 229–58, and Alfred Pijpers's *The Vicissitudes of European Political Cooperation* (n. p., 1990).

Two collections of essays provide a historical account of EPC, one in the 1970s, the other in the 1980s. These are D. Allen, R. Rummel, and W. Wessels (eds.), *European Political Cooperation* (London, 1982) (the English edition of *Die Europäische Politische Zusammenarbeit: Leistungsvermögen und Struktur der EPZ* (Bonn, 1978)), and the book edited by Pijpers, Regelsberger, and Wessels cited above.

C. Hill (ed.), *National Foreign Policies and European Political Cooperation* (London, 1983), investigates national attitudes to EPC, a subject which has been insufficiently explored.

A number of journals, including the *Yearbook of European Law*, publish annual reviews of EPC.

SELECTED READING

The reader will find at the end of each chapter a guide to further reading, to facilitate following up any particular topic discussed in the chapter. The works cited, with their respective bibliographies and footnotes, will point to the complete literature on the subject.

For ease of reference, all the works cited are listed here in alphabetical order by author.

ALLEN, D., 'Foreign Policy at the European Level: Beyond the Nation-State?', in W. Wallace and W. Paterson (eds.), *Foreign Policy Making in Western Europe* (Farnborough, 1978), 135–54.

—— 'Political Cooperation and the Euro-Arab Dialogue', in D. Allen, R. Rummel, and W. Wessels (eds.), *European Political Cooperation* (London, 1982), 69–82. An updated version appears as 'The Euro-Arab Dialogue', in *Journal of Common Market Studies*, 16 (1978), 323–42.

AL-MANI', S., *The Euro-Arab Dialogue* (London, 1983).

BERGER, R., 'Von der Wiedergeburt Europas à la Wiener Kongress?', *Europa-Archiv*, 19 (1971), 665–72.

BLOES, R., *Le 'Plan Fouchet' et le problème de l'Europe politique* (Bruges, 1970).

BODENHEIMER, S., *Political Union: A Microcosm of European Politics, 1960–66* (Leiden, 1967).

BONVICINI, G., 'Mechanisms and Procedures of EPC: More than Traditional Diplomacy?', in A. Pijpers, E. Regelsberger, and W. Wessels (eds.), *European Political Cooperation in the 1980s* (Dordrecht, 1988), 49–70.

—— 'The Genscher–Colombo Plan and the "Solemn Declaration on European Union" (1981–83)', in R. Pryce (ed.), *The Dynamics of European Union* (London, 1989), 174–87.

BOT, B. R., 'Co-operation between the Diplomatic Missions of the Ten in Third Countries and International Organisations', *Legal Issues of European Integration*, 1 (1984), 149–69.

BOURRINET, J. (ed.), *Le Dialogue Euro-Arabe* (Paris, 1979).

BULMER, S., and WESSELS, W., *The European Council* (London, 1987).

BURGESS, M., 'Altiero Spinelli, Federalism and the EUT', in J. Lodge (ed.), *European Union: The European Community in Search of its Future* (London, 1986), 174–85.

Bibliography 325

CARDOZO, R., 'The Project for a Political Community (1952–54)', in Pryce, *The Dynamics of European Union*, 49–77.

CARRINGTON, P. A. R. C. (Lord), 'European Political Cooperation: America should Welcome It', *International Affairs*, 58 (Winter 1981–2), 1–6.

CATTANI, A., 'Essai de coopération politique entre les Six, 1960–62, et échec des négociations pour un statut politique' *Chronique de politique étrangère*, 11/4 (July 1967).

CORBETT, R., 'The 1985 Intergovernmental Conference and the single European Act', in Pryce, *Dynamics of European Union*, 238–72.

COSTA PEREIRA, P. DA, 'The Use of a Secretariat', in Pijpers, *et al.*, *European Political Cooperation*, 85–103.

COUSTE, P., and VISINE, F., *Pompidou et l'Europe* (Paris, 1974).

DEHOUSSE, R., and WEILER, J., *EPC and the Single Act: From Soft Law to Hard Law?*, EUI Working Paper, EPU No. 90/1 (Florence, 1990).

DE RUYT, J., *L'Acte unique européen* (Brussels, 1987).

EDWARDS, G., 'Europe and the Falklands Crisis', *Journal of Common Market Studies*, 22/4 (June 1984), 295–313.

FONSECA WOLLHEIM, H. DA, 'Zehn Jahre Europäische Politische Zusammenarbeit (EPZ)', *Integration* (Feb. 1981), 17–66.

FOUCHET, C., 'Le Plan Fouchet et l'union politique de l'Europe', *La Comunità internazionale* (n. d.), 327–39.

FREESTONE, D., 'The EEC Treaty and Common Action on Terrorism', *Yearbook of European Law 1984* (Oxford, 1985), 207–30.

—— and DAVIDSON, S., 'Community Competence and Part III of the Single European Act', *Common Market Law Review*, 23 (1986), 793–801.

FURSDON, E., *The European Defence Community: A History* (London, 1980).

GÉRARD, Y., 'La Coopération politique européenne: Méthodes et résultats', *Revue du Marché commun*, 309 (Aug. -Sept. 1987), 466–70.

GERBET, P., *La Construction de l'Europe* (Paris, 1975).

—— 'The Origins: Early Attempts and the Emergence of the Six (1945–52', in Pryce, *The Dynamics of European Union*, 35–48.

—— 'In Search of Political Union: The Fouchet Plan Negotiations (1960–62)', in Pryce, *The Dynamics of European Union*, 105–29.

GRÄBENDORFF, W., 'Relations with Central and Southern America: A Question of Over-Reach?', in G. Edwards and E. Regelsberger (eds.), *Europe's Global Links* (London, 1990), 84–96.

GREILSAMMER, I. *Israël et l'Europe* (Lausanne, 1981).

—— and WEILER, J., *Europe's Middle East Dilemma: The Quest for a Unified Stance* (Boulder, Colo., 1987).

—— —— 'European Political Cooperation and the Palestinian–Israeli Conflict: An Israeli Perspective', in D. Allen and A. Pijpers (eds.), *European Foreign Policy-Making and the Arab-Israeli Conflict* (The Hague, 1984), 121–56.

GROLL, G. VON, 'The Nine at the Conference on Security and Cooperation in Europe', in Allen, et al. 60–8.

HANSEN, N., 'Die Europäische Politische Zusammenarbeit bei den Vereinten Nationen', Europa Archiv, 15 (1975), 493–500.

—— 'Plädoyer für eine Europäische Union', Europa Archiv, 5 (1981), 141–8.

HILL, C., 'Changing Gear in Political Co-operation', Political Quarterly, 53/1 (1982), 47–60.

—— 'European Foreign Policy: Power Bloc, Civilian Model—or Flop?', in R. Rummel (ed.) The Evolution of an International Actor (Boulder, Colo., 1990), 31–55; (= Die Europäische Gemeinschaft zwischen nationaler interressenbefriedigung und weltweiter Mitverantwortung) (Ebenhausen, 1987), 29–57.

—— 'European Preoccupations with Terrorism', in Pijpers, et al., European Political Cooperation, 166–89.

HOLLAND, M., The European Community and South Africa (London, 1988).

HURD, D., 'Political Co-operation', International Affairs, 57/3 (Summer 1981).

IFESTOS, P., European Political Cooperation (Aldershot, 1987).

'ISTÉVÈNE GAIUS', 'L'Unione europea e la cooperazione politica dopo Lussemburgo', Affari esteri, 70 (Spring 1986), 3–15.

JAGOW, P. VON, 'European Political Cooperation: Concerted Diplomacy in an Interregional Context', in Edwards and Regelsberger, Europe's Global Links 188–97.

JANSEN, T., Europa: Von der Gemeinschaft zur Union (Bonn, 1986).

JANNUZZI, G. 'Comunità Europea e politica estera: al di là dell'Atto Unico', Rivista di studi politici internazionali, 227 (1990), 371–80.

KEATINGE, P. and MURPHY, A., 'The European Council's ad hoc Committee on Institutional Affairs (1984–1985)', in Pryce, Dynamics of European Union, 217–37.

KISSINGER, H., Years of Upheaval (Boston, Mass., 1982).

KÖHLER, B., 'Euro-American Relations and European Political Co-operation', in Allen, et al., European Political Cooperation, 83–133.

KRENZLER, H. G., 'Die Einheitliche Europäische Akte als Schritt auf dem Wege zu einer gemeinsamen europäischen Aussenpolitik', Europarecht, 4 (1986), 384–91.

KUYPER, P. J., 'Community Sanctions against Argentina: Lawfulness under Community and International Law', in D. O'Keeffe, and H. G. Schermers (eds.), Essays in European Law and Integration (Deventer, 1982), 141–66.

—— 'New Developments in Trade Sanctions and Export Controls by the EEC', in K. M. Meessen (ed.), The International Law of Export Controls: Prolems of Extraterritoriality (Dordrecht, 1991).

LAK, M., 'Het Secretariaat van de EPS', *Internationale Spectator*, 42/2 (Feb. 1988), 87–92.
LAY, F., *L'iniziativa italo-tedesca per il rilancio dell'Unione europea* (Padua, 1983).
—— 'Il Segretariato Permanente della Cooperazione Europea', *Rivista di studi politici internazionali*, 53/4 (1986), 555–74.
LEGROS, J., 'L'Europe des Dix face à l'invasion israélienne du Liban', in B. Khader (ed.), *Coopération euro-arabe, diagnostic et prospective* (Louvain-la-Neuve, 1982), i. 220–76.
LIEBER, R. J., *Oil and the Middle East War: Europe in the Energy Crisis*, Harvard Studies in International Affairs, No. 35 (Cambridge, Mass., 1976).
LOUIS, J. V. 'La Communauté et ses États membres dans les relations extérieures', *Revue d'intégration européenne* 6/2–3 (1983).
MASCLET, J. -C., *L'Union politique de l'Europe* (Paris, 1986).
MASLEN, J. 'The European Community's Relations with the State-Trading Countries 1981–1983', *Yearbook of European Law 1983* (Oxford, 1984), 323–46.
—— 'The European Community's Relations with the State-Trading Countries of Europe 1984–1986', *Yearbook of European Law 1986* (Oxford, 1987), 335–56.
MAULL, H., *Europe and World Energy* (London, 1980), 284–92.
—— 'The Strategy of Avoidance: Europe's Middle East Policies after the October War', in J. C. Hurewitz (ed.), *Oil, the Arab–Israel Dispute and the Industrial World* (Boulder, Colo., 1976).
MEENAN, K., 'The Work of the Dooge Committee', *Administration*, 33/4 (1985), 580–9.
MISCHO, J., 'Les efforts en vue d'organiser sur le plan juridique la coopération des États membres de la Communauté en matière de politique étrangère', in *Liber amicorum Pierre Pescatore* (Baden-Baden, 1987).
MOÏSI, D., 'L'Europe et le conflit Israélo-Arabe', *Politique étrangère*, 4 (1980), 835–47.
MOREAU DEFARGES, P., ' ". . . J'ai fait un rêve . . .": Le Président François Mitterrand, artisan de l'union européenne', *Politique étrangère*, (autumn 1985), 359–75.
—— 'Twelve Years of European Council History (1974–1986): The Crystallizing Forum', in J. M. Hoscheit and W. Wessels (eds.), *The European Council 1974–1986: Evaluation and Prospects* (Maastricht, 1988), 35–60.
NEVILLE-JONES, P., 'The Genscher/Colombo Proposals on European Union', *Common Market Law Review*, 20 (1983), 657–99.
NUTTALL, S., 'European Political Co-operation and the Single European Act', *Yearbook of European Law 1985* (Oxford, 1986), 203–32.

—— 'Interaction between European Political Co-operation and the European Community', *Yearbook of European Law 1987*, (Oxford, 1988), 211–49.

—— 'Interaction between European Political Co-operation and the European Community', *Yearbook of European Law 1988* (Oxford, 1989), 171–3.

—— 'Where the European Commission comes in', in Pijpers, *et al.*, *European Political Cooperation*, 104–17.

PARDALIS, A., 'European Political Cooperation and the United States', *Journal of Common Market Studies*, 25/4 (June 1987), 271–94.

PIERRE, A. J., 'What Happened to the Year of Europe?', *The World Today* (March 1974), 110–19.

PIJPERS, A., 'European Political Cooperation and the CSCE Process', *Legal Issues of European Integration*, 1 (1984), 135–48; a slightly revised version of this article appears as ch. 4 of A. Pijpers, *The Vicissitudes of European Political Cooperation* (n.p., 1990).

—— 'European Participation in the Sinai Peace-Keeping Force (MFO)', in Allen and Pijpers, *European Foreign Policy-Making*, 211–23.

PRAAG, N. VAN, 'European Political Cooperation and Southern Africa', in Allen, *et al.*, *European Political Cooperation*, 134–6.

—— 'Political Cooperation and Southern Europe: Case Studies in Crisis Management', in Allen, *et al.*, *European Political Cooperation*, 94–109.

REGELSBERGER, E. 'European Political Cooperation (EPC) Contacts with Third Countries: Past and Present', in E. Regelsberger, P. de Schoutheete, S. J. Nuttall, and G. Edwards, *The External Relations of European Political Cooperation and the Future of EPC*, EUI Working Paper No. 85/172 (Florence, 1985), 1–32.

RUMMEL, R. and WESSELS, W., 'Of Falling Pillars and the Genscher Initiative', in C. Hill (ed.), *National Foreign Policies and European Political Cooperation* (London, 1983), 34–55.

SALMON, T. C., 'Ireland: A Neutral in the Community?', *Journal of Common Market Studies*, 3 (March 1982), 205–27.

SCHEEL, W., 'Europäische Erfahrungen und Erwartungen—Ein Rückblick auf die EPZ', *Integration 9* (Jan. 1986), 3–10.

SCHMUCK, O., 'The European Parliament's Draft Treaty Establishing the European Union (1979–1984)', in Pryce, *Dynamics of European Union*, 188–216.

SCHOUTHEETE, P. DE, 'European Political Cooperation: Achievements and Prospects', *European Documents*, 1061 (3 July 1979).

—— *La Coopération politique européenne* (2nd edn., Brussels, 1986).

—— 'The Presidency and the Management of Political Cooperation' in Pijpers, *et al.*, *Europe Political Cooperation*, 71–83.

SCHWERIN, O. (Graf), 'Die Solidarität der EG-Staaten in der KSZE', *Europa Archiv*, 15 (1975), 483–92.

Bibliography

SERRE, F. DE LA, 'L'Europe des Neuf et le conflit israèlo-arabe', *Revue française de science politique*, 24/4 (1974), 801–11.

—— 'La Politique européenne de la France: new look or new deal?', *Politique étrangère*, 47/1 (1982), 125–37.

—— and MOREAU DEFARGES, P., 'France: A Penchant for Leadership', in Hill, *National Foreign Policies and European Political Cooperation*, 56–70.

SICHERMAN, H., 'Europe's Role in the Middle East: Illusions and Realities', *Orbis* (Winter 1985), 803–28.

SILJ, A., *Europe's Political Puzzle: A Study of the Fouchet Negotiations and the 1963 Veto* (Cambridge, Mass., 1967).

SMITH, S., 'Policy Preferences and Bureaucratic Position: The Case of the American Hostage Rescue Mission', *International Affairs*, 61/1 (Winter 1984-5), 9–25.

SOUTOU, G. -H., 'Le Général de Gaulle et le plan Fouchet', contribution to the Journées Internationales organized by the Institut Charles de Gaulle (Paris, 19–24 Nov. 1990).

SPÄTH, W. 'Die Arbeit des EPZ-Sekretariats: Eine Bilanz', *Europa Archiv*, 6 (1990), 213–20.

STADLER, K. -D., *Die Europäische Politische Zusammenarbeit in der Generalversammlung der Vereinten Nationen zu Beginn der Achtziger Jahre*, EUI Working Paper No. 89/371 (Florence, 1989) (= Europ Archiv 7/88).

TANAKA, T., 'Euro-Japanese Political Cooperation: In Search for New Roles in International Politics', *Keio Journal of Politics*, 5 (1984), 81–91.

TEMPLE LANG, J., 'The Irish Court Case which Delayed the Single European Act: Crotty v. an Taoiseach and Others', *Common Market Law Review*, 24 (1987), 709–18.

TOMKYS, R., 'European Political Cooperation and the Middle East: A Personal Perspective', *International Affairs*, 63/3 (1987), 425–37.

VERNANT, J., 'Chypre et la coopération politique des Neuf', *Défense nationale* (Dec. 1974), 99–104.

WEILER, J., 'The Genscher–Colombo Draft European Act: The Politics of Indecision', *Revue d'intégration européenne/Journal of European Integration*, 6/2-3 (1983), 129–53.

WELL, G. VAN, 'Le Développement d'une politique commune des Neuf au Proche-Orient', *Politique étrangère*, 2 (1967), 113–25.

WESSELS, W., 'Die Einheitliche Europäische Akte: Die europäische Zusammenarbeit in der Ausenpolitik', *Integration 9*, (March 1986), 126–32.

INDEX

Adenauer, Conrad 40–1
ad hoc Committee on Institutional
 Affairs, *see* Dooge Committee
Afghanistan:
 EC aid 272–3
 Soviet invasion and EPC reaction 7,
  151, 154–8
 stimulus to EPC 272–3
Andersen, K. B. 80
Angola 128–30
Argentina, *see* Falkland Islands
Association of South-East Asian
 Nations (ASEAN):
 dialogue 289
 economic ties with EC 270

Bad Godesberg declaration 42
Badinter, Robert 297
Baker, James 286
Basque terrorists 6, 125–7
de Beaumarchais, Étienne 51
Brandt, Willy:
 at the Hague Summit 49
 resigns 92, 141
Bulgaria 276

Caribbean Basin Intitiative (CBI), *see*
 United States
Carrington, Lord:
 and Afghanistan 8, 156–8, 175
 and EPC 8, 176
 on Middle East 163, 167, 215–16
 on Poland 204
 resignation 221
Carter, Jimmy:
 on EPC and the Middle East 164
 and Iran hostages 169–71
 Middle East policy 159–61
 policy mystifies Europeans 3
 weak leadership 8, 191
Cattani, Attilio 40
Central America:
 Contadora 224–30
 declarations an effective tool 13
 dialogue with 9, 288, 290
 EC aid 222–4, 270–1
 and EC budget 9, 13
 EPC policy 222–30
 San José Conferences 226–8, 290
chemical weapons, precursors of:
 export control 266–7
Cheysson, Claude:
 on Central America 222
 Foreign Minister 177, 222
 on Middle East 168
 premature announcement on
  MFO 215
China, People's Republic of:
 aid after Tiananmen 269
 dialogue with 287
Code of Conduct, *see* South Africa
Colombo, Emilio 8, 185
 see also Genscher-Colombo
  initiative
Comecon, *see* Council for Mutual
 Economic Assistance
Commission of the EC:
 in Copenhagen Report 78
 in EPC 24–5, 180, 246
 in Euro-Arab Dialogue 105
 in London Report 8, 177, 180
 in Luxembourg Report 53
 opinion on Single European
  Act 250
 responsible for consistency 24–5,
  293
 in Troika 19
Committee of Permanent
 Representatives (Coreper):
 and CSCE 115–16
 and Falkland Islands 209
 prepares Council 15
 resists guidance from Political
  Committee 118
 and sanctions against Soviet
  Union 202–4
Conference on Disarmament in
 Europe (CDE) 196
Conference on Security and Co-
 operation in Europe (CSCE):
 attitude of Soviet Union 112–13,
  114, 115, 117
 Basket II 110, 112, 115–16
 Belgrade meeting 114–16

Conference on Security (CSCE) (cont.):
  Commission participation 111, 112, 114
  co-operation continues (1978–81) 152–3
  discussed at Munich Conference 55–8
  EC statements at Helsinki 65–6, 117
  EPC relations with EC 58, 64–6, 110–11, 115–16
  EPC relations with NATO 63–4, 153
  Final Act 111, 114
  France makes proposal without consultation 113
  France opposes maintaining EPC structures 114
  Helsinki meeting 113–14
  inviolability of frontiers 112
  Madrid meeting 115, 152–3
  most-favoured-nation treatment 112
  preparation and first phase 59–66
  second phase 110–13, 116–17
  sets pattern for EPC 6, 58, 62, 116
  sharing out of responsibilities in EPC 112
  Sub-committee and ad hoc Group 59–60, 61, 62–3, 76, 111
  support for after collapse of Communism 279–80
  Working Group 114
consensus:
  Italy proposes should be built round majority view 249
  and KAL airliner 194
  objections of Greece do not prevent 307
  and Poland 204, 262
  Presidency to assist search for 306
  rule of in EPC 12, 313–15
  in Single European Act 253
  and South Africa 233
  and US raid on Libya 305
consistency:
  and Association Agreement with Cyprus 122–3
  in CSCE 117
  on Eastern Europe 276, 280, 293
  and EC Agreement with Israel 106
  of EPC with EC 10
  need for recognized by Paris Summit 74
  responsibility of Presidency and Commission 24–5, 293
  in Single European Act 253–5, 319–20
  in speech at UN General Assembly 138
  in Stuttgart Declaration 189
Contact Group of Five, *see* Namibia
Contadora, *see* Central America
Copenhagen Report (1973):
  consolidates EPC 6, 11
  origins and content 71–80
Copenhagen Summit (1973) 94, 96–7
Coreper, *see* Committee of Permanent Representatives
Coreu network:
  function and origin 23–4, 77
  urgent decisions taken by 17
Correspondents, Group of European:
  origins 70, 76
  prepares London Report 176
  and relations with Parliament 146
  role and organization 22–3
  and setting up of EPC Secretariat 258
Council of Europe:
  Convention on the Suppression of Terrorism 294–5, 296, 298
  Convention on the transfer of sentenced persons 297
  EPC co-ordination 69
  EPC meeting in Lisbon 170
Council for Mutual Economic Assistance (CMEA, Comecon):
  in CSCE 114, 117
  relationship with EC 61, 117–18, 197, 274
Court of Justice, European 12
coutumier 147, 174
Craxi, Bettino:
  chairs Milan European Council 247
  visits Moscow 197
crisis management mechanism, *see* European Political Co-operation
cultural co-operation:
  in Genscher-Colombo proposals 187
Cyprus:
  Association Agreement 122–3
  Community aid 122
  invasion by Turkey and EPC reaction 6, 119–23, 127
Czechoslovakia:
  dialogue with 293
  trade agreement 276

Index 333

Davignon Report, *see* Luxembourg Report
Davignon, Vicomte Étienne:
  chairs Committee preparing Luxembourg Report 51
  tables paper for Copenhagen Report 74
Debré, Michel 45
démarche:
  carried out by Presidency or Troika 13
  on human rights 13
Denmark:
  delays signature of Single European Act 255
  dissenting UN vote 139
  and Falkland Islands 208–12
  inter-governmental view of EPC 2, 310
  legal reservations on EC sanctions 203, 209, 212, 233, 262
  objects to Commission role in EPC 180
  referendum on Single European Act 255
  reticent on security in EPC 8, 188
  and South Africa 231
dialogue with third countries:
  ASEAN 289
  Australia 292
  Austria 292
  Canada 292
  Central America 227–9, 290
  Contadora 224–5
  Cyprus 292
  Czechoslovakia 293
  GCC 290–1
  Group of Rio 290
  Hungary 293
  Japan 287
  in London Report 287
  Malta 292
  New Zealand 292
  Norway 283, 287, 292
  overview 282–93
  Poland 293
  regional 288–91
  in Single European Act 292
  Soviet Union 197, 292
  United States 284–7
  Yugoslavia 288, 292
disarmament 195–6
Dooge Committee 10, 240–4, 314

Dublin Agreement, *see* judicial co-operation
'Dublin formula', *see* Euro-Arab Dialogue
Ducci, Roberto 113

Eastern Europe:
  dialogue with 292–3
  EC reaction to collapse of Communism 274–81
  PHARE 277, 278
East-West relations:
  EPC fails to discuss 150
  EPC policy 191–207
  gas pipeline 193–4
  trade 193–4
enlargement:
  consultations with applicants (first enlargement) 54, 172
  effect on EPC 314–15, 320–2
  to Greece 8, 171–4
  to Spain and Portugal 8
Ethiopia 268–9
Euro-Arab Dialogue:
  ad hoc Group 105
  Arab League 104, 106–7, 108, 109, 161
  Commission involved 99, 103
  Co-ordinating Group 105
  'Dublin formula' 106, 107
  General Committee 103, 108
  important aim of French diplomacy 92
  inception 97–100
  Kissinger not informed 93
  Ministerial Meeting 103–4
  PLO 105–6, 108
  relations with EC 100, 105
  relaunched 163, 165
  structure 103–9, 288
  Summit convened 312
  suspended 161, 291
  Troika formula 108
European Correspondents, *see* Correspondents, Group of European
European Council:
  at apex of EPC 14
  fails on South Africa sanctions 14
  in Genscher-Colombo proposals 187
  makes aid to Portugal conditional 124
  at Milan 10, 244–7

European Council (*cont.*):
  resistance to rubber-stamping 14
  Rhodes Declaration 275
  set up 139–43
  in Stuttgart Declaration 189
European Defence Community (EDC):
  draft Treaty signed 33
  launched by France 3, 33
  rejected by France 5, 36
European Identity, Document on the:
  and co-operation at UN 136
  drafting and final agreement 75, 88–90
European Political Community 5, 30–7
European Political Co-operation (EPC):
  acquis 173–4
  the 'alibi' dividend 310
  assessment 309–22
  attraction to third countries 317
  basis 11–13
  control of development aid 267–9
  in Copenhagen Report 79
  crisis mechanism 147, 176, 177, 180, 201, 219, 304, 305
  declaratory diplomacy 13, 317
  definition 1, 11
  diplomatic club 11–12
  evolving machinery 4
  institutional, political, and organizational strands 2
  inter-governmental nature 12, 141, 184
  limited penetration in national administrations 312
  machinery 14–18
  management functions 18–25
  not lowest common denominator 314
  solidarity 213
  stagnation 7, 149–54
  see also consensus; consistency; dialogue with third countries; planning; Presidency; sanctions; security

Falkland Islands:
  invasion and EPC reaction 9, 207–13
  sanctions 13, 262–3
Fouchet Plans:
  failure influences Luxembourg Report 53
  launch, negotiation, and failure 5, 37–46
France:
  diminished interest in EPC 7
  inter-governmental view of EPC 2, 53, 64, 71–2, 118, 317
  and judicial co-operation 297
  launches EDC 3, 33
  lukewarm on Genscher–Colombo initiative 8, 185, 191
  maintains bilateral policies towards Eastern Europe 118
  and Middle East policy 56, 95, 213–14, 221
  national measures against South Africa 231
  need for policies different from US 3, 56
  and PLO 106
  position in EPC 309
  and precursors of chemical weapons 266
  promotes Euro-Arab Dialogue 98–9
  recognizes Angola 130
  rejects EDC Treaty 36
  sensitive about extradition 295
  succeeds with German support 3
  welcomes Greece's application to join EC 121
  see also Giscard d'Estaing; Mitterrand; Pompidou
Front Line States:
  meeting with EPC 234, 288
  programmes to assist 233

G 24 277
gas pipeline, *see* East–West relations
de Gaulle, Charles:
  and Adenauer 40–1
  agreement with Germany 46
  changes Fouchet Plan 44–5
  initiative for a political Europe 37–8
  inter-governmental view 2, 3
  vision of independent European foreign policy 38, 82
Genscher, Hans Dietrich:
  initiative for dialogue with Soviet Union 193
  launches dialogue: with ASEAN 289–90; with GCC 291
  launches initiative with Colombo 8, 183–9

Index

meets Kissinger 91
and precursors of chemical
    weapons 267
sets tone on US raid on Libya 305
and South Africa 232, 236
Stuttgart speech 176, 178, 183–5
supports co-operation with Central
    America 225, 290
takes lead on Poland 199
urges Code of Conduct 133
Genscher–Colombo initiative, *see*
    Genscher
Germany, Federal Republic of:
    agreement with France 46
    initiative for co-operation at
        UN 136–7
    integrationist view of EPC 2
    joins UN 136
    Ostpolitik and CSCE 57
    and PLO 106
    position in EPC 310
    restrictions on deployment of
        forces 214
    reunification 279
Giscard d'Estaing, Valéry:
    Guadeloupe Summit 151
    and judicial co-operation 295, 298
    on Middle East 163
    noncommittal on Genscher–
        Colombo initiative 185
    prefers groupings of world
        statesmen 7
    President 92, 141
    role in setting up European
        Council 139, 141
    separate declaration on
        Afghanistan 155
Global Mediterranean Approach, *see*
    Mediterranean
Gorbachev, Mikhail:
    comes to power 195
    Craxi luncheon 197
    EPC evaluation 197
    Reykjavik summit 198
Greece:
    accepts *acquis* of EPC 173–4
    applies to join EC 120–1
    consultation before accession 174
    hampers co-operation at UN 28
    and Hindawi case 306–7
    inter-governmental view of EPC 2,
        310
    and MFO 216

radical views on Middle East 221
reticent on security in EPC 8, 188,
    249
and shooting-down of KAL
    airliner 194–5
withdraws from Poland
    consensus 202, 262
Guinea-Bissau 128
Gulf Co-operation Council
    (GCC) 290–1
Gulf War:
    EC aid to neighbouring
        countries 273–4
    invasion of Kuwait 9, 264–5
    Trevi meeting 300
Gymnich arrangement:
    allows Euro-Arab Dialogue to
        begin 100
    application 102, 284
    arrived at 90–3
Gymnich-type meetings 15

Hague Summit, The (1969) 46–9
Haig, Al:
    and Falkland Islands 210
    and Middle East 214–15
Harmel, Pierre:
    launches discussion on CSCE 57
    proposals on political union 73, 82
Haughey, Charles 211
Heath, Edward 140
Howe, Sir Geoffrey:
    agrees structure for dialogue with
        US 285
    circulates draft agreement on
        EPC 245
    and Hindawi case 306
    South Africa mission 235–6
    and US raid on Libya 304–5
human rights:
    conditionality 279
    démarches 13
    and development aid 268–9
    and Eastern Europe 278
Hungary:
    aid for 277
    dialogue with 293
    Trade and Co-operation
        Agreement 275
Hurd, Douglas 175–6

immigration:
    ad hoc Group 301

336 Index

interaction of EPC with EC:
  Afghanistan 155, 272–3
  aid 135–6, 199–200, 205–7, 222–3, 270–4
  ASEAN 270
  Central America 9, 13, 223–9, 270–1
  Comecon 117–18
  as 'consistency' 319–20
  CSCE 58, 60
  Cyprus 121–3
  Eastern Europe 117–18, 274–81
  Euro-Arab Dialogue 99, 105, 106–7, 108–9
  Falkland Islands 9, 13, 207–13
  Gulf War 273–4
  inadequacy of EC financing 206
  institutional *rapprochement* 9, 24, 105
  Israel 106–7, 220
  Member States' attitudes to 260
  Portugal 123–5
  precursors of chemical weapons 266–7
  proposal for joint Embassy 128
  South Africa 9, 13, 232–7, 271–2
  Spain 126–7
Inter-governmental Conference on Political Union 1, 2
inter-governmentalism:
  versus integrationism 2
Iran hostage crisis:
  EPC disappoints US 8
  EPC reaction 168–71, 261–2
  EPC fails to impose sanctions 151
Iran–Iraq war:
  clearing of sea-lanes 218
  gives rise to GCC 291
Iraq:
  sanctions 264–5
Ireland:
  and Central America 226
  and Falkland Islands 209, 211, 212
  and MF0 215–16, 217
  neutrality 196
  position in EPC 310
  ratification of Single European Act 256–7
  reticent on security in EPC 8, 188, 198, 217, 249
  sensitive about extradition 295
Israel:
  EC Agreement and Protocol 106, 220
  invasion of Lebanon 13, 218–20
  and MFO 215–16
Italy:
  and Falkland Islands 209, 211–12
  integrationist view of EPC 2
  and PLO 106
  position in EPC 310
  and terrorism 303

Jannuzzi, Gianni 258
Japan:
  dialogue with 287
  and Iran sanctions 171
  judicial co-operation:
    Dublin Agreement 296, 298
    European Legal Space 295, 297
    in Genscher–Colombo proposals 187
    origins and content 154, 294–301

KAL airliner 194–5
Kissinger, Henry:
  and Genscher 91
  lets Europeans handle CSCE 57
  not informed of Euro-Arab Dialogue 93
  offers joint initiative on Cyprus 121
  promotes Geneva Conference 94
  and recognition of Angola and Mozambique 129–30
  speech to Society of Pilgrims 96–7
  see also 'Year of Europe'
van der Klaauw C. A. 167–8, 213

Lebanon:
  crisis mechanism used 180
  Israeli invasion 13, 218–20
  Multinational Force in Beirut 218
Libya:
  bombing of La Belle discothèque 303–4
  killing in St James's Square 302–3
  and terrorism 302
  US raid on 9, 304, 312
Lomé Convention:
  channel for aid 135
  EC aid apolitical 267–8
  EC economic ties 270
  human rights 268–9
London Report (1981):
  codifies EPC 8, 11
  co-operation in third countries 26
  dialogue with third countries 287
  drafted by Correspondents 23
  origins and content 172, 175–80

Index

sets up Troika support team 19
Luns, Josef:
  blocks de Gaulle 41–2
  at Munich Conference 58
Luxembourg Report (1970):
  avoids errors of Fouchet Plan 45–6
  establishes EPC 5, 11
  origins and content 51–5

Malfatti, Franco Maria:
  at Munich Conference 58
  at Paris Conference (1971) 58–9, 62
Mediterranean:
  Commission excluded from Working Group 121–2
  EPC policy 119
  Global Mediterranean Approach handled by EC 70, 98
  Spain included in Global Mediterranean Approach 126
  Working Group 69–70
Middle East:
  Camp David agreement 109, 159–68, 214
  Declaration by London European Council 102, 159
  declaration not published following US pressure 101–2
  discussed at Munich Conference 55–6
  Energy Conference in Washington 97
  October War 89–96
  oil embargo on Netherlands 94–6
  policy 66–9, 93–109, 213–22
  rights of Palestinians 95, 100–1, 102, 159, 162–3, 214, 220–1
  Schumann document 68, 93, 95, 121
  Six Day War 67
  see also Multinational Force and Observers in Sinai; Occupied Territories; Venice Declaration
Ministerial Meetings:
  cancelled 149
  in Copenhagen (1973) 75, 88, 89
  first Ministerial Conference in Munich 55–8, 68, 69, 71
  frequency 14, 54, 76
  in The Hague (1972) 61, 65
  in Paris (1971) 59, 64–5
  precursor meetings initiated by de Gaulle 39–40
  in Rome (1971) 59, 72, 82
  shared agenda with Council 15
  in Stuttgart Declaration 190
  in tandem with EC Council 14–15, 120, 154–5, 190, 249, 254, 278
Ministers' Decision of 28 February 1986:
  content 253
  co-operation in third countries 26
  defines role of EPC Secretariat 20
  drafted by Correspondents 23
Missions in third countries:
  co-operation among 25–7, 71, 147–8
  in Copenhagen Report 77–8
  instructions to drafted by Correspondents 23, 147
  in London Report 179
  in Teheran on Iran hostages 169
Mitterrand, François:
  convenes Euro-Arab Dialogue Summit 312
  policy: on Central America 222; on Middle East 168, 213–15
  President 157, 168, 177, 213, 222, 297
  supports draft Treaty on European Union 240–1
  visits Moscow 198
Moro, Aldo 113, 117
Mozambique 128–9
Multinational Force and Observers in Sinai (MFO) 13, 214–18
Munich, first Ministerial Conference, *see* Ministerial Meetings

Namibia 132, 149, 152
NATO:
  'double-track' decision 192
  East–West trade 192
Netherlands:
  and human rights 269
  oppose de Gaulle 3
  and South Africa 230–1, 234
  want UK in EC 39
Nicaragua:
  EC aid 223–4
  EPC reaction to Sandinista revolution 222
  US trade embargo 228

Occupied Territories 272
oral reports, *see* Working Groups
Ortoli, François-Xavier 103–4
Ostpolitik, *see* Germany
Owen, David:

Owen, David (cont.):
  on aid to Uganda 136, 268
  and Code of Conduct 133-4
  policy on Rhodesia 131
Pakistan 69
Palestine Liberation Organization
  (PLO), see Middle East
Paris Summit:
  (1972): gives mandate on European
    Union 6; increases frequency of
    Ministerial Meetings 76; links
    CSCE with EC policy 60;
    preparation, postponement, and
    results 71-4, 82, 140
  (1974): commissions Tindemans
    Report 143; role of Presidency
    and Parliament 145-6; sets up
    European Council 139-43
Parliament, European:
  colloquy with Political
    Committee 53
  in Copenhagen Report 78
  demands sanctions against South
    Africa 231
  Draft Treaty on European
    Union 239-40, 245
  finances Polish Church scheme for
    agriculture 206
  opinion on aid to neighbouring
    countries in Gulf War 274
  role defined by Paris Summit 145-6
  in Stuttgart Declaration 190
PHARE, see Eastern Europe
planning:
  capacity installed 147
  in Copenhagen Report 77
  lacunae 77, 316, 318
Pléven Plan 33
Poland:
  Church scheme for agriculture
    205-7, 271
  crisis mechanism not used 180
  dialogue with 293
  EC aid 199-201, 205, 270, 277
  imposition of martial law and EPC
    reaction 9, 199-207, 262
  trade and co-operation
    agreement 276
Political Committee:
  in Copenhagen Report 76
  and directives on co-operation in
    third countries 26

  hub of EPC 16-17
  meets in capital of Presidency 17
  power to strike a deal 16
  precursor of 40
  prepares Ministerial Meetings 15
  seeks to guide Coreper 118
  set up by Luxembourg Report 54
Polticial Directors 16
Pompidou, Georges:
  affirms Europe's separate
    identity 82
  calls for meetings of Heads of
    Government 140
  condemns EPC inertia on Middle
    East 94
  dies 92
  at The Hague Summit 5
  launches new European policy 47
  motives 47-8
Poos, Jacques 232
Portugal:
  break-up of colonial empire 127-30
  political decisions taken by EC not
    EPC 125
  revolution and EPC reaction 123-5
  Trade Agreement and financial
    assistance from EC 123-4
Presidency:
  carries out *démarches* 13
  in Copenhagen Report 78
  and Cyprus coup 119-20
  leading role 18-19, 313, 315-16
  in London Report 178-9
  Political Director attends Gymnich
    meetings 15
  responsibility for consistency 24
  role defined by Paris Summit 145-6
  spokesman for EPC 18, 146, 178-9,
    282
Protocol, Heads of:
  Working Group 70
Pym, Francis:
  and Falkland Islands 210

Reagan, Ronald:
  campaign to isolate Libya 303
  'Evil Empire' policies 9, 191
  policy: on Central America 222,
    225; on Middle East 167, 221;
    uncongenial to Europeans 3, 191
  Reykjavik Summit 198
  SDI 196-7
recueil 147, 174

Index

Reykjavik Summit, *see* Reagan
Rhodesia:
  EPC support for UK policy 128, 130–1, 152
  Security Council sanctions 261
Rifkind, Malcolm:
  Member of Dooge Committee 244, 245
  on South Africa 232
Rio, Group of 290–1
Rumor, Mariano:
  at the Hague Summit 49
  speech at UN 138

Sadat, Anwar al-:
  pressure on EPC 160
  speech to European Parliament 168
  visits Jerusalem 158–9
sanctions:
  Argentina 208–13, 262–3
  Denmark's legal reservations 203
  development of resort to 260–5
  Iran 151, 169–71, 261–2
  Iraq 264
  not resorted to over Cyprus 120
  Poland 202–5, 262
  South Africa 132–3, 232–7, 263–4
  Syria 307
San José Conferences, *see* Central America
Sauvagnargues, Jean 103–4
Scheel, Walter;
  chairs Munich Conference 55, 58, 66
  and Euro-Arab Dialogue 100
  on Luxembourg Report 53
  rapprochement with Arabs 66–7
Schluter, Paul:
  referendum on Single European Act 255
Schmidt, Helmut:
  role in setting up European Council 139–41
  separate declaration on Afghanistan 155
de Schoutheete, Philippe:
  chairs *ad hoc* Group to study Genscher–Colombo proposals 168
Schumann document, *see* Middle East
Schumann, Maurice:
  launches Pompidou's European policy 47
  at Munich Conference 58
  and Presidency 58, 63
Secretariat of EPC:
  begins operations 257
  in British proposal 246
  drafts replies to Parliamentary questions 21
  in Franco-German proposal 246–7
  Head of: appointed by Ministers 20; attends Gymnich meetings 15
  liaison with Presidency 21
  no planning function 316
  origins and role 19–21, 176, 186, 255, 257–8
  proposed in Dooge Report 243
  set up by Single European Act 255
secretariat, political:
  idea revived by Pompidou 72
  proposed by General de Gaulle 39
  spectre raised by Mitterrand 241–2
Secretariat-General of the Commission:
  co-ordinating powers 25
Secretariat-General of the Council:
  provides office services for EPC 21
  provides secretariat for *ad hoc* Group on Immigration 301
  Secretary-General attends Gymnich meetings 15
  transmits replies to PQs for EPC Secretariat 22
security:
  debate on in preparation for Single European Act 249–50
  economic aspects of 190
  extension of EPC to 176–8, 311–12
  extension proposed by Genscher 184
  Italy proposes links with WEU 249
  in Stuttgart Declaration 190–1
Single European Act (1987):
  codification of EPC 22
  Commission opinion 250
  covers EC and EPC 10, 252
  and dialogue with third countries 292
  Italian proposal for shared agenda with Council rejected 15
  origins and content 239–55
  Political Committee meetings foreseen in Brussels 17
  ratification and implementation 198, 255–9

Single European Act (1987) (*cont.*):
　Title III governing EPC 12
Soames, Sir Christopher 124
socialization:
　of European Correspondents 23, 313
　of officials in EPC 14, 312–13
　in Political Committee 16, 113, 313
South Africa:
　Code of Conduct 7, 133–5, 152, 230–1, 233
　EPC policy 132–5, 152, 230–7
　Howe mission 235–6
　Kagiso Trust 233–4
　Political Committee discusses in Strasbourg 17
　positive measures 9, 232, 271–2
　restrictive measures (sanctions) 9, 13, 152, 231–7, 263–4
　Troika mission 231–2
　see also Front Line States; Southern African Development Co-ordination Conference
Southern Africa:
　EPC concern over Marxist influence 127–9
　EPC interest in 6–7
　EPC policy 127–32
Southern African Development Co-ordination Conference (SADCC) 233
Spaak, Paul-Henri 43
Spain:
　executions of Basque terrorists 125–7
　Middle East policy 315
　position in EPC 310
Spinelli, Altiero:
　draft Treaty on European Union 239–40, 245
von Staden, Berndt 52
Strategic Defence Initiative (SDI) 196–7
Stuttgart Solemn Declaration (1983) 8, 189–91
Syria:
　and terrorism 302, 305–7

terrorism:
　bombing of La Belle discothèque 303–4
　and EPC 302–7
　Hindawi case 305–7
　killing in St James's Square 302–3
　spread of international 294, 299
　state-sponsored 302
Thatcher, Margaret:
　receptive to US views on Middle East 221–2
　and terrorism 303
　and US raid on Libya 304, 312
Thorn, Gaston 166–7, 213
Tindemans, Leo:
　report on European Union 7, 143–5
Trevi:
　origins and content 299–301
　weak co-ordination with EPC 294
Troika:
　ASEAN 289
　carries out *démarches* 13
　China 287
　Commission participation 19
　for consultations with Turkey 173, 284
　Contadora 225
　distinguishing feature of EPC 316
　Eastern Europe 278, 284
　in Euro-Arab Dialogue 108
　GCC 291
　India 287
　Japan 287
　in London Report 179
　mission to South Africa 232
　not firmly established 166
　origins and role 19
　Soviet Union 292
　Trevi 300
　United States 285
Troika support team:
　activities 202
　forerunner of EPC Secretariat 19–20, 255
　origins 172
　set up by London Report 19, 177, 179
Turkey:
　dialogue with 283–4
　treatment on Greek accession 172–3, 284

Uganda 136, 268
Union of Soviet Socialist Republics: (USSR):
　dialogue 197–8, 292
　and EC–Comecon relations 117–18, 198

Index 341

Gromyko deals with Carrington as
  EPC spokesman 157–8
invades Afghanistan 7, 154
recognition of EPC 197
trade and co-operation
  agreement 276
see also Conference on Security and
  Co-operation in Europe
United Kingdom:
  accession to EC made condition by
    Spaak 43
  de Gaulle's veto 46
  initiates directives on co-operation
    in third countries 26
  inter-governmental view of EPC 2
  opposes aid to Nicaragua 223
  policy lead on Cyprus 119
  position in EPC 309
  and terrorism 302–3
United Nations:
  EC observer status 137
  EPC co-ordination at 27–8, 70–1, 76,
    78, 136–9
  New International Economic
    Order 137
  permanent members of Security
    Council 28, 221, 311
  Presidency speech in General
    Assembly 13
  voting in General Assembly 28,
    138–9, 315
United States:
  Caribbean Basin Initiative 224
  deterioration in relations with
    EPC 9
  dialogue with 284–7
  disappointed by EPC reaction to
    terrorism 302, 303–5
  discourages Gulf States from
    discussing energy with EPC 107
  influence on EPC 2–4
  influence on European Defence
    Community 31–3, 37
  lets Europeans handle CSCE 57
  measures against Poland 201
  Nixon accuses Europeans of
    ganging up 90
  and PLO 106
  policy on Central America 222
  and postponement of Paris
    Summit 73
  presses EPC not to publish Middle
    East declaration 101–2

raid on Libya 305
relations with EPC on East-West
  questions 191–8
sees EPC Declaration on Middle
  East as challenge 95
trade embargo against
  Nicaragua 228
Transatlantic Declaration 286
transatlantic dilemma 82–3
see also European Identity,
  Document on the; Iran hostage
  crisis; Multinational Force and
  Observers in Sinai

Venice Delcaration (1980):
  effective EPC tool 13
  origins and content 158–68
  role of European Council 14
  weakened by US 8
Vietnam 268

Waldheim, Kurt 121
Western European Union (WEU):
  discusses Reykjavik Summit 198
  discusses SDI 196
  and Iran-Iraq war 218
  revival after Stuttgart
    Declaration 191
Working Groups:
  Africa 127, 135, 151–2, 271
  Asia 151, 154–5
  contacts with US 285–6
  East European 118, 150–1
  foreshadowed in Luxembourg
    Report 54
  Latin America 222
  in London Report 178
  meet in Brussels 17
  Middle East 151
  oral reports 17
  organization 17–18
  pattern set by CSCE Working
    Groups 63
  Planners 147, 316
  tendency to manage EC policy 25
Terroism 294, 302
UN-Disarmament 138, 151
United Nations 137–8, 151

'Year of Europe' (1973):
  holds up Copenhagen Report 75
  Kissinger's speech 84–6, 284
  launched by Kissinger 4, 6

'Year of Europe' (1973) (*cont.*):
  not covered by Luxembourg
    Report 46
  origins and purpose 83–93

Zaïre:
  independent French initiative 128,
    131
  invasion of Shaba 131